EVERYMAN, I will go with thee,

and be thy guide,

In thy most need to go by thy side

JOHN MILTON, 1608–1674

(*See* chronology of his life, page xiv.)

Milton's Prose Writings

INTRODUCTION BY
K. M. BURTON

DENT: LONDON
EVERYMAN'S LIBRARY
DUTTON: NEW YORK

© *Introduction and editing, J. M. Dent & Sons Ltd, 1958*
All rights reserved
Made in Great Britain
at the
Aldine Press · Letchworth · Herts
for
J. M. DENT & SONS LTD
Aldine House · Albemarle Street · London
First included in Everyman's Library 1927
Revised edition 1958
Last reprinted 1974

No. 795   Hardback ISBN 0 460 00795 5
No. 1795   Paperback ISBN 0 460 01795 0

INTRODUCTION

'No ordinance, human or from heaven, can bind against the good of man.' So Milton, in *Tetrachordon*, made his position clear: the good of man was his standard of reference. Commandments were valid and obligatory only in so far as they promoted this good; where they did not do so they must be overridden, regardless of their apparent origin. Milton felt it was supremely important that man should be left free to discipline himself in virtue, unhindered by the State or the Church. Between 1640 and 1660 he worked to bring about a state of affairs in which Englishmen were enabled to realize the highest potentialities of their natures. Since men were sons of God, having free access to Him through the words of the Bible, they did not need an intermediary in the person of priest or bishop. The only law for a Christian to obey was the law in his heart, conscience. Milton wanted for men the right to be independently moral, without the prison protection of law which made virtuous action impossible. Only in a state of liberty were men able to ascertain truth and to develop in goodness.

It was typical of Milton that he handled this question of liberty on a public level: he did not want to solve problems for himself alone, but for the community. The isolated freedom of a mystic would not have satisfied him. He felt his responsibility to the rest of his mature countrymen, and for their sakes he wanted to rebuild the City of Destruction, instead of escaping from it. So he concerned himself with the functions of the Church and the State in promoting the liberty of Englishmen, in the religious, civil, and domestic spheres. The State must serve the people, and refrain from putting stumbling-blocks in their way; the Church must effect spiritual discipline by purely spiritual means—exhortation and shame. The fetters of ignorance and custom were to be removed by education. 'To govern well, is to train up a nation in true wisdom and virtue, and that which springs from thence, magnanimity (take heed of that), and that which is our beginning, regeneration, and happiest end, likeness to God, which in one word we call godliness.' (*Of Reformation.*) Until the course of events during the civil wars and the Commonwealth made him lose his faith in the average run of men, he thought the whole nation could be roused to 'the flourishing deeds of a free commonwealth.'

The prerequisites of liberty as Milton understood it were submission to God, and a living faith, not imposed by any church, but apprehended by personal knowledge of the Bible. A man could be truly free only when he had dedicated his life to God. Liberty depended, not on swords and muskets, but on integrity of life. Inward sanctity must be attained by using 'all diligence and sincerity of heart, by reading, by learning, by study, by prayer for illumination of the Holy Spirit.' (*Of True Religion*.) Salvation was to be worked out in fear and trembling—but its direction was clear. The means to salvation were plainly set out for all to understand, in the words of the Bible. 'The wisdom of God created understanding, fit and proportionable to truth.' (*Of Reformation*.) The Holy Spirit in the heart was incorruptible, and every man must use this inward scripture to discover the truth in the written testaments. No one else could give it to him ready-made. The true Protestant had not only the right but the duty of interpreting Scripture for himself, and no one was justified in saying that he must believe another interpretation. All Protestants were bound by their own principles to respect the sincere beliefs of other Protestants who differed from them, since 'no man, no synod, no session of men though called the Church can judge definitively the sense of scripture to another man's conscience.' Here Milton was more tolerant than most of his contemporaries, who were inclined to argue that their own rectitude of interpretation justified them in imposing it on others.

In the early years of the dispute Milton thought that the bishops were the source of tyranny in the Church, since they laid down the law on matters of doctrine, liturgy, and ceremony. He prophesied that Presbyterianism would bring freedom to the Church, but he came to find as much tyranny in Presbyterianism itself. In the end he felt the only solution to be a spiritual priesthood of all believers in the invisible church. His views on church government became increasingly radical. He thought that the invidious distinction between clergy and laity should be abolished. Neither doctrines nor sacraments were a mystery too high for the ordinary man's capacity; all should be empowered to preach and to administer the sacraments as a normal part of life. The people should select and install their own ministers without the meaningless ceremony of the laying-on of hands: it was God's call, not the bishop's touch, that made a man fit to be a minister.

A living faith and a will to virtue could not be imposed on men by the priesthood, and it could not be stimulated by ritual means. Church ceremony was as cramping to it as Chinese foot-binding. The invisible church was the one that mattered. Man's duty was to 'walk as ever in His presence,' not to dissect life into days holy and days profane, or to rely for merit on the dull repetition of set words and gestures. In the *Apology against a Pamphlet* he denounced the liturgy as a kind of Dalila or Salmacis, taking away all individual strength: those who relied on it came 'in the end to such a pass by overmuch leaning as to lose even the legs of their devotion.' Formalism led to a 'numb and chill stupidity of soul' in the Church. A soul that found ease in 'gewgaws' 'shifted off from herself the labour of high soaring any more, forgot her heavenly flight,' and ended by losing all real sense of religion. (*Of Reformation.*) Milton, in common with most Puritans, could not understand the temperament that found spiritual aid in the forms and ceremonies of the Anglican or Catholic Church.

The whole trend of Milton's thought was towards self-discipline, since this was the only kind of discipline consonant with the dignity of man. State legislation in the realm of religion or morality defeated its own ends, since actions done in mere obedience to the law were not virtuous. 'If every action, which is good or evil in man at ripe years, were to be under pittance and prescription and compulsion, what were virtue but a name, what praise could then be due to well-doing, what gramercy to be sober, just or continent?' (*Areopagitica.*) Only liberty could make morality possible. Christ had loosed men from the bondage of the law; it was sinful of governments to attempt to bind them again. Christ had made them sons of God instead of servants unadopted; they must take up this gift. 'If we turn again to those weak and beggarly rudiments we are not free, yea though willingly and with a misguided conscience we desire to be in bondage to them.' (*Of Civil Power.*)

The liberty Milton wanted was very far from licence; it was the liberty to face danger and difficulty and overcome them without the help of anyone but God. He must have felt it as a real stimulus to have been created 'sufficient to have stood, though free to fall.' Such freedom made immense demands on self-discipline. 'For there is not that thing in the world of more grave and urgent importance throughout the whole life of man than is discipline.' (*Reason of Church Government.*) This discipline was valuable in so far as it was self-imposed. Other men could help a human being to discipline himself, but they must never constrain him—that prevented him from being virtuous. They could use all forms of spiritual persuasion. 'If he exhort this, I hear him as an angel, though he speak without warrant; but if he would compel me, I know him for Satan.' (*Doctrine and Discipline of Divorce.*) True liberty was liberty to constrain oneself to good. This good was a positive self-fulfilment: self-discipline was not ascetic in purpose. Order and control were directed towards the right enjoyment of God's plenty: they were the means whereby 'our happiness may orb itself into a thousand vagancies of glory and delight.' (*Reason of Church Government.*)

Milton had hoped that the nation could be educated in self-discipline. The people were to be guided out of the superstition of 'imaginary and scarecrow sins.' Schools and libraries must be set up to combat malice and ignorance. When he was writing his pamphlets *Of Education* and *Areopagitica* Milton obviously believed in the capacity of all men to grow in spiritual freedom towards the full dignity of man; but by the time that the Commonwealth was drawing to a close he was disillusioned. Even in the *Tenure* he mistrusted the moral constancy of the majority of the nation. In his official second defence of the English people he considered that only those who had attained inner liberty should have the right to vote. By the time he wrote *The Ready and Easy Way*, on the eve of the Restoration, he had come to disbelieve in democracy. He felt that the people, by their blind servility, had lost the right to govern themselves; the aristocracy of virtue, who were in a minority, had the right to impose their will on the unbridled and licentious majority. Those who would not discipline themselves must be disciplined for the sake of the rest. He had shifted from the picture of a noble and puissant nation shaking her invincible locks to one of a nation consisting in the main of lazy and servile individuals who were to be governed by a perpetual grand council. Milton had reached the paradoxical position of wanting to force men to be free. This pamphlet was a concession to expediency: Milton's basic principles made the government the servant of the people, not their despot.

Until he wrote *The Ready and Easy Way*, Milton had consistently portrayed the civil law as a positively immoral force. More laws always meant worse laws. They crippled the soul and reduced her to blind acquiescence. Milton was diametrically opposed to the Puritan policy of restrictive legislation. It was a sign of pusillanimity and insecurity in the government, and it was ridiculous in its ineffectiveness. 'If we think to regulate printing, thereby to rectify manners, we must regulate all recreations and pastimes, all that is delightful to man. . . . And who shall silence all the airs and madrigals that whisper softness in chambers?' (*Areopagitica*.) God never meant man to be kept 'under a perpetual childhood of prescription.' The function of the State was not to create petty laws, but to remove restraints that hindered man in his struggle towards virtue. 'Not that we have dominion over your faith, but are helpers of your joy.' The State must allow complete freedom of speech to all Protestants. They must loosen the intolerable bonds of the marriage and divorce laws which tied a man for life to a completely incompatible wife—a situation in which 'he shall be forced to love against a possibility, and to use dissimulation against his soul . . . doubtless his whole duty of serving God must needs be blurred and tainted.' (*Doctrine and Discipline of Divorce*.) Milton, in common with many other Puritan writers, valued most in marriage the companionship of 'a fit conversing soul'; this was the foundation of good citizenship. The household unhappiness caused by its absence precluded true reformation in the country as a whole. The State must improve on the present position by reforming the divorce laws. It was not the duty of the State to support the Church; temporal support was both an insult and a limitation to a spiritual entity. Its priests would tend to become mere servants of the government. In the same way, government control of the press was injurious to the pursuit of truth: 'such authorized books are but the language of the times.' The needs of the people were of paramount importance; the State had value only in so far as it served man.

Given that this was the end of government, a commonwealth was the best form of government. It was 'most magnanimous, most fearless and confident of its own fair proceedings,' whereas a king was full of fears and jealousies. Moreover, kings could not be controlled; they claimed to derive their power directly from God and to be responsible to no one but God. Milton held that power was given by the people to the magistrate; they could therefore justly deprive him of it if he became a tyrant. A commonwealth was less likely to become tyrannical, since individual members of the grand council acted as a check on the potential tyranny of the rest. Milton's desire for a commonwealth was based on his admiration of classical and Venetian republics, but he was well aware that the free self-governing community which he visualized depended on the existence of a Christian society. Its members must realize that the true function of government was service. Each man must recognize his duty 'to place everyone his private welfare and happiness in the public peace, liberty, and safety.' In such a society there would be no climbing after wealth and power and possessions; the rulers would not expect to be worshipped as demi-gods, but would be 'perpetual servants and drudges to the public at their own cost and charges . . . yet not elevated above their brethren.'

Milton was conscious of his own responsibility to promote such a state. That was why he gave up his retired life of study, postponed the composition of his epic, and embarked on contro-versial writing. He felt that the gifts entrusted to him by God must be employed for the moment in the service of the cause he knew to be just. He would have reason to reproach himself if he neglected to do so, although he did not feel perfectly adapted to the task. Considering the general run of pamphlets pub-lished between 1640 and 1660, his contributions did not always bear directly on the central controversy, but his output both as a private individual and as a government employee was relatively large. He began by concerning himself entirely with what he considered to be prelatical tyranny, and wrote five pamphlets on this subject between April 1641 and March 1642. The case of Strafford did not interest him enough to make him write about it. In fact he published no strictly political pamphlet until February 1649, when the king had been executed. In the early years of the war the majority of the pamphleteers were concentrating on the debate about the lawfulness of taking up arms against the king. Once the power of the bishops was curbed, Milton turned his attention to domestic liberty. He said he felt free to leave the question of civil liberty since the magistrates were strenuously active in obtaining it. He side-stepped the central debate to discuss questions of divorce and censorship, feeling that no effect of tyranny could 'sit more heavy on the commonwealth, than this household unhappiness on the family'; and that 'he who destroys a good book, kills reason itself.' His later pamphlets were nearly all concerned with an official defence of the remains of the Long Parliament in their trial and execution of the king, and with exalting a common-wealth above a monarchy. He returned to the question of the Church: its relation with the State, the selection of its ministers. His final pamphlet considered the problems of heresy and toleration.

Milton's most valuable contribution lies in the realm of ideals. As a political theorist he cannot be compared with Henry Parker or Lilburne. He was impractical: he could not see difficulties or admit real obstacles. He was too much inclined to think that only the best men mattered. But his essential concerns for the dignity of man and his respect for individuality set him above most controversialists of his time. His language may be abusive at times, but his work seems animated by a genuine love of the best qualities in men—in strong contrast to the work of writers such as Prynne and the host of anonymous pamphleteers whose chief joy came from the downfall of their enemies. Few men of his time were as tolerant as he of differences in personal faith, even though he did not extend this toleration to Catholics. For every man, he contended, the individual conscience was the last court of appeal. He stood for the central freedoms—freedom of conscience, freedom of speech and thought. On these questions he wrote with an imagination and a depth of principle which compel respect from the reader.

KATHLEEN BURTON.

1958.

SELECT BIBLIOGRAPHY

SEPARATE WORKS. *A Maske presented at Ludlow Castle, 1634, on Michaelmasse Night*, etc., 1637 (*Comus*); *Lycidas* (published in *Obsequies to the Memorie of Mr Edward King*, 1638); *Of Reformation Touching Church-Discipline in England: and the Causes that hitherto have hindred it: Two Bookes, written to a Freind*, 1641; *Of Prelatical Episcopacy, and Whether it may be deduc'd from the Apostolical Times by vertue of those Testimonies which are alledg'd to that purpose in some late Treatises; One whereof goes under the Name of James Archbishop of Armagh*, 1641; *Animadversions upon The Remonstrants Defence against Smectymnuus*, 1641; *The Reason of Church-governement Urg'd against Prelaty*, 1642; *An Apology Against a Pamphlet call'd A Modest Confutation of the Animadversions upon the Remonstrant against Smectymnuus*, 1642; *The Doctrine and Discipline of Divorce: Restor'd to the good of both Sexes, From the Bondage of Canon Law, and other Mistakes, to Christian Freedom, guided by the Rule of Charity*, etc., 1643; second edition, 1644; *Of Education. To Master Samuel Hartlib*, 1644; *The Judgement of Martin Bucer concerning Divorce: Writt'n to Edward the Sixt, in his Second Book of the Kingdom of Christ: And now Englisht*, etc., 1644; *Areopagitica; A Speech of Mr John Milton for the Liberty of Unlicens'd Printing, to the Parliament of England*, 1644; *Tetrachordon: Expositions upon The foure chief Places in Scripture which treat of Mariage, or Nullities in*

Mariage, etc., 1645; *Colasterion: A Reply to a Nameles Answer against The Doctrine and Discipline of Divorce*, etc., 1645; *Poems of Mr John Milton, both English and Latin*, 1645; *The Tenure of Kings and Magistrates: Proving that it is Lawfull, and hath been held so through all Ages, for any, who have the Power, to call to account a Tyrant, or wicked King*, etc., 1649; second edition, 1650; *Observations on the Articles of Peace made and Concluded with the Irish Rebels, and Papists*, etc., 1649; *Eikonoklastes in Answer to a Book intitl'd Eikon Basilike*, 1649; *Joannis Miltoni Angli pro Populo Anglicano Defensio contra Claudii Anonymi, alias Salmasii, Defensionem Regiam*, 1651; *Joannis Miltoni Angli pro Populo Anglicano Defensio Secunda*, etc., 1654; *Joannis Miltoni Angli pro se Defensio contra Alexandrum Morum, Ecclesiasten*, etc., 1655; *A Treatise of Civil Power in Ecclesiastical Causes: Shewing that it is not lawfull for any power on Earth to compell in matters of Religion*, 1659; *Considerations touching the likeliest Means to remove Hirelings out of the Church*, etc., 1659; *The Readie and Easie Way to establish a Free Commonwealth, and the excellence thereof*, etc., 1660; second edition, 1660; *The Present Means and Brief Delineation of a Free Commonwealth . . . in a Letter to General Monck*, 1660 (published 1697, in Toland's edition); *Brief Notes Upon a late Sermon, titl'd The Fear of God and the King; Preach'd, and since publish'd, by Matthew Griffith, D.D.*, etc., 1660; *Paradise Lost. A Poem Written in Ten Books by John Milton*, 1667, 1668, 1669; *Accidence Commenc't Grammar*, etc., 1669; *The History of Britain, That part especially now call'd England*, etc., 1670; *Paradise Regain'd. A poem. In IV Books. To which is added Samson Agonistes*, 1671; *Johannis Miltoni Angli, Artis Logicae Plenior Institutio, ad Petri Rami Methodum concinnata*, etc., 1672; *Of True Religion, Haeresie, Schism, Toleration, And what best means may be us'd against the growth of Popery*, 1673; *Paradise Lost. A Poem in Twelve Books*, 1674; *Joannis Miltoni Angli, Epistolarum Familiarum Liber Unus*, etc., 1674; *A Declaration, Or, Letters Patents for the Election Of this present King of Poland John the Third . . . Now faithfully translated from the Latin Copy*, 1674; *Literae Pseudo-Senatus, Anglicani, Cromwellii Reliquorumque Perduellium nomine ac jussu conscriptae a Joanne Miltono*, 1676; *Character of the Long Parliament and Assembly of Divines. In MDCXLI*, 1681 (authorship questioned); *A Brief History of Moscovia*, etc., 1682; *Joannis Miltoni Angli De Doctrina Christiana. Libri Duo Posthumi*, ed. C. R. Sumner, 1825; *A Commonplace Book*, ed. A. J. Horwood, 1876; *Facsimile of the Manuscript of Milton's Minor Poems preserved in the Library of Trinity College*, ed. W. A. Wright, 1899; *Private Correspondence and Academic Exercises:* translated from the Latin by P. B. Tillyard with an introduction by E. M. W. Tillyard, 1932.

COLLECTED WORKS. *Verse and Prose*, ed. J. Mitford, 8 vols., London, 1851; *Complete Works*, ed. F. A. Patterson, 18 vols., with variants and translations, New York, 1931–8, the Columbia Edition; *Poetical Works*, ed. Patrick Hume, 5 pts., London, 1695; *Poetical Works*, ed. H. J. Todd, Variorum edition, 6 vols., London, 1801; *Poetical Works*, ed. W. A. Wright, Cambridge, 1903; *Poetical Works*, ed. H. C. Beeching, Oxford, 1904; *The Poems of John Milton*, ed. H. J. C. Grierson, London, 1925; *Paradise Lost*, ed. M. Y. Hughes, New York, 1935; *Paradise Regained, the Minor Poems, and Samson Agonistes*, ed. M. Y. Hughes, New York, 1937; *Poetical Works*, ed. H. Darbishire, Oxford, vol. i, 1952, in progress; *Poetical Works*, ed. B. A. Wright (Everyman's Library), 1955; *Prose Works*, ed. J. Toland, 3 vols., London, 1694–8; *Prose Works*, ed. C. Symmons, 7 vols., London, 1806; *Complete Prose Works*, ed. D. M. Wolfe, 7 vols., New Haven, vol. i, 1953, vol. ii, 1959, vol. iv, 1966, in progress.

BIOGRAPHY AND CRITICISM. *The Early Lives of Milton*, ed. H. Darbishire, London, 1932; Samuel Johnson: *Lives of the Poets*, London, 1779; D. Masson: *Life of John Milton, narrated in connection with the political, ecclesiastical, and literary history of his time*, 6 vols., London, 1859–94; M. Pattison: *Milton* (English Men of Letters), London, 1879; E. M. W. Tillyard:

Milton, London, 1934; D. L. Clark: *The Education of Milton at St Paul's School*, Columbia, New York, 1948; J. M. French: *The Life Records of John Milton*, vol. i, New Brunswick, 1949, in progress; J. H. Hanford: *John Milton, Englishman*, London, 1950; T. B. Macaulay: *Critical and Historical Essays*, London, 1843; E. Dowden: *Puritan and Anglican*, London, 1900; Sir C. Firth: *Milton as Historian*, Proceedings of the British Academy, IV, London, 1907–8; D. Saurat: *Milton, Man and Thinker*, London, 1925; H. J. C. Grierson: *Milton and Wordsworth*, Cambridge, 1937; W. J. Allen: *English Political Ideas 1603–1660*, vol. i, London, 1938; W. H. Haller: *The Rise of Puritanism*, Columbia, New York, 1938; A. Sewell: *A Study in Milton's Christian Doctrine*, London, 1939; W. R. Parker: *Milton's Contemporary Reputation*, Columbus, 1940; D. M. Wolfe: *Milton in the Puritan Revolution*, New York, 1941; M. W. Kelley: *This Great Argument*, Princeton, 1941; A. F. Barker: *Milton and the Puritan Dilemma*, New York, 1942; D. Bush: *English Literature in the Earlier Seventeenth Century*, Oxford, 1945; Z. S. Fink: *The Classical Republicans*, Evanston, 1945; E. M. W. Tillyard: *Studies in Milton*, London, 1951; K. Muir: *John Milton*, London, 1955; H. F. Robins: *If This Be Heresy: a Study of Milton and Origen*, Urbana, 1963; T. Krarnidas: *The Fierce Equation: a Study of Milton's Decorum*, The Hague, 1965; C. A. Patrides: *Milton and the Christian Tradition*, London, 1966; W. R. Parker: *Milton: A Biography*, 2 vols., Columbus, 1968.

CHRONOLOGY OF MILTON'S LIFE

1608, December 9. Born in Bread Street, Cheapside, London.

1620. Entered St Paul's School.

1625, February 12. Matriculated at Christ's College, Cambridge.

1629, March. Took B.A. degree.

1629, December. *On the Morning of Christ's Nativity.*

1632, July. Took M.A. degree.

1632, July–1638, April. Lived at Horton.

1634, September 29. *Comus* performed at Ludlow.

1637, November. *Lycidas.*

1638, April–1639, August. Continental tour.

1639–1640. Settled in London.

1641–1642. Begins pamphleteering. Five anti-prelatical tracts: *Of Reformation in England*; *Of Prelatical Episcopacy*; *Animadversions upon the Remonstrant's Defence*; *The Reason of Church Government*; *Apology for Smectymnuus.*

1642, May–June. Married Mary Powell, who left him about a month later.

1643–1645. *The Doctrine and Discipline of Divorce; Of Education; The Judgement of Martin Bucer Concerning Divorce; Areopagitica; Tetrachordon; Colasterion.*

1645. Milton's wife returns. *Miscellaneous Poems* published.

1649. *The Tenure of Kings and Magistrates* (February). Appointed Secretary for Foreign Tongues to the Council of State (March). *Eikonoklastes* (October).

1651. *Defensio pro Populo Anglicano.*

1652. Milton totally blind. Death of his first wife.

1654. *Defensio Secunda.*

1655. *Defensio Pro Se.*

1656, November. Married Katherine Woodcock.

1658, February. Death of Katherine Woodcock.

1660, March. *The Ready and Easy Way to Establish a Free Commonwealth.*

1663, February. Married Elizabeth Minshull.

1667. *Paradise Lost* published.

1671. *Paradise Regained* and *Samson Agonistes* published.

1673. Second edition of *Miscellaneous Poems.*

1674. Second edition of *Paradise Lost.*

1674, November 8. Died; buried in St Giles's Church, Cripplegate.

CONTENTS

ON
RELIGIOUS LIBERTY

OF REFORMATION IN ENGLAND

AND THE

CAUSES THAT HITHERTO HAVE HINDERED IT

IN TWO BOOKS

WRITTEN TO A FRIEND

Milton's first pamphlet, written in the spring of 1641, was an attempt to promote religious liberty for Puritans by taking away the authority of Anglican bishops. The Scots had won their war against Archbishop Laud, who had tried to impose the Anglican system of church government and belief on the Scottish church. The Long Parliament had already impeached the Archbishop, and some of its members were preparing a scheme to abolish episcopacy in England. The alternative system entertained was Presbyterianism. At this stage Milton thought it embodied the best qualities of Puritanism.

Bishops were, to him, temporal lords, wolves preying on the community rather than shepherds tending it. Their existence was an insult to the dignity of the individual soul in its relationship with God. They were also an impairment of the King's dignity: a rotten prop to heroic virtue. Once episcopacy was abolished, the millennium would be attained.

The other hindrance to perfect reformation was the revival of the 'gewgaws' of ceremony: the insistence on certain kinds of bodily gesture and apparel, rather than on spiritual service. 'The soul . . . finding the ease she had from her visible and sensuous colleague, the body, in performance of religious duties, her pinions now broken and flagging, shifted off from herself the labour of high soaring any more, forgot her heavenly flight, and left the dull and droiling carcass to plod on in the old road and drudging trade of outward conformity.'

Milton ended his pamphlet with an apocalyptic vision. He foresaw the glorification of the just, and the damnation of the bishops and their party. Five years later, he had come to fear that New Presbyter was but Old Priest writ large.

THE FIRST BOOK

SIR,—Amidst those deep and retired thoughts, which, with every man Christianly instructed, ought to be most frequent of God, and of his miraculous ways and works amongst men, and of our religion and works, to be performed to him; after

3

the story of our Saviour Christ, suffering to the lowest bent of weakness in the flesh, and presently triumphing to the highest pitch of glory in the spirit, which drew up his body also; till we in both be united to him in the revelation of his kingdom, I do not know anything more worthy to take up the whole passion of pity on the one side, and joy on the other, than to consider first the foul and sudden corruption, and then, after many a tedious age, the long deferred, but much more wonderful and happy reformation of the church in these latter days. Sad it is to think how that doctrine of the gospel, planted by teachers divinely inspired, and by them winnowed and sifted from the chaff of overdated ceremonies, and refined to such a spiritual height and temper of purity, and knowledge of the Creator, that the body with all the circumstances of time and place, were purified by the affections of the regenerate soul, and nothing left impure but sin; faith needing not the weak and fallible office of the senses, to be either the ushers or interpreters of heavenly mysteries, save where our Lord himself in his sacraments ordained; that such a doctrine should, through the grossness and blindness of her professors, and the fraud of deceivable traditions, drag so downwards, as to backslide one way into the Jewish beggary of old cast rudiments, and stumble forward another way into the new-vomited paganism of sensual idolatry, attributing purity or impurity to things indifferent, that they might bring the inward acts of the spirit to the outward and customary eye-service of the body, as if they could make God earthly and fleshly, because they could not make themselves heavenly and spiritual; they began to draw down all the divine intercourse betwixt God and the soul, yea, the very shape of God himself, into an exterior and bodily form, urgently pretending a necessity and obligement of joining the body in a formal reverence and worship circumscribed; they hallowed it, they fumed up, they sprinkled it, they bedecked it, not in robes of pure innocency, but of pure linen, with other deformed and fantastic dresses, in palls and mitres, gold, and gewgaws fetched from Aaron's old wardrobe, or the flamins' vestry; then was the priest set to con his motions and his postures, his liturgies and his lurries, till the soul by this means of overbodying herself, given up justly to fleshly delights, bated her wing apace downward: and finding the ease she had from her visible and sensuous colleague, the body, in performance of religious duties, her pinions now broken and flagging, shifted off from herself the labour of high soaring any more, forgot her heavenly flight, and left the dull and droiling carcass to plod on in the old road and drudging trade of outward conformity. And here out of question from her perverse conceiting of God and holy things, she had fallen to believe no God at all, had not custom and the worm of conscience nipped her incredulity: hence to all the duties of evangelical grace, instead of the adoptive and cheerful boldness which our new alliance with God requires, came servile and thrall-like fear: for in very deed, the superstitious man by his goodwill is an atheist; but being scared from thence by the pangs and gripes of a boiling conscience, all in a pudder shuffles up to himself such a God and such a worship as is most agreeable to remedy his fear; which fear of his, as also is his hope, fixed only upon the flesh, renders likewise the whole faculty of his apprehension carnal; and all the inward acts of worship, issuing from the native strength of the soul, run out lavishly to the upper skin, and there harden into a crust of formality. Hence men came to scan the scriptures by the letter, and in the covenant of our redemption, magnified the external signs more than the quickening power of the Spirit; and yet, looking on them through their own guiltiness with a servile fear, and finding as little comfort, or rather terror from them again, they knew not how to hide their slavish approach to God's behests, by them not understood, nor worthily received, but by cloaking their servile crouching to all religious presentments, sometimes lawful, sometimes idolatrous, under the name of humility, and terming the piebald frippery and ostentation of ceremonies, decency.

Then was baptism changed into a kind of exorcism, and water, sanctified by Christ's institute, thought little enough to wash off the original spot, without the scratch or cross impression of a priest's forefinger: and that feast of free grace and adoption to which Christ invited his disciples to sit as brethren, and coheirs of the happy covenant, which at that table was to be sealed to them, even that feast of love and heavenly admitted fellowship, the seal of filial grace, became the subject of horror, and glouting adoration, pageanted about like a dreadful idol; which sometimes deceives well-meaning men, and beguiles them of their reward, by their voluntary humility; which indeed is fleshly pride, preferring a foolish sacrifice, and the rudiments of the world, as St Paul to the Colossians explaineth, before a savoury obedience to Christ's example. Such was Peter's unseasonable humility, as then his knowledge was small, when Christ came to wash his feet; who at an impertinent time would needs strain courtesy with his master, and falling troublesomely upon the lowly, all-wise, and unexaminable intention of Christ, in what he went with resolution to do, so provoked by his interruption the meek Lord, that he threatened to exclude him from his heavenly portion, unless he could be content to be less arrogant and stiff-necked in his humility.

But to dwell no longer in characterizing the depravities of the church, and how they sprung, and how they took increase; when I recall to mind at last, after so many dark ages, wherein the huge overshadowing train of error had almost swept all the stars out of the firmament of the church; how the bright and blissful Reformation (by divine power) struck through the black and settled night of ignorance and antichristian tyranny, methinks a sovereign and reviving joy must needs rush into the bosom of him that reads or hears; and the sweet odour of the returning gospel imbathe his soul with the fragrancy of heaven. Then was the sacred Bible sought out of the dusty corners where profane falsehood and neglect had thrown it, the schools opened, divine and human learning raked out of the embers of forgotten tongues, the princes and cities trooping apace to the new erected banner of salvation; the martyrs, with the unresistible might of weakness, shaking the powers of darkness, and scorning the fiery rage of the old red dragon.

The pleasing pursuit of these thoughts hath ofttimes led me into a serious question and debatement with myself, how it should come to pass that England (having had this grace and honour from God, to be the first that should set up a standard for the recovery of lost truth, and blow the first evangelic trumpet to the nations, holding up, as from a hill, the new lamp of saving light to all Christendom) should now be last and most unsettled in the enjoyment of that peace, whereof she taught the way to others; although indeed our Wickliff's preaching, at which all the succeeding reformers more effectually lighted their tapers, was to his countrymen but a short blaze, soon damped and stifled by the pope and prelates for six or seven kings' reigns; yet methinks the precedency which God gave this island, to be first restorer of buried truth, should have been followed with more happy success, and sooner attained perfection; in which as yet we are amongst the last: for, albeit in purity of doctrine we agree with our brethren; yet in discipline, which is the execution and applying of doctrine home, and laying the salve to the very orifice of the wound, yea, tenting and searching to the core, without which pulpit preaching is but shooting at rovers; in this we are no better than a schism from all the Reformation, and a sore scandal to them: for while we hold ordination to belong only to bishops, as our prelates do, we must of necessity hold also their ministers to be no ministers, and shortly after their church to be no church: not to speak of those senseless ceremonies which we only retain, as a dangerous earnest of sliding back to Rome, and serving merely, either as a mist to cover nakedness where true grace is extinguished, or as an interlude to set out the pomp of prelatism. Certainly it would be worth the while therefore, and the pains, to inquire more particularly, what, and how many the chief causes have been, that have still hindered our uniform consent to the rest of the churches abroad, at this time especially when the kingdom is in a good propensity thereto, and all men in prayers, in hopes, or in disputes, either for or against it.

Yet I will not insist on that which may seem to be the cause on God's part; as his judgment on our sins, the trail of his own, the unmasking of hypocrites: nor shall I stay to speak of the continual eagerness and extreme diligence of the pope and papists to stop the furtherance of reformation, which know they have no hold or hope of England, their lost darling, longer than the government of bishops bolsters them out; and therefore plot all they can to uphold them, as may be seen by the book of Santa Clara, the popish priest, in defence of bishops, which came out piping hot much about the time that one of our own prelates, out of an ominous fear, had writ on the same argument; as if they had joined their forces, like good confederates, to support one falling Babel.

But I shall chiefly endeavour to declare those causes that hinder the forwarding of true discipline, which are among ourselves. Orderly proceeding will divide our inquiry into our forefathers' days, and into our times. Henry VIII was the first that rent this kingdom from the pope's subjection totally; but his quarrel being more about supremacy, than other faultiness in religion that he regarded, it is no marvel if he stuck where he did. The next default was in the bishops, who though they had renounced the pope, they still hugged the popedom, and shared the authority among themselves, by their six bloody articles, persecuting the protestants no slacker than the pope would have done. And doubtless, whenever the pope shall fall, if his ruin be not like the sudden downcome of a tower, the bishops, when they see him tottering, will leave him, and fall to scrambling, catch who may, he a patriarchdom, and another what comes next hand; as the French cardinal of late and the see of Canterbury hath plainly affected.

In Edward VI's days, why a complete reformation was not effected, to any considerate man may appear. First, he no sooner entered into his kingdom, but into a war with Scotland; from whence the protector returning with victory, had but newly put his hand to repeal the six articles, and throw the images out of churches, but rebellions on all sides, stirred up by obdurate papists, and other tumults, with a plain war in Norfolk, holding tack against two of the king's generals, made them of force content themselves with what they had already done. Hereupon followed ambitious contentions among the peers, which ceased not but with the protector's death, who was the most zealous in this point: and then Northumberland was he that could do most in England, who little minding religion (as his apostasy well showed at his death), vent all his wit how to bring the right of the crown into his own line. And for the bishops they were so far any such worthy attempts, as that they suffered themselves to be the common stales, to countenance with their prostituted gravities every politic fetch that was then on foot, as oft as the potent statists pleased to employ them. Never do we read that they made use of their authority and high place of access to bring the jarring nobility to Christian peace, or to withstand their disloyal projects: but if a toleration for mass were to be begged of the king for his sister Mary, lest Charles V should be angry, who but the grave prelates, Cranmer and Ridley, must be sent to extort it from the young king? But out of the mouth of that godly and royal child, Christ himself returned such an awful repulse to those halting and time-serving prelates, that after much bold importunity, they went their way not without shame and tears.

Nor was this the first time that they discovered to be followers of this world; for when the protector's brother, Lord Dudley, the admiral, through private malice and malengine was to lose his life, no man could be found fitter than Bishop Latimer (like another Dr Shaw) to divulge in his sermon the forged accusations laid to his charge, thereby to defame him with the people, who else it was thought would take ill the innocent man's death, unless the reverend bishop could warrant them there was no foul play. What could be more impious than to debar the children of the king from their right to the crown? to comply with the ambitious usurpation of a traitor, and to make void the last will of Henry VIII, to which the breakers had sworn observance? Yet Bishop Cranmer, one of the executors, and the other bishops, none refusing (lest they should resist the Duke of

Northumberland), could find in their consciences to set their hands to the disenabling and defeating not only the princess Mary the papist, but of Elizabeth the protestant, and (by the bishop's judgment) the lawful issue of King Henry.

Who then can think (though these prelates had sought a further reformation) that the least wry face of a politician would not have hushed them? But it will be said, these men were martyrs: what then? though every true Christian will be a martyr when he is called to it, not presently does it follow, that every one suffering for religion is, without exception. St Paul writes, that 'a man may give his body to be burnt (meaning for religion), and yet not have charity': he is not therefore above all possibility of erring, because he burns for some points of truth.

Witness the Arians and Pelagians, which were slain by the heathen for Christ's sake, yet we take both these for no true friends of Christ. If the martyrs (said Cyprian in his 30th epistle) decree one thing, and the gospel another, either the martyrs must lose their crown by not observing the gospel for which they are martyrs, or the majesty of the gospel must be broken and lie flat, if it can be overtopped by the novelty of any other decree.

And here withal I invoke the Immortal Deity, revealer and judge of secrets, that wherever I have in this book plainly and roundly (though worthily and truly) laid open the faults and blemishes of fathers, martyrs, or Christian emperors, or have otherwise inveighed against error and superstition with vehement expressions; I have done it neither out of malice, nor list to speak evil, nor any vainglory, but of mere necessity to vindicate the spotless truth from an ignominious bondage, whose native worth is now become of such a low esteem, that she is likely to find small credit with us for what she can say, unless she can bring a ticket from Cranmer, Latimer, and Ridley; or prove herself a retainer to Constantine, and wear his badge. More tolerable it were for the church of God, that all these names were utterly abolished, like the brazen serpent, than that men's fond opinion should thus idolize them, and the heavenly truth be thus captivated.

Now to proceed, whatsoever the bishops were, it seems they themselves were unsatisfied in matters of religion as they then stood, by that commission granted to eight bishops, eight other divines, eight civilians, eight common lawyers, to frame ecclesiastical constitutions; which no wonder if it came to nothing, for (as Hayward relates) both their professions and their ends were different. Lastly, we all know by example, that exact reformation is not perfected at the first push, and those un-wieldy times of Edward VI may hold some plea by this excuse. Now let any reasonable man judge whether that king's reign be a fit time from whence to pattern out the constitution of a church discipline, much less that it should yield occasion from whence to foster and establish the continuance of imperfection, with the commendatory subscriptions of confessors and martyrs, to entitle and engage a glorious name to a gross corruption. It was not episcopacy that wrought in them the heavenly fortitude of martyrdom, as little is it that martyrdom can make good episcopacy; but it was episcopacy that led the good and holy men, through the temptation of the enemy, and the snare of this present world, to many blameworthy and opprobrious actions. And it is still episcopacy that before all our eyes worsens and slugs the most learned and seeming religious of our ministers, who no sooner advance to it, but, like a seething pot set to cool, sensibly exhale the reek out the greatest part of that zeal and those gifts which were formerly in them, settling in a skinny congealment of ease and sloth at the top; and if they keep their learning by some potent sway of nature, it is a rare chance; but their devotion most commonly comes to that queazy temper of lukewarmness, that gives a vomit to God himself.

But why do we suffer misshapen and enormous prelatism, as we do, thus to blanch and varnish her deformities with the fair colours, as before of martyrdom, so now of episcopacy? They are not bishops, God and all good men know they are not, that have filled this land with late confusion and violence; but a tyrannical crew and corporation of impostors, that have blinded and abused the world so long under that name. He that, enabled with gifts from God, and the lawful and primitive choice of the church assembled in convenient number, faithfully from that time forward feeds his parochial flock, has his coequal and compresbyterial power to ordain ministers and deacons by public prayer, and vote of Christ's congregation in like sort as he himself was ordained, and is a true apostolic bishop. But when he steps up into the chair of pontifical pride, and changes a moderate and exemplary house for a misgoverned and haughty palace, spiritual dignity for carnal precedence, and secular high office and employment for the high negotiations of his heavenly embassage, then he degrades, then he unbishops himself; he that makes him bishop, makes him no bishop. No marvel there-fore if St Martin complained to Sulpitius Severus, that since he was bishop he felt inwardly a sensible decay of those virtues and graces that God had given him in great measure before; although the same Sulpitius write that he was nothing tainted or altered in his habit, diet, or personal demeanour from that simple plainness to which he first betook himself. It was not therefore that thing alone which God took displeasure at in the bishops of those times, but rather an universal rottenness and gangrene in the whole function.

From hence then I pass to Queen Elizabeth, the next protestant princess, in whose days why religion attained not a perfect reducement in the beginning of her reign, I suppose the hindering causes will be found to be common with some formerly alleged for King Edward VI: the greenness of the times, the weak estate which Queen Mary left the realm in, the great places and offices executed by papists, the judges, the lawyers, the justices of peace for the most part popish, the bishops firm to Rome; from whence was to be expected the furious flashing of excommunications, and absolving the people from their obedience. Next, her private counsellors, whoever they were, persuaded her (as Camden writes) that the altering of ecclesiastical policy would move sedition. Then was the liturgy given to a number of moderate divines, and Sir Thomas Smith, a statesman, to be purged and physicked: and surely they were moderate divines indeed, neither hot nor cold; and Grindal, the best of them, afterwards Archbishop of Canterbury, lost favour in the court, and I think was discharged the government of his see, for favouring the ministers, though Camden seems willing to find another cause: therefore about her second year, in a parliament of men and minds some scarce well grounded, others belching the sour crudities of yesterday's popery, those constitutions of Edward VI, which, as you heard before, no way satisfied the men that made them, are now established for best, and not to be mended. From that time followed nothing but imprisonments, troubles, disgraces on all those that found fault with the decrees of the convocation, and straight were they branded with the name of puritans. As for the queen herself, she was made believe that by putting down bishops her prerogative would be infringed, of which shall be spoken anon as the course of method brings it in: and why the prelates laboured it should be so thought, ask not them, but ask their bellies. They had found a good tabernacle, they sat under a spreading vine, their lot was fallen in a fair inheritance. And these perhaps were the chief impeachments of a more sound rectifying the church in the queen's time.

From this period I count to begin our times, which because they concern us more nearly, and our own eyes and ears can give us the ampler scope to judge, will require a more exact search, and to effect this the speedier, I shall distinguish such as I esteem to be the hinderers of reformation into three sorts, Antiquitarians (for so I had rather call them than antiquaries, whose labours are useful and laudable). 2. Libertines. 3. Politicians.

To the votarists of antiquity I shall think to have fully answered, if I shall be able to prove out of antiquity, First, that if they will conform our bishops to the purer times, they must mew their feathers and their pounces, and make but curtailed bishops of them; and we know they hate to be docked and clipped, as much as to be put down outright. Secondly, that those purer times were corrupt, and their books corrupted soon after. Thirdly, that the best of those that then wrote disclaim that any man should repose on them, and send all to the scriptures.

First, therefore, if those that over-affect antiquity will follow the square thereof, their bishops must be elected by the hands of the whole church. The ancientest of the extant fathers, Ignatius, writing to the Philadelphians, saith 'that it belongs to them as to the church of God to choose a bishop.' Let no man cavil, but take the church of God as meaning the whole consistence of orders and members, as St Paul's epistles express, and this likewise being read over: besides this, it is there to be marked, that those Philadelphians are exhorted to choose a bishop of Antioch. Whence it seems by the way that there was not that wary limitation of diocese in those times, which is confirmed even by a fast friend of episcopacy, Camden, who cannot but love bishops as well as old coins, and his much lamented monasteries, for antiquity's sake. He writes in his description of Scotland, that 'over all the world bishops had no certain diocese till Pope Dionysius about the year 268 did cut them out; and that the bishops of Scotland executed their function in what place soever they came indifferently, and without distinction, till King Malcolm III, about the year 1070.' Whence may be guessed what their function was: was it to go about circled with a band of rooking officials, with cloakbags full of citations, and processes to be served by a corporality of griffonlike promoters and apparitors? Did he go about to pitch down his court, as an empiric does his bank, to inveigle in all the money of the country? No, certainly, it would not have been permitted him to exercise any such function indifferently wherever he came. And verily some such matter it was as want of a fat diocese that kept our Britain bishops so poor in the primitive times, that being called to the council of Ariminum in the year 359, they had not where-withal to defray the charges of their journey, but were fed and lodged upon the emperor's cost; which must needs be no acci-dental but usual poverty in them: for the author, Sulpitius Severus, in his 2nd book of Church History, praises them, and avouches it praiseworthy in a bishop to be so poor as to have nothing of his own. But to return to the ancient election of bishops, that it could not lawfully be without the consent of the people is so express in Cyprian, and so often to be met with, that to cite each place at large were to translate a good part of the volume; therefore touching the chief passages, I refer the rest to whom so list peruse the author himself. In the 24th epistle, 'If a bishop,' saith he, 'be once made and allowed by the testi-mony and judgment of his colleagues and the people, no other can be made.' In the 55th, 'When a bishop is made by the suff-rage of all the people in peace.' In the 68th mark but what he says: 'The people chiefly hath power either of choosing worthy ones, or refusing unworthy'; this he there proves by authorities out of the Old and New Testament, and with solid reasons: these were his antiquities.

This voice of the people, to be had ever in episcopal elections, was so well known before Cyprian's time, even to those that were without the church, that the emperor Alexander Severus desired to have his governors of provinces chosen in the same manner, as Lampridius can tell; so little thought it he offensive to monarchy. And if single authorities persuade not, hearken what the whole general council of Nicaea, the first and famousest of all the rest, determines, writing a synodical epistle to the African churches, to warn them of Arianism: it exhorts them to choose orthodox bishops in the place of the dead, so they be worthy, and the people choose them; whereby they seem to make the people's assent so necessary, that merit without their free choice were not sufficient to make a bishop. What would ye say now, grave fathers, if you should wake and see unworthy bishops, or rather no bishops, but Egyptian taskmasters of cere-monies thrust purposely upon the groaning church, to the affliction and vexation of God's people? It was not of old that a conspiracy of bishops could frustrate and fob off the right of the people; for we may read how St Martin, soon after Con-stantine, was made Bishop of Turon in France, by the people's consent from all places thereabout, maugre all the opposition that the bishops could make. Thus went matters of the church almost 400 years after Christ, and very probably far lower: for Nicephorus Phocas, the Greek emperor, whose reign fell near the 1,000th year of our Lord, having done many things tyrannically, is said by Cedrenus to have done nothing more grievous and displeasing to the people, than to have enacted that no bishop should be chosen without his will; so long did this right remain to the people in the midst of other palpable corruptions. Now for episcopal dignity, what it was, see out of Ignatius, who, in his epistle to those of Trallis, confesseth that 'the presbyters are his fellow-counsellors and fellow-benchers.' And Cyprian in many places, as in the 6th, 41st, 52nd epistles, speaking of presbyters, calls them his compresbyters, as if he deemed himself no other, whenas by the same place it appears he was a bishop; he calls them brethren, but that will be thought his meekness; yea, but the presbyters and deacons writing to him think they do him honour enough, when they phrase him no higher than brother Cyprian, and dear Cyprian, in the 26th epistle. For their authority it is evident not to have been single, but depending on the counsel of the presbyters, as from Ignatius was erewhile alleged; and the same Cyprian acknowledges as much in the 6th epistle, and adds thereto, that he had determined, from his entrance into the office of bishop, to do nothing without the consent of his people; and so in the 31st epistle, for it were tedious to course through all his writings, which are so full of the like assertions, insomuch that even in the womb and centre of apostasy, Rome itself, there yet remains a glimpse of this truth; for the pope himself, as a learned English writer notes well, performeth all ecclesiastical jurisdiction as in consistory among his cardinals, which were originally but the parish priests of Rome. Thus then did the spirit of unity and meekness inspire and animate every joint and sinew of the mystical body: but now the gravest and worthiest minister, a true bishop of his fold, shall be reviled and ruffled by an insulting and only canon-wise prelate, as if he were some slight paltry companion: and the people of God, redeemed and washed with Christ's blood, and dignified with so many glorious titles of saints and sons in the gospel, are now no better reputed than impure ethnics and lay dogs; stones, and pillars, and crucifixes, have now the honour and the alms due to Christ's living members; the table of communion, now become a table of separation, stands like an exalted platform upon the brow of the quire, fortified with bulwark and barricado, to keep off the profane touch of the laics, whilst the obscene and surfeited priest scruples not to paw and mammoc the sacramental bread as familiarly as his tavern biscuit. And thus the people, vilified, and rejected by them, give over the earnest study of virtue and godliness, as a thing of greater purity than they need, and the search of divine knowledge as a mystery too high for their capacities, and only for churchmen to meddle with; which is what the prelates desire, that when they have brought us back to popish blindness, we might commit to their dispose the whole managing of our salvation; for they think it was never fair world with them since that time. But he that will mould a modern bishop into a primitive, must yield him to be elected by the popular voice, undiocesed, unrevenued, unlorded, and leave him nothing but brotherly equality, matchless temperance, frequent fasting, incessant prayer and preaching, continual watchings and labours in his ministry; which what a rich booty it would be, what a plump endowment to the many-beneficed gaping-mouth of a prelate, what a relish it would give to his canary-sucking and swam-eating palate, let old Bishop Mountain judge for me.

How little therefore those ancient times make for modern bishops hath been plainly discoursed; but let them make for them as much as they will, yet why we ought not to stand to their arbitrement, shall now appear by a threefold corruption which will be found upon them. 1. The best times were spreadingly infected. 2. The best men of those times foully tainted. 3. The best writings of those men dangerously adulterated. These positions are to be made good out of those times witnessing of themselves. First, Ignatius in his early days testifies to the churches of Asia, that even then heresies were sprung up, and rife everywhere, as Eusebius relates in his 3rd book, 35th chap. after the Greek number. And Hegesippus, a grave church writer of prime antiquity, affirms in the same book of Eusebius, c. 32, 'that while the apostles were on earth, the depravers of doctrine did but lurk; but they once gone, with open forehead they durst preach down the truth with falsities.' Yea, those that are reckoned for orthodox, began to make sad and shameful rents in the church about the trivial celebration of feasts, not agreeing when to keep Easter-day; which controversy grew so hot, that Victor, the Bishop of Rome, excommunicated all the churches of Asia for no other cause, and was worthily thereof reproved by Irenaeus. For can any sound theologer think, that these great fathers understood what was gospel, or what was excommunication? Doubtless that which led the good men into fraud and error was, that they attended more to the near tradition of what they heard the apostles sometimes did, than to what they had left written, not considering that many things which they did were by the apostles themselves professed to be done only for the present, and of mere indulgence to some scrupulous converts of the circumcision, but what they writ was of firm decree to all future ages. Look but a century lower in the 1st chap. of Eusebius's 8th book. What a universal tetter of impurity had envenomed every part, order, and degree of the church! to omit the lay herd, which will be little regarded, 'Those that seem to be our pastors,' saith he, 'overturning the law of God's worship, burnt in contentions one towards another, and increasing in hatred and bitterness, outrageously sought to uphold lordship and command as it were a tyranny.' Stay but a little, magnanimous bishops, suppress your aspiring thoughts, for there is nothing wanting but Constantine to reign, and then tyranny herself shall give up all her citadels into your hands, and count ye thenceforward her trustiest agents. Such were these that must be called the ancientest and most virgin times between Christ and Constantine. Nor was this general contagion in their actions, and not in their writings. Who is ignorant of the foul errors, the ridiculous wresting of Scripture, the heresies, the vanities thick sown through the volumes of Justin Martyr, Clemens, Origen, Tertullian, and others of eldest time? Who would think him fit to write an apology for Christian faith to the Roman senate, that would tell them 'how of the angels,' which he must needs mean those in Genesis, called the sons of God, 'mixing with women were begotten the devils,' as good Justin Martyr in his Apology told them? But more indignation would it move to any Christian that shall read Tertullian, terming St Paul a novice, and raw in grace, for reproving St Peter at Antioch, worthy to be blamed, if we believe the epistle to the Galatians. Perhaps from this hint the blasphemous Jesuits presumed in Italy to give their judgment of St Paul, as of a hot-headed person, as Sandys in his relations tells us.

Now besides all this, who knows not how many superstitious works are ingraffed into the legitimate writings of the fathers? And of those books that pass for authentic, who knows what hath been tempered withal, what hath been razed out, what hath been inserted? Besides the late legerdemain of the papists, that which Sulpitius writes concerning Origen's books gives us cause vehemently to suspect there hath been packing of old. In the third chapter of his 1st Dialogue we may read what wrangling the bishops and monks had about the reading or not reading of Origen; some objecting that he was corrupted by heretics; others answering that all such books had been so dealt with. How then shall I trust these times to lead me, that testify so ill of leading themselves? Certainly of their defects their own witness may be best received, but of the rectitude and sincerity of their life and doctrine, to judge rightly we must judge by that which was to be their rule.

But it will be objected, that this was an unsettled state of the church, wanting the temporal magistrate to suppress the licence of false brethren, and the extravagancy of still new opinions; a time not imitable for church government, where the temporal and spiritual power did not close in one belief, as under Constantine. I am not of opinion to think the church a vine in this respect, because, as they take it, she cannot subsist without clasping about the elm of worldly strength and felicity, as if the heavenly city could not support itself without the props and buttresses of secular authority. They extol Constantine because he extolled them; as our home-bred monks in their histories blanch the kings their benefactors, and brand those that went about to be their correctors. If he had curbed the growing pride, avarice, and luxury of the clergy, then every page of his story should have swelled with his faults, and that which Zozimus the heathen writes of him should have come in to boot; we should have heard then in every declamation how he slew his nephew Commodus, a worthy man, his noble and eldest son Crispus, his wife Fausta, besides numbers of his friends: then his cruel exactions, his unsoundness in religion, favouring the Arians that had been condemned in a council, of which himself sat as it were president; his hard measure and banishment of the faithful and invincible Athanasius; his living unbaptized almost to his dying day: these blurs are too apparent in his life. But since he must needs be the loadstar of reformation, as some men clatter, it will be good to see further his knowledge of religion what it was, and by that we may likewise guess at the sincerity of his times in those that were not heretical, it being likely that he would converse with the famousest prelates (for so he had made them) that were to be found for learning.

Of his Arianism we heard, and for the rest a pretty scantling of his knowledge may be taken by his deferring to be baptized so many years, a thing not usual, and repugnant to the tenor of scripture; Philip knowing nothing that should hinder the eunuch to be baptized after profession of his belief. Next, by the excessive devotion, that I may not say superstition, both of him and his mother Helena, to find out the cross on which Christ suffered, that had long lain under the rubbish of old ruins (a thing which the disciples and kindred of our Saviour might with more ease have done, if they had thought it a pious duty); some of the nails whereof he put into his helmet, to bear off blows in battle; others he fastened among the studs of his bridle, to fulfil (as he thought or his court bishops persuaded him) the prophecy of Zechariah: 'And it shall be that which is in the bridle shall be holy to the Lord.' Part of the cross, in which he thought such virtue to reside, as would prove a kind of palladium to save the city wherever it remained, he caused to be laid up in a pillar of porphyry by his statue. How he or his teachers could trifle thus with half an eye open upon St Paul's principles, I know not how to imagine.

How should then the dim taper of this emperor's age that had such need of snuffing, extend any beam to our times, wherewith we might hope to be better lighted, than by those luminaries that God hath set up to shine to us far nearer hand? And what reformation he wrought for his own time, it will not be amiss to consider. He appointed certain times for fasts and feasts, built stately churches, gave large immunities to the clergy, great riches and promotions to bishops, gave and ministered occasion to bring in a deluge of ceremonies, thereby either to draw in the heathen by a resemblance of their rites, or to set a gloss upon the simplicity and plainness of Christianity; which, to the gorgeous solemnities of paganism, and the sense of the world's children, seemed but a homely and yeomanly religion; for the beauty of inward sanctity was not within their prospect.

So that in this manner the prelates, both then and ever since, coming from a mean and plebeian life on a sudden to be lords of stately palaces, rich furniture, delicious fare, and princely attendance, thought the plain and homespun verity of Christ's gospel unfit any longer to hold their lordships' acquaintance, unless the poor threadbare matron were put into better clothes: her chaste and modest veil, surrounded with celestial beams, they overlaid with wanton tresses, and in a flaring tire bespeckled her with all the gaudy allurements of a whore.

Thus flourished the church with Constantine's wealth, and thereafter were the effects that followed: his son Constantius proved a flat Arian, and his nephew Julian an apostate, and there his race ended; the church that before by insensible degrees

welked and impaired, now with large steps went downhill decaying; at this time antichrist began first to put forth his horn,
and that saying was common, that former times had wooden
chalices and golden priests, but they, golden chalices and wooden
priests. 'Formerly,' saith Sulpitius, 'martyrdom by glorious
death was sought more greedily than now bishoprics by vile
ambition are hunted after,' speaking of these times. And in
another place, 'They gape after possession, they tend lands and
livings, they cower over their gold, they buy and sell: and if there
be any that neither possess nor traffic, that which is worse, they
sit still, and expect gifts, and prostitute every endowment of
grace, every holy thing, to sale.' And in the end of his history
thus he concludes: 'All things went to wrack by the faction,
wilfulness, and avarice of the bishops; and by this means God's
people, and every good man, was had in scorn and derision';
which St Martin found truly to be said by his friend Sulpitius;
for, being held in admiration of all men, he had only the bishops
his enemies, found God less favourable to him after he was
bishop than before, and for his last sixteen years would come at
no bishops' meeting. Thus you see, sir, what Constantine's
doings in the church brought forth, either in his own or in his
son's reign.

Now, lest it should be thought that something else might ail
this author thus to hamper the bishops of those days, I will
bring you the opinion of three the famousest men for wit and
learning that Italy at this day glories of, whereby it may be
concluded for a received opinion, even among men professing
the Romish faith, that Constantine married all in the church.
Dante, in his 19th canto of Inferno, hath thus, as I will render
it you in English blank verse:

> Ah Constantine! of how much ill was cause,
> Not thy conversion, but those rich domains
> That the first wealthy pope receiv'd of thee!

So, in his 20th canto of Paradise, he makes the like complaint;
and Petrarch seconds him in the same mind in his 108th sonnet,
which is wiped out by the inquisitor in some editions; speaking
of the Roman antichrist as merely bred up by Constantine:

> Founded in chaste and humble poverty,
> 'Gainst them that rais'd thee dost thou lift thy horn,
> Impudent whore, where hast thou plac'd thy hope?
> In they adulterers, or thy ill-got wealth?
> Another Constantine comes not in haste.

Ariosto of Ferrara, after both these in time, but equal in fame, following the scope of his poem in a difficult knot how to restore Orlando, his chief hero, to his lost senses, brings Astolfo, the English knight, up into the moon, where St John, as he feigns, met him.   Cant. 34:

> And, to be short, at last his guide him brings
> Into a goodly valley, where he sees
> A mighty mass of things strangely confus'd,
> Things that on earth were lost, or were abus'd.

And amongst these so abused things listen what he met withal, under the conduct of the Evangelist:

> Then pass'd he to a flowery mountain green,
> Which once smelt sweet, now stinks as odiously:
> This was that gift (if you the truth will have)
> That Constantine to good Sylvestro gave.

And this was a truth well known in England before this poet was born, as our Chaucer's Ploughman shall tell you by and by upon another occasion.   By all these circumstances laid together, I do not see how it can be disputed what good this emperor Constantine wrought to the church; but rather whether ever any, though perhaps not wittingly, set open a door to more mischief in Christendom.   There is just cause therefore, that when the prelates cry out, Let the church be reformed according to Constantine, it should sound to a judicious ear no otherwise than if they should say, Make us rich, make us lofty, make us lawless; for if any under him were not so, thanks to those ancient remains of integrity which were not yet quite worn out, and not to his government.

Thus finally it appears, that those purer times were not such as they are cried up, and not to be followed without suspicion, doubt, and danger.   The last point wherein the antiquary is to be dealt with at his own weapon, is to make it manifest that the ancientest and best of the fathers have disclaimed all sufficiency in themselves that men should rely on, and sent all comers to the scriptures, as all-sufficient: that this is true, will not be unduly gathered, by showing what esteem they had of antiquity themselves, and what validity they thought in it to prove doctrine or discipline.   I must of necessity begin from the second rank of fathers, because till then antiquity could have no plea.   Cyprian in his 63rd epistle: 'If any,' saith he, 'of our ancestors, either ignorantly or out of simplicity, hath not observed that which the Lord taught us by his example,' speaking of the Lord's supper, 'his simplicity God may pardon of his mercy; but we cannot be excused for following him, being instructed by the Lord.' And have not we the same instructions? and will not this holy man, with all the whole consistory of saints and martyrs that lived of old, rise up and stop our mouths in judgment, when we shall go about to father our errors and opinions upon their authority? In the 73rd epistle he adds: 'In vain do they oppose custom to us, if they be overcome by reason: as if custom were greater than truth, or that in spiritual things that were not to be followed which is revealed for the better by the Holy Ghost.' In the 74th: 'Neither ought custom to hinder that truth should not prevail; for custom without truth is but agedness of error.'

Next Lactantius, he that was preferred to have the bringing up of Constantine's children, in his second book of Institutions, chaps. 7 and 8, disputes against the vain trust in antiquity, as being the chiefest argument of the heathen against the Christians: 'They do not consider,' saith he, 'what religion is, but they are confident it is true, because the ancients delivered it; they count it a trespass to examine it.' And in the eighth: 'Not because they went before us in time, therefore in wisdom; which being given alike to all ages, cannot be prepossessed by the ancients: wherefore, seeing that to seek the truth is inbred to all, they bereave themselves of wisdom, the gift of God, who without judgment, follow the ancients, and are led by others like brute beasts.' St Justin writes to Fortunatian, that 'he counts it lawful, in the books of whomsoever, to reject that which he finds otherwise than true; and so he would have others deal by him.' He neither accounted, as it seems, those fathers that went before, nor himself, nor others of his rank, for men of more than ordinary spirit, that might equally deceive, and be deceived: and oft-times setting our servile humours aside, yea, God so ordering, we may find truth with one man, as soon as in a council, as Cyprian agrees, 71st epistle: 'Many things,' saith he, 'are better revealed to single persons.' At Nicaea, in the first and best reputed council of all the world, there had gone out a canon to divorce married priests, had not one old man, Paphnutius, stood up and reasoned against it.

Now remains it to show clearly that the fathers refer all decision of controversy to the scriptures, as all-sufficient to direct, to resolve, and to determine. Ignatius, taking his last leave of the Asian churches, as he went to martyrdom, exhorted them to adhere close to the written doctrine of the apostles, necessarily written for posterity: so far was he from unwritten traditions, as may be read in the 36th chap. of Eusebius, 3rd book. In the 74th epistle of Cyprian against Stefan, bishop of Rome, imposing upon him a tradition: 'Whence,' quoth he, 'is this tradition? Is it fetched from the authority of Christ in the gospel, or of the apostles in their epistles? for God testifies that those things are to be done which are written.' And then thus: 'What obstinacy, what presumption is this, to prefer human tradition before divine ordinance?' And in the same epistle: 'If we shall return to the head and beginning of divine tradition (which we all know means the Bible) human error ceases; and the reason of heavenly mysteries unfolded, whatsoever was obscure becomes clear.' And in the 14th distinct. of the same epistle, directly against our modern fantasies of a still visible church, he teaches, 'that succession of truth may fail; to renew which, we must have recourse to the fountains'; using this excellent similitude: 'If a channel, or conduit-pipe, which brought in water plentifully before, suddenly fail, do we not go to the fountain to know the cause, whether the spring affords no more, or whether the vein be stopped, or turned aside in the mid course? Thus ought we to do, keeping God's precepts that if in aught the truth shall be changed, we may repair to the gospel and to the apostles, that thence may arise the reason of our doings, from whence our order and beginning arose.' In the 75th he inveighs bitterly against pope Stephanus, 'for that he could boast his succession from Peter, and yet foist in traditions that were not apostolical.' And in his book of the unity of the church, he compares those that, neglecting God's word, follow the doctrines of men, to Corah, Dathan, and Abiram. The very first page of Athanasius against the Gentiles avers the scriptures to be sufficient of themselves for the declaration of truth; and that if his friend Macarius read other religious writers, it was but φιλοκάλος (come un vertuoso, as the Italians say), as a lover of elegance: and in his second tome, the 39th page, after he hath reckoned up the canonical books, 'In these only,' saith he, 'is the doctrine of godliness taught; let no man add to these, or take from these.' And in his Synopsis, having again set down all the writers of the Old and New Testament, 'These,' said he, 'be the anchors and props of our faith.' Besides these, millions of other books have been written by great and wise men according to rule, and agreement with these, of which I will not now speak, as being of infinite number and mere dependence on the canonical books. Basil, in his 2nd tome, writing of true faith, tells his auditors, he is bound to teach them that which he hath learned out of the Bible: and in the same treatise he saith, 'that seeing the commandments of the Lord are faithful, and sure for ever, it is a plain falling from the faith, and a high pride, either to make void anything therein, or to introduce anything not there to be found': and he gives the reason: 'For Christ saith, My sheep hear my voice: they will not follow another, but fly from him, because they know not his voice.' But not to be endless in quotations, it may chance to be objected, that there be many opinions in the fathers which have no ground in scripture; so much the less, may I say, should we follow them, for their own words shall condemn them, and acquit us, that lean not on them; otherwise these their words will acquit them, and condemn us. But it will be replied, The scriptures are difficult to be understood, and therefore require the explanation of the fathers. It is true, there be some books, and especially some places in these books, that remain clouded; yet ever that which is most necessary to be known is most easy; and that which is most difficult, so far expounds itself ever, as to tell us how little it imports our saving knowledge. Hence, to infer a general obscurity over all the text, is a mere suggestion of the devil to disuade men from reading it, and casts an aspersion of dishonour both upon the mercy, truth, and wisdom of God. We count it no gentleness or fair dealing in a man of power amongst us, to require strict and punctual obedience, and yet give out all his commands ambiguous and obscure: we should think he had a plot upon us; certainly such commands were no commands, but snares. The very essence of truth is plainness and brightness; the darkness and crookedness is our own. The wisdom of God created understanding, fit and proportionable to truth, the object and end of it, as the eye to the thing visible. If our understanding have a film of ignorance over it, or be blear with gazing on other false glisterings, what is that to truth? If we will but purge with sovereign eyesalve that intellectual ray which God hath planted in us, then we would believe the scriptures protesting their own plainness and perspicuity, calling to them to be instructed, not only the wise and learned, but the simple, the poor, the babes, foretelling an extraordinary effusion of God's Spirit upon every age and sex, attributing to all men, and requiring from them the ability of searching, trying, examining all things, and by the Spirit discerning that which is good; and as the scriptures themselves pronounce their own plainness, so do the fathers testify of them.

I will not run into a paroxysm of citations again in this point, only instance Athanasius in his forementioned first page: 'The knowledge of truth,' saith he, 'wants no human lore, as being evident in itself, and by the preaching of Christ now opens brighter than the sun.' If these doctors, who had scarce half the light that we enjoy, who all, except two or three, were ignorant of the Hebrew tongue, and many of the Greek, blundering upon the dangerous and suspectful translations of the apostate Aquila, the heretical Theodotion, the judaized Symmachus, the erroneous Origen; if these could yet find the Bible so easy, why should we doubt, that have all the helps of learning and faithful industry that man in this life can look for, and the assistance of God as near now to us as ever? But let the scriptures be hard; are they more hard, more crabbed, more abstruse than the fathers? He that cannot understand the sober, plain, and unaffected style of the scriptures, will be ten times more puzzled with the knotty Africanisms, the pampered metaphors, the intricate and involved sentences of the fathers, besides the fantastic and declamatory flashes, the cross-jingling periods which cannot but disturb and come thwart a settled devotion, worse than the din of bells and rattles.

Now, sir, for the love of holy reformation, what can be said more against these importunate clients of antiquity than she herself their patroness hath said? Whether, think ye, would she approve still to dote upon immeasurable, innumerable, and therefore unnecessary and unmerciful volumes, choosing rather to err with the specious name of the fathers, or to take a sound truth at the hand of a plain upright man, that all his days hath been diligently reading the holy scriptures, and thereto imploring God's grace, while the admirers of antiquity have been beating their brains about their ambones, their diptychs, and meniaias? Now, he that cannot tell of stations and indictions, nor has wasted his precious hours in the endless conferring of councils and conclaves that demolish one another (although I know many of those that pretend to be great rabbis in these studies, have scarce saluted them from the strings and the title page; or, to give them more, have been but the ferrets and mousehunts of an index): yet what pastor or minister, how learned, religious, or discreet soever, does not now bring both his cheeks full blown with oecumenical and synodical, shall be counted a lank, shallow, insufficient man, yea, a dunce, and not worthy to speak about reformation of church discipline.   But I trust they for whom God hath reserved the honour of reforming this church, will easily perceive their adversaries' drift in thus calling for antiquity: they fear the plain field of the scriptures; the chase is too hot; they seek the dark, the bushy, the tangled forest, they would imbosk: they feel themselves struck in the transparent streams of divine truth; they would plunge, and tumble, and think to lie hid in the foul weeds and muddy waters, where no plummet can reach the bottom.   But let them beat themselves like whales, and spend their oil till they be dragged ashore: though wherefore should the ministers give them so much line for shifts and delays? wherefore should they not urge only the gospel, and hold it ever in their faces like a mirror of diamond, till it dazzle and pierce their misty eyeballs? maintaining it the honour of its absolute sufficiency and supremacy inviolable: for if the scriptures be for reformation and antiquity to boot, it is but an advantage to the dozen, it is no winning cast: and though antiquity be against it, while the scriptures be for it, the cause is as good as ought to be wished, antiquity itself sitting judge.

But to draw to an end: the second sort of those that may be justly numbered among the hinderers of reformation, are libertines; these suggest that the discipline sought would be intolerable: for one bishop now in a diocese, we should then have a pope in every parish.   It will not be requisite to answer these men, but only to discover them; for reason they have none, but lust and licentiousness, and therefore answer can have none. It is not any discipline that they could live under, it is the corruption and remissness of discipline that they seek.   Episcopacy duly executed, yea, the Turkish and Jewish rigour against whoring and drinking, the dear and tender discipline of a father, the sociable and loving reproof of a brother, the bosom admonition of a friend, is a presbytery and a consistory to them.   It is only the merry Friar in Chaucer can dispel them.

> Full sweetly heard he confession,
> And pleasant was his absolution,
> He was an easy man to give penance.

And so I leave them; and refer the political discourse of episcopacy to a second book.

The Second Book

Sir,—It is a work good and prudent to be able to guide one man; of larger extended virtue to order well one house: but to govern a nation piously and justly, which only is to say happily, is for a spirit of the greatest size and divinest mettle. And certainly of no less a mind, nor of less excellence in another way, were they who by writing laid the solid and true foundations of this science, which being of greatest importance to the life of man, yet there is no art that hath been more cankered in her principles, more soiled and slubbered with aphorising pedantry, than the art of policy; and that most, where a man would think should least be, in Christian commonwealths. They teach not, that to govern well is to train up a nation in true wisdom and virtue, and that which springs from thence, magnanimity (take heed of that), and that which is our beginning, regeneration, and happiest end, likeness to God, which in one word we call godliness; and that this is the true flourishing of a land, other things follow as the shadow does the substance: to teach thus were mere pulpitry to them. This is the masterpiece of a modern politician, how to qualify and mould the sufferance and sub-jection of the people to the length of that foot that is to tread on their necks; how rapine may serve itself with the fair and honourable pretences of public good; how the puny law may be brought under the wardship and control of lust and will: in which attempt if they fall short, then must a superficial colour of repu-tation by all means, direct or indirect, be gotten to wash over the unsightly bruise of honour. To make men governable in this manner, their precepts mainly tend to break a national spirit and courage, by countenancing open riot, luxury, and ignorance, till having thus disfigured and made men beneath men, as Juno in the fable of Io, they deliver up the poor trans-formed heifer of the commonwealth to be stung and vexed with the breeze and goad of oppression, under the custody of some Argus with a hundred eyes of jealousy. To be plainer, sir, how to solder, how to stop a leak, how to keep up the floating carcass of a crazy and diseased monarchy or state, betwixt wind and water, swimming still upon her own dead lees, that now is the deep design of a politician. Alas, sir! a commonwealth ought to be but as one huge Christian personage, one mighty growth and stature of an honest man, as big and compact in virtue as in body; for look what the grounds and causes are of single happiness to one man, the same ye shall find them to a whole state, as Aristotle, both in his Ethics and Politics, from the principles of reason, lays down: by consequence, therefore, that which is good and agreeable to monarchy, will appear soonest to be so, by being good and agreeable to the true welfare of every Christian; and that which can be justly proved hurtful and offensive to every true Christian, will be evinced to be alike hurtful to monarchy: for God forbid that we should separate and distinguish the end and good of a monarch, from the end and good of the monarchy, or of that, from Christianity. How then this third and last sort that hinder reformation will justify that it stands not with reason of state, I must muse, for certain I am, the Bible is shut against them, as certain that neither Plato nor Aristotle is for their turns. What they can bring us now from the schools of Loyola with his Jesuits, or their Malvezzi, that can cut Tacitus into slivers and steaks, we shall presently hear. They allege, 1. That the church-government must be conformable to the civil polity; next, That no form of church-government is agreeable to monarchy, but that of bishops. Must church-government that is appointed in the gospel, and has chief respect to the soul, be conformable and pliant to civil, that is arbitrary, and chiefly conversant about the visible and external part of man? This is the very maxim that moulded the calves of Bethel and of Dan; this was the quintessence of Jeroboam's policy, he made religion conform to his politic interests; and this was the sin that watched over the Israelites till their final captivity. If this state principle come from the prelates, as they affected to be counted statists, let them look back to Eleutherius Bishop of Rome, and see what he thought of the policy of England; being required by Lucius, the first Christian king of this island, to give his counsel for the founding of religious laws, little thought he of this sage caution, but bids him betake himself to the Old and New Testament, and receive direction from them how to administer both church and commonwealth; that he was God's vicar, and therefore to rule by God's laws; that the edicts of Caesar we may at all times disallow, but the statutes of God for no reason we may reject. Now certain, if church-government be taught in the gospel, as the bishops dare not deny, we may well conclude of what late standing this position is, newly calculated for the altitude of bishop-elevation, and lettuce for their lips. But by what example can they show, that the form of church-discipline must be minted and modelled out to secular pretences? The ancient republic of the Jews is evident to have run through all the changes of civil estate, if we survey the story from the giving of the law to the Herods; yet did one manner of priestly government serve without inconvenience to all these temporal mutations; it served the mild aristocracy of elective dukes, and heads of tribes joined with them; the dictatorship of the judges, the easy or hardhanded monarchies, the domestic or foreign tyrannies: lastly, the Roman senate from without, the Jewish senate at home, with the Galilean tetrarch; yet the Levites had some right to deal in civil affairs: but seeing the evangelical precept forbids churchmen to intermeddle with worldly employments, what interweavings or interworkings can knit the minister and the magistrate in their several functions, to the regard of any precise correspondency! Seeing that the churchman's office is only to teach men the Christian faith, to exhort all, to encourage the good, to admonish the bad, privately the less offender, publicly the scandalous and stubborn; to censure and separate, from the communion of Christ's flock, the contagious and incorrigible, to receive with joy and fatherly compassion the penitent: all this must be done, and more than this is beyond any church-authority. What is all this either here or there, to the temporal regiment or weal public, whether it be popular, princely, or monarchical? Where doth it entrench upon the temporal governor? where does it come in his walk? where doth it make inroad upon his jurisdiction? Indeed if the minister's part be rightly discharged, it renders him the people more conscionable, quiet, and easy to be governed; if otherwise, his life and doctrine will declare him. If, therefore, the constitution of the church be already set down by divine prescript, as all sides confess, then can she not be a handmaid to wait on civil commodities and respects; and if the nature and limits of church-discipline be such, as are either helpful to all political estates indifferently, or have no particular relation to any, then is there no necessity, nor indeed possibility, of linking the one with the other in a special conformation.

Now for their second conclusion, 'That no form of church-government is agreeable to monarchy, but that of bishops,' although it fall to pieces of itself by that which hath been said; yet to give them play, front and rear, it shall be my task to prove that episcopacy, with that authority which it challenges in England, is not only not agreeable, but tending to the destruction of monarchy. While the primitive pastors of the church of God laboured faithfully in their ministry, tending only their sheep, and not seeking, but avoiding all worldly matters as clogs, and indeed derogations and debasements to their high calling, little needed the princes and potentates of the earth, which way soever the gospel was spread, to study ways how to make a coherence between the church's polity and theirs: therefore, when Pilate heard once our Saviour Christ professing that 'his kingdom was not of this world,' he thought the man could not stand much in Caesar's light nor much endamage the Roman empire; for if the life of Christ be hid to this world, much more is his sceptre inoperative, but in spiritual things. And thus lived, for two or three ages, the successors of the apostles. But when, through Constantine's lavish superstition, they forsook their first love, and set themselves up two gods instead, Mammon and their belly; then taking advantage of the spiritual power which they had on men's consciences, they began to cast a longing eye to get the body also, and bodily things into their command: upon which their carnal desires, the spirit daily quenching and dying in them, knew no way to keep themselves up from falling to nothing, but by bolstering and supporting their inward rottenness by a carnal and outward strength. For a while they rather privily sought opportunity, than hastily disclosed their project; but when Constantine was dead, and three or four emperors more, their drift became notorious and offensive to the whole world; for while Theodosius the younger reigned, thus writes Socrates the historian, in his 7th book, chap. 11: 'Now began an ill name to stick upon the bishops of Rome and Alexandria, who beyond their priestly bounds now long ago had stepped into principality': and this was scarce eighty years since their raising from the meanest worldly condition. Of courtesy now let any man tell me, if they draw to themselves a temporal strength and power out of Caesar's dominion, is not Caesar's empire thereby diminished? But this was a stolen bit, hitherto he was but a caterpillar secretly gnawing at monarchy; the next time you shall see him a wolf, a lion, lifting his paw against his raiser, as Petrarch expressed it, and finally an open enemy and subverter of the Greek empire. Philippicus and Leo, with divers other emperors after them, not without the advice of their patriarchs, and at length of a whole eastern council of three hundred and thirty-eight bishops, threw the images out of the churches as being decreed idolatrous.

Upon this goodly occasion the Bishop of Rome not only seizes the city, and all the territory about, into his own hands, and makes himself lord thereof, which till then was governed by a Greek magistrate, but absolves all Italy of their tribute and obedience due to the emperor, because he obeyed God's commandment in abolishing idolatry.

Mark, sir, here, how the pope came by St Peter's patrimony, as he feigns it; not the donation of Constantine, but idolatry and rebellion got it him. Ye need but read Sigonius, one of his own sect, to know the story at large. And now to shroud himself against a storm from the Greek continent, and provide a champion to bear him out in these practices, he takes upon him by papal sentence to unthrone Chilpericus, the rightful king of France and gives the kingdom to Pepin, for no other cause, but that he seemed to him the more active man. If he were a friend herein to monarchy, I know not; but to the monarch I need not ask what he was.

Having thus made Pepin his fast friend, he calls him into Italy against Aistulphus the Lombard, that warred upon him for his late usurpation of Rome, as belonging to Ravenna, which he had newly won. Pepin, not unobedient to the pope's call, passing into Italy, frees him out of danger, and wins for him the whole exarchate of Ravenna; which though it had been almost immediately before the hereditary possession of that monarchy, which was his chief patron and benefactor, yet he takes and keeps it to himself as lawful prize, and given to St Peter. What a dangerous fallacy is this, when a spiritual man may snatch to himself any temporal dignity or dominion, under pretence of receiving it for the church's use? Thus he claims Naples, Sicily, England, and what not. To be short, under show of his zeal against the errors of the Greek church, he never ceased baiting and goring the successors of his best lord Constantine, what by his barking curses and excommunications, what by his hindering the western princes from aiding them against the Saracens and Turks, unless when they humoured him; so that it may be truly affirmed, he was the subversion and fall of that monarchy which was the hoisting of him. This, besides Petrarch, whom I have cited, our Chaucer also hath observed, and gives from hence a caution to England, to beware of her bishops in time, for that their ends and aims are no more friendly to monarchy than the pope's.

This he begins in the Ploughman speaking, part ii. stanza 28:

> The emperor yafe the pope sometime
> So high lordship him about,
> That at last the silly kime,
> The proud pope put him out;
> So of this realm is no doubt.

> But lords beware and them defend;
> For now these folks be wonders stout,
> The king and lords now this amend.

And in the next stanza, which begins the third part of the tale, he argues that they ought not to be lords:

> Moses law forbode it tho
> That priests should no lordship welde,
> Christ's gospel biddeth also
> That they should no lordships held;
> Ne Christ's apostles were never so bold
> No such lordships to hem embrace,
> But smeren her sheep and keep her fold.

And so forward. Whether the bishops of England have deserved thus to be feared by men so wise as our Chaucer is esteemed; and how agreeable to our monarchy and monarchs their demeanour has been, he that is but meanly read in our chronicles needs not be instructed. Have they not been as the Canaanites and Philistines to this kingdom? What treasons, what revolts to the pope, what rebellions, and those the basest and most pretenceless, have they not been chief in? What could monarchy think, when Becket durst challenge the custody of Rochester Castle, and the Tower of London, as appertaining to his signory? to omit his other insolencies and affronts to regal majesty, until the lashes inflicted on the anointed body of the king washed off the holy unction with his blood drawn by the polluted hands of bishops, abbots, and monks.

What good upholders of royalty were the bishops, when, by their rebellious opposition against King John, Normandy was lost, he himself deposed, and this kingdom made over to the pope? When the Bishop of Winchester durst tell the nobles, the pillars of the realm, that there were no peers in England, as in France, but that the king might do what he pleased, what could tyranny say more? It would be pretty now if I should insist upon the rendering up of Tournay by Wolsey's treason, the excommunications, cursings, and interdicts upon the whole land; for haply I shall be cut off short by a reply, that these were the faults of men and their popish errors, not of episcopacy, that hath now renounced the pope, and is a protestant. Yes, sure; as wise and famous men have suspected and feared the protestant episcopacy in England, as those that have feared the papal.

You know, sir, what was the judgment of Padre Paolo, the great Venetian antagonist of the pope, for it is extant in the hands of many men, whereby he declares his fear, that when the hierarchy of England shall light into the hands of busy and audacious men, or shall meet with princes tractable to the prelacy, then much mischief is like to ensue. And can it be nearer hand than when bishops shall openly affirm that, 'No bishop no king'? A trim paradox, and that ye may know where they have been a-begging for it, I will fetch you the twin brother to it out of the Jesuits' cell: they feeling the axe of God's reformation hewing at the old and hollow trunk of papacy, and finding the Spaniard their surest friend and safest refuge, to soothe him up in his dream of a fifth monarchy, and withal to uphold the decrepit papalty, have invented this superpolitic aphorism, as one terms it, 'One pope and one king.'

Surely there is not any prince in Christendom, who, hearing this rare sophistry, can choose but smile; and if we be not blind at home, we may as well perceive that this worthy motto, 'No bishop no king,' is of the same batch, and infanted out of the same fears, a mere ague-cake, coagulated of a certain fever they have, presaging their time to be but short: and now, like those that are sinking, they catch round of that which is likeliest to hold them up; and would persuade regal power that if they dive, he must after. But what greater debasement can there be to royal dignity, whose towering and steadfast height rests upon the unmovable foundations of justice and heroic virtue, than to chain it in a dependence of subsisting, or ruining, to the painted battlements and gaudy rottenness of prelatry, which want but one puff of the king's to blow them down like a pasteboard house built of court-cards? Sir, the little ado which methinks I find in untacking these pleasant sophisms, puts me into the mood to tell you a tale ere I proceed further; and Menenius Agrippa speed us.

Upon a time the body summoned all the members to meet in the guild, for the common good (as Aesop's chronicles aver many stranger accidents): the head by right takes the first seat, and next to it a huge and monstrous wen, little less than the head itself, growing to it by a narrower excrescency. The members, amazed, began to ask one another what he was that took place next their chief? None could resolve. Whereat the wen, though unwieldy, with much ado gets up, and bespeaks the assembly to this purpose: 'That as in place he was second to the head, so by due of merit; that he was to it an ornament, and strength, and of special near relation; and that if the head should fail, none were fitter than himself to step into his place:

therefore he thought it for the honour of the body, that such dignities and rich endowments should be decreed him, as did adorn and set out the noblest members.' To this was answered, that it should be consulted. Then was a wise and learned philosopher sent for, that knew all the charters, laws, and tenures of the body. On him it is imposed by all, as chief committee, to examine and discuss the claim and petition of right put in by the wen; who soon perceiving the matter, and wondering at the boldness of such a swoln tumour, 'Wilt thou,' quoth he, 'that art but a bottle of vicious and hardened excrements, contend with the lawful and freeborn members, whose certain number is set by ancient and unrepealable statute? Head thou art none, though thou receive this huge substance from it. What office bearest thou? what good canst thou show by thee done to the common weal?' The wen, not easily dashed, replies that his office was his glory; for so oft as the soul would retire out of the head from over the steaming vapours of the lower parts to divine contemplation, with him she found the purest and quietest retreat, as being most remote from soil and disturbance. 'Lourdan,' quoth the philosopher, 'thy folly is as great as thy filth: know that all the faculties of the soul are confined of old to their several vessels and ventricles, from which they cannot part without dissolution of the whole body; and that thou containest no good thing in thee, but a heap of hard and loathsome uncleanness, and art to the head a foul disfigurement and burden, when I have cut thee off, and opened thee, as by the help of these implements I will do, all men shall see.'

But to return whence was disgressed: seeing that the throne of a king, as the wise King Solomon often remembers us, 'is established in justice,' which is the universal justice that Aristotle so much praises, containing in it all other virtues, it may assure us that the fall of prelacy, whose actions are so far distant from justice, cannot shake the least fringe that borders the royal canopy; but that their standing doth continually oppose and lay battery to regal safety, shall by that which follows easily appear. Amongst many secondary and accessory causes that support monarchy, these are not of least reckoning, though common to all other states; the love of the subjects, the multitude and valour of the people, and store of treasure. In all these things hath the kingdom been of late sore weakened, and chiefly by the prelates. First, let any man consider, that if any prince shall suffer under him a commission of authority to be exercised, till all the land groan and cry out, as against a whip of scorpions, whether this

be not likely to lesson and keel the affections of the subject.
Next, what numbers of faithful and freeborn Englishmen, and
good Christians, have been constrained to forsake their dearest
home, their friends and kindred, whom nothing but the wide
ocean, and the savage deserts of America, could hide and shelter
from the fury of the bishops? O, sir, if we could but see the
shape of our dear mother England, as poets are wont to give a
personal form to what they please, how would she appear,
think ye, but in a mourning weed, with ashes upon her head,
and tears abundantly flowing from her eyes, to behold so many
of her children exposed at once, and thrust from things of dearest
necessity, because their conscience could not assent to things
which the bishops thought indifferent? What more binding than
conscience? What more free than indifferency? Cruel then
must that indifferency needs be, that shall violate the strict
necessity of conscience; merciless and inhuman that free choice
and liberty that shall break asunder the bonds of religion! Let
the astrologer be dismayed at the portentous blaze of comets
and impressions in the air, as foretelling troubles and changes
to states: I shall believe there cannot be a more ill-boding sign
to a nation (God turn the omen from us!) than when the inhabitants, to avoid insufferable grievances at home, are enforced
by heaps to forsake their native country. Now, whereas the
only remedy and amends against the depopulation and thinness
of a land within, is the borrowed strength of firm alliance from
without, these priestly policies of theirs having thus exhausted
our domestic forces, have gone the way also to leave us as naked
of our firmest and faithfullest neighbours abroad, by disparaging
and alienating from us all protestant princes and commonwealths;
who are not ignorant that our prelates, and as many as they can
infect, account them no better than a sort of sacrilegious and
puritanical rebels, preferring the Spaniard, our deadly enemy,
before them, and set all orthodox writers at nought in comparison
of the Jesuits, who are indeed the only corrupters of youth and
good learning: and I have heard many wise and learned men in
Italy say as much. It cannot be that the strongest knot of
confederacy should not daily slacken, when religion, which is the
chief engagement of our league, shall be turned to their reproach.
Hence it is that the prosperous and prudent states of the United
Provinces (whom we ought to love, if not for themselves, yet
for our own good work in them, they having been in a manner
planted and erected by us, and having been since to us the faithful watchmen and discoverers of many a popish and Austrian

complotted treason, and with us the partners of many a bloody
and victorious battle), whom the similitude of manners and
language, the commodity of traffic, which founded the old
Burgundian league betwixt us, but chiefly religion, should bind
to us immortally; even such friends as these, out of some of the
principles instilled into us by the prelates, have been often dis-
missed with distasteful answers, and sometimes unfriendly actions:
nor is it to be considered to the breach of confederate nations,
whose mutual interest is of such high consequence, though their
merchants bicker in the East Indies; neither is it safe, or wary,
or indeed Christianly, that the French king, of a different faith,
should afford our nearest allies as good protection as we. Sir, I
persuade myself, if our zeal to true religion, and the brotherly
usage of our truest friends, were as notorious to the world as
our prelatical schism and captivity to rochet apophthegms, we
had ere this seen our old conquerors, and afterwards liegemen,
the Normans, together with the Britains, our proper colony, and
all the Gascoins that are the rightful dowry of our ancient kings,
come with cap and knee, desiring the shadow of the English
sceptre to defend them from the hot persecutions and taxes of
the French. But when they come hither, and see a tympany of
Spaniolized bishops swaggering in the foretop of the state, and
meddling to turn and dandle the royal ball with unskilful and
pedantic palms, no marvel though they think it as unsafe to
commit religion and liberty to their arbitrating as to a synagogue
of Jesuits.

But what do I stand reckoning upon advantages and gains
lost by the misrule and turbulency of the prelates? What do
I pick up so thriftily their scatterings and diminishings of the
meaner subject, whilst they by their seditious practices have
endangered to lose the king one-third of his main stock? What
have they not done to banish him from his own native country?
But to speak of this as it ought, would ask a volume by
itself.

Thus as they have unpeopled the kingdom by expulsion of
so many thousands, as they have endeavoured to lay the skirts
of it bare by disheartening and dishonouring our loyalest
confederates abroad, so have they hamstrung the valour of the
subject by seeking to effeminate us all at home. Well knows
every wise nation, that their liberty consists in manly and honest
labours, in sobriety and rigorous honour to the marriage-bed,
which in both sexes should be bred up from chaste hopes to loyal
enjoyments; and when the people slacken, and fall to looseness

and riot, then do they as much as if they laid down their necks for some wild tyrant to get up and ride. Thus learnt Cyrus to tame the Lydians, whom by arms he could not whilst they kept themselves from luxury; with one easy proclamation to set up stews, dancing, feasting, and dicing, he made them soon his slaves. I know not what drift the prelates had, whose brokers they were to prepare, and supple us either for a foreign invasion or domestic oppression: but this I am sure, they took the ready way to despoil us both of manhood and grace at once, and that in the shamefullest and ungodliest manner, upon that day which God's law and even our own reason hath consecrated, that we might have one day at least of seven set apart wherein to examine and increase our knowledge of God, to meditate and commune of our faith, our hope, our eternal city in heaven, and to quicken withal the study and exercise of charity; at such a time that men should be plucked from their soberest and saddest thoughts, and by bishops, the pretended fathers of the church, instigated, by public edict, and with earnest endeavour pushed forward to gaming, jigging, wassailing, and mixed dancing, is a horror to think! Thus did the reprobate hireling priest Balaam seek to subdue the Israelites to Moab, if not by force, then by this devilish policy, to draw them from the sanctuary of God to the luxurious and ribald feasts of Baal-peor. Thus have they trespassed not only against the monarchy of England, but of Heaven also, as others, I doubt not, can prosecute against them.

I proceed within my own bounds to show you next what good agents they are about the revenues and riches of the kingdom, which declare of what moment they are to monarchy, or what avail. Two leeches they have that still suck and suck the kingdom—their ceremonies and their courts. If any man will contend that ceremonies be lawful under the gospel, he may be answered otherwhere. This doubtless, that they ought to be many and overcostly, no true protestant will affirm. Now I appeal to all wise men, what an excessive waste of treasure hath been within these few years in this land, not in the expedient, but in the idolatrous erection of temples beautified exquisitely to out-vie the papists, the costly and dear-bought scandals and snares of images, pictures, rich copes, gorgeous altar-cloths: and by the courses they took, and the opinions they held, it was not likely any stay would be, or any end of their madness, where a pious pretext is so ready at hand to cover their insatiate desires. What can we suppose this will come to? What other materials than these have built up the spiritual Babel to the height of her abominations? Believe it, sir, right truly it may be said, that Antichrist is Mammon's son. The sour leaven of human traditions, mixed in one putrefied mass with the poisonous dregs of hypocrisy in the hearts of prelates, that lie basking in the sunny warmth of wealth and promotion, is the serpent's egg that will hatch an Antichrist wheresoever, and engender the same monster as big, or little, as the lump is which breeds him. If the splendour of gold and silver begin to lord it once again in the church of England, we shall see Antichrist shortly wallow here, though his chief kennel be at Rome. If they had one thought upon God's glory, and the advancement of Christian faith, they would be a means that with these expenses thus profusely thrown away in trash, rather churches and schools might be built, where they cry out for want, and more added where too few are; a moderate maintenance distributed to every painful minister, that now scarce sustains his family with bread, while the prelates revel like Belshazzar with their full carouses in goblets and vessels of gold snatched from God's temple; which (I hope) the worthy men of our land will consider. Now then for their courts. What a mass of money is drawn from the veins into the ulcers of the kingdom this way; their extortions, their open corruptions, the multitude of hungry and ravenous harpies that swarm about their offices, declare sufficiently. And what though all this go not over sea? It were better it did: better a penurious kingdom, than where excessive wealth flows into the graceless and injurious hands of common sponges, to the impoverishing of good and loyal men, and that by such execrable, such irreligious courses.

If the sacred and dreadful works of holy discipline, censure, penance, excommunication, and absolution, where no profane thing ought to have access, nothing to be assistant but sage and Christianly admonition, brotherly love, flaming charity and zeal; and then according to the effects, paternal sorrow, or paternal joy, mild severity, melting compassion: if such divine ministries as these, wherein the angel of the church represents the person of Christ Jesus, must lie prostitute to sordid fees, and not pass to and fro between our Saviour, that of free grace redeemed us, and the submissive penitent, without the truckage of perishing coin, and the butcherly execution of tormentors, rooks, and rakeshames sold to lucre; then have the Babylonish merchants of souls just excuse. Hitherto, sir, you have heard how the prelates have weakened and withdrawn the external accomplishments of kingly prosperity, the love of the people, their multitude, their valour, their wealth; mining and sapping the outworks and redoubts of monarchy. Now hear how they strike at the very heart and vitals.

We know that monarchy is made up of two parts, the liberty of the subject, and the supremacy of the king. I begin at the root. See what gentle and benign fathers they have been to our liberty! Their trade being, by the same alchemy that the pope uses, to extract heaps of gold and silver out of the drossy bullion of the people's sins; and justly fearing that the quick-sighted protestant's eye, cleared in great part from the mist of superstition, may at one time or another look with a good judgment into these their deceitful pedleries; to gain as many associates of guiltiness as they can, and to infect the temporal magistrate with the like lawless, though not sacrilegious extortion, see awhile what they do! they engage themselves to preach and persuade an assertion for truth the most false, and to this monarchy the most pernicious and destructive that could be chosen. What more baneful to monarchy than a popular commotion? for the dissolution of monarchy slides aptest into a democracy; and what stirs the Englishmen, as our wisest writers have observed, sooner to rebellion, than violent and heavy hands upon their goods and purses? Yet these devout prelates, spite of our Great Charter, and the souls of our progenitors that wrested their liberties out of the Norman gripe with their dearest blood and highest prowess, for these many years have not ceased in their pulpits wrenching and spraining the text, to set at nought and trample under foot all the most sacred and lifeblood laws, statutes, and acts of parliament, that are the holy covenant of union and marriage between the king and his realm, by proscribing and confiscating from us all the right we have to our own bodies, goods, and liberties. What is this but to blow a trumpet, and proclaim a firecross to an hereditary and perpetual civil war? Thus much against the subjects' liberty hath been assaulted by them. Now how they have spared supremacy, or are likely hereafter to submit to it, remains lastly to be considered.

The emulation that under the old law was in the king towards the priest, is now so come about in the gospel, that all the danger is to be feared from the priest to the king. Whilst the priest's office in the law was set out with an exterior lustre of pomp and glory, kings were ambitious to be priests; now priests, not perceiving the heavenly brightness and inward splendour of their more glorious evangelic ministry, with as great ambiton affect to be kings, as in all their courses is easy to be observed. Their eyes ever eminent upon worldly matters, their desires ever thirting after worldly employments, instead of diligent and fervent study in the Bible, they covet to be expert in canons and decretals, which may enable them to judge and interpose in temporal causes, however pretended ecclesiastical. Do they not hoard up pelf, seek to be potent in secular strength, in state affairs, in lands, lordships, and domains, to sway and carry all before them in high courts and privy-councils, to bring into their grasp the high and principal offices of the kingdom? Have they not been bold of late to check the common law, to slight and brave the indiminishable majesty of our highest court, the lawgiving and sacred parliament? Do they not plainly labour to exempt churchmen from the magistrate? Yea, so presumptuously as to question and menace officers that represent the king's person for using their authority against drunken priests? The cause of protecting murderous clergymen was the first heart-burning that swelled up the audacious Becket to the pestilent and odious vexation of Henry the Second. Nay, more: have not some of their devoted scholars begun, I need not say to nibble, but openly to argue against the king's supremacy? Is not the chief of them accused out of his own book, and his late canons, to affect a certain unquestionable patriarchate, independent, and unsubordinate to the crown? From whence having first brought us to a servile state of religion and manhood, and having predisposed his condition with the pope, that lays claim to this land, or some Pepin of his own creating, it were all as likely for him to aspire to the monarchy among us, as that the pope could find means so on the sudden both to bereave the emperor of the Roman territory with the favour of Italy, and by an unexpected friend out of France, while he was in danger to lose his new-got purchase, beyond hope to leap into the fair exarchate of Ravenna.

A good while the pope subtly acted the lamb, writing to the emperor, 'my lord Tiberius, my lord Mauritius'; but no sooner did this his lord pluck at the images and idols, but he threw off his sheep's clothing, and started up a wolf, laying his paws upon the emperor's right, as forfeited to Peter. Why may not we as well, having been forewarned at home by our renowned Chaucer, and from abroad by the great and learned Padre Paolo, from the like beginnings, as we see they are, fear the like events? Certainly a wise and provident king ought to suspect a hierarchy in his realm, being ever attended, as it is, with two such greedy purveyors, ambition and usurpation; I say he ought to suspect a hierarchy to be as dangerous and derogatory from his crown as a tetrarchy or a heptarchy. Yet now that the prelates had almost attained to what their insolent and unbridled minds had hurried them; to thrust the laity under the despotical rule of the monarch, that they themselves might confine the monarch to a kind of pupilage under their hierarchy, observe but how their own principles combat one another, and supplant each one his fellow.

Having fitted us only for peace, and that a servile peace, by lessening our numbers, draining our estates, enfeebling our bodies, cowing our free spirits by those ways as you have heard, their impotent actions cannot sustain themselves the least moment, unless they would rouse us up to a war fit for Cain to be the leader of, an abhorred, a cursed, a fraternal war. England and Scotland, dearest brothers both in nature and in Christ, must be set to wade in one another's blood; and Ireland, our free denizen, upon the back of us both, as occasion should serve: a piece of service that the pope and all his factors have been compassing to do ever since the Reformation.

But ever blessed be He, and ever glorified, that from his high watch-tower in the heavens, discerning the crooked ways of perverse and cruel men, hath hitherto maimed and infatuated all their damnable inventions, and deluded their great wizards with a delusion fit for fools and children: had God been so minded, he could have sent a spirit of mutiny amongst us, as he did between Abimelech and the Sechemites, to have made our funerals, and slain heaps more in number than the miserable surviving remnant; but he, when we least deserved, sent out a gentle gale and message of peace from the wings of those his cherubims that fan his mercy-seat. Nor shall the wisdom, the moderation, the Christian piety, the constancy of our nobility and commons of England, be ever forgotten, whose calm and temperate connivance could sit still and smile out the stormy bluster of men more audacious and precipitant than of solid and deep reach, until their own fury had run itself out of breath, assailing by rash and heady approaches the impregnable situation of our liberty and safety, that laughed such weak enginery to scorn, such poor drifts to make a national war of a surplice brabble, a tippet scuffle, and engage the untainted honour of English knighthood to unfurl the streaming red cross, or to rear the horrid standard of those fatal guly dragons, for so unworthy a purpose, as to force upon their fellow-subjects that which themselves are weary of, the skeleton of a mass-book. Nor must the patience, the fortitude, the firm obedience of the nobles and people of Scotland, striving against manifold provocations; not must their sincere and moderate proceedings hitherto be unremembered, to the shameful conviction of all their detractors.

Go on both hand in hand, O nations, never to be disunited; be the praise and the heroic song of all posterity; merit this, but seek only virtue, not to extend your limits (for what needs to win a fading triumphant laurel out of the tears of wretched men?); but to settle the pure worship of God in his church, and justice in the state: then shall the hardest difficulties smooth out themselves before ye; envy shall sink to hell, craft and malice be confounded, whether it be homebred mischief or outlandish cunning: yea, other nations will then covet to serve ye, for lordship and victory are but the pages of justice and virtue. Commit security to true wisdom the vanquishing and uncasing of craft and subtlety, which are but her two runagates: join your invincible might to do worthy and godlike deeds; and then he that seeks to break your union, a cleaving curse be his inheritance to all generations.

Sir, you have now at length this question for the time, and as my memory would best serve me in such a copious and vast theme, fully handled, and you yourself may judge whether prelacy be the only church-government agreeable to monarchy. Seeing therefore the perilous and confused state into which we are fallen, and that, to the certain knowledge of all men, through the irreligious pride and hateful tyranny of prelates (as the innumerable and grievous complaints of every shire cry out), if we will now resolve to settle affairs either according to pure religion or sound policy, we must first of all begin roundly to cashier and cut away from the public body the noisome and diseased tumour of prelacy, and come from schism to unity with our neighbour reformed sister-churches, which with the blessing of peace and pure doctrine have now long time flourished; and doubtless with all hearty joy and gratulation will meet and welcome our Christian union with them, as they have been all this while grieved at our strangeness and little better than separation from them. And for the discipline propounded, seeing that it hath been inevitably proved, that the natural and fundamental causes of political happiness in all governments are the same and that this church-discipline is taught in the word of God, and, as we see, agrees according to wish with all such states as have received it; we may infallibly assure ourselves that it will as well agree with monarchy, though all the tribe of Aphorismers and Politicasters would persuade us there be secret and mysterious reasons against it. For upon the settling hereof mark what nourishing and cordial restorements to the state will follow, the ministers of the gospel attending only to the work of salvation, every one within his limited charge; besides the diffusive blessing of God upon all our actions, the king shall sit without an old disturber, a daily encroacher and intruder: shall rid his kingdom of a strong sequestered and collateral power; a confronting mitre, whose potent wealth and wakeful ambition he had just cause to hold in jealousy: not to repeat the other present evils which only their removal will remove, and because things simply pure are inconsistent in the mass of nature, nor are the elements or humours in a man's body exactly homogeneal; and hence the best-founded commonwealths and least barbarous have aimed at a certain mixture and temperament, partaking the several virtues of each other state, that each part drawing to itself may keep up a steady and even uprightness in common.

There is no civil government that hath been known, no not the Spartan, not the Roman, though both for this respect so much praised by the wise Polybius, more divinely and harmoniously tuned, more equally balanced as it were by the hand and scale of justice, than is the commonwealth of England; where, under a free and untutored monarch, the noblest, worthiest, and most prudent men, with full approbation and suffrage of the people, have in their power the supreme and final determination of highest affairs. Now if conformity of church-discipline to the civil be so desired, there can be nothing more parallel, more uniform, than when under the sovereign prince, Christ's vicegerent, using the sceptre of David, according to God's law, the godliest, the wisest, the learnedest ministers in their several charges have the instructing and disciplining of God's people, by whose full and free election they are consecrated to that holy and equal aristocracy. And why should not the piety and conscience of Englishmen, as members of the church, be trusted in the election of pastors to functions that nothing concern a monarch as well as their worldly wisdoms are privileged as members of the state in suffraging their knights and burgesses to matters that concern him nearly? And if in weighing these several offices, their difference in time and quality be cast in, I know they will not turn the beam of equal judgment the moiety of a scruple. We therefore having already a kind of apostolical and ancient church election in our state, what a perverseness would it be in us of all others to retain forcibly a kind of imperious and stately election in our church! And what a blindness to think that what is already evangelical, as it were by a happy chance in our polity, should be repugnant to that which is the same by divine command in the ministry! Thus then we see that our ecclesiastical and political choices may consent and sort as well together without any rupture in the state, as Christians and freeholders. But as for honour, that ought indeed to be different and distinct, as either office looks a several way; the minister whose calling and end is spiritual, ought to be honoured as a father and physician to the soul (if he be found to be so) with a son-like and disciple-like reverence, which is indeed the dearest and most affectionate honour, most to be desired by a wise man, and such as will easily command a free and plentiful provision of outward necessaries, without his further care of this world.

The magistrate, whose charge is to see to our persons and estates, is to be honoured with a more elaborate and personal courtship, with large salaries and stipends, that he himself may abound in those things whereof his legal justice and watchful care give us the quiet enjoyment. And this distinction of honour will bring forth a seemly and graceful uniformity over all the kingdom.

Then shall the nobles possess all the dignities and offices of temporal honour to themselves, sole lords without the improper mixture of scholastic and pusillanimous upstarts; the parliament shall void her upper house of the same annoyances; the common and civil laws shall be both set free, the former from the control, the other from the mere vassalage and copyhold of the clergy.

And whereas temporal laws rather punish men when they have transgressed, than form them to be such as should transgress seldomest, we may conceive great hopes, through the showers of divine benediction watering the unmolested and watchful pains of the ministry, that the whole inheritance of God will grow up so straight and blameless, that the civil magistrate may with far less toil and difficulty, and far more ease and delight, steer the tall and goodly vessel of the commonwealth through all the gusts and tides of the world's mutability.

Here I might have ended, but that some objections, which I have heard commonly flying about, press me to the endeavour of an answer. We must not run, they say, into sudden extremes. This is a fallacious rule, unless understood only of the actions of virtue about things indifferent: for if it be found that those two extremes be vice and virtue, falsehood and truth, the greater extremity of virtue and superlative truth we run into, the more virtuous and the more wise we become; and he that, flying from degenerate and traditional corruption, fears to shoot himself too far into the meeting embraces of a divinely warranted reformation, had better not have run at all. And for the suddenness, it cannot be feared. Who should oppose it? The papists? They dare not. The protestants otherwise affected? They were mad. There is nothing will be removed but what to them is professedly indifferent. The long affection which the people have borne to it, what for itself, what for the odiousness of prelates, is evident: from the first year of Queen Elizabeth it hath still been more and more propounded, desired, and beseeched, yea, sometimes, favourably forwarded by the parliaments themselves. Yet if it were sudden and swift, provided still it be from worse to better, certainly we ought to hie us from evil like a torrent, and rid ourselves of corrupt discipline, as we would shake fire out of our bosoms.

Speedy and vehement were the reformations of all the good kings of Judah, though the people had been nuzzled in idolatry ever so long before; they feared not the bugbear danger nor the lion in the way that the sluggish and timorous politician thinks he sees; no more did our brethren of the reformed churches abroad, they ventured (God being their guide) out of rigid popery into that which we in mockery call precise puritanism, and yet we see no inconvenience befell them.

Let us not dally with God when he offers us a full blessing, to take as much of it as we think will serve our ends, and turn him back the rest upon his hands, lest in his anger he snatch all from us again. Next, they allege the antiquity of episcopacy through all ages. What it was in the apostles' time, that questionless it must be still; and therein I trust the ministers will be able to satisfy the parliament. But if episcopacy be taken for prelacy, all the ages they can deduce it through, will make it no more venerable than papacy.

Most certain it is (as all our stories bear witness), that ever since their coming to the see of Canterbury, for near twelve hundred years, to speak of them in general, they have been in England to our souls a sad and doleful succession of illiterate and blind guides; to our purses and goods a wasteful band of robbers, a perpetual havock and rapine; to our state a continual hydra of mischief and molestation, the forge of discord and rebellion; this is the trophy of their antiquity, and boasted succession through so many ages. And for those prelate-martyrs they glory of, they are to be judged what they were by the gospel, and not the gospel to be tried by them.

And it is to be noted, that if they were for bishoprics and ceremonies, it was in their prosperity and fulness of bread; but in their persecution, which purified them, and near their death, which was their garland, they plainly disliked and condemned the ceremonies, and threw away those episcopal ornaments wherein they were installed as foolish and detestable; for so the words of Ridley at his degradement, and his letter to Hooper, expressly show. Neither doth the author of our church-history spare to record sadly the fall (for so he terms it) and infirmities of these martyrs, though we would deify them. And why should their martyrdom more countenance corrupt doctrine or discipline, than their subscriptions justify their treason to the royal blood of this realm, by diverting and entailing the right of the crown from the true heirs, to the houses of Northumberland and Suffolk? which had it took effect, this present king had, in all likelihood, never sat on this throne, and the happy union of this island had been frustrated.

Lastly, whereas they add that some the learnedest of the reformed abroad admire our episcopacy; it had been more for the strength of the argument to tell us that some of the wisest statesmen admire it, for thereby we might guess them weary of the present discipline, as offensive to their state, which is the bug we fear, but being they are churchmen, we may rather suspect them for some prelatizing spirits that admire our bishoprics, not episcopacy.

The next objection vanishes of itself, propounding a doubt, whether a greater inconvenience would not grow from the corruption of any other discipline than from that of episcopacy. This seems an unseasonable foresight, and out of order, to defer and put off the most needful constitution of one right discipline, while we stand balancing the discommodities of two corrupt ones. First constitute that which is right, and of itself it will discover and rectify that which swerves, and easily remedy the pretended fear of having a pope in every parish, unless we call the zealous and meek censure of the church a popedom, which whoso does, let him advise how he can reject the pastorly rod and sheep-hook of Christ, and those cords of love, and not fear to fall under the iron sceptre of his anger, that will dash him to pieces like a potsherd.

At another doubt of theirs I wonder, whether this discipline which we desire be such as can be put in practice within this kingdom; they say it cannot stand with the common law nor with the king's safety, the government of episcopacy is now so weaved into the common law. In God's name let it weave out again; let not human quillets keep back divine authority. It is not the common law, nor the civil, but piety and justice that are our foundresses; they stoop not, neither change colour for aristocracy, democracy, or monarchy, nor yet at all interrupt their just courses; but far above the taking notice of these inferior niceties, with perfect sympathy, wherever they meet, kiss each other. Lastly, they are fearful that the discipline which will succeed cannot stand with the king's safety. Wherefore? it is but episcopacy reduced to what it should be: were it not that the tyranny or prelates under the name of bishops had made our ears tender and startling, we might call every good minister a bishop, as every bishop, yea, the apostles themselves, are called ministers, and the angels ministering spirits, and the ministers again angels. But wherein is this propounded government so shrewd? Because the government of assemblies will succeed. Did not the apostles govern the church by assemblies? How should it else be catholic? How should it have communion? We count it sacrilege to take from the rich prelates their lands and revenues, which is sacrilege in them to keep, using them as they do; and can we think it safe to defraud the living church of God of that right which God has given her in assemblies? O but the consequence! assemblies draw to them the supremacy of ecclesiastical jurisdiction. No, surely, they draw no supremacy, but that authority which Christ, and St Paul in his name, confers upon them. The king may still retain the same supremacy in the assemblies as in the parliament; here he can do nothing alone against the common law, and there neither alone, nor with consent, against the scriptures. But is this all? No: this ecclesiastical supremacy draws to it the power to excommunicate kings; and then follows the worst that can be imagined. Do they hope to avoid this, by keeping prelates that have so often done it? Not to exemplify the malapert insolence of our own bishops in this kind towards our kings, I shall turn back to the primitive and pure times, which the objectors would have the rule of reformation to us.

Not an assembly, but one bishop alone, St Ambrose of Milan, held Theodosius, the most Christian emperor, under excommunication above eight months together, drove him from the church in the presence of his nobles; which the good emperor bore with heroic humility, and never ceased by prayers and tears, till he was absolved; for which coming to the bishop with supplication into the salutatory, some outporch of the church, he was charged by him with tyrannical madness against God, for coming into holy ground. At last, upon conditions absolved, and after great humiliation approaching to the altar to offer (as those thrice pure times then thought meet), he had scarce withdrawn his hand, and stood awhile, when a bold archdeacon comes in the bishop's name, and chases him from within the rails, telling him peremptorily, that the place wherein he stood was for none but the priests to enter, or to touch: and this is another piece of pure primitive divinity! Think ye, then, our bishops will forgo the power of excommunication on whomsoever? No, certainly, unless to compass sinister ends, and then revoke when they see their time. And yet this most mild, though withal dreadful and inviolable prerogative of Christ's diadem, excommunication, serves for nothing with them, but to prog and pander for fees, or to display their pride, and sharpen their revenge, debarring men the protection of the law; and I remember not whether in some cases it bereaves not men all right to their worldly goods and inheritances, besides the denial of Christian burial. But in the evangelical and reformed use of this sacred censure, no such prostitution, no such Iscariotical drifts are to be doubted, as that spiritual doom and sentence should invade worldly possession, which is the rightful lot and portion even of the wickedest men, as frankly bestowed upon them by the all-dispensing bounty as rain and sunshine. No, no, it seeks not to bereave or destroy the body; it seeks to save the soul by humbling the body, not by imprisonment, or pecuniary mulct, much less by stripes, or bonds, or disinheritance, but by fatherly admonishment, and Christian rebuke to cast it into godly sorrow, whose end is joy, and ingenuous bashfulness to sin: if that cannot be wrought, then as a tender mother takes her child and holds it over the pit with scaring words, that it may learn to fear where danger is; so doth excommunication as dearly and as freely, without money, use her wholesome and saving terrors; she is instant, she beseeches, by all the dear and sweet promises of salvation she entices and woos; by all the threatenings and thunders of the law, and rejected gospel, she charges and adjures: this is all her armoury, her munition, her artillery; then she awaits with long-sufferance, and yet ardent zeal. In brief, there is no act in all the errand of God's ministers to mankind wherein passes more loverlike contestation between Christ and the soul of a regenerate man lapsing, than before, and in, and after the sentence of excommunication. As for the fogging proctorage of money, with such an eye as struck Gehazi with leprosy and Simon Magnus with a curse, so does she look, and so threaten her fiery whip against that banking den of thieves that dare thus baffle, and buy and sell the awful and majestic wrinkles of her brow. He that is rightly and apostolically sped with her invisible arrow, if he can be at peace in his soul, and not smell within him the brimstone of hell, may have fair leave to tell all his bags over undiminished of the least farthing, may eat his dainties, drink his wine, use his delights, enjoy his lands and liberties, not the least skin raised, not the least hair misplaced, for all that excommunication has done: much more may a king enjoy his rights and prerogatives undeflowered, untouched, and be as absolute and complete a king, as all his royalties and revenues can make him. And therefore little did Theodosius fear a plot upon his empire, when he stood excommunicate by St Ambrose, though it were done either with much haughty pride, or ignorant zeal. But let us rather look upon the reformed churches beyond the seas, the Grizons, the Swisses, the Hollanders, the French, that have a supremacy to live under, as well as we: where do the churches in all these places strive for supremacy? Where do they clash and justle supremacies with the civil magistrate? In France, a more severe monarchy than ours, the protestants under this church government carry the name of the best subjects the king has; and yet presbytery, if it must be so called, does there all that it desires to do: how easy were it, if there be such great suspicion, to give no more scope to it in England! But let us not for fear of a scarecrow, or else through hatred to be reformed, stand hankering and politizing, when God with spread hands testifies to us, and points us out the way to our peace.

Let us not be so over-credulous, unless God hath blinded us, as to trust our dear souls into the hands of men that beg so devoutly for the pride and gluttony of their own backs and bellies, that sue and solicit so eagerly, not for the saving of souls, the consideration of which can have here no place at all, but for their bishoprics, deaneries, prebends, and canonries: how can these men not be corrupt, whose very cause is the bribe of their own pleading, whose mouths cannot open without the strong breath and loud stench of avarice, simony, and sacrilege, embezzling the treasury of the church on painted and gilded walls of temples wherein God hath testified to have no delight, warming their palace kitchens, and from thence their unctuous and epicurean paunches, with the alms of the blind, the lame, the impotent, the aged, the orphan, the widow? for with these the treasury of Christ ought to be, here must be his jewels bestowed, his rich cabinet must be emptied here; as the constant martyr St Lawrence taught the Roman praetor. Sir, would you know what the remonstrance of these men would have, what their petition implies? They entreat us that we would not be weary of those insupportable grievances that our shoulders have hitherto cracked under; they beseech us that we would think them fit to be our justices of peace, our lords, our highest officers of state, though they come furnished with no more experience than they learnt between the cook and the manciple, or more profoundly at the college audit, or the regent house, or to come to their deepest insight, at their patron's table; they would request us to endure still the rustling of their silken cassocks, and that we would burst our midriffs, rather than laugh to see them under sail in all their lawn and sarcenet, their shrouds and tackle, with a geometrical rhomboides upon their heads: they would bear us in hand that we must of duty still appear before them once a year in Jerusalem, like good circumcised males and females, to be taxed by the poll, to be sconced our head-money, our two pences, in their chandlerly shopbook of Easter. They pray us that it would please us to let them still hale us, and worry us with their bandogs and pursuivants; and that it would please the parliament that they may yet have the whipping, fleecing, and flaying of us in their diabolical courts, to tear the flesh from our bones, and into our wide wounds instead of balm, to pour in the oil of tartar, vitriol, and mercury: surely, a right reasonable, innocent, and softhearted petition. O the relenting bowels of the fathers! Can this be granted them, unless God have smitten us with frenzy from above, and with a dazzling giddiness at noonday? Should not those men rather be heard that come to plead against their own preferments, their worldly advantages, their own abundance; for honour and obedience to God's word, the conversion of souls, the Christian peace of the land, and union of the reformed catholic church, the unappropriating and unmonopolizing the rewards of learning and industry, from the greasy clutch of ignorance and high feeding? We have tried already, and miserably felt what ambition, worldly glory, and immoderate wealth, can do; what the boisterous and contradictional hand of a temporal, earthly, and corporeal spirituality can avail to

the edifying of Christ's holy church; were it such a desperate
hazard to put to the venture the universal votes of Christ's
congregation, and fellowly and friendly yoke of a teaching and
laborious ministry, the pastorlike and apostolic imitation of
meek and unlordly discipline, the gentle and benevolent medio-
crity of church-maintenance, without the ignoble hucksterage
of piddling tithes? Were it such an incurable mischief to make
a little trial, what all this would do to the flourishing and growing
up of Christ's mystical body? as rather to use every poor shift,
and if that serve not, to threaten uproar and combustion, and
shake the brand of civil discord?

O, sir, I do now feel myself inwrapped on the sudden into
those mazes and labyrinths of dreadful and hideous thoughts,
that which way to get out, or which way to end, I know not,
unless I turn mine eyes, and with your help lift up my hands
to that eternal and propitious throne, where nothing is readier
than grace and refuge to the distresses of mortal suppliants:
and it were a shame to leave these serious thoughts less piously
than the heathen were wont to conclude their graver discourses.

Thou, therefore, that sittest in light and glory unapproach-
able, parent of angels and men! next, thee I implore, omnipotent
King, Redeemer of that lost remnant whose nature thou didst
assume, ineffable and everlasting Love! and thou, the third
subsistence of divine infinitude, illumining Spirit, the joy and
solace of created things! one Tripersonal godhead! look upon
this thy poor and almost spent and expiring church, leave her
not thus a prey to these importunate wolves, that wait and
think long till they devour thy tender flock; these wild boars
that have broke into thy vineyard, and left the print of their
polluting hoofs on the souls of thy servants. O let them not
bring about their damned designs, that stand now at the entrance
of the bottomless pit, expecting the watchword to open and let
out those dreadful locusts and scorpions, to reinvolve us in that
pitchy cloud of infernal darkness, where we shall never more
see the sun of thy truth again, never hope for the cheerful dawn,
never more hear the bird of morning sing. Be moved with pity
at the afflicted state of this our shaken monarchy, that now lies
labouring under her throes, and struggling against the grudges
of more dreaded calamities.

O thou, that, after the impetuous rage of five bloody inunda-
tions, and the succeeding sword of intestine war, soaking the
land in her own gore, didst pity the sad and ceaseless revolution
of our swift and thick-coming sorrows; when we were quite

breathless, of thy free grace didst motion peace and terms of covenant with us; and having first wellnigh freed us from antichristian thraldom, didst build up this Britannic empire to a glorious and enviable height, with all her daughter-islands about her; stay us in this felicity, let not the obstinacy of our half-obedience and will-worship bring forth that viper of sedition, that for these fourscore years hath been breeding to eat through the entrails of our peace; but let her cast her abortive spawn without the danger of this travailing and throbbing kingdom: that we may still remember in our solemn thanksgivings, how for us the northern ocean even to the frozen Thule was scattered with the proud shipwrecks of the Spanish armada, and the very maw of hell ransacked, and made to give up her concealed destruction, ere she could vent it in that horrible and damned blast.

O how much more glorious will those former deliverances appear, when we shall know them not only to have saved us from greatest miseries past, but to have reserved us for greatest happiness to come! Hitherto thou hast but freed us, and that not fully, from the unjust and tyrannous claim of thy foes; now unite us entirely, and appropriate us to thyself, tie us everlastingly in willing homage to the prerogative of thy eternal throne.

And now we know, O thou our most certain hope and defence, that thine enemies have been consulting all the sorceries of the great whore, and have joined their plots with that sad intelligencing tyrant that mischiefs the world with his mines of Ophir, and lies thirsting to revenge his naval ruins that have larded our seas: but let them all take counsel together, and let it come to nought; let them decree, and do thou cancel it; let them gather themselves, and be scattered; let them embattle themselves, and be broken; let them embattle, and be broken, for thou art with us.

Then, amidst the hymns and hallelujahs of saints, some one may perhaps be heard offering at high strains in new and lofty measure to sing and celebrate thy divine mercies and marvellous judgments in this land throughout all ages; whereby this great and warlike nation, instructed and inured to the fervent and continual practice of truth and righteousness, and casting far from her the rags of her whole vices, may press on hard to that high and happy emulation to be found the soberest, wisest, and most Christian people at that day, when thou, the eternal and shortly expected King, shalt open the clouds to judge the several kingdoms of the world, and distributing national honours and rewards to religious and just commonwealths, shalt put an end to all earthly tyrannies, proclaiming thy universal and mild monarchy through heaven and earth; where they undoubtedly, that by their labours, counsels, and prayers, have been earnest for the common good of religion and their country, shall receive above the inferior orders of the blessed, the regal addition of principalities, legions, and thrones into their glorious titles, and in supereminence of beatific vision, progressing the dateless and irrevoluble circle of eternity, shall clasp inseparable hands with joy and bliss, in overmeasure for ever.

But they contrary, that by the impairing and diminution of the true faith, the distresses and servitude of their country, aspire to high dignity, rule, and promotion here, after a shameful end in this life (which God grant them), shall be thrown down eternally into the darkest and deepest gulf of hell, where, under the despiteful control, the trample and spurn of all the other damned, that in the anguish of their torture, shall have no other ease than to exercise a raving and bestial tyranny over them as their slaves and negroes, they shall remain in that plight for ever, the basest, the lowermost, the most dejected, most under foot, and down-trodden vassals of perdition.

AN APOLOGY FOR SMECTYMNUUS

In defence of episcopacy, Bishop Hall composed *An Humble Remonstrance to the High Court of Parliament*. The most famous of the replies to this was the one published in March 1641 by five Presbyterian clergymen, under the name of Smectymnuus, a pseudonym composed of their initials (Stephen Marshal, Edmund Calamy, Thomas Young, Matthew Newcomen, William Spurstow). Next month came Hall's reply, his *Defence of the Humble Remonstrance*. This provoked Milton, in July, to the publication of an angry pamphlet entitled *Animadversions upon the Remonstrant's Defence against Smectymnuus. A Modest Confutation* of Milton's attack, probably written by Hall's son, was published the following February. This evoked a further answer from Milton in March: *An Apology against a Pamphlet call'd A Modest Confutation of the Animadversions of the Remonstrant against Smectymnuus*.

In *A Modest Confutation*, Milton's opponent made use of the classical weapon of ethical rhetoric. He tried to persuade his audience of the justice of his own point of view by showing himself to be an admirable and trustworthy character and his opponent vile and dissipated. An ethical appeal of this kind was justified by Aristotle in his treatise on rhetoric. Milton himself frequently made use of it, particularly in his *Defensiones*. In the *Apology* he took seriously the charges that had been made against him, and refuted them by a detailed account of his own life. His satirical counter-attack was vivid and pointed. It must be admitted that Milton hit harder in personal attack than most of his educated opponents allowed themselves to do. His idea of decorum was classical rather than contemporary.

IF, readers, to that same great difficulty of well-doing what we certainly know, were not added in most men as great a carelessness of knowing what they and other ought to do, we had been long ere this, no doubt but all of us, much further on our way to some degree of peace and happiness in this kingdom. But since our sinful neglect of practising that which we know to be undoubtedly true and good, hath brought forth among us, through God's just anger, so great a difficulty now to know that which otherwise might be soon learnt, and hath divided us by a controversy of great importance indeed, but of no hard solution, which is the more our punishment; I resolved (of what small moment soever I might be thought) to stand on that side where I saw both the plain authority of scripture leading, and the reason of justice and equity persuading; with this opinion, which esteems it more unlike a Christian to be a cold neuter in the cause of the church, than the law of Solon made it punishable after a sedition in the state.

And because I observe that fear and dull disposition, lukewarmness and sloth, are not seldomer wont to cloak themselves under the affected name of moderation, than true and lively zeal is customably disparaged with the term if indiscretion, bitterness, and choler; I could not to my thinking honour a good cause more from the heart, than by defending it earnestly, as oft as I could judge it to behove me, notwithstanding any false name that could be invented to wrong or undervalue an honest meaning. Wherein although I have not doubted to single forth more than once such of them as were thought the chief and most nominated opposers on the other side, whom no man else undertook; if I have done well either to be confident of the truth, whose force is best seen against the ablest resistance, or to be jealous and tender of the hurt that might be done among the weaker by the entrapping authority of great names titled to false opinions; or that it be lawful to attribute somewhat to gifts of God's imparting, which I boast not, but thankfully acknowledge, and fear also lest at my certain account they be reckoned to me rather many than few; or if lastly it be but justice not to defraud of due esteem the wearisome labours and studious watchings, wherein I have spent and tired out almost a whole youth, I shall not distrust to be acquitted of presumption: knowing, that if heretofore all ages have received with favour and good acceptance the early industry of him that hath been hopeful, it were but hard measure now if the freedom of any timely spirit should be oppressed merely by the big and blunted fame of his elder adversary; and that his sufficiency must be now sentenced, not by pondering the reason he shows, but by calculating the years he brings.

However, as my purpose is not, nor hath been formerly, to look on my adversary abroad through the deceiving glass of other men's great opinion of him, but at home, where I may find him in the proper light of his own worth, so now against the rancour of an evil tongue, from which I never thought so absurdly, as that I of all men should be exempt, I must be forced to proceed from the unfeigned and diligent inquiry of my own conscience at home (for better way I know not, readers) to give a more true account of myself abroad than this modest confuter, as he calls himself, hath given of me. Albeit, that in doing this I shall be sensible of two things which to me will be nothing pleasant; the one is, that not unlikely I shall be thought too much a party in mine own cause, and therein to see least: the other, that I shall be put unwillingly to molest the public view with the vindication of a private name; as if it were worth the while that the people should care whether such a one were thus, or thus. Yet those I entreat who have found the leisure to read that name, however of small repute, unworthily defamed, would be so good and so patient as to hear the same person not unneedfully defended.

I will not deny but that the best apology against false accusers is silence and sufferance, and honest deeds set against dishonest words. And that I could at this time most easily and securely, with the least loss of reputation, use no other defence, I need not despair to win belief; whether I consider both the foolish contriving and ridiculous aiming of these his slanderous bolts, shot so wide of any suspicion to be fastened on me, that I have oft with inward contentment perceived my friends congratulating themselves in my innocence, and my enemies ashamed of their partner's folly: or whether I look at these present times, wherein most men, now scarce permitted the liberty to think over their own concernments, have removed the seat of their thoughts more outward to the expectation of public events: or whether the examples of men, either noble or religious, who have sat down lately with a meek silence and sufferance under many libellous endorsements, may be a rule to others, I might well appease myself to put up any reproaches in such a honourable society of fellow-sufferers, using no other defence.

And were it that slander would be content to make an end where it first fixes, and not seek to cast out the like infamy upon each thing that hath but any religion to the person traduced, I should have pleaded against this confuter by no other advocates than those which I first commended, silence and sufferance, and speaking deeds against faltering words. But when I discerned his intent was not so much to smite at me, as through me to render odious the truth which I had written, and to stain with ignominy that evangelic doctrine which opposes the tradition of prelacy, I conceived myself to be now not as mine own person, but as a member incorporate into that truth whereof I was persuaded, and whereof I had declared openly to be a partaker. Whereupon I thought it my duty, if not to myself, yet to the religious cause I had in hand, not to leave on my garment the least spot or blemish in good name, so long as God should give me to say that which might wipe it off; lest those disgraces which I ought to suffer, if it so befall me, for my religion, through my default religion be made liable to suffer for me. And, whether it might not something reflect upon those reverent men, whose friend I may be thought in writing the Animadversions, was not my last care to consider: if I should rest under these reproaches, having the same common adversary with them, it might be counted small credit for their cause to have found such an assistant, as this babbler hath devised me. What other thing in his book there is of dispute or question, in answering thereto I doubt not to be justified; except there be who will condemn me to have wasted time in throwing down that which could not keep itself up. As for others, who notwithstanding what I can allege have yet decreed to misinterpret the intents of my reply, I suppose they would have found as many causes to have misconceived the reasons of my silence.

To begin, therefore, an Apology for those Animadversions, which I wrote against the Remonstrant in defence of Smectymnuus; since the preface, which was purposely set before them, is not thought apologetical enough, it will be best to acquaint ye, readers, before other things, what the meaning was to write them in that manner which I did. For I do not look to be asked wherefore I wrote the book, it being no difficulty to answer, that I did it to those ends which the best men propose to themselves when they write; but wherefore in that manner, neglecting the main bulk of all that specious antiquity, which might stun children, and not men, I chose rather to observe some kind of military advantages, to await him at his foragings, at his waterings, and whenever he felt himself secure, to solace his vein in derision of his more serious opponents.

And here let me have pardon, readers, if the remembrance of that which he hath licensed himself to utter contemptuously of those reverend men, provoke me to do that over again, which some expect I should excuse as too freely done, since I have two provocations—his latest insulting in his short answer, and their final patience. I had no fear, but that the authors of Smectymnuus, to all the show of solidity which the Remonstrant could bring, were prepared both with skill and purpose to return a sufficing answer, and were able enough to lay the dust and pudder in antiquity, which he and his, out of stratagem, are wont to raise. But when I saw his weak arguments headed with sharp taunts, and that his design was if he could not refute them, yet at least with quips and snapping adages to vapour them out, which they, bent only upon the business, were minded to let pass; by how much I saw them taking little thought for their own injuries, I must confess I took it as my part the less to endure that my respected friends, through their own unnecessary patience, should thus lie at the mercy of a coy flirting style; to be girded with frumps and curtal gibes by one who makes sentences by the statute, as if all above three inches long were confiscate. To me it seemed an indignity, that whom his whole wisdom could not move from their place, them his impetuous folly should presume to ride over. And if I were more warm than was meet in any passage of that book, which yet I do not yield, I might use therein the patronage of no worse an author than Gregory Nyssen, who mentioning his sharpness against Eunomius in the defence of his brother Basil, holds himself irreprovable in that 'it was not for himself, but in the cause of his brother; and in such cases,' saith he, 'perhaps it is worthier pardon to be angry than to be cooler.'

And whereas this confuter taxes the whole discourse of levity, I shall show ye, readers, wheresoever it shall be objected in particular, that I have answered with as little lightness as the Remonstrant hath given example. I have not been so light as the palm of a bishop, which is the lightest thing in the world when he brings out his book of ordination: for then, contrary to that which is wont in releasing out of prison, any one that will pay his fees is laid hands on. Another reason, it would not be amiss though the Remonstrant were told, wherefore he was in that unusual manner beleaguered; and this was it, to pluck out of the heads of his admirers the conceit that all who are not prelatical, are gross-headed, thick-witted, illiterate, shallow. Can nothing then but episcopacy teach men to speak good English, to pick and order a set of words judiciously? Must we learn from canons and quaint sermonings, interlined with barbarous Latin, to illumine a period, to wreathe an enthymema with masterous dexterity? I rather incline, as I have heard it observed, that a Jesuit's Italian, when he writes, is ever naught, though he be born and bred a Florentine, so to think, that from like causes we may go near to observe the same in the style of a prelate.

For doubtless that indeed according to art is most eloquent, which turns and approaches nearest to nature, from whence it came; and they express nature best, who in their lives least wander from her safe leading, which may be called regenerate reason. So that how he should be truly eloquent who is not withal a good man, I see not. Nevertheless, as oft as is to be dealt with men who pride themselves in their supposed art, to leave them inexcusable wherein they will not be bettered; there be of those that esteem prelacy a figment, who yet can pipe if they can dance, nor will be unfurnished to show, that what the prelates admire and have not, others have and admire not. The knowledge whereof, and not of that only, but of what the scripture teacheth us how we ought to withstand the perverters of the gospel, were those other motives which gave the Animadversions no leave to remit a continual vehemence throughout the book. For as in teaching doubtless the spirit of meekness is most powerful, so are the meek only fit persons to be taught: as for the proud, the obstinate, and false doctors of men's devices, be taught they will not, but discovered and laid open they must be.

For how can they admit of teaching, who have the condemnation of God already upon them for refusing divine instruction? That is, to be filled with their own devices, as in the Proverbs we may read: therefore we may safely imitate the method that God uses, 'with the froward to be froward, and to throw scorn upon the scorner,' whom if any thing, nothing else will heal. And if the 'righteous shall laugh at the destruction of the ungodly,' they may also laugh at the pertinacious and incurable obstinacy, and at the same time be moved with detestation of their seducing malice, who employ all their wits to defend a prelacy usurped, and to deprave that just government which pride and ambition, partly by fine fetches and pretences, partly by force, hath shouldered out of the church. And against such kind of deceivers openly and earnestly to protest, lest any one should be inquisitive wherefore this or that man is forwarder than others, let him know that this office goes not by age or youth, but to whomsoever God shall give apparently the will, the spirit, and the utterance. Ye have heard the reason for which I thought not myself exempted from associating with good men in their labours towards the church's welfare; to which if any one brought opposition, I brought my best resistance. If in requital of this, and for that I have not been negligent toward the reputation of my friends, I have gained a name bestuck, or as I may say, bedecked with the reproaches and reviles of this modest confuter; it shall be to me neither strange nor unwelcome, as that which could not come in a better time.

Having rendered an account what induced me to write those Animadversions in that manner as I writ them, I come now to see what the Confutation hath to say against them; but so as the confutor shall hear first what I have to say against his Confutation. And because he pretends to be a great conjector at other men by their writings, I will not fail to give ye, readers, a present taste of him from his title, hung out like a tolling signpost to call passengers, not simply a confutation, but 'a Modest Confutation,' with a laudatory of itself obtruded in the very first word. Whereas a modest title should only inform the buyer what the book contains without further insinuation; this officious epithet so hastily assuming the modesty which others are to judge of by reading, not the author to anticipate to himself by forestalling, is a strong presumption that his modesty, set there to sale in the frontispiece, is not much addicted to blush. A surer sign of his lost shame he could not have given, than seeking thus unseasonably to prepossess men of his modesty. And seeing he hath neither kept his word in the sequel, nor omitted any kind of boldness in slandering, it is manifest his purpose was only to rub the forehead of his title with this word Modest, that he might not want colour to be the more impudent throughout his whole Confutation.

Next, what can equally savour of injustice and plain arrogance, as to prejudice and forecondemn his adversary in the title for 'slanderous and scurrilous,' and as the Remonstrant's fashion is, for frivolous, tedious, and false, not staying till the reader can hear him proved so in the following discourse? Which is one cause of a suspicion that in setting forth this pamphlet the Remonstrant was not unconsulted with. Thus his first address was, 'An humble Remonstrance by a dutiful Son of the Church,' almost as if he had said, her Whiteboy. His next was 'a Defence' (a wonder how it escaped some praising adjunct) 'against the frivolous and false Exceptions of Smectymnuus,' sitting in the chair of his title-page upon his poor cast adversaries both as a judge and party, and that before the jury of readers can be impanelled. His last was 'A short Answer to a tedious Vindication'; so little can he suffer a man to measure, either with his eye or judgment, what is short or what tedious, without his preoccupying direction: and from hence is begotten this 'Modest Confutation against a slanderous and scurrilous Libel.'

I conceive, readers, much may be guessed at the man and his book, what depth there is, by the framing of his title; which being in this Remonstrant so rash and unadvised as ye see, I conceit him to be near akin to him who set forth a passion sermon with a formal dedicatory in great letters to our Saviour. Although I know that all we do ought to begin and end in his praise and glory, yet to inscribe him in a void place with flourishes, as a man in compliment uses to trick up the name of some esquire, gentleman, or lord paramount at common law, to be his book-patron, with the appendant form of a ceremonious presentment, will ever appear among the judicious to be but an insulse [1] and frigid affectation. As no less was that before his book against the Brownists, to write a letter to a Prosopopoeia, a certain rhetorized woman whom he calls mother, and complains of some that laid whoredom to her charge; and certainly had he folded his epistle with a superscription to be delivered to that female figure by any post or carrier, who were not an ubiquitary, it had been a most miraculous greeting. We find the primitive doctors, as oft as they wrote to churches, speaking to them as to a number of faithful brethren and sons; and not to make a cloudy transmigration of sexes in such a familiar way of writing as an epistle ought to be, leaving the tract of common address, to run up, and tread the air in metaphorical compellations, and many fond utterances better let alone.

But I step again to this emblazoner of his title-page, (whether it be the same man or no, I leave it in the midst), and here I find him pronouncing without reprieve those Animadversions to be a slanderous and scurrilous libel. To which I, readers, that they are neither slanderous, nor scurrilous, will answer in what place of his book he shall be found with reason, and not ink only, in his mouth. Nor can it be a libel more than his own, which is both nameless and full of slanders; and if in this that it freely speaks of things amiss in religion, but established by act of state, I see not how Wickliff and Luther, with all the first martyrs and reformers, could avoid the imputation of libelling. I never thought the human frailty of erring in cases of religion, infamy to a state, no more than to a council. It had therefore been neither civil nor Christianly, to derogate the honour of the state for that cause, especially when I saw the parliament itself piously and magnanimously bent to supply and reform the defects and oversights of their forefathers; which to the godly and repentant ages of the Jews were often matter of humble confessing and bewailing, not of confident asserting and maintaining. Of the state therefore I found good reason to speak all honourable things and to join in petition with good men that petitioned: but against the prelates, who were the only seducers and misleaders of the state to constitute the government of the church not rightly, methought I had not vehemence enough. And thus, readers, by the example which he hath set me, I have given yet two or

[1] Insipid.

three notes of him out of his title-page; by which his firstlings fear not to guess boldly at his whole lump, for that guess will not fail ye; and although I tell him keen truth, yet he may bear with me, since I am like to chase him into some good knowledge, and others, I trust, shall not misspend their leisure. For this my aim is, if I am forced to be unpleasing to him whose fault it is, I shall not forget at the same time to be useful in something to the stander-by.

As therefore he began in the title, so in the next leaf he makes it his first business to tamper with his reader by sycophanting, and misnaming the work of his adversary. He calls it 'a mime thrust forth upon the stage, to make up the breaches of those solemn scenes between the prelates and the Smectymnuans.' Wherein while he is so over-greedy to fix a name of ill sound upon another, note how stupid he is to expose himself or his own friends to the same ignominy, likening those grave controversies to a piece of stagery, or scene-work, where his own Remonstrant, whether in buskin or sock, must of all right be counted the chief player, be it boasting Thraso or Davus that troubles all things, or one who can shift into any shape, I meddle not; let him explicate who hath resembled the whole argument to a comedy, for 'tragical,' he says, 'were too ominous.' Nor yet doth he tell us what a mime is, whereof we have no pattern from ancient writers, except some fragments, which contain many acute and wise sentences. And this we know in Laertius, that the mimes of Sophron were of such reckoning with Plato, as to take them nightly to read on, and after make them his pillow. Scaliger describes a mime to be a poem imitating any action to stir up laughter. But this being neither poem, nor yet ridiculous, how is it but abusively taxed to be a mime? For if every book, which may chance excite to laugh here and there, must be termed thus, then may the dialogues of Plato, who for those his writings hath obtained the surname of divine, be esteemed as they are by that detractor in Athenaeus, no better than mimes: because there is scarce one of them, especially wherein some notable sophister lies sweating and turmoiling under the inevitable and merciless dilemmas of Socrates, but that he who reads, were it Saturn himself, would be often robbed of more than a smile. And whereas he tells us, that 'scurrilous Mime was a personated grim lowering fool,' his foolish language unwittingly writes fool upon his own friend, for he who was there personated was only the Remonstrant, the author is ever distinguished from the person he introduces.

But in an ill hour hath this unfortunate rashness stumbled upon the mention of miming, that he might at length cease, which he hath not yet since he stepped in, to gall and hurt him whom he would aid. Could he not beware, could he not bethink him, was he so uncircumspect as not to foresee, that no sooner would that word mime be set eye on in the paper, but it would bring to mind that wretched pilgrimage over Minsheu's dictionary[1] called *Mundus alter et idem*, the idlest and the paltriest mime that ever mounted upon bank? Let him ask 'the author of those toothless satires,' who was the maker, or rather the anti-creator of that universal foolery, who he was, who like that other principal of the Manichees, the arch evil one, when he had looked upon all that he had made and mapped out, could say no other but contrary to the divine mouth, that it was all very foolish. That grave and noble invention, which the greatest and sublimest wits in sundry ages, Plato in Critias, and our two famous countrymen, the one in his *Utopia*, the other in his *New Atlantis*, chose, I may not say as a field, but as a mighty continent, wherein to display the largeness of their spirits, by teaching this our world better and exacter things than were yet known or used; this petty prevaricator of America, the zany of Columbus (for so he must be till his world's end), having rambled over the huge topography of his own vain thoughts, no marvel if he brought us home nothing but a mere tankard drollery, a venereous parjetory for stews. Certainly, he that could endure with a sober pen to sit and devise laws for drunkards to carouse by, I doubt me whether the very soberness of such a one, like an unliquored Silenus, were not stark drunk. Let him go now and brand another man injuriously with the name of mime, being himself the loosest and most extravagant mime that hath been heard of, whom no less than almost half the world could serve

---

[1] This is a bitter satire on Bishop Hall's Latin romance, entitled *Mundus Alter et Idem*, said, on the title-page, to have been printed at Utrecht, by Johannis à Waesberg, in 1643. The frontispiece represents a company of coarse revellers at a feast, an apt illustration of the book, which is a satire on gluttony, drunkenness, and immodesty. The *Civitas Solis* of Thomas Campanella, and Lord Bacon's *Nova Atlantis* are included in the same volume. As both in the text and notes the author scatters round with a lavish hand proofs of his acquaintance with various languages, Milton, to humble his pride, represents him painfully picking up his knowledge from *Minsheu's Dictionary*, a very curious book, now little known. It is entitled, *The Guide into the Tongues, with their agreement and consent one with another, as also their Etymologies, that is, the reasons and derivations of all or the most part of Words, in these Nine Languages, viz. English, Low Dutch, High Dutch, French, Italian, Spanish, Latin, Greek, Hebrew, etc. By the industry, study, labour, and at the charges of John Minsheu.*

for stage-room to play the mime in. And let him advise again with Sir Francis Bacon, whom he cites to confute others, what it is 'to turn the sins of Christendom into a mimical mockery, to rip up the saddest vices with a laughing countenance,' especially where neither reproof not better teaching is adjoined. Nor is my meaning, readers, to shift off a blame from myself, by charging the like upon my accuser, but shall only desire that sentence may be respited till I can come to some instance whereto I may give answer.

Thus having spent his first onset, not in confuting, but in a reasonless defaming of the book, the method of his malice hurries him to attempt the like against the author; not by proofs and testimonies, but 'having no certain notice of me,' as he professes, 'further than what he gathers from the Animadversions,' blunders at me for the rest, and flings out stray crimes at a venture, which he could never, though he be a serpent, suck from anything that I have written, but from his own stuffed magazine and hoard of slanderous inventions, over and above that which he converted to venom in the drawing. To me, readers, it happens as a singular contentment, and let it be to good men no light satisfaction, that the slanderer here confesses he has 'no further notice of me than his own conjecture.' Although it had been honest to have inquired, before he uttered such infamous words, and I am credibly informed he did inquire; but finding small comfort from the intelligence which he received, whereon to ground the falsities which he had provided, thought it his likeliest course, under a pretended ignorance, to let drive at random, lest he should lose his odd ends, which from some penurious book of characters he had been culling out and would fain apply. Not caring to burden me with those vices, whereof, among whom my conversation hath been, I have been ever least suspected; perhaps not without some subtlety to cast me into envy, by bringing on me a necessity to enter into mine own praises. In which argument I know every wise man is more unwillingly drawn to speak, than the most repining ear can be averse to hear.

Nevertheless, since I dare not wish to pass this life unpersecuted of slanderous tongues, for God hath told us that to be generally praised is woeful, I shall rely on his promise to free the innocent from causeless aspersions: whereof nothing sooner can assure me, than if I shall feel him now assisting me in the just vindication of myself, which yet I could defer, it being more meet, that to those other matters of public debatement in this book I should give attendance first, but that I fear it would but harm the truth for me to reason in her behalf, so long as I should suffer my honest estimation to lie unpurged from these insolent suspicions. And if I shall be large or unwonted in justifying myself to those who know me not, for else it would be needless, let them consider that a short slander will ofttimes reach further than a long apology; and that he who will do justly to all men, must begin from knowing how, if it so happen, to be not unjust to himself. I must be thought, if this libeller (for now he shows himself to be so) can find belief, after an inordinate and riotous youth spent at the university, to have been at length 'vomited out thence.' For which commodious lie, that he may be encouraged in the trade another time, I thank him; for it hath given me an apt occasion to acknowledge publicly with all grateful mind, that more than ordinary favour and respect which I found above any of my equals at the hands of those courteous and learned men, the fellows of that college wherein I spent some years: who at my parting, after I had taken two degrees, as the manner is, signified many ways how much better it would content them that I would stay; as by many letters full of kindness and loving respect, both before that time, and long after, I was assured of their singular good affection towards me. Which being likewise propense to all such as were for their studious and civil life worthy of esteem, I could not wrong their judgments and upright intentions, so much as to think I had that regard from them for other cause, than that I might be still encouraged to proceed in the honest and laudable courses, of which they apprehended I had given good proof. And to those ingenuous and friendly men, who were ever the countenancers of virtuous and hopeful wits, I wish the best and happiest things that friends in absence wish one to another.

As for the common approbation or dislike of that place, as now it is, that I should esteem or disesteem myself, or any other the more for that, too simple and too credulous is the confuter, if he think to obtain with me, or any right discerner. Of small practice were that physician, who could not judge by what both she or her sister hath of long time vomited, that the worser stuff she strongly keeps in her stomach, but the better she is ever kecking at, and is queasy. She vomits now out of sickness; but ere it will be well with her, she must vomit by strong physic. In the meantime that suburb sink, as this rude scavenger calls it, and more than scurrilously taunts it with the plague, having a worse plague in his middle entrail, that suburb wherein I dwell shall be in my account a more honourable place than his university. Which as in the time of her better health, and mine own younger judgment, I never greatly admired, so now much less. But he follows me to the city, still usurping and forging beyond his book notice, which only he affirms to have had; 'and where my morning haunts are, he wisses not.' It is wonder that, being so rare an alchymist of slander, he could not extract that, as well as the university vomit, and the suburb sink which his art could distil so cunningly; but because his lembec fails him, to give him and envy the more vexation, I will tell him.

Those morning haunts are where they should be, at home; not sleeping, or concocting the surfeits of an irregular feast, but up and stirring, in winter often ere the sound of any bell awake men to labour, or to devotion; in summer as oft with the bird that first rouses, or not much tardier, to read good authors, or cause them to be read, till the attention be weary, or memory have its full fraught: then, with useful and generous labours preserving the body's health and hardiness to render lightsome, clear, and not lumpish obedience to the mind, to the cause of religion, and our country's liberty, when it shall require firm hearts in sound bodies to stand and cover their stations, rather than to see the ruin of our protestation, and the enforcement of a slavish life.

These are the morning practices: proceed now to the afternoon; 'in playhouses,' he says, 'and the bordelloes.' Your intelligence, unfaithful spy of Canaan? He gives in his evidence, that 'there he hath traced me.' Take him at his word, readers; but let him bring good sureties ere ye dismiss him, that while he pretended to dog others, he did not turn in for his own pleasure: for so much in effect he concludes against himself, not contented to be caught in every other gin, but he must be such a novice as to be still hampered in his own hemp. In the Animadversions, saith he, I find the mention of old cloaks, false beards, night-walkers, and salt lotion;[1] therefore, the animadverter haunts

[1] This refers to a fine passage in his *Animadversions*, where we discover the first seeds of the *Areopagitica*. In opposition to Hall, who would gladly, notwithstanding his boasted learning, have been protected by a censorship from the rough eloquence of his adversary, he maintains the wisdom and necessity of leaving the press free. Even Lord Bacon, he observes, 'in one of his discourses, complains of the bishops' uneven hand over these pamphlets, confining those against bishops to darkness, but licensing those against puritans to be uttered openly.' He then, after a sneer at their wigs, continues: 'The Romans had a time, once every year, when their slaves might freely speak their minds; it were hard if the free-born people of England, with whom the voice of truth for these many years, even against the proverb, hath not been heard but in corners, after all your monkish prohibitions, and expurgatorious indexes, your gags

playhouses and bordelloes; for if he did not, how could he speak
of such gear? Now that he may know what it is to be a child,
and yet to meddle with edged tools, I turn his antistrophon upon
his own head; the confuter knows that these things are the
furniture of playhouses and bordelloes, therefore, by the same
reason, 'the confuter himself hath been traced in those places.'
Was it such a dissolute speech, telling of some politicians who
were wont to eavesdrop in disguises, to say they were often liable
to a nightwalking cudgeller, or the emptying of a urinal? What
if I had written as your friend the author of the aforesaid mime,
Mundus alter et idem, to have been ravished like some young
Cephalus or Hylas, by a troop of camping housewives in Vira-
ginea, and that he was there forced to swear himself an uxorious
varlet; then after a long servitude to have come into Aphrodisia
that pleasant country, that gave such a sweet smell to his nostrils
among the shameless courtesans of Desvergonia? Surely he
would have then concluded me as constant at the bordello, as the
galley-slave at his oar.

But since there is such necessity to the hearsay of a tire, a
periwig, or a vizard, that plays must have been seen, what
difficulty was there in that? when in the colleges so many of
the young divines, and those in next aptitude to divinity, have
been seen so often upon the stage, writhing and unboning their
clergy limbs to all the antic and dishonest gestures of Trinculoes,

---

and snaffles, your proud Imprimatura, not to be obtained without the
shallow surview, but *not shallow hand* of some mercenary, narrow-souled,
and illiterate chaplain, when liberty of speaking, than which nothing is
more sweet to man, was girded and strait-laced almost to a broken-winded
phthisic, if now, at a good time, our time of parliament, the very jubilee
and resurrection of the state, if now the concealed, the aggrieved, and
long-persecuted truth, could not be suffered to speak.' Having thus
described the pleasure of this freedom, he proceeds to enumerate its advantages, among which he instances its delivering princes and statesmen from
the necessity of disguising themselves and becoming eavesdroppers, 'that
they might hear everywhere the utterances of private breasts, and amongst
them find out the precious gem of truth, as amongst the numberless pebbles
of the shore; whereby they might be the abler to discover and avoid that
deceitful and close-couched evil of flattery, that ever attends them, and
misleads them, and might skilfully know how to apply the several redresses
to each malady of state, without trusting the disloyal information of para-
sites and sycophants; whereas now this permission of free writing, were
there no good else in it, yet at some times thus licensed, is such an unripping,
such an anatomy of the shyest and tenderest particular truths, as makes
not only the whole nation in many points the wiser, but also presents and
carries home to princes, men most remote from vulgar concourse, such
a full insight of every lurking evil, or restrained good among the commons,
as that they shall not need hereafter, in old cloaks and false beards, to stand
to the courtesy of a night-walking cudgeller for eavesdropping, nor to
accept quietly as a perfume the overhead emptying of some salt lotion.'

buffoons, and bawds; prostituting the shame of that ministry, which either they had, or were nigh having, to the eyes of courtiers and court ladies, with their grooms and mademoiselles. There, while they acted and overacted, among other young scholars, I was a spectator they thought themselves gallant men, and I thought them fools; they made sport, and I laughed; they mispronounced, and I misliked; and, to make up the atticism, they were out, and I hissed. Judge now whether so many good textmen were not sufficient to instruct me of false beards and vizards, without more expositors; and how can this confuter take the face to object to me the seeing of that which his reverend prelates allow, and incite their young disciples to act? For if it be unlawful to sit and behold a mercenary comedian personating that which is least unseemly for a hireling to do, how much more blameful is it to endure the sight of as vile things acted by persons either entered, or presently to enter, into the ministry; and how much more foul and ignominious for them to be the actors!

But because as well by this upbraiding to me the bordelloes, as by other suspicious glancings in his book, he would seem privily to point me out to his readers as one whose custom of life were not honest, but licentious, I shall entreat to be borne with, though I digress; and in a way not often trod, acquaint ye with the sum of my thoughts in this matter, through the course of my years and studies: although I am not ignorant how hazardous it will be to do this under the nose of the envious, as it were in skirmish to change the compact order, and instead of outward actions, to bring inmost thoughts into front. And I must tell ye, readers, that by this sort of men I have been already bitten at; yet shall they not for me know how slightly they are esteemed, unless they have so much learning as to read what in Greek ἀπειροκαλία is, which, together with envy, is the common disease of those who censure books that are not for their reading. With me it fares now, as with him whose outward garment hath been injured and ill-bedighted; for having no other shift, what help but to turn the inside outwards, especially if the lining be of the same, or, as it is sometimes, much better? So if my name and outward demeanour be not evident enough to defend me, I must make trial if the discovery of my inmost thoughts can: wherein of two purposes, both honest and both sincere, the one perhaps I shall not miss; although I fail to gain belief with others, of being such as my perpetual thoughts shall here disclose me, I may yet not fail of success in persuading some to be such really themselves, as they cannot believe me to be more than what I feign.

I had my time, readers, as others have, who have good learning bestowed upon them, to be sent to those places where, the opinion was, it might be soonest attained; and as the manner is, was not unstudied in those authors which are most commended. Whereof some were grave orators and historians, whose matter methought I loved indeed, but as my age then was, so I understood them; others were the smooth elegiac poets, whereof the schools are not scarce, whom both for the pleasing sound of their numerous writing, which in imitation I found most easy, and most agreeable to nature's part in me, and for their matter, which what it is, there be few who know not, I was so allured to read, that no recreation came to me better welcome. For that it was then those years with me which are excused, though they be least severe, I may be saved the labour to remember ye. Whence having observed them to account it the chief glory of their wit, in that they were ablest to judge, to praise, and by that could esteem themselves worthiest to love those high perfections, which under one or other name they took to celebrate; I thought with myself by every instinct and presage of nature, which is not wont to be false, that what emboldened them to this task, might with such diligence as they used embolden me; and that what judgment, wit, or elegance was my share, would herein best appear, and best value itself, by how much more wisely and with more love of virtue I should choose (let rude ears be absent) the object of not unlike praises. For albeit these thoughts to some will seem virtuous and commendable, to others only pardonable, to a third sort perhaps idle; yet the mentioning of them now will end in serious.

Nor blame it, readers, in those years to propose to themselves such a reward, as the noblest dispositions above other things in this life have sometimes preferred: whereof not to be sensible when good and fair in one person meet, argues both a gross and shallow judgment, and withal an ungentle and swainish breast. For by the firm settling of these persuasions, I became, to my best memory, so much a proficient, that if I found those authors anywhere speaking unworthy things of themselves, or unchaste of those names which before they had extolled, this effect it wrought with me, from that time forward their art I still applauded, but the men I deplored; and above them all, preferred the two famous renowners of Beatrice and Laura,[1]

---

[1] Dante and Petrarch.

who never write but honour of them to whom they devote their verse, displaying sublime and pure thoughts, without transgression. And long it was not after, when I was confirmed in this opinion, that he who would not be frustrate of his hope to write well hereafter in laudable things, ought himself to be a true poem; that is, a composition and pattern of the best and honourablest things; not presuming to sing high praises of heroic men, or famous cities, unless he have in himself the experience and the practice of all that which is praiseworthy. These reasonings, together with a certain niceness of nature, an honest haughtiness, and self-esteem either of what I was, or what I might be (which let envy call pride), and lastly that modesty, whereof, though not in the title-page, yet here I may be excused to make some beseeming profession; all these uniting the supply of their natural aid together, kept me still above those low descents of mind, beneath which he must deject and plunge himself, that can agree to saleable and unlawful prostitutions.

Next (for hear me out now, readers), that I may tell ye whither my younger feet wandered; I betook me among those lofty fables and romances which recount in solemn cantos the deeds of knighthood founded by our victorious kings, and from hence had in renown over all Christendom. There I read it in the oath of every knight, that he should defend to the expense of his best blood, or of his life, if it so befell him, the honour and chastity of virgin or matron; from whence even then I learned what a noble virtue chastity sure must be, to the defence of which so many worthies, by such a dear adventure of themselves, had sworn. And if I found in the story afterward, any of them, by word or deed, breaking that oath, I judged it the same fault of the poet as that which is attributed to Homer, to have written indecent things of the gods.[1] Only this my mind gave me, that every free and gentle spirit, without that oath, ought to be born a knight, nor needed to expect the gilt spur, or the laying of a

[1] He here alludes to a passage in the second book of Plato's *Republic* (t. vi. 69, *et seqq. edit. Bekk.*), where the philosopher introduces Adeimantus animadverting with just severity on the absurdity and immorality sometimes found in the works of the poets, 'who, though they praise virtue, represent it, nevertheless, as difficult and laborious, and much inferior to vice in administering delight. They agree also with the multitude in considering injustice more profitable than justice; and, while they despise the poor and uninfluential, whom, at the same time, perhaps, they admit to be superior in virtue, all their praise and admiration, both in public and private, are lavished on the rich and powerful. But most extraordinary of all are their discourses concerning virtue and the gods, who, according to them, frequently overwhelm the good with misfortune, and rain plenty and prosperity upon the impiously wicked.'

sword upon his shoulder to stir him up both by his counsel and
his arms, to secure and protect the weakness of any attempted
chastity. So that even these books, which to many others have
been the fuel of wantonness and loose living, I cannot think how,
unless by divine indulgence, proved to me so many incitements,
as you have heard, to the love and steadfast observation of that
virtue which abhors the society of bordelloes.

Thus, from the laureat fraternity of poets, riper years and the
ceaseless round of study and reading led me to the shady spaces
of philosophy; but chiefly to the divine volumes of Plato, and
his equal Xenophon: where, if I should tell ye what I learnt of
chastity and love, I mean that which is truly so, whose charming
cup is only virtue, which she bears in her hand to those who are
worthy (the rest are cheated with a thick intoxicating potion,
which a certain sorceress, the abuser of love's name, carries
about); and how the first and chiefest office of love begins and
ends in the soul, producing those happy twins of her divine
generation, knowledge and virtue. With such abstracted sub-
limities as these, it might be worth your listening, readers, as
I may one day hope to have ye in a still time, when there shall
be no chiding; not in these noises, the adversary, as ye know,
barking at the door, or searching for me at the bordelloes, where
it may be he had lost himself, and raps up without pity the sage
and rheumatic old prelates, with all Corinthian laity, to inquire
for such a one.

Last of all, not in time, but as perfection is last, that care was
ever had of me, with my earliest capacity, not to be negligently
trained in the precepts of the Christian religion: this that I have
hitherto related, hath been to show, that though Christianity
had been but slightly taught me, yet a certain reservedness of
natural disposition, and moral discipline, learnt out of the
noblest philosophy, was enough to keep me in disdain of far less
incontinences than this of the bordello. But having had the
doctrine of holy scripture unfolding those chaste and high mysteries, with timeliest care infused, that 'the body is for the Lord,
and the Lord for the body'; thus also I argued to myself, that
if unchastity in a woman, whom St Paul terms the glory of man,
be such a scandal and dishonour, then certainly in a man, who
is both the image and glory of God, it must, though commonly
not so thought, be much more deflouring and dishonourable; in
that he sins both against his own body, which is the perfecter
sex, and his own glory, which is in the woman; and, that which
is worst, against the image and glory of God, which is in himself.

Nor did I slumber over that place expressing such high rewards of ever accompanying the Lamb with those celestial songs to others inapprehensible, but not to those who were not defiled with women, which doubtless means fornication; for marriage must not be called a defilement.

Thus large I have purposely been, that if I have been justly taxed with this crime, it may come upon me, after all this my confession, with a tenfold shame: but if I have hitherto deserved no such opprobrious word, or suspicion, I may hereby engage myself now openly to the faithful observation of what I have professed. I go on to show you the unbridled impudence of this loose railer, who, having once begun his race, regards not how far he flies out beyond all truth and shame; who from the single notice of the Animadversions, as he protests, will undertake to tell ye the very clothes I wear, though he be much mistaken in my wardrobe: and like a son of Belial, without the hire of Jezebel, charges me 'blaspheming God and the king,' as ordinarily as he imagines 'me to drink sack and swear,' merely because this was a shred in his commonplace book, and seemed to come off roundly, as if he were some empiric of false accusations, to try his poisons upon me, whether they would work or not. Whom what should I endeavour to refute more, whenas that book, which is his only testimony, returns the lie upon him; not giving him the least hint of the author to be either a swearer or a sack-drinker. And for the readers, if they can believe me, principally for those reasons which I have alleged, to be of life and purpose neither dishonest nor unchaste, they will be easily induced to think me sober both of wine and of word; but if I have been already successless in persuading them, all that I can further say will be but vain; and it will be better thrift to save two tedious labours, mine of excusing, and theirs of needless hearing.

Proceeding further, I am met with a whole gang of words and phrases not mine, for he hath maimed them, and, like a sly depraver, mangled them in this his wicked limbo, worse than the ghost of Deiphobus appeared to his friend Aeneas. I scarce know them; and he that would, let him repair to the place in that book where I set them: for certainly this tormentor of semicolons is as good at dismembering and slitting sentences, as his grave fathers the prelates have been at stigmatizing and slitting noses. By such handicraft as this what might he not traduce? Only that odour, which being his own must needs offend his sense of smelling, since he will needs bestow his foot among us, and not allow us to think he wears a sock, I shall endeavour it may be offenceless to other men's ears. The Remonstrant having to do with grave and reverend men his adversaries, though it became him to tell them in scorn, that 'the bishop's foot had been in their book and confuted it'; which when I saw him arrogate to have done that with his heels that surpassed the best consideration of his head, to spurn a confutation among respected men, I questioned not the lawfulness of moving his jollity to bethink him, what odour a sock would have in such painful business. And this may have chanced to touch him more nearly than I was aware, for indeed a bishop's foot that hath all his toes maugre the gout, and a linen sock over it, is the aptest emblem of the prelate himself; who being a pluralist, may under one surplice, which is also linen, hide four benefices, besides the metropolitan toe, and sends a fouler stench to heaven than that which this young queasiness retches at. And this is the immediate reason here why our enraged confuter, that he may be as perfect a hypocrite as Caiaphas, ere he be a high-priest, cried out, 'Horrid blasphemy!' and, like a recreant Jew, calls for stones. I beseech ye, friends, ere the brick-bats fly, resolve me and yourselves, is it blasphemy, or any whit disagreeing from Christian meekness, whenas Christ himself, speaking of unsavoury traditions, scruples not to name the dunghill and the jakes, for me to answer a slovenly wincer of a confutation, that if he would needs put his foot to such a sweaty service, the odour of his sock was like to be neither musk nor benjamin? Thus did that foolish monk in a barbarous declamation accuse Petrarch of blasphemy for dispraising the French wines.

But this which follows is plain bedlam stuff; this is the demoniac legion indeed, which the Remonstrant feared had been against him, and now he may see, is for him. 'You that love Christ,' saith he, 'and know this miscreant wretch, stone him to death, lest you smart for his impunity.' What thinks the Remonstrant? does he like that such words as these should come out of his shop, out of his *Trojan horse*? to give the watchword like a Guisian of Paris, to a mutiny or massacre; to proclaim a crusade against his fellow-christian now in this troublous and divided time of the kingdom? If he do, I shall say that to be the Remonstrant is no better than to be a Jesuit; and that if he and his accomplices could do as the rebels have done in Ireland to the protestants, they would do in England the same to them that would no prelates. For a more seditious and butcherly speech no cell of

Loyola could have belched against one who in all his writing spake not, that any man's skin should be rased.

And yet this cursing Shimei, a hurler of stones, as well as a railer, wants not the face instantly to make as though he 'despaired of victory, unless a modest defence would get it him.' Did I err at all, readers, to foretell ye, when first I met with his title, that the epithet of modest there was a certain red portending sign, that he meant ere long to be most tempestuously bold and shameless? Nevertheless, he dares not say but there may be hid in his nature as much venomous atheism and profanation, as he thinks hath broke out at his adversary's lips; but he hath not 'the sore running upon him,' as he would intimate I have. Now trust me not, readers, if I be not already weary of pluming and footing this sea-gull, so open he lies to strokes, and never offers at another but brings home the dorre himself. For if the sore be running upon me, in all judgment I have escaped the disease; but he who hath as much hid in him as he hath voluntarily confessed, and cannot expel it, because he is dull (for venomous atheism were no treasure to be kept within him else), let him take the part he hath chosen, which must needs follow, to swell and burst with his own inward venom.

But mark, readers, there is a kind of justice observed among them that do evil; but this man loves injustice in the very order of his malice. For having all this while abused the good name of his adversary with all manner of licence in revenge of his Remonstrant, if they be not both one person, or as I am told, father and son, yet after all this he calls for satisfaction, whenas he himself hath already taken the utmost farthing. 'Violence hath been done,' says he, 'to the person of a holy and religious prelate.' To which, something in effect to what St Paul answered of Ananias, I answer, 'I wist not, brethren, that he was a holy and religious prelate'; for evil is written of those who would be prelates. And finding him thus in disguise without his superscription or phylactery either of holy or prelate, it were no sin to serve him as Longchamp Bishop of Ely was served in his disguise at Dover: he hath begun the measure nameless, and when he pleases we may all appear as we are. And let him be then what he will, he shall be to me so as I find him principled. For neither must prelate or archprelate hope to exempt himself from being reckoned as one of the vulgar, which is for him only to hope whom true wisdom and the contempt of vulgar opinions exempts, it being taught us in the Psalms, that he who is in honour and understandeth not, is as the beasts that perish.

And now first 'the manner of handling that cause,' which I undertook, he thinks is suspicious, as if the wisest and the best words were not ever to some or other suspicious. But where is the offence, the disagreement from Christian meekness, or the precept of Solomon in answering folly? When the Remonstrant talks of froth and scum, I tell him there is none, and bid him spare his ladle; when he brings in the mess with keal, beef, and brewess, what stomach in England could forbear to call for flanks and briskets? Capon and white broth having been likely sometimes in the same room with Christ and his apostles, why does it trouble him, that it should be now in the same leaf, especially where the discourse is not continued, but interrupt? And let him tell me, is he wont to say grace, doth he not then name holiest names over the steam of costliest superfluities? Does he judge it foolish or dishonest, to write that among religious things, which, when he talks of religious things, he can devoutly chew? Is he afraid to name Christ where those things are written in the same leaf, whom he fears not to name while the same things are in his mouth? Doth not Christ himself teach the highest things by the similitude of old bottles and patched clothes? Doth he not illustrate best things by things most evil? his own coming to be as a thief in the night, and the righteous man's wisdom to that of an unjust steward? He might therefore have done better to have kept in his canting beggars, and heathen altar, to sacrifice his threadbare criticism of Bomolochus to an unseasonable goddess fit for him called Importunity, and have reserved his Greek derivation till he lecture to his freshmen, for here his itching pedantry is but flouted.

But to the end that nothing may be omitted, which may farther satisfy any conscionable man, who, notwithstanding what I could explain before the Animadversions, remains yet unsatisfied concerning that way of writing which I there defended, but this confuter, whom it pinches, utterly disapproves; I shall assay once again, and perhaps with more success. If therefore the question were in oratory, whether a vehement vein throwing out indignation or scorn upon an object that merits it, were among the aptest *ideas* of speech to be allowed, it were my work, and that an easy one, to make it clear both by the rules of best rhetoricians, and the famousest examples of the Greek and Roman orations. But since the religion of it is disputed, and not the art, I shall make use only of such reasons and authorities as religion cannot except against. It will be harder to gainsay, than for me to evince, that in the teaching of men diversely tempered, different ways are to be tried. The Baptist, we know, was a strict man, remarkable for austerity and set order of life. Our Saviour, who had all gifts in him, was Lord to express his indoctrinating power in what sort him best seemed; sometimes by a mild and familiar converse; sometimes with plain and impartial home-speaking, regardless of those whom the auditors might think he should have had in more respect; otherwhile, with bitter and ireful rebukes, if not teaching, yet leaving excuseless those his wilful impugners.

What was all in him, was divided among many others the teachers of his church; some to be severe and ever of a sad gravity, that they may win such, and check sometimes those who be of nature over-confident and jocund; others were sent more cheerful, free, and still as it were at large, in the midst of an untrespassing honesty; that they who are so tempered, may have by whom they might be drawn to salvation, and they who are too scrupulous, and dejected of spirit, might be often strengthened with wise consolation and revivings: no man being forced wholly to dissolve that groundwork of nature which God created in him, the sanguine to empty out all his sociable liveliness, the choleric to expel quite the unsinning predominance of his anger; but that each radical humour and passion, wrought upon and corrected as it ought, might be made the proper mould and foundation of every man's peculiar gifts and virtues. Some also were indued with a staid moderation and soundness of argument, to teach and convince the rational and sober-minded; yet not therefore that to be thought the only expedient course of teaching, for in times of opposition, when either against new heresies arising, or old corruptions to be reformed, this cool unpassionate mildness of positive wisdom is not enough to damp and astonish the proud resistance of carnal and false doctors, then (that I may have leave to soar awhile as the poets use) Zeal, whose substance is ethereal, arming in complete diamond, ascends his fiery chariot, drawn with two blazing meteors, figured like beasts, but of a higher breed than any the zodiac yields, resembling two of those four which Ezekiel and St John saw; the one visaged like a lion, to express power, high authority, and indignation; the other of countenance like a man, to cast derision and scorn upon perverse and fraudulent seducers: with these the invincible warrior, Zeal, shaking loosely the slack reins, drives over the heads of scarlet prelates, and such as are insolent to maintain traditions, bruising their stiff necks under his flaming wheels.

Thus did the true prophet of old combat with the false; thus Christ, himself the fountain of meekness, found acrimony enough to be still galling and vexing the prelatical pharisees. But ye will say, these had immediate warrant from God to be thus bitter; and I say, so much the plainer is it proved, that there may be a sanctified bitterness against the enemies of truth. Yet that ye may not think inspiration only the warrant thereof, but that it is as any other virtue, of moral and general observation, the example of Luther may stand for all, whom God made choice of before others to be of highest eminence and power in reforming the church; who, not of revelation, but of judgment, writ so vehemently against the chief defenders of old untruths in the Romish church, that his own friends and favourers were many times offended with the fierceness of his spirit; yet he being cited before Charles the Fifth to answer for his books, and having divided them into three sorts, whereof one was of those which he had sharply written, refused, though upon deliberation given him, to retract or unsay any word therein, as we may read in Sleidan. Yea, he defends his eagerness, as being 'of an ardent spirit, and one who could not write a dull style': and affirmed, 'he thought it God's will, to have the inventions of men thus laid open, seeing that matters quietly handled were quickly forgot'.

And herewithal how useful and available God hath made his tart rhetoric in the church's cause, he often found by his own experience. For when he betook himself to lenity and moderation, as they call it, he reaped nothing but contempt both from Cajetan and Erasmus, from Cocleus, from Ecchius, and others; insomuch that blaming his friends, who had so counselled him, he resolved never to run into the like error. If at other times he seem to excuse his vehemence, as more than what was meet, I have not examined through his works, to know how far he gave way to his own fervent mind; it shall suffice me to look to mine own. And this I shall easily aver, though it may seem a hard saying, that the Spirit of God, who is purity itself, when he would reprove any fault severely, or but relate things done or said with indignation by others, abstains not from some words not civil at other times to be spoken. Omitting that place in Numbers at the killing of Zimri and Cosbi, done by Phineas in the height of zeal, related, as the rabbins expound, not within an obscene word; we may find in Deuteronomy and three of the prophets, where God, denouncing bitterly the punishments of idolaters, tells them in a term immodest to be uttered in cool blood, that their wives shall be defiled openly.

But these, they will say, were honest words in that age when they were spoken. Which is more than any rabbin can prove; and certainly had God been so minded, he could have picked such words as should never have come into abuse. What will they say to this? David going against Nabal, in the very same breath when he had just before named the name of God, he vows not 'to leave any alive of Nabal's house that pisseth against the wall.' But this was unadvisedly spoken, you will answer, and set down to aggravate his infirmity. Turn then to the First of Kings, where God himself uses the phrase, 'I will cut off from Jeroboam him that pisseth against the wall'; which had it been an unseemly speech in the heat of an earnest expression, then we must conclude that Jonathan or Onkelos the targumists were of cleaner language than he that made the tongue; for they render it as briefly, 'I will cut off all who are at years of discretion,' that is to say, so much discretion as to hide nakedness. Whereas God, who is the author both of purity and eloquence, chose this phrase as fittest in that vehement character wherein he spake. Otherwise that plain word might have easily been forborne: which the mazoreths and rabbinical scholiasts, not well attending, have often used to blur the margin with Keri instead of Ketiv, and gave us this insulse rule out of their Talmud, 'That all words which in the law are written obscenely, must be changed to more civil words': fools, who would teach men to read more decently than God thought good to write. And thus I take it to be manifest, that indignation against men and their actions notoriously bad hath leave and authority ofttimes to utter such words and phrases, as in common talk were not so mannerly to use. That ye may know, not only as the historian speaks, 'that all those things for which men plough, build, or sail, obey virtue,' but that all words, and whatsoever may be spoken, shall at some time in an unwonted manner wait upon her purposes.

Now that the confutant may also know as he desires, what force of teaching there is sometimes in laughter, I shall return him in short, that laughter, being one way of answering 'a fool according to his folly,' teaches two sorts of persons: first, the fool himself, 'not to be wise in his own conceit,' as Solomon affirms; which is certainly a great document to make an unwise man know himself. Next, it teacheth the hearers, inasmuch as scorn is one of those punishments which belong to men carnally wise, which is oft in scripture declared; for when such are punished, 'the simple are thereby made wise,' if Solomon's

rule be true. And I would ask, to what end Eliah mocked the
false prophets? was it to show his wit, or to fulfil his humour?
Doubtless we cannot imagine that great servant of God had any
other end, in all which he there did, but to teach and instruct
the poor misled people. And we may frequently read, that many
of the martyrs in the midst of their troubles were not sparing
to deride and scoff their superstitious persecutors. Now may
the confutant advise again with Sir Francis Bacon, whether
Eliah and the martyrs did well to turn religion into a comedy
or satire; 'to rip up the wounds of idolatry and superstition with
a laughing countenance': so that for pious gravity the author
here is matched and overmatched, and for wit and morality in
one that follows:

> ——laughing to teach the truth
> What hinders? as some teachers give to boys
>   Junkets and knacks, that they may learn apace.

Thus Flaccus in his first satire, and his tenth:

> ——Jesting decides great things
> Stronglier and better oft than earnest can.

I could urge the same out of Cicero and Seneca, but he may
content him with this. And henceforward, if he can learn, may
know as well what are the bounds and objects of laughter and
vehement reproof, as he hath known hitherto how to deserve
them both. But lest some may haply think, or thus expostulate
with me after this debatement, who made you the busy almoner
to deal about this dole of laughter and reprehension, which no
man thanks your bounty for? To the urbanity of that man I
should answer much after this sort: that I, friend objector,
having read of heathen philosophers, some to have taught,
that whosoever would but use his ear to listen, might hear the
voice of his guiding genius ever before him, calling, and as it
were pointing to that way which is his part to follow; others,
as the stoics, to account reason, which they call the Hegemoni-
con, to be the common Mercury conducting without error those
that give themselves obediently to be led accordingly. Having
read this, I could not esteem so poorly of the faith which I profess
that God had left nothing to those who had forsaken all other
doctrines for his, to be an inward witness and warrant of what
they have to do, as that they should need to measure themselves
by other men's measures, how to give scope or limit to their
proper actions; for that were to make us the most at a stand, the

most uncertain and accidental wanderers in our doings, of all religions in the world. So that the question erewhile moved, who is he that spends thus the benevolence of laughter and reproof so liberally upon such men as the prelates, may return with a more just demand, who is he not of place and knowledge never so mean, under whose contempt and jerk these men are not deservedly fallen? Neither can religion receive any wound by disgrace thrown upon the prelates, since religion and they surely were never in such amity. They rather are the men who have wounded religion, and their stripes must heal her. I might also tell them what Electra in Sophocles, a wise virgin, answered her wicked mother, who thought herself too violently reproved by her the daughter:

> 'Tis you that say it, not I; you do the deeds,
> And your ungodly deeds find me the words.

If therefore the Remonstrant complain of libels, it is because he feels them to be right aimed. For I ask again, as before in the Animadversions, how long is it since he hath disrelished libels? We never heard the least mutter of his voice against them while they flew abroad without control or check, defaming the Scots and Puritans. And yet he can remember of none but Lysimachus Nicanor, and 'that he misliked and censured.' No more but of one can the Remonstrant remember? What if I put him in mind of one more? What if of one more whereof the Remonstrant in many likelihoods may be thought the author? Did he never see a pamphlet intitled after his own fashion, 'A Survey of that foolish, seditious, scandalous, pro-phane Libel, the Protestation protested'? The child doth not more expressly refigure the visage of his father, than that book resembles the style of the Remonstrant, in those idioms of speech wherein he seems most to delight: and in the seventeenth page three lines together are taken out of the Remonstrance word for word, not as a citation, but as an author borrows from himself. Whoever it be, he may as justly be said to have libelled, as he against whom he writes: there ye shall find another man than is here made show of, there he bites as fast as this whines. 'Vinegar in the ink,' is there 'the antidote of vipers.' Laughing in a religious controversy is there 'a thrifty physic to expel his melancholy.'

In the meantime the testimony of Sir Francis Bacon was not misalleged, complaining that libels on the bishop's part were uttered openly; and if he hoped the prelates had not intelligence with the libellers, he delivers it but as his favourable opinion. But had he contradicted himself, how could I assoil him here, more than a little before, where I know not how, by entangling himself, he leaves an aspersion upon Job, which by any else I never heard laid to his charge? For having affirmed that 'there is no greater confusion than the confounding of jest and earnest,' presently he brings the example of Job, 'glancing at conceits of mirth, when he sat among the people with the gravity of a judge upon him.' If jest and earnest be such a confusion, then were the people much wiser than Job, for 'he smiled, and they believed him not.' To defend libels, which is that whereof I am next accused, was far from my purpose. I had not so little share in good name, as to give another that advantage against myself. The sum of what I said was, that a more free permission of writing at some times might be profitable, in such a question especially wherein the magistrates are not fully resolved; and both sides have equal liberty to write, as now they have. Not as when the prelates bore sway, in whose time the books of some men were confuted, when they who should have answered were in close prison, denied the use of pen or paper. And the divine right of episcopacy was then valiantly asserted, when he who would have been respondent must have bethought himself withal how he could refute the Clink or the Gatehouse.[1] If now therefore they be pursued with bad words, who persecuted others with bad deeds, it is a way to lessen tumult rather than to increase it; whenas anger thus freely vented spends itself ere it break out into action, though Machiavel, whom he cites, or any other Machiavellian priest, think the contrary.

Now, readers, I bring ye to his third section; wherein very cautiously and no more than needs, lest I should take him for some chaplain at hand, some squire of the body to his prelate, one that serves not at the altar only, but at the court cupboard, he will bestow on us a pretty model of himself; and he sobs me out half a dozen phthisical mottoes, wherever he had them, hopping short in the measure of convulsion-fits; in which labour the agony of his wit having escaped narrowly, instead of well-sized periods, he greets us with a quantity of thumb-ring posies. 'He has a fortune therefore good, because he is content with it.' This is a piece of sapience not worth the brain of a fruit trencher; as if content were the measure of what is good or bad in the gift of fortune: for by this rule a bad man may have a good fortune, because he may be ofttimes content with it for

[1] The Newgate and Coldbath Fields of those days.

many reasons which have no affinity with virtue, as love of
ease, want of spirit to use more, and the like. 'And therefore
content,' he says, 'because it neither goes before, nor comes
behind his merit.' Belike then if his fortune should go before
his merit, he would not be content, but resign, if we believe
him; which I do the less, because he implies, that if it came
behind his merit, he would be content as little. Whereas if a
wise man's content should depend upon such a therefore,
because his fortune came not behind his merit, how many wise
men could have content in this world?

In his next pithy symbol I dare not board him, for he passes
all the seven wise masters of Greece, attributing to himself that
which, on my life, Solomon durst not: 'to have affections so
equally tempered, that they neither too hastily adhere to the
truth before it be fully examined, nor too lazily afterward':
which unless he only were exempted out of the corrupt mass of
Adam, born without sin original, and living without actual, is
impossible. Had Solomon (for it behoves me to instance in the
wisest, dealing with such a transcendent sage as this), had
Solomon affections so equally tempered, as 'not adhering too
lazily to the truth,' when God warned him of his halting in
idolatry? do we read that he repented hastily? did not his affections lead him hastily from an examined truth, how much more
would they lead him slowly to it? Yet this man, beyond a stoic
apathy, sees truth as in a rapture, and cleaves to it; not as
through the dim glass of his affections, which, in this frail
mansion of flesh, are ever unequally tempered, pushing forward
to error, and keeping back from truth ofttimes the best of men.
But how far this boaster is from knowing himself, let his preface
speak. Something I thought it was that made him so quick-
sighted to gather such strange things out of the Animadversions,
whereof the least conception could not be drawn from thence,
of 'suburb sinks,' sometimes 'out of wit and clothes,' sometimes 'in new serge, drinking sack, and swearing'; now I know
it was this equal temper of his affections that gave him to see
clearer than any fennel-rubbed serpent. Lastly, he has resolved
'that neither person nor cause shall improper him.' I may
mistake his meaning, for the word ye hear is 'improper.' But
whether if not a person, yet a good parsonage or impropriation
bought out for him, would not 'improper' him, because there
may be a quirk in the word, I leave it for a canonist to resolve.

And thus ends this section, or rather dissection, of himself,
short ye will say both in breadth and extent, as in our own praises

it ought to be, unless wherein a good name hath been wrong-fully attained.   Right; but if ye look at what he ascribes to him-self, 'that temper of his affections,' which cannot anywhere be but in Paradise, all the judicious panegyrics in any language extant are not half so prolix.   And that well appears in his next removal.   For what with putting his fancy to the tiptoe in this description of himself, and what with adventuring presently to stand upon his own legs without the crutches of his margin, which is the sluice most commonly that feeds the drought of his text, he comes so lazily on in a simile, with his 'armful of weeds,' and demeans himself in the dull expression so like a dough-kneaded thing, that he has not spirit enough left him so far to look to his syntax, as to avoid nonsense.   For it must be under-stood there that the stranger, and not he who brings the bundle, would be deceived in censuring the field, which this hipshot grammarian cannot set into right frame of construction, neither here in the similitude, nor in the following reddition thereof; which being to this purpose, that 'the faults of the best picked out, and presented in gross, seem monstrous; this,' saith he, 'you have done, in pinning on his sleeve the faults of others'; as if to pick out his own faults, and to pin the faults of others upon him, were to do the same thing.

To answer therefore how I have culled out the evil actions of the Remonstrant from his virtues, I am acquitted by the dexterity and conveyance of his nonsense, losing that for which he brought his parable.   But what of other men's faults I have pinned upon his sleeve, let him show.   For whether he were the man who termed the martyrs 'Foxian confessors,' it matters not; he that shall step up before others to defend a church government, which wants almost no circumstance, but only a name, to be a plain popedom, a government which changes the fatherly and ever-teaching discipline of Christ into that lordly and uninstructing jurisdiction which properly makes the pope Antichrist, makes himself an accessory to all the evil committed by those who are armed to do mischief by that undue govern-ment; which they, by their wicked deeds, do, with a kind of passive and unwitting obedience to God, destroy; but he, by plausible words and traditions against the scripture, obstinately seeks to maintain.   They, by their own wickedness ruining their own unjust authority, make room for good to succeed; but he, by a show of good upholding the evil which in them undoes itself, hinders the good which they by accident let in.   Their manifest crimes serve to bring forth an ensuring good, and hasten a remedy against themselves; and his seeming good tends to reinforce their self-punishing crimes and his own, by doing his best to delay all redress. Shall not all the mischief which other men do be laid to his charge, if they do it by that un-church-like power which he defends? Christ saith, 'He that is not with me is against me; and he that gathers not with me, scatters.' In what degree of enmity to Christ shall we place that man, then, who so is with him, as that it makes more against him; and so gathers with him, that it scatters more from him? Shall it avail that man to say he honours the martyrs' memory, and treads in their steps? No; the pharisees confessed as much of the holy prophets. Let him, and such as he, when they are in their best actions, even at their prayers, look to hear that which the pharisees heard from John the Baptist when they least expected, when they rather looked for praise from him: 'Generation of vipers, who hath warned ye to flee from the wrath to come?'

Now that ye have started back from the purity of scripture, which is the only rule of reformation, to the old vomit of your traditions; now that ye have either troubled or leavened the people of God, and the doctrine of the gospel, with scandalous ceremonies and mass-borrowed liturgies, do ye turn the use of that truth which ye profess, to countenance that falsehood which ye gain by? We also reverence the martyrs, but rely only upon the scriptures. And why we ought not to rely upon the martyrs, I shall be content with such reasons as my confuter himself affords me; who is, I must needs say for him, in that point as officious an adversary as I would wish to any man. For, 'first,' saith he, 'there may be a martyr in a wrong cause, and as courageous in suffering as the best; sometimes in a good cause with a forward ambition displeasing to God. Other whiles they that story of them out of blind zeal or malice, may write many things of them untruly.' If this be so, as ye hear his own con-fession, with what safety can the Remonstrant rely upon the martyrs as 'patrons of his cause,' whenas any of those who are alleged for the approvers of our ligurgy or prelacy, might have been, though not in a wrong cause, martyrs? Yet whether not vainly ambitious of that honour, or whether not misreported or misunderstood in those their opinions, God only knows. The testimony of what we believe in religion must be such as the conscience may rest on to be infallible and incorruptible, which is only the word of God.

His fifth section finds itself aggrieved that the Remonstrant should be taxed with the illegal proceeding of the high commission, and oath *ex officio*: and first, 'whether they were illegal or no, it is more than he knows.' See this malevolent fox! that tyranny which the whole kingdom cried out against as stung with adders and scorpions, that tyranny which the parliament, in compassion of the church and commonwealth, hath dissolved and fetched up the roots, for which it hath received the public thanks and blessings of thousands, this obscure thorn-eater of malice and detraction as well as of quodlibets and sophisms, knows not whether it were illegal or not. Evil, evil would be your reward, ye worthies of the parliament, if this sophister and his accomplices had the censuring or the sounding forth of your labours. And that the Remonstrant cannot wash his hands of all the cruelties exercised by the prelates, is past doubting. They scourged the confessors of the gospel; and he held the scourgers' garments. They executed their rage; and he, if he did nothing else, defended the government with the oath that did it, and the ceremonies which were the cause of it: does he think to be counted guiltless?

In the following section I must foretell ye, readers, the doings will be rough and dangerous, the baiting of a satire. And if the work seem more trivial or boisterous than for this discourse, let the Remonstrant thank the folly of this confuter, who could not let a private word pass, but he must make all this blaze of it. I had said, that because the Remonstrant was so much offended with those who were tart against the prelates, sure he loved toothless satires, which I took were as improper as a toothed sleekstone. This champion from behind the arras cries out, that those toothless satires were of the Remonstrant's making; and arms himself here tooth and nail, and horn to boot, to supply the want of teeth, or rather of gums in the satires; and for an onset tells me, that the simile of a sleekstone 'shows I can be as bold with a prelate as familiar with a laundress.' But does it not argue rather the lascivious promptness of his own fancy, who, from the harmless mention of a sleekstone, could neigh out the remembrance of his old conversation among the viragian trollops? For me, if he move me, I shall claim his own oath, the oath *ex officio*, against any priest or prelate in the kingdom, to have ever as much hated such pranks as the best and chastest of them all. That exception which I made against toothless satires, the confuter hopes I had from the satirist, but is far deceived: neither have I ever read the hobbling distich which he means.

For this good hap I had from a careful education, to be inured and seasoned betimes with the best and elegantest authors of the learned tongues, and thereto brought an ear that could measure a just cadence, and scan without articulating: rather nice and humorous in what was tolerable, than patient to read every drawling versifier. Whence lighting upon this title of 'toothless satires,' I will not conceal ye what I thought, readers, that sure this must be some sucking satyr, who might have done better to have used his coral, and made an end of teething, ere he took upon him to wield a satire's whip. But when I heard him talk of 'scouring the rusty swords of elvish knights,' do not blame me if I changed my thought, and concluded him some desperate cutler. But why 'his scornful muse could never abide with tragic shoes her ancles for to hide,' the pace of the verse told me that her mawkin knuckles were never shapen to that royal buskin. And turning by chance to the sixth satire of his second book, I was confirmed; where having begun loftily 'in heaven's universal alphabet,' he falls down to that wretched poorness and frigidity, as to talk of 'Bridge-street in heaven, and the ostler of heaven,' and there wanting other matter to catch him a heat (for certain he was in the frozen zone miserably nebumbed), with thoughts lower than any beadle betakes him to whip the signposts of Cambridge ale-houses, the ordinary subject of freshmen's tales, and in a strain as pitiful. Which for him who would be counted the first English satire, to abuse himself to, who might have learned better among the Latin and Italian satirists, and in our own tongue from the *Vision and Creed of Pierce Plowman*, besides others before him, manifested a presumptuous undertaking with weak and unexamined shoulders. For a satire as it was born out of a tragedy, so ought to resemble his parentage, to strike high, and adventure dangerously at the most eminent vices among the greatest persons, and not to creep into every blind tap-house, that fears a constable more than a satire. But that such a poem should be toothless, I still affirm it to be a bull, taking away the essence of that which it calls itself. For if it bite neither the persons nor the vices, how is it a satire? And if it bite either, how is it toothless? So that toothless satires are as much as if he had said toothless teeth. What we should do, therefore, with this learned comment upon teeth and horns, which hath brought this confutant into his pedantic kingdom of cornucopia, to reward him for glossing upon horns even to the Hebrew root, I know not; unless we should commend him to be lecturer in Eastcheap upon St Luke's day, when they send their tribute to that famous haven by Deptford. But we are not like to escape him so; for now the worm of criticism works in him, he will tell us the derivation of 'German rutters, of meat, and of ink,' which doubtless, rightly applied with some gall in it, may prove good to heal this tetter of pedagogism that bespreads him, with such a tenesmus of originating, that if he be an Arminian, and deny original sin, all the etymologies of his book shall witness that his brain is not meanly tainted with that infection.

His seventh section labours to cavil out the flaws which were found in the Remonstrant's logic; who having laid down for a general proposition, that 'civil polity is variably and arbitrary,' from whence was inferred logically upon him that he had concluded the polity of England to be arbitrary, for general includes particular; here his defendant is not ashamed to confess, that the Remonstrant's proposition was sophistical by a fallacy called *ad plures interrogationes*, which sounds to me somewhat strange, that a Remonstrant of that pretended sincerity should bring deceitful and double-dealing propositions to the parliament. The truth is, he had let slip a shrewd passage ere he was aware, not thinking the conclusion would turn upon him with such a terrible edge, and not knowing how to wind out of the briers, he, or his substitute, seems more willing to lay the integrity of his logic to pawn, and grant a fallacy in his own major, where none is, than to be forced to uphold the inference. For that distinction of possible and lawful, is ridiculous to be sought for in that proposition; no man doubting that it is possible to change the form of civil polity; and that it is held lawful by that major, the word 'arbitrary' implies. Nor will this help him to deny that it is arbitrary, 'at any time, or by any undertakers' (which are the limitations invented by him since), for when it stands as he would have it now by his second edition, 'civil polity is variable, but not at any time or by any undertakers,' it will result upon him, belike then at some time, and by some undertakers it may. And so he goes on mincing the matter, till he meets with something in Sir Francis Bacon; then he takes heart again, and holds his major at large. But by and by, as soon as the shadow of Sir Francis hath left him, he falls off again, warping and warping, till he come to contradict himself in diameter; and denies flatly that it is 'either variable or arbitrary, being once settled.' Which third shift is no less a piece of laughter: for, before the polity was settled, how could it be variable, whenas it was no polity at all, but either an anarchy or a tyranny? That limitation, therefore, of after-settling, is a mere tautology. So that, in fine, his former assertion is now recanted, and 'civil polity is neither variable nor arbitrary.'

Whatever else may persuade me that this Confutation was not made without some assistance or advice of the Remonstrant, yet in this eighth section that his hand was not greatly intermixed, I can easily believe. For it begins with this surmise, that 'not having to accuse the Remonstrant to the king, I do it to the parliament': which conceit of the man clearly shoves the king out of the parliament, and makes two bodies of one. Whereas the Remonstrant, in the epistle to his last 'Short Answer,' gives his supposal, 'that they cannot be severed in the rights of their several concernments.' Mark, readers, if they cannot be severed in what is several (which casts a bull's eye to go yoke with the toothless satires), how should they be severed in their common concernments, the welfare of the land, by due accusation of such as are the common grievancers, among which I took the Remonstrant to be one? And therefore if I accused him to the parliament, it was the same as to accuse him to the king.

Next he casts it into the dish of I know not whom, 'that they flatter some of the house, and libel others whose consciences made them vote contrary to some proceedings.' Those some proceedings can be understood of nothing else but the deputy's execution.[1] And can this private concoctor of malecontent, at the very instant when he pretends to extol the parliament, afford thus to blur over, rather than to mention that public triumph of their justice and constancy, so high, so glorious, so reviving to the fainted commonwealth, with such a suspicious and murmuring expression as to call it some proceedings? And yet immediately he falls to glossing, as if he were the only man that rejoiced at these times. But I shall discover to ye, readers, that this his praising of them is as full of nonsense and scholastic foppery, as his meaning he himself discovers to be full of close malignity. His first encomium is, 'that the sun looks not upon a braver, nobler convocation than is that of king, peers, and commons.'

One thing I beg of ye, readers, as ye bear any zeal to learning, to elegance, and that which is called decorum in the writing of praise, especially on such a noble argument, ye would not be offended, though I rate this cloistered lubber according to his

---

[1] The Earl of Strafford's execution in 1640.

deserts. Where didst thou learn to be so aguish, so pusillanimous, thou losel bachelor of art, as against all custom, and use
of speech to term the high and sovereign court of parliament a
convocation? Was this the flower of all the synonimas and
voluminous papers, whose best folios are predestined to no better
end than to make winding-sheets in Lent for pilchers? Couldst
thou presume thus, with one word's speaking, to clap, as it were
under hatches, the king with all his peers and gentry into square
caps and monkish hoods? How well dost thou now appear to
be a chip of the old block, that could find 'Bridge-street and
alehouses in heaven'? Why didst thou not, to be his perfect
imitator, liken the king to the vice-chancellor, and the lords to
the doctors? Neither is this an indignity only, but a reproach,
to all that inviolable residence of justice and liberty by such
an odious name as now a 'convocation' is become, which
would be nothing injured, though it were styled the house of
bondage, whereout so many cruel tasks, so many unjust burdens
have been laden upon the bruised consciences of so many
Christians throughout the land.

But which of those worthy deeds, whereof we and our posterity
must confess this parliament to have done so many and so noble,
which of those memorable acts comes first into his praises?
None of all, not one. What will he then praise them for? Not
for anything doing, but for deferring to do, for deferring to
chastise his lewd and insolent compriests: not that they have
deferred all, but that he hopes they will remit what is yet behind.
For the rest of his oratory that follows, so just is it in the language
of stall epistle nonsense, that if he who made it can understand
it, I deny not but that he may deserve for his pains a cast doublet.
When a man would look he should vent something of his own,
as ever in a set speech the manner is with him that knows anything; he, lest we should not take notice enough of his barren
stupidity, declares it by alphabet, and refers us to odd remnants
in his topics. Nor yet content with the wonted room of his
margin, but he must cut out large docks and creeks into his text,
to unlade the foolish frigate of his unseasonable authorities,
not therewith to praise the parliament, but to tell them what he
would have them do. What else there is, he jumbles together
in such a lost construction, as no man, either lettered or unlettered, will be able to piece up. I shall spare to transcribe him,
but if I do him wrong let me be so dealt with.

Now although it be a digression from the ensuing matter,
yet because it shall not be said I am apter to blame others than

to make trial myself, and that I may, after this harsh discord, touch upon a smoother string, awhile to entertain myself and him that list with some more pleasing fit, and not the least to testify the gratitude which I owe to those public benefactors of their country, for the share I enjoy in the common peace and good by their incessant labours; I shall be so troublesome to this disclaimer for once, as to show him what he might have better said in their praise; wherein I must mention only some few things of many, for more than that to a digression may not be granted. Although certainly their actions are worthy not thus to be spoken of by the way, yet if hereafter it befall me to attempt something more answerable to their great merits, I perceive how hopeless it will be to reach the height of their praises at the accomplishment of that expectation that waits upon their noble deeds, the unfinishing whereof already surpasses what others before them have left enacted with their utmost performance through many ages. And to the end we may be confident that what they do proceeds neither from uncertain opinion nor sudden counsels, but from mature wisdom, deliberate virtue, and dear affection to the public good, I shall begin at that which made them likeliest in the eyes of good men to effect those things for the recovery of decayed religion and the common-wealth, which they who were best minded had long wished for, but few, as the times then were desperate, had the courage to hope for.

First, therefore, the most of them being either of ancient and high nobility, or at least of known and well-reputed ancestry, which is a great advantage towards virtue one way, but in respect of wealth, ease, and flattery, which accompany a nice and tender education, is as much a hinderance another way: the good which lay before them they took, in imitating the worthiest of their progenitors: and the evil which assaulted their younger years by the temptation of riches, high birth, and that usual bringing up, perhaps too favourable and too remiss, through the strength of an inbred goodness, and with the help of divine grace, that had marked them out for no mean purposes, they nobly overcame. Yet had they a greater danger to cope with; for being trained up in the knowledge of learning, and sent to those places which were intended to be the seed-plots of piety and the liberal arts, but were become the nurseries of superstition and empty speculation, as they were prosperous against those vices which grow upon youth out of idleness and superfluity, so were they happy in working off the harms of their abused studies and labours; correcting, by the clearness of their own judgment, the errors of their misinstruction, and were, as David was, wiser than their teachers. And although their lot fell into such times, and to be bred in such places, where if they chanced to be taught anything good, or of their own accord had learnt it, they might see that presently untaught them by the custom and ill example of their elders; so far in all probability was their youth from being misled by the single power of example, as their riper years were known to be unmoved with the baits of preferment, and undaunted for any discouragement and terror, which appeared often to those that loved religion and their native liberty; which two things God hath inseparably knit together, and hath disclosed to us, that they who seek to corrupt our religion, are the same that would enthral our civil liberty.

Thus in the midst of all disadvantages and disrespects (some also at last not without imprisonment and open disgraces in the cause of their country), having given proof of themselves to be better made and framed by nature to the love and practice of virtue, than others under the holiest precepts and best examples have been headstrong and prone to vice; and having, in all the trials of a firm ingrafted honesty, not oftener buckled in the conflict than given every opposition the foil; this moreover was added by favour from Heaven, as an ornament and happiness to their virtue, that it should be neither obscure in the opinion of men, nor eclipsed for want of matter equal to illustrate itself; God and man consenting in joint approbation to choose them out as worthiest above others to be both the great reformers of the church, and the restorers of the commonwealth. Nor did they deceive that expectation which with the eyes and desires of their country was fixed upon them: for no sooner did the force of so much united excellence meet in one globe of brightness and efficacy, but encountering the dazzled resistance of tyranny, they gave not over, though their enemies were strong and subtle, till they had laid her grovelling upon the fatal block; with one stroke winning again our lost liberties and charters, which our forefathers after so many battles could scarce maintain.

And meeting next, as I may so resemble, with the second life of tyranny (for she was grown an ambiguous monster, and to be slain in two shapes), guarded with superstition, which hath no small power to captivate the minds of men otherwise most wise, they neither were taken with her mitred hypocrisy, nor terrified with the push of her bestial horns, but breaking them, immediately forced her to unbend the pontifical brow, and recoil; which repulse only given to the prelates (that we may imagine how happy their removal would be) was the producement of such glorious effects and consequences in the church, that if I should compare them with those exploits of highest fame in poems and panegyrics of old, I am certain it would but diminish and impair their worth, who are now my argument; for those ancient worthies delivered men from such tyrants as were content to enforce only an outward obedience, letting the mind be as free as it could; but these have freed us from a doctrine of tyranny, that offered violence and corruption even to the inward persuasion. They set at liberty nations and cities of men good and bad mixed together; but these, opening the prisons and dungeons, called out of darkness and bonds the elect matryrs and witnesses of their Redeemer. They restored the body to ease and wealth; but these, the oppressed conscience to that freedom which is the chief prerogative of the gospel; taking off those cruel burdens imposed not by necessity, as other tyrants are wont for the safeguard of their lives, but laid upon our necks by the strange wilfulness and wantonness of a needless and jolly persecutor, called Indifference. Lastly, some of those ancient deliverers have had immortal praises for preserving their citizens from a famine of corn. But these, by this only repulse of an unholy hierarchy, almost in a moment replenished with saving knowledge their country, nigh famished for want of that which should feed their souls. All this being done while two armies in the field stood gazing on: the one in reverence of such nobleness quietly gave back and dislodged; the other, spite of the unruliness and doubted fidelity in some regiments, was either persuaded or compelled to disband and retire home.

With such a majesty had their wisdom begirt itself, that whereas others had levied war to subdue a nation that sought for peace, they sitting here in peace could so many miles extend the force of their single words, as to overawe the dissolute stoutness of an armed power, secretly stirred up and almost hired against them. And having by a solemn protestation vowed themselves and the kingdom anew to God and his service, and by a prudent foresight above what their fathers thought on, prevented the dissolution and frustrating of their designs by an untimely breaking up; notwithstanding all the treasonous plots against them, all the rumours either of rebellion or invasion, they have not been yet brought to change their constant resolution, ever to think fearlessly of their own safeties, and hopefully of the commonwealth: which hath gained them such an admiration from all good men, that now they hear it as their ordinary surname, to be saluted the fathers of their country, and sit as gods among daily petitions and public thanks flowing in upon them. Which doth so little yet exalt them in their own thoughts, that, with all gentle affability and courteous acceptance, they both receive and return that tribute of thanks which is tendered them; testifying their zeal and desire to spend themselves as it were piecemeal upon the grievances and wrongs of their distressed nation; insomuch that the meanest artisans and labourers, at other times also women, and often the younger sort of servants assembling with their complaints, and that sometimes in a less humble guise than for petitioners, have gone with confidence, that neither their meanness would be rejected, nor their simplicity contemned; nor yet their urgency distasted either by the dignity, wisdom, or moderation of that supreme senate; nor did they depart unsatisfied.

And, indeed, if we consider the general concourse of suppliants, the free and ready admittance, the willing and speedy redress in what is possible, it will not seem much otherwise, than as if some divine commission from heaven were descended to take into hearing and commiseration the long and remediless afflictions of this kingdom; were it not that none more than themselves labour to remove and divert such thoughts, lest men should place too much confidence in their persons, still referring us and our prayers to him that can grant all, and appointing the monthly return of public fasts and supplications. Therefore the more they seek to humble themselves, the more does God, by manifest signs and testimonies, visibly honour their proceedings; and sets them as the mediators of this his covenant, which he offers us to renew. Wicked men daily conspire their hurt, and it comes to nothing; rebellion rages in our Irish province, but, with miraculous and lossless victories of few against many, is daily discomfited and broken; if we neglect not this early pledge of God's inclining towards us, by the slackness of our needful aids. And whereas at other times we count it ample honour when God vouchsafes to make men the instrument and subordinate worker of his gracious will, such acceptation have their prayers found with him, that to them he hath been pleased to make himself the agent and immediate performer of their desires; dissolving their difficulties when they are thought inexplicable, cutting out ways for them where no passage could be seen; as who is there so regardless of divine Providence, that from late occurrences will not confess? If, therefore, it be so high a grace when men are preferred to be but the inferior officers of good things from God, what is it when God himself condescends, and works with his own hands to fulfil the requests of men? Which I leave with them as the greatest praise that can belong to human nature: not that we should think they are at the end of their glorious progress, but that they will go on to follow his Almighty leading, who seems to have thus covenanted with them; that if the will and the endeavour shall be theirs, the performance and the perfecting shall be his. Whence only it is that I have not feared, though many wise men have miscarried in praising great designs before the utmost event, because I see who is their assistant, who is their confederate, who hath engaged his omnipotent arm to support and crown with success their faith, their fortitude, their just and magnanimous actions, till he have brought to pass all that expected good which, his servants trust, is in his thoughts to bring upon this land in the full and perfect reformation of his church.

Thus far I have digressed, readers, from my former subject; but into such a path, as I doubt not ye will agree with me, to be much fairer and more delightful than the roadway I was in. And how to break off suddenly into those jarring notes which this confuter hath set me, I must be wary, unless I can provide against offending the ear, as some musicians are wont skilfully to fall out of one key into another, without breach of harmony. By good luck, therefore, his ninth section is spent in mournful elegy, certain passionate soliloquies, and two whole pages of interrogatories that praise the Remonstrant even to the sonneting of 'his fresh cheek, quick eyes, round tongue, agile hand, and nimble invention.'

In his tenth section he will needs erect figures and tell fortunes: 'I am no bishop,' he says; 'I was never born to it.' Let me tell, therefore, this wizard, since he calculates so right, that he may know there be in the world, and I among those, who nothing admire his idol—a bishopric; and hold that it wants so much to be a blessing, as that I rather deem it the merest, the falsest, the most unfortunate gift of fortune. And were the punishment and misery of being a prelate bishop terminated only in the person, and did not extend to the affliction of the whole diocess, if I would wish anything in the bitterness of soul to mine enemy, I would wish him the biggest and fattest bishopric. But he proceeds, and the familiar belike informs him, that 'a rich widow, or a lecture, or both, would content me': whereby

I perceive him to be more ignorant in his art of divining then any gipsy. For this I cannot omit without ingratitude to that Providence above, who hath ever bred me up in plenty, although my life hath not been unexpensive in learning, and voyaging about; so long as it shall please him to lend me what he hath hitherto thought good, which is enough to serve me in all honest and liberal occasions, and something over besides, I were unthankful to that highest bounty, if I should make myself so poor, as to solicit needily any such kind of rich hopes as this fortune-teller dreams of. And that he may further learn how his astrology is wide all the houses of heaven in spelling marriages, I care not if I tell him thus much professedly, though it be the losing of my rich hopes, as he calls them, that I think with them who, both in prudence and elegance of spirit, would choose a virgin of mean fortunes, honestly bred, before the wealthiest widow. The fiend, therefore, that told our Chaldean the contrary, was a lying fiend.

His next venom he utters against a prayer, which he found in the Animadversions, angry it seems to find any prayers but in the service-book; he dislikes it, and I therefore like it the better. 'It was theatrical,' he says; and yet it consisted most of scripture language; it had no rubric to be sung in an antic cope upon the stage of a high altar. 'It was big-mouthed,' he says; no marvel, if it were framed as the voice of three kingdoms; neither was it a prayer, so much as a hymn in prose, frequent both in the prophets and in human authors; therefore, the style was greater than for an ordinary prayer. 'It was an astonishing prayer.' I thank him for that confession, so it was intended to astound and to astonish the guilty prelates; and this confuter confesses, that with him it wrought that effect. But in that which follows, he does not play the soothsayer, but the diabolic slanderer of prayers. 'It was made,' he says, 'not so much to please God, or to benefit the weal public' (how dares the viper judge that?), 'but to intimate,' saith he, 'your good abilities to her that is your rich hopes, your Maronilla.'

How hard is it when a man meets with a fool to keep his tongue from folly! That were miserable indeed to be a courtier of Maronilla, and withal of such a hapless invention, as that no way should be left me to present my meaning but to make myself a canting probationer of orisons. The Remonstrant, when he was young as I, could

> Teach each hollow grove to sound his love,
> Wearying echo with one changeless word.
>
> *Toothless Satires.*

And so he well might and all his auditory besides, with his 'teach each.'

> Whether so me list my lovely thoughts to sing,
> Come dance ye nimble dryads by my side,
> Whiles I report my fortunes or my loves.
> *Toothless Satires.*

Delicious! he had that whole bevy at command whether in morrice or at maypole; whilst I by this figure-caster must be imagined in such distress as to sue to Maronilla, and yet left so impoverished of what to say, as to turn my liturgy into my lady's psalter. Believe it, graduate, I am not altogether so rustic, and nothing so irreligious, but as far distant from a lecturer as the merest laic, for any consecrating hand of a prelate that shall ever touch me. Yet I shall not decline the more for that, to speak my opinion in the controversy next moved, 'whether the people may be allowed for competent judges of a minister's ability.' For how else can be fulfilled that which God hath promised, to pour out such abundance of knowledge upon all sorts of men in the times of the gospel? How should the people examine the doctrine which is taught them, as Christ and his apostles continually bid them do? How should they 'discern and beware of false prophets, and try every spirit,' if they must be thought unfit to judge of the minister's abilities? The apostles ever laboured to persuade the Christian flock, that they 'were called in Christ to all perfectness of spiritual knowledge, and full assurance of understanding in the mystery of God.' But the non-resident and plurality-gaping prelates, the gulfs and whirlpools of benefices, but the dry pits of all sound doctrine, that they may the better preach what they list to their sheep, are still possessing them that they are sheep indeed, without judgment, without understanding, 'the very beasts of Mount Sinai,' as this confuter calls them; which words of theirs may serve to condemn them out of their own mouths, and to show the gross contrarieties that are in their opinions. For while none think the people so void of knowledge as the prelates think them, none are so backward and malignant as they to bestow knowledge upon them; both by suppressing the frequency of sermons, and the printed explanations of the English Bible.

No marvel if the people turn beasts, when their teachers themselves, as Isaiah calls them, 'are dumb and greedy dogs that can never have enough; ignorant, blind, and cannot understand; who, while they all look their own way, every one for his

gain from his quarter,' how many parts of the land are fed with
windy ceremonies instead of sincere milk; and while one prelate
enjoys the nourishment and right of twenty ministers, how many
waste places are left as dark as 'Galilee of the Gentiles, sitting
in the region and shadow of death,' without preaching minister,
without light. So little care they of beasts to make them men,
that by their sorcerous doctrine of formalities, they take the
way to transform them out of Christian men into judaizing
beasts. Had they but taught the land or suffered it to be taught,
as Christ would it should have been in all plenteous dispensation of the word; then the poor mechanic might have so accustomed his ear to good teaching, as to have discerned between
faithful teachers and false. But now, with a most inhuman
cruelty, they who have put out the people's eyes, reproach them
of their blindness; just as the pharisees their true fathers were
wont, who could not endure that the people should be thought
competent judges of Christ's doctrine, although we know they
judged far better than those great rabbis: yet 'this people,' said
they, 'that knows not the law is accursed.'

We need not the authority of Pliny brought to tell us the
people cannot judge of a minister: yet that hurts not. For as
none can judge of a painter, or statuary, but he who is an artist
that is either in the practice or theory, which is often separated
from the practice, and judges learnedly without it; so none can
judge of a Christian teacher, but he who hath either the practice
or the knowledge of Christian religion, though not so artfully
digested in him. And who almost of the meanest Christians hath
not heard the scriptures often read from his childhood, besides
so many sermons and lectures, more in number than any student
hath heard in philosophy, whereby he may easily attain to know
when he is wisely taught, and when weakly? whereof, three ways
I remember are set down in scripture; the one is to read often
that best of books written to this purpose, that not the wise only,
but the simple and ignorant, may learn by them; the other way
to know of a minister is, by the life he leads, whereof the meanest
understanding may be apprehensive. The last way to judge
aright in this point is, when he who judges, lives a Christian life
himself. Which of these three will the confuter affirm to exceed
the capacity of a plain artisan? And what reason then is there
left, wherefore he should be denied his voice in the election of
his minister, as not thought a competent discerner?

It is but arrogance therefore, and the pride of a metaphysical
fume, to think that 'the mutinous rabble' (for so he calls the

Christian congregation) 'would be so mistaken in a clerk of the university,' that were to be their minister. I doubt me those clerks, that think so, are more mistaken in themselves; and what with truanting and debauchery, what with false grounds and the weakness of natural faculties in many of them (it being a maxim in some men to send the simplest of their sons thither), perhaps there would be found among them as many unsolid and corrupted judgments, both in doctrine and life, as in any other two corporations of like bigness. This is undoubted, that if any carpenter, smith, or weaver were such a bungler in his trade, as the greatest number of them are in their profession, he would starve for any custom. And should he exercise his manufacture as little as they do their talents, he would forget his art; and should he mistake his tools as they do theirs, he would mar all the work he took in hand. How few among them that know to write or speak in a pure style; much less to distinguish the ideas and various kinds of style in Latin barbarous, and oft not without solecisms, declaiming in rugged and miscellaneous gear blown together by the four winds, and in their choice preferring the gay rankness of Apuleius, Arnobius, or any modern fustianist, before the native Latinisms of Cicero. In the Greek tongue most of them unlettered, or 'unentered to any sound proficiency in those Attic masters of moral wisdom and eloquence.' In the Hebrew text, which is so necessary to be understood, except it be some few of them, their lips are utterly uncircumcized.

No less are they out of the way in philosophy, pestering their heads with the sapless dotages of old Paris and Salamanca. And that which is the main point, in their sermons affecting the comments and postils of friars and jesuits, but scorning and slighting the reformed writers; insomuch that the better sort among them will confess it a rare matter to hear a true edifying sermon in either of their great churches: and that such as are most hummed and applauded there, would scarcely be suffered the second hearing in a grave congregation of pious Christians. Is there cause why these men should overwean, and be so queasy of the rude multitude, lest their deep worth should be undervalued for want of fit umpires? No, my matriculated confutant, there will not want in any congregation of this island, that hath not been altogether famished or wholly perverted with prelatish leaven; there will not want divers plain and solid men, that have learned by the experience of a good conscience what it is to be well taught, who will soon look through and through both the lofty nakedness of your Latinizing barbarian. and the finical goosery of your neat sermon actor. And so I leave you and your fellow 'stars,' as you term them, 'of either horizon,' meaning I suppose either hemisphere, unless you will be ridiculous in your astronomy; for the rational horizon in heaven is but one, and the sensible horizons in earth are innumerable; so that your allusion was as erroneous as your stars. But that you did well to prognosticate them all at lowest in the horizon; that is, either seeming bigger than they are through the mist and vapour which they raise, or else sinking and wasted to the snuff in their western socket.

His eleventh section intends I know not what, unless to clog us with the residue of his phlegmatic sloth discussing with a heavy pulse the 'expedience of set forms'; which no question but to some, and for some time, may be permitted, and perhaps there may be usefully set forth by the church a common directory of public prayer, especially in the administration of the sacraments. But that it should therefore be enforced where both minister and people profess to have no need, but to be scandalized by it, that, I hope, every sensible Christian will deny; and the reasons of such denial the confuter himself, as his bounty still is to his adversary, will give us out of his affirmation. First, saith he, 'God in his providence hath chosen some to teach others, and pray for others, as ministers and pastors.' Whence I gather, that however the faculty of others may be, yet that they whom God hath set apart to his ministry, are by him endued with an ability of prayer; because their office is to pray for others, and not to be the lip-working deacons of other men's appointed words. Nor is it easily credible, that he who can preach well, should be unable to pray well; whenas it is indeed the same ability to speak affirmatively, or doctrinally, and only by changing the mood, to speak prayingly.

In vain, therefore, do they pretend to want utterance in prayer, who can find utterance to preach. And if prayer be the gift of the Spirit, why do they admit those to the ministry who want a main gift of their function, and prescribe gifted men to use that which is the remedy of another man's want; setting them their tasks to read, whom the Spirit of God stands ready to assist in his ordinance with the gift of free conceptions? What if it be granted to the infirmity of some ministers (though such seem rather to be half-ministers) to help themselves with a set form, shall it therefore be urged upon the plenteous graces of others? And let it be granted to some people while they are

babes in Christian gifts, were it not better to take it away soon
after, as we do loitering books and interlineary translations from
children: to stir up and exercise that portion of the Spirit which is
in them, and not impose it upon congregations who not only
deny to need it, but as a thing troublesome and offensive, refuse
it?

Another reason which he brings for liturgy, is 'the preserving
of order, unity, and piety'; and the same shall be my reason
against liturgy. For I, readers, shall always be of this opinion,
that obedience to the Spirit of God, rather than to the fair
seeming pretences of men, is the best and most dutiful order
that a Christian can observe. If the Spirit of God manifest the
gift of prayer in his minister, what more seemly order in the
congregation than to go along with that man in our devoutest
affections? For him to abridge himself by reading, and to fore-
stall himself in those petitions, which he must either omit, or
vainly repeat, when he comes into the pulpit under a show of
order, is the greatest disorder. Nor is unity less broken,
especially by our liturgy, though this author would almost bring
the communion of saints to a communion of litergical words.
For what other reformed church holds communion with us by
our liturgy, and does not rather dislike it? And among ourselves, who knows it not to have been a perpetual cause of
disunion?

Lastly, it hinders piety rather than sets it forward, being
more apt to weaken the spiritual faculties, if the people be not
weaned from it in due time; as the daily pouring in of hot waters
quenches the natural heat. For not only the body and the mind,
but also the improvement of God's Spirit, is quickened by using.
Whereas they who will ever adhere to liturgy, bring themselves
in the end to such a pass, by overmuch learning, as to lose even
the legs of their devotion. These inconveniences and dangers
follow the compelling of set forms: but that the toleration of
the English liturgy now in use is more dangerous than the
compelling of any other, which the reformed churches use, these
reasons following may evince. To contend that it is fantastical,
if not senseless in some places, were a copious argument, especially in the Responsories. For such alternations as are there
used must be by several persons; but the minister and the
people cannot so sever their interests, as to sustain several
persons; he being the only mouth of the whole body which he
presents. And if the people pray, he being silent, or they ask
any one thing, and he another, it either changes the property,

making the priest the people, and the people the priest, by turns, or else makes two persons and two bodies representatives where there should be but one. Which, if it be nought else, must needs be a strange quaintness in ordinary prayer.

The like, or worse, may be said of the litany, wherein neither priest nor people speak any entire sense of themselves throughout the whole, I know not what to name it; only by the timely contribution of their parted stakes, closing up as it were the schism of a sliced prayer, they pray not in vain, for by this means they keep life between them in a piece of gasping sense, and keep down the sauciness of a continual rebounding nonsense. And hence it is, that as it hath been far from the imitation of any warranted prayer, so we all know it hath been obvious to be the pattern of many a jig. And he who hath but read in good books of devotion, and no more, cannot be so either of ear or judgment unpractised to distinguish what is grave, pathetical, devout, and what not, but will presently perceive this liturgy all over in conception lean and dry, of affections empty and unmoving; of passion, or any height whereto the soul might soar upon the wings of zeal, destitute and barren; besides errors, tautologies, impertinencies, as those thanks in the woman's churching for her delivery from sunburning and moonblasting, as if she had been travailing not in her bed, but in the deserts of Arabia.

So that while some men cease not to admire the incomparable frame of our liturgy, I cannot but admire as fast what they think is become of judgment and taste in other men, that they can hope to be heard without laughter. And if this were all, perhaps it were a compliable matter. But when we remember this our liturgy, where we found it, whence we had it, and yet where we left it, still serving to all the abominations of the antichristian temple, it may be wondered how we can demur whether it should be done away or no, and not rather fear we have highly offended in using it so long. It hath indeed been pretended to be more ancient than the mass; but so little proved, that whereas other corrupt liturgies have had withal such a seeming antiquity, as that their publishers have ventured to ascribe them, with their worst corruptions, either to St Peter, St James, St Mark, or at least to Chrysostom or Basil, ours hath been never able to find either age or author allowable, on whom to father those things therein which are least offensive, except the two creeds, for Te Deum has a snatch in it of Limbus Patrum: as if Christ had not 'opened the kingdom of heaven' before he had 'overcome the sharpness of death.'   So that having received it from the papal church as an original creature, for aught can be shown to the contrary, formed and fashioned by workmasters ill to be trusted, we may be assured that if God loathe the best of an idolater's prayer, much more the conceited fangle of his praise.

This confuter himself confesses that a community of the same set form in prayers, is that which 'makes church and church truly one'; we then using a liturgy far more like to the mass-book than to any Protestant set form, by his own words must have more communion with the Romish church, than with any of the reformed.   How can we then not partake with them the curse and vengeance of their superstition, to whom we come so near in the same set form and dress of our devotion? Do we think to sift the matter finer than we are sure God in his jealousy will, who detested both the gold and the spoil of idolatrous cities, and forbade the eating of things offered to idols? Are we stronger than he, to brook that which his heart cannot brook?   It is not surely because we think that prayers are nowhere to be had but at Rome!   That were a foul scorn and indignity cast upon all the reformed churches and our own: if we imagine that all the godly ministers of England are not able to new mould a better and more pious liturgy than this which was conceived and infanted by an idolatrous mother, how basely were that to esteem of God's Spirit, and all the holy blessings and privileges of a true church above a false!

Hark ye, prelates, is this your glorious mother of England, who, whenas Christ hath taught her to pray, thinks it not enough unless she add thereto the teaching of Antichrist?   How can we believe ye would refuse to take the stipend of Rome, when ye shame not to live upon the alms-basket of her prayers?   Will ye persuade us that ye can curse Rome from your hearts, when none but Rome must teach ye to pray?   Abraham disdained to take so much as a thread or a shoe-latchet from the king of Sodom, though no foe of his, but a wicked king; and shall we receive our prayers at the bounty of our more wicked enemies, whose gifts are no gifts, but the instruments of our bane?   Alas! that the Spirit of God should blow as an uncertain wind, should so mistake his inspiring, so misbestow his gifts, promised only to the elect, that the idolatrous should find words acceptable to present God with, and abound to their neighbours, while the true professors of the gospel can find nothing of their own worth the constituting, wherewith to worship God in public!

Consider if this be to magnify the church of England, and not rather to display her nakedness to all the world.

Like, therefore, as the retaining of this Romish liturgy is a provocation to God, and a dishonour to our church, so is it by those ceremonies, those purifyings and offerings at the altar, a pollution and disturbance to the gospel itself; and a kind of driving us with the foolish Galatians to another gospel. For that which the apostles taught hath freed us in religion from the ordinances of men, and commands that 'burdens be not laid' upon the redeemed of Christ; though the formalist will say, 'What! no decency in God's worship?' Certainly, readers, the worship of God singly in itself, the very act of prayer and thanksgiving, with those free and unimposed expressions which from a sincere heart unbidden come into the outward gesture, is the greatest decency that can be imagined. Which to dress up and garnish with a devised bravery abolished in the law, and disclaimed by the gospel, adds nothing but a deformed ugliness; and hath ever afforded a colourable pretence to bring in all those traditions and carnalities that are so killing to the power and virtue of the gospel. What was that which made the Jews, figured under the names of Aholah and Aholibah, go a whoring after all the heathen's inventions, but that they saw a religion gorgeously attired and desirable to the eye? What was all that the false doctors of the primitive church and ever since have done, but 'to make a fair show in the flesh,' as St Paul's words are?

If we have indeed given a bill of divorce to popery and super-stition, why do we not say as to a divorced wife, 'Those things which are yours take them all with you, and they shall sweep after you'? Why were not we thus wise at our parting from Rome? Ah! like a crafty adulteress, she forgot not all her smooth looks and enticing words at her parting: 'Yet keep these letters, these tokens, and these few ornaments; I am not all so greedy of what is mine, let them preserve with you the memory' —of what I am? No, but—'of what I was; once fair and lovely in your eyes.' Thus did those tender-hearted reformers dotingly suffer themselves to be overcome with harlot's language. And she, like a witch, but with a contrary policy, did not take some-thing of theirs, that she still might have power to bewitch them, but for the same intent left something of her own behind her. And that her whorish cunning should prevail to work upon us her deceitful ends, though it be sad to speak, yet, such is our blindness, that we deserve. For we are deep in dotage. We cry out sacrilege and misdevotion against those who in zeal have demolished the dens and cages of her unclean wallowings. We stand for a popish liturgy as for the ark of our covenant. And so little does it appear our prayers are from the heart, that multitudes of us declare they know not how to pray but by rote. Yet they can learnedly invent a prayer of their own to the parliament, that they may still ignorantly read the prayers of other men to God. They object, that if we must forsake all that is Rome's, we must bid adieu to our creed; and I had thought our creed had been of the apostles, for so it bears title. But if it be hers, let her take it. We can want no creed, so long as we want not the scriptures. We magnify those who, in reforming our church, have inconsiderately and blamefully permitted the old leaven to remain and sour our whole lump. But they were martyrs: true; and he that looks well into the book of God's providence, if he read there that God, for this their negligence and halting, brought all that following persecution upon this church, and on themselves, perhaps will be found at the last day not to have read amiss.

But now, readers, we have the port within sight; his last section, which is no deep one, remains only to be forded, and then the wished shore. And here first it pleases him much, that he had descried me, as he conceives, to be unread in the councils. Concerning which matter it will not be unnecessary to shape him this answer; that some years I had spent in the stories of those Greek and Roman exploits, wherein I found many things both nobly done and worthily spoken: when, coming in the method of time to that age wherein the church had obtained a Christian emperor, I so prepared myself, as being now to read examples of wisdom and goodness among those who were foremost in the church, not elsewhere to be paralleled; but to the amazement of what I expected I found it all quite contrary: excepting in some very few, nothing but ambition, corruption, contention, combustion; insomuch that I could not but love the historian, Socrates, who, in the proem to his fifth book professes, 'he was fain to intermix affairs of state; for that it would be else an extreme annoyance to hear, in a continued discourse, the endless brabbles and counter-plottings of the bishops.'

Finding, therefore, the most of their actions in single to be weak, and yet turbulent, full of strife and yet flat of spirit; and the sum of their best council there collected, to be most commonly in questions either trivial or vain, or else of short and easy decision, without that great bustle which they made; I concluded that if their single ambition and ignorance was such, then certainly united in a council it would be much more; and if the compendious recital of what they there did was so tedious and unprofitable, then surely to set out the whole extent of their tattle in a dozen volumes would be a loss of time irrecoverable. Besides that which I had read of St Martin, who for his last sixteen years could never be persuaded to be at any council of the bishops. And Gregory Nazianzen betook him to the same resolution, affirming to Procopius, 'that of any council or meeting of bishops he never saw good end; nor any remedy thereby of evil in the church, but rather an increase. For,' saith he, 'their contentions and desire of lording no tongue is able to express.'

I have not therefore, I confess, read more of the councils, save here and there; I should be sorry to have been such a prodigal of my time; but, that which is better, I can assure this confuter, I have read into them all. And if I want anything yet I shall reply something toward that which in the defence of Murena was answered by Cicero to Sulpitius the lawyer. If ye provoke me (for at no hand else will I undertake such a frivolous labour) I will in three months be an expert councilist.[1] For, be not deceived, readers, by men that would overawe your ears with big names and huge tomes that contradict and repeal one another, because they can cram a margin with citations. Do but winnow their chaff from their wheat, ye shall see their great heap shrink and wax thin, past belief.

From hence he passes to inquire wherefore I should blame the vices of the prelates only, seeing the inferior clergy is known to be as faulty. To which let him hear in brief; that those priests whose vices have been notorious, are all prelatical, which argues both the impiety of that opinion, and the wicked remissness of that government. We hear not of any which are called nonconformists, that have been accused of scandalous living; but are known to be pious or at least sober men: which is a great good argument that they are in the truth and prelates in the error. He would be resolved next, 'What the corruptions of the universities concern the prelates?' And to that let him take this, that the Remonstrant having spoken as if learning would

---

[1] In that admirable speech, Pro L. Murena, sparkling with wit and eloquence, Cicero, to humble the pride of Sulpitius, who valued himself greatly on his knowledge of the civil law, jocularly threatens in *three days* to profess himself a lawyer: 'Itaque, si mihi, homini vehementer occupato, stomachum moveritis, triduo me jurisconsultum esse profitebor.' c. xiii. § 28, *Oper*, t. v. p. 333, *edit. Barb.*

decay with the removal of prelates, I showed him that while
books were extant and in print, learning could not readily be
at a worse pass in the universities than it was now under their
government.   Then he seeks to justify the pernicious sermons
of the clergy, as if they upheld sovereignty; whenas all Christian
sovereignty is by law, and to no other end but to the maintenance
of the common good.   But their doctrine was plainly the dissolution of law, which only sets up sovereignty, and the erecting
of an arbitrary sway, according to private will, to which they
would enjoin a slavish obedience without law; which is the
known definition of a tyrant, and a tyrannized people.

A little beneath he denies that great riches in the church are
the baits of pride and ambition; of which error to undeceive him
I shall allege a reputed divine authority, as ancient as Constantine, which his love to antiquity must not except against;
and to add the more weight, he shall learn it rather in the words
of our old poet, Gower, than in mine, that he may see it is no
new opinion, but a truth delivered of old by a voice from heaven,
and ratified by long experience.

> This Constantine which heal hath found,
> Within Rome anon let found
> Two churches which he did make
> For Peter and for Paul's sake:
> Of whom he had a vision,
> And yafe thereto possession
> Of lordship and of world's good;
> But how so that his will was good
> Towards the pope and his franchise,
> Yet it hath proved otherwise
> To see the working of the deed;
> For in cronick thus I read,
> Anon as he hath made the yeft,
> A voice was heard on high the left,
> Of which all Rome was adrad,
> And said, this day venim is shad
> In holy Church, of temporall
> That meddleth with the spiritual;
> And how it stant in that degree,
> Yet may a man the sooth see,
> God amend it when he will,
> I can thereto none other skill.

But there were beasts of prey, saith he, before wealth was
bestowed on the church.   What, though, because the vultures
had then but small picking, shall we therefore go and fling them

a full gorge? If they, for lucre, use to creep into the church undiscernibly, the more wisdom will it be so to provide than no revenue there may exceed the golden mean; for so good pastors will be content, as having need of no more, and knowing withal the precept and example of Christ and his apostles, and also will be less tempted to ambition. The bad will have but small matter whereon to set their mischief awork; and the worst and subtlest heads will not come at all, when they shall see the crop nothing answerable to their capacious greediness; for small temptations allure but dribbling offenders; but a great purchase will call such as both are most able of themselves, and will be most enabled hereby to compass dangerous projects.

'But,' saith he, 'a widow's house will tempt as well as a bishop's palace.' Acutely spoken! because neither we nor the prelates can abolish widows' houses, which are but an occasion taken of evil without the church, therefore we shall set up within the church a lottery of such prizes as are the direct inviting causes of avarice and ambition, both unnecessary and harmful to be proposed, and most easy, most convenient, and needful to be removed. 'Yea, but they are in a wise dispenser's hand.' Let them be in whose hand they will, they are most apt to blind, to puff up, and pervert the most seeming good. And how they have been kept from vultures, whatever the dispenser's care hath been, we have learned by our miseries.

But this which comes next in view, I know not what good vein or humour took him when he let drop into his paper; I that was erewhile the ignorant, the loiterer, on the sudden by his permission am now granted 'to know something.' And that 'such a volley of expressions' he hath met withal, 'as he would never desire to have them better clothed.' For me, readers, although I cannot say that I am utterly untrained in those rules which best rhetoricians have given, or unacquainted with those examples which the prime authors of eloquence have written in any learned tongue; yet true eloquence I find to be none, but the serious and hearty love of truth: and that whose mind soever is fully possessed with a fervant desire to know good things, and with the dearest charity to infuse the knowledge of them into others, when such a man would speak, his words (by what I can express), like so many nimble and airy servitors, trip about him at command, and in well-ordered files, as he would wish, fall aptly into their own places.

But now to the remainder of our discourse. Christ refused great riches and large honours at the devil's hand. But why?

saith he, 'as they were tendered by him from whom it was a sin to receive them.' Timely remembered: why is it not therefore as much a sin to receive a liturgy of the masses' giving, were it for nothing else but for the giver? 'But he could make no use of such a high estate,' quoth the confuter, opportunely. For why then should the servant take upon him to use those things which his master had unfitted himself to use, that he might teach his ministers to follow his steps in the same ministry? But 'they were offered him to a bad end.' So they prove to the prelates, who, after their preferment, most usually change the teaching labour of the word, into the unteaching ease of lordship over consciences and purses. But he proceeds: 'God enticed the Israelites with the promise of Canaan'; did not the prelates bring as slavish minds with them, as the Jews brought out of Egypt, they had left out that instance. Besides that it was then the time whenas the best of them, as St Paul saith, 'was shut up unto the faith under the law, their schoolmaster,' who was forced to entice them as children with childish enticements. But the gospel is our manhood, and the ministry should be the manhood of the gospel, not to look after, much less so basely to plead for earthly rewards.

'But God incited the wisest man, Solomon, with these means.' Ah, confuter of thyself, this example hath undone thee; Solomon asked an understanding heart, which the prelates have little care to ask. He asked no riches, which is their chief care; therefore was the prayer of Solomon pleasing to God: he gave him wisdom at his request, and riches without asking, as now he gives the prelates riches at their seeking, and no wisdom, because of their perverse asking. But he gives not over yet. 'Moses had an eye to the reward.' To what reward, thou man that lookest with Balaam's eyes? To what reward had the faith of Moses an eye? He that had forsaken all the greatness of Egypt, and chose a troublesome journey in his old age through the wilderness, and yet arrived not at his journey's end. His faithful eyes were fixed upon that incorruptible reward, promised to Abraham and his seed in the Messiah; he sought a heavenly reward, which could make him happy, and never hurt him; and to such a reward every good may have a respect; but the prelates are eager of such rewards as cannot make them happy, but can only make them worse. Jacob, a prince born, vowed that if God would 'but give him bread to eat, and raiment to put on, then the Lord should be his God.' But the prelates of mean birth, and ofttimes of lowest, making show as if they were called to the spiritual and humble ministry of the gospel, yet murmur, and think it a hard service, unless, contrary to the tenor of their profession, they may eat the bread and wear the honours of princes: so much more covetous and base they are than Simon Magus, for he proffered a reward to be admitted to that work, which they will not be meanly hired to.

But, saith he, 'Are not the clergy members of Christ? why should not each member thrive alike?' Carnal text man! as if worldly thriving were one of the privileges we have by being in Christ, and were not a providence ofttimes extended more liberally to the infidel than to the Christian. Therefore must the ministers of Christ not be over rich or great in the world, because their calling is spiritual, not secular; because they have a special warfare, which is not to be entangled with many impediments; because their master, Christ, gave them his precept, and set them this example, told them this was the mystery of his coming, by mean things and persons to subdue mighty ones; and lastly, because a middle estate is most proper to the office of teaching, whereas higher dignity teaches far less, and blinds the teacher. Nay, saith the confuter, fetching his last endeavour, 'the prelates will be very loath to let go their baronies, and votes in parliament,' and calls it, 'God's cause,' with an insufferable impudence. 'Not that they love the honours and the means,' good men and generous! 'but that they would not have their country made guilty of such a sacrilege and injustice!'

A worthy patriot for his own corrupt ends. That which he imputes as sacrilege to his country, is the only way left them to purge that abominable sacrilege out of the land, which none but the prelates are guilty of; who for the discharge of one single duty, receive and keep that which might be enough to satisfy the labours of many painful ministers better deserving than themselves; who possess huge benefices for lazy performances, great promotions only for the execution of a cruel disgospelling jurisdiction; who engross many pluralities under a non-resident and slubbering dispatch of souls; who let hundreds of parishes famish in one diocess, while they, the prelates, are mute, and yet enjoy that wealth that would furnish all those dark places with able supply: and yet they eat, and yet they live at the rate of earls, and yet hoard up; they who chase away all the faithful shepherds of the flock, and bring in a dearth of spiritual food, robbing thereby the church of her dearest treasure, and sending herds of souls starveling to hell, while they feast and riot upon the labours of hireling curates, consuming and purloining even that which by their foundation is allowed, and left to the poor, and to reparations of the church. These are they who have bound the land with the sin of sacrilege, from which mortal engagement we shall never be free, till we have totally removed, with one labour, as one individual thing, prelacy and sacrilege. And herein will the king be a true defender of the faith, not by paring or lessening, but by distributing in due proportion the maintenance of the church, that all parts of the land may equally partake the plentiful and diligent preaching of the faith; the scandal of ceremonies thrown out that delude and circumvent the faith; and the usurpation of prelates laid level, who are in words the fathers, but in their deeds the oppugners of the faith. This is that which will best confirm him in that glorious title.

Thus ye have heard, readers, how many shifts and wiles the prelates have invented to save their ill-got booty. And if it be true, as in scripture it is foretold, that pride and covetousness are the sure marks of those false prophets which are to come; then boldly conclude these to be as great seducers as any of the latter times. For between this and the judgment-day do not look for any arch-deceivers, who in spite of reformation will use more craft or less shame to defend their love of the world and their ambition, than these prelates have done. And if ye think that soundness of reason, or what force of argument soever, will bring them to an ingenuous silence, ye think that which will never be. But if ye take that course which Erasmus was wont to say Luther took against the pope and monks; if ye denounce war against their mitres and their bellies, ye shall soon discern that turban of pride, which they wear upon their heads, to be no helmet of salvation, but the mere metal and hornwork of papal jurisdiction; and that they have also this gift, like a certain kind of some that are possessed, to have their voice in their bellies, which being well-drained and taken down, their great oracle, which is only there, will soon be dumb; and the divine right of episcopacy, forthwith expiring, will put us no more to trouble with tedious antiquities and disputes.

A TREATISE

OF

CIVIL POWER IN ECCLESIASTICAL CAUSES:

SHEWING THAT IT IS NOT LAWFUL FOR ANY POWER ON EARTH TO COMPEL IN MATTERS OF RELIGION

Cromwell, as Lord Protector, had allowed his major-generals to enforce religious decrees with the aid of the army. After the death of Cromwell in 1658, Milton felt he had an opportunity to plead with the government for a complete separation of civil and ecclesiastical power. In February 1659 he published *A Treatise of Civil Power in Ecclesiastical Causes.*

Milton maintained that the enforcement of church discipline by civil magistrates defeated the ends of the church. Even a minister had no right to impose his views on the consciences of his congregation; what right had a magistrate to do so? Civil discipline in matters of religion induced only an implicit or a hypocritical assent that might well damn those who were compelled. Under the new covenant of the Gospel, men were sons of God, not servants unadopted. Now, conscience, the voice of the Holy Spirit, not external authority, was the final court of appeal in each individual. The Church might persuade, but only God could judge and condemn. Christ's spiritual kingdom was strong in dispensing with the weapon of worldly force, 'able . . . to subdue all the powers and kingdoms of this world, which are upheld by outward force only.' Here, again, the reader is conscious of Milton's respect for the spiritual life of individual human beings, and of his sense of the futility of using force in such a sphere.

Two things there be, which have been ever found working much mischief to the church of God and the advancement of truth: force on one side restraining, and hire on the other side corrupting, the teachers thereof. Few ages have been since the ascension of our Saviour, wherein the one of these two, or both together, have not prevailed. It can be at no time, therefore, unseasonable to speak of these things; since by them the church is either in continual detriment and oppression, or in continual danger. The former shall be at this time my argument: the latter as I shall find God disposing me, and opportunity inviting. What I argue shall be drawn from the scripture only; and therein

110

from true fundamental principles of the gospel, to all knowing Christians undeniable. And if the governors of this commonwealth, since the rooting out of prelates, have made least use of force in religion, and most have favoured Christian liberty of any in this island before them since the first preaching of the gospel, for which we are not to forget our thanks to God, and their due praise; they may, I doubt not, in this treatise, find that which not only will confirm them to defend still the Christian liberty which we enjoy, but will incite them also to enlarge it, if in aught they yet straiten it. To them who perhaps hereafter, less experienced in religion, may come to govern or give us laws, this or other such, if they please, may be a timely instruction: however, to the truth it will be at all times no unneedful testimony, at least some discharge of that general duty, which no Christian, but according to what he hath received, knows is required of him, if he have aught more conducing to the advancement of religion, than what is usually endeavoured, freely to impart it.

It will require no great labour of exposition to unfold what is here meant by matters of religion; being as soon apprehended as defined, such things as belong chiefly to the knowledge and service of God; and are either above the reach and light of nature without revelation from above, and therefore liable to be variously understood by human reason, or such things as are enjoined or forbidden by divine precept, which else by the light of reason would seem indifferent to be done or not done; and so likewise must needs appear to very man as the precept is understood. Whence I here mean by conscience or religion that full persuasion, whereby we are assured, that our belief and practice, as far as we are able to apprehend and probably make appear, is according to the will of God and his Holy Spirit within us, which we ought to follow much rather than any law of man, as not only his word everywhere bids us, but the very dictate of reason tells us (Acts iv. 19): 'Whether it be right in the sight of God, to hearken to you more than to God, judge ye.' That for belief or practice in religion, according to this conscientious persuasion, no man ought to be punished or molested by any outward force on earth whatsoever, I distrust not, through God's implored assistance, to make plain by these following arguments.

First, it cannot be denied, being the main foundation of our protestant religion, that we of these ages, having no other divine rule or authority from without us, warrantable to one another as a common ground, but the holy scripture, and no other within us but the illumination of the Holy Spirit, so interpreting that scripture as warrantable only to ourselves, and to such whose consciences we can so persuade, can have no other ground in matters of religion but only from the scriptures. And these being not possible to be understood without this divine illumination, which no man can know at all times to be in himself, much less to be at any time for certain in any other, it follows clearly, that no man or body of men in these times can be the infallible judges or determiners in matters of religion to any other men's consciences but their own. And therefore those Bereans are commended, Acts xvii. 11, who after the preaching even of St Paul, 'searched the scriptures daily, whether those things were so.' Nor did they more than what God himself in many places commands us by the same apostle, to search, to try, to judge of these things ourselves: and gives us reason also (Gal. vi. 4, 5): 'Let every man prove his own work, and then shall he have rejoicing in himself alone, and not in another: for every man shall bear his own burden.' If then we count it so ignorant and irreligious in the papist, to think himself discharged in God's account, believing only as the church believes, how much greater condemnation will it be to the protestant his condemner, to think himself justified, believing only as the state believes? With good cause, therefore, it is the general consent of all sound protestant writers, that neither traditions, councils, nor canons of any visible church, much less edicts of any magistrate or civil session, but the scripture only, can be the final judge or rule in matters of religion, and that only in the conscience of every Christian to himself. Which protestation made by the first public reformers of our religion against the imperial edicts of Charles the Fifth, imposing church traditions without scripture, gave first beginning to the name of Protestant; and with that name hath ever been received this doctrine, which prefers the scripture before the church, and acknowledges none but the scripture sole interpreter of itself to the conscience. For if the church be not sufficient to be implicitly believed, as we hold it is not, what can there else be named of more authority than the church but the conscience, than which God only is greater? 1 John iii. 20. But if any man shall pretend that the scripture judges to his conscience for other men, he makes himself greater not only than the church, but also than the scripture, than the consciences of other men: a presumption too high for any mortal, since every true Christian, able to give a reason of his faith, hath the word of God before him, the promised Holy Spirit, and the mind of Christ within him,

1 Cor. ii. 16; a much better and safer guide of conscience, which as far as concerns himself he may far more certainly know, than any outward rule imposed upon him by others, whom he inwardly neither knows nor can know; at least knows nothing of them more sure than this one thing, that they cannot be his judges in religion (1 Cor. ii. 15): 'The spiritual man judgeth all things, but he himself is judged of no man.' Chiefly for this cause do all true protestants account the pope antichrist, for that he assumes to himself this infallibility over both the conscience and the scripture; 'sitting in the temple of God,' as it were opposite to God, 'and exalting himself above all that is called God, or is worshipped,' 2 Thes. ii. 4. That is to say, not only above all judges and magistrates, who though they be called gods, are far beneath infallible; but also above God himself, by giving law both to the scripture, to the conscience, and to the Spirit itself of God within us. Whenas we find (James iv. 12): 'There is one lawgiver, who is able to save and to destroy: Who art thou that judgest another?' That Christ is the only lawgiver of his church, and that it is here meant in religious matters, no well-grounded Christian will deny. Thus also St Paul (Rom. xiv. 4): 'Who art thou that judgest the servant of another? to his own lord he standeth or falleth: but he shall stand; for God is able to make him stand.' As therefore of one beyond expression bold and presumptous, both these apostles demand, 'Who art thou,' that presumest to impose other law or judgment in religion than the only lawgiver and judge, Christ, who only can save and destroy, gives to the conscience? And the forecited place to the Thessalonians, by compared effects, resolves us, that be he or they who or wherever they be or can be, they are of far less authority than the church, whom in these things as protestants they receive not, and yet no less antichrist in this main point of antichristianism, no less a pope or popedom than he at Rome, if not much more, by setting up supreme interpreters of scripture either those doctors whom they follow. or, which is far worse, themselves as a civil papacy assuming unaccountable supremacy to themselves, not in civil only, but in ecclesiastical causes. Seeing then that in matters of religion, as hath been proved, none can judge or determine here on earth, no, not church governors themselves, against the consciences of other believers, my inference is, or rather not mine but our Saviour's own, that in those matters they neither can command nor use constraint, lest they run rashly on a pernicious consequence, forewarned in that parable (Matt. xiii. from ver.

29 to 31): 'Lest while ye gather up the tares, ye root up also the wheat with them. Let both grow together until the harvest: and in the time of harvest I will say to the reapers, Gather ye together first the tares,' etc. Whereby he declares, that this work neither his own ministers nor any else can discerningly enough or judgingly perform without his own immediate direction, in his own fit season; and that they ought till then not to attempt it. Which is further confirmed (2 Cor. i. 24): 'Not that we have dominion over your faith, but are helpers of your joy.' If apostles had no dominion or constraining power over faith or conscience, much less have ordinary ministers (1 Pet. v. 2, 3): 'Feed the flock of God, etc., not by constraint, neither as being lords over God's heritage.' But some will object, that this overthrows all church discipline, all censure of errors, if no man can determine. My answer is, that what they hear is plain scripture, which forbids not church sentence or determining, but as it ends in violence upon the conscience unconvinced. Let whoso will interpret or determine, so it be according to true church discipline, which is exercised on them only who have willingly joined themselves in that covenant of union, and proceeds only to a separation from the rest, proceeds never to any corporal enforcement or forfeiture of money, which in all spiritual things are the two arms of Antichrist, not of the true church; the one being an inquisition, the other no better than a temporal indulgence of sin for money, whether by the church exacted or by the magistrate; both the one and the other a temporal satisfaction for what Christ hath satisfied eternally; a popish commuting of penalty, corporal for spiritual; a satisfaction to man, especially to the magistrate, for what and to whom we owe none: these and more are the injustices of force and fining in religion, besides what I most insist on, the violation of God's express commandment in the gospel, as hath been shewn. Thus then, if church governors cannot use force in religion, though but for this reason, because they cannot infallibly determine to the conscience without convincement, much less have civil magistrates authority to use force where they can much less judge; unless they mean only to be the civil executioners of them who have no civil power to give them such commission, no, nor yet ecclesiastical, to any force or violence in religion. To sum up all in brief, if we must believe as the magistrate appoints, why not rather as the church? If not as either without convincement, how can force be lawful? But some are ready to cry out, what shall then be done to blasphemy? Them I would first exhort, not thus to terrify and pose

the people with a Greek word; but to teach them better what it is, being a most usual and common word in that language to signify any slander, any malicious or evil speaking, whether against God or man, or anything to good belonging: blasphemy or evil speaking against God maliciously, is far from conscience in religion, according to that of Mark ix. 39: 'There is none who doth a powerful work in my name, and can lightly speak evil of me.' If this suffice not, I refer them to that prudent and well deliberated act, 9th August 1650, where the parliament defines blasphemy against God, as far as it is a crime belonging to civil judicature, 'plenius ac melius Chrysippo et Crantore'; in plain English, more warily, more judiciously, more orthodoxally than twice their number of divines have done in many a prolix volume: although in all likelihood they whose whole study and profession these things are, should be most intelligent and authentic therein, as they are for the most part; yet neither they nor these unerring always, or infallible. But we shall not carry it thus; another Greek apparition stands in our way, Heresy and Heretic; in like manner also railed at to the people as in a tongue unknown. They should first interpret to them that heresy, by what it signifies in that language, is no word of evil note, meaning only the choice or following of any opinion, good or bad, in religion, or any other learning; and thus not only in heathen authors, but in the New Testament itself, without censure or blame; Acts xv. 5: 'Certain of the heresy of the pharisees which believed'; and xxvi. 5: 'After the exactest heresy of our religion I lived a Pharisee.' In which sense presbyterian or independent may without reproach be called a heresy. Where it is mentioned with blame, it seems to differ little from schism (1 Cor. xi. 18, 19): 'I hear that there be schisms among you,' etc. 'for there must also heresies be among you,' etc. Though some, who write of heresy after their own heads, would make it far worse than schism; whenas on the contrary, schism signifies division, and in the worse sense; heresy, choice only of one opinion before another, which may be without discord. In apostolic times, therefore, ere the scripture was written, heresy was a doctrine maintained against the doctrine by them delivered; which in these times can be no otherwise defined than a doctrine maintained against the light which we now only have of the scripture. Seeing, therefore, that no man, no synod, no session of men, though called the church, can judge definitely the sense of scripture to another man's conscience, which is well known to be a general maxim of the protestant religion; it follows plainly, that he who holds in religion that belief; or those opinions, which to his consciences and utmost understanding appear with most evidence or probability in the scripture, though to others he seem erroneous, can no more be justly censured for a heretic than his censurers; who do but the same thing themselves, while they censure him for so doing. For ask them, or any protestant, which hath most authority, the church or the scripture? They will answer, doubtless, that the scripture: and what hath most authority, that no doubt but they will confess is to be followed. He then, who to his best apprehension follows the scripture, though against any point of doctrine by the whole church received, is not the heretic; but he who follows the church against his conscience and persuasion grounded on the scripture.

·　　　·　　　·　　　·　　　·

From the riddance of these objections, I proceed yet to another reason why it is unlawful for the civil magistrate to use force in matters of religion; which is, because to judge in those things, though we should grant him able, which is proved he is not, yet as a civil magistrate he hath no right. Christ hath a government of his own, sufficient of itself to all his ends and purposes in governing his church, but much different from that of the civil magistrate; and the difference in this very thing principally consists, that it governs not by outward force; and that for two reasons: First, Because it deals only with the inward man and his actions, which are all spiritual, and to outward force not liable. Secondly, To show us the divine excellence of his spiritual kingdom, able, without worldly force, to subdue all the powers and kingdoms of this world, which are upheld by outward force only. That the inward man is nothing else but the inward part of man, his understanding and his will; and that his actions thence proceeding, yet not simply thence, but from the work of divine grace upon them, are the whole matter of religion under the gospel, will appear plainly by considering what that religion is; whence we shall perceive yet more plainly that it cannot be forced. What evangelic religion is, is told in two words, —faith and charity, or belief and practice. That both these flow, either, the one from the understanding, the other from the will, or both jointly from both, once indeed naturally free, but now only as they are regenerate and wrought on by divine grace, is in part evident to common sense and principles unquestioned, the rest by scripture: concerning our belief. Matt. xvi. 17: 'Flesh and blood hath not revealed it unto thee, but my Father which is in heaven'; concerning our practice, as it is religious, and not merely civil, Gal. v. 22, 23, and other places, declare it to be the fruit of the spirit only. Nay, our whole practical duty in religion is contained in charity, or the love of God and our neighbour, no way to be forced, yet the fulfilling of the whole law; that is to say, our whole practice in religion. If then both our belief and practice, which comprehend our whole religion, flow from faculties of the inward man, free and unconstrainable of themselves by nature, and our practice not only from faculties endued with freedom, but from love and charity besides, incapable of force, and all these things by transgression lost, but renewed and regenerated in us by the power and gift of God alone; how can such religion as this admit of force from man, or force be any way applied to such religion, especially under the free offer of grace in the gospel, but it must forthwith frustrate and make of no effect both the religion and the gospel? And that to compel outward profession, which they will say perhaps ought to be compelled, though inward religion cannot, is to compel hypocrisy, not to advance religion, shall yet, though of itself clear enough, be ere the conclusion, further manifest. The other reason why Christ rejects outward force in the government of his church, is, as I said before, to show us the divine excellence of his spiritual kingdom, able without worldly force to subdue all the powers and kingdoms of this world, which are upheld by outward force only: by which to uphold religion otherwise than to defend the religious from outward violence, is no service to Christ or his kingdom, but rather a disparagement, and degrades it from a divine and spiritual kingdom, to a kingdom of this world: which he denies it to be, because it needs not force to confirm it (John xviii. 36): 'If, my kingdom were of this world, then would my servants fight that I should not be delivered to the Jews.' This proves the kingdom of Christ not governed by outward force, as being none of this world, whose kingdoms are maintained all by force only; and yet disproves not that a Christian commonwealth may defend itself against outward force, in the cause of religion as well as in any other: though Christ himself coming purposely to die for us, would not be so defended. 1 Cor. i. 27: 'God hath chosen the weak things of the world, to confound the things which are mighty.' Then surely he hath not chosen the force of this world to subdue conscience, and conscientious men, who in this world are counted weakest; but rather conscience, as being weakest, to subdue and regulate force, his adversary, not his aid or instrument in governing the church (2 Cor. x. 3–6): 'For though we walk in the flesh, we do not war after the flesh: for the weapons of our warfare are not carnal, but mighty through God to the pulling down of strongholds, casting down imaginations, and every high thing that exalts itself against the knowledge of God, and bringing into captivity every thought to the obedience of Christ: and having in a readiness to avenge all disobedience.' It is evident by the first and second verses of this chapter, and the apostle here speaks of that spiritual power by which Christ governs his church, how all-sufficient it is, how powerful to reach the conscience, and the inward man with whom it chiefly deals, and whom no power else can deal with. In comparison of which, as it is here thus magnificently described, how ineffectual and weak is outward force with all her boisterous tools, to the shame of those Christians, and especially those churchmen, who to the exercising of church-discipline, never cease calling on the civil magistrate to interpose his fleshly force? An argument that all true ministerial and spiritual power is dead within them; who think the gospel, which both began and spread over the whole world for above three hundred years, under heathen and persecuting emperors, cannot stand or continue, supported by the same divine presence and protection, to the world's end, much easier under the defensive favour only of a Christian magistrate, unless it be enacted and settled, as they call it, by the state, a statute or a state religion; and understand not that the church itself cannot, much less the state, settle or impose one title of religion upon our obedience implicit, but can only recommend or propound it to our free and conscientious examination: unless they mean to set the state higher than the church in religion, and with a gross contradiction give to the state in their settling petition that command of our implicit belief which they deny in their settled confession both to the state and to the church. Let them cease then to importune and interrupt the magistrate from attending to his own charge in civil and moral things, the settling of things just, things honest, the defence of things religious, settled by the churches within themselves; and the repressing of their contraries, determinable by the common light of nature; which is not to constrain or to repress religion probable by scripture, but the violaters and persecuters thereof: of all which things he hath enough and more than enough to do, left yet undone; for which the land groans, and justice goes to wrack the while. Let him also forbear force where he hath no right to judge, for the conscience is not his province, lest a worse woe arrive him, for worse offending, than was denounced by our Saviour (Matt. xxiii. 23) against the pharisees: Ye have forced the conscience, which was not to be forced; but judgment and mercy ye have not executed; this ye should have done, and the other let alone.

.   .   .   .   .

Gal. iv. 3, etc. 'Even so we, when we were children, were in bondage under the rudiments of the world: but when the fulness of time was come, God sent forth his Son, etc., to redeem them that were under the law, that we might receive the adoption of sons, etc. Wherefore thou art no more a servant, but a son, etc. But now, etc. how turn ye again to the weak and beggarly rudiments, whereunto ye desire again to be in bondage? Ye observe days,' etc. Hence it plainly appears, that if we be not free, we are not sons, but still servants unadopted; and if we turn again to those weak and beggarly rudiments, we are not free; yea, though willingly, and with a misguided conscience, we desire to be in bondage to them; how much more then if unwillingly and against our conscience? Ill was our condition changed from legal to evangelical, and small advantage gotten by the gospel, if for the spirit of adoption to freedom promised us, we receive again the spirit of bondage to fear; if our fear, which was then servile towards God only, must be now servile in religion towards men: strange also and preposterous fear, if when and wherein it hath attained by the redemption of our Saviour to be filial only towards God, it must be now servile towards the magistrate: who, by subjecting us to his punishment in these things, brings back into religion that law of terror and satisfaction belonging now only to civil crimes; and thereby in effect abolishes the gospel, by establishing again the law to a far worse yoke of servitude upon us than before. It will therefore not misbecome the meanest Christian to put in mind Christian magistrates, and so much the more freely by how much the more they desire to be thought Christian (for they will be thereby, as they ought to be in these things, the more our brethren and the less our lords), that they meddle not rashly with Christian liberty, the birthright and outward testimony of our adoption; lest while they little think it, nay, think they do God service, they themselves, like the sons of that bondwoman, be found persecuting them who are freeborn of the Spirit, and by a sacrilege of not the least aggravation, bereaving them of that sacred liberty, which our Saviour with his own blood purchased for them.

A fourth reason why the magistrate ought not to use force in religion, I bring from the consideration of all those ends which he can likely pretend to the interposing of his force therein; and those hardly can be other than first the glory of God; next, either the spiritual good of them whom he forces, or the temporal punishment of their scandal to others. As for the promoting of God's glory, none, I think, will say that his glory ought to be promoted in religious things by unwarrantable means, much less by means contrary to what he hath commanded. That outward force is such, and that God's glory in the whole administration of the gospel according to his own will and counsel ought to be fulfilled by weakness, at least so refuted, not by force; or if by force, inward and spiritual, not outward and corporeal, is already proved at large. That outward force cannot tend to the good of him, who is forced in religion, is unquestionable. For in religion whatever we do under the gospel, we ought to be thereof persuaded without scruple; and are justified by the faith we have, not by the work we do (Rom. xiv. 5): 'Let every man be fully persuaded in his own mind.' The other reason which follows necessarily is obvious (Gal. ii. 16), and in many other places of St Paul, as the groundwork and foundation of the whole gospel, that we are 'justified by the faith of Christ, and not by the works of the law.' If not by the works of God's law, how then by the injunctions of man's law? Surely force cannot work persuasion, which is faith; cannot therefore justify nor pacify the conscience, and that which justifies not in the gospel, condemns; is not only not good, but sinful to do (Rom, xiv. 23): 'Whatsoever is not of faith, is sin.' It concerns the magistrate, then, to take heed how he forces in religion conscientious men, lest by compelling them to do that whereof they cannot be persuaded, that wherein they cannot find themselves justified, but by their own consciences condemned, instead of aiming at their spiritual good, he force them to do evil; and while he thinks himself Asa, Josiah, Nehemiah, he be found Jeroboam, who caused Israel to sin; and thereby draw upon his own head all those sins and shipwrecks of implicit faith and conformity, which he hath forced, and all the wounds given to those little ones, whom to offend he will find worse one day than that violent drowning mentioned Matt. xviii. 6.

A TREATISE ON CHRISTIAN DOCTRINE,

COMPILED FROM THE

HOLY SCRIPTURES ALONE

Shortly after his return from Italy, Milton began to compile his treatise *De Doctrina Christiana*. It was intended as a full statement of his theological beliefs. Professor Kelley thinks that the treatise was substantially in its final form by 1660, and that his theology was already distinctly heterodox before the completion of *Paradise Lost*.

More than any other work of Milton's, the treatise *On Christian Doctrine* relied on the Bible. All his statements were followed by texts to prove their validity. His handling of the texts was consistently scholarly and critical; there was no tendency towards fundamentalism. He reserved the right of every believer to 'interpret the Scripture for himself, inasmuch as he has the Spirit for his guide, and the mind of Christ is in him.'

The excerpt from the treatise which follows is, in a sense, the key to the whole work. In this chapter Milton asserted that it was the duty of every Christian to discover, by studying the Bible for himself, the terms of his own faith. His Arianism and his mortalism are of less importance than this basic principle of his Protestantism.

The text is taken from Bishop Sumner's translation, first published in 1825.

BOOK I

CHAPTER XXX

THE Holy Scriptures were not written for occasional purposes only, as is the doctrine of the Papists, but for the use of the church throughout all ages, as well under the gospel as under the law. Exod. xxxiv. 27: 'write thou these words; for after the tenour of these words I have made a covenant with thee and with Israel.' Deut. xxxi. 19: 'write ye this song for you . . . that this song may be a witness for me.' Isai. viii. 20; 'to the law and to the testimony; if they speak not according to this word, it is because there is no light in them.' xxx. 8: 'write it . . . that it may be for the time to come for ever and ever.' Habak. ii. 2: 'write . . . for the vision is yet for an appointed time.' Luke

xvi. 29: 'they have Moses and the prophets; let them hear them.'
John v. 39: 'search the scriptures, for in them ye think ye have
eternal life.' Rom. xv. 4: 'whatsoever things were written afore-
time were written for our learning, that we through patience
and comfort of the scriptures might have hope.' 1 Cor. x. 11:
'they are written for our admonition, upon whom the ends of
the world are come.'

Almost everything advanced in the New Testament is proved
by citations from the Old. The use of the New Testament
writings themselves is declared John xx. 31: 'these are written
that ye might believe . . .' Eph. ii. 20: 'built upon the foundation of the apostles and prophets.' Philipp. iii. 1: 'to write the
same things to you, to me indeed is not grievous, but for you it
is safe.' 1 Thess. v. 27: 'I charge you by the Lord, that this
epistle be read unto all the holy brethren.' 1 Tim. iii. 15: '—if
I tarry long, that thou mayest know how thou oughtest to behave
thyself in the house of God.' 2 Tim. iii. 15–17: 'from a child thou
hast known the holy scriptures, which are able to make thee wise
unto salvation through faith which is in Christ Jesus: all scripture is given by inspiration of God, and is profitable for doctrine,
for reproof, for correction, for instruction in righteousness.'
It is true that the Scriptures which Timothy is here said to have
'known from a child,' and which were of themselves 'able to
make him wise unto salvation through faith in Christ,' were
probably those of the Old Testament alone, since no part of the
New Testament appears to have existed during the infancy of
Timothy; the same is, however, predicted of the whole of Scripture in the succeeding verse, namely, that it is 'profitable for
doctrine'; even to such as are already wise and learned (1 Cor.
x. 15): 'I speak as unto wise men, judge ye what I say,' to men
arrived at Christian maturity (Philipp. iii. 15): 'let us therefore,
as many as be perfect, be thus minded,' such as Timothy himself,
and Titus, to whom Paul wrote; and to the strong in faith (1 John
ii. 14): 'I have written unto you, young men, because ye are
strong, and the word of God abideth in you.' 2 Pet. i. 12, 15:
'wherefore I will not be negligent to put you always in remembrance of these things, though ye know them, and be established
in the present truth: moreover I will endeavour that he may be
able after my decease to have these things always in remembrance.' iii. 15, 16: 'even as our beloved brother Paul also,
according unto the wisdom given unto him, hath written unto
you.' For although the epistle of Paul here alluded to was more
immediately directed to the Romans (Rom. i. 7, 15), Peter in

the above passage expressly intimates that it was addressed not to that church alone, but to believers generally. 2 Pet. iii. 1, 2: 'this second epistle, beloved, I now write unto you; in both which I stir up your minds by way of remembrance.' 1 John ii. 21: 'I have not written unto you, because ye know not the truth, but because ye know it.' Rev. i. 19: 'write the things which thou hast seen, and the things which are, and the things which shall be hereafter.'

From all these passages it is evident, that the use of the Scriptures is prohibited to no one; but that, on the contrary, they are adapted for the daily hearing or reading of all classes and orders of men; of princes, Deut. xvii. 19, of magistrates, Josh. i. 8, of men of all descriptions, Deut. xxxi. 9–11: 'Moses wrote this law, and delivered it unto the priests the sons of Levi . . . and unto all the elders of Israel: and Moses commanded them, saying . . . Thou shalt read this law before all Israel.' xi. 18–20: 'therefore shall ye lay up these my words in your heart, and in your soul, and bind them for a sign upon your hand . . . and thou shalt write them upon the door-posts of thine house.' xxix. 29: 'those things which are revealed belong unto us and to our children for ever, that we may do all the words . . .' xxx. 11: 'for this commandment which I command thee this day it is not hidden from thee, neither is it far off.' 2 Chron. xxxiv. 30: 'he read in their ears all the words of the book of the covenant.' Isa. viii. 20: 'to the law and to the testimony.' Nehem. ix. 3: 'they stood up in their place and read in the book of the law of Jehovah'; that is, the whole people, as appears from the second verse of the chapter. To the same purpose may be adduced the testimony of a writer whom the opponents of this opinion regard as canonical. 1 Macc. i. 56, 57: 'wheresoever was found with any the book of the testament, the king's commandment was that they should put him to death.'

The New Testament is still more explicit. Luke x. 26: 'what is written in the law? how readest thou?' This was the question of Christ to one of the interpreters of the law, of whom there were many at that time, Pharisees and others, confessedly neither priests nor Levites; neither was Christ himself, whom we cannot suppose to have been considered as particularly learned in the law, forbidden to expound in the synagogue; much less therefore could it have been unlawful to read the Scriptures at home. xvi. 29: 'they have Moses and the prophets; let them hear them.' John v. 39: 'search the scriptures.' Acts viii. 28: 'he read Esaias the prophet.' xvii. 11: 'they searched the scriptures daily.' xviii. 24: 'mighty in the scriptures.' 2 Tim. iii. 15: 'from a child thou hast known the holy scriptures.' Rev. i. 3: 'blessed is he that readeth.'

The Scriptures, therefore, partly by reason of their own simplicity, and partly through the divine illumination, are plain and perspicuous in all things necessary to salvation, and adapted to the instruction even of the most unlearned, through the medium of diligent and constant reading. Psal. xix. 7: 'the law of Jehovah is perfect, converting the soul; the testimony of Jehovah is sure, making wise the simple.' cxix. 105: 'thy word is a lamp unto my feet, and a light unto my path.' v. 130: 'the entrance of thy words giveth light, it giveth understanding unto the simple'; whence it follows that the liberty of investigating Scripture thoroughly is granted to all. v. 18: 'open thou mine eyes, that I may behold wondrous things out of thy law.' Luke xxiv. 45: 'then opened he their understanding, that they might understand the scriptures.' Acts xviii. 28: 'he mightily convinced the Jews, and that publicly, shewing by the scriptures that Jesus was Christ.' 2 Pet. i. 20, 21: 'no prophecy of the scripture is of any private interpretation; for the prophecy came not in the old time by the will of man'; neither therefore is it to be interpreted by the judgment of men, that is, by our own unassisted judgment, but by means of that Holy Spirit promised to all believers. Hence the gift of prophecy, mentioned 1 Cor. i. 4.

If then the Scriptures be in themselves so perspicuous, and sufficient of themselves 'to make men wise unto salvation through faith,' and that 'the man of God may be perfect, thoroughly furnished unto all good works,' through what infatuation is it, that even Protestant divines persist in darkening the most momentous truths of religion by intricate metaphysical comments, on the plea that such explanation is necessary; stringing together all the useless technicalities and empty distinctions of scholastic barbarism, for the purpose of elucidating those Scriptures, which they are continually extolling as models of plainness? As if Scripture, which possesses in itself the clearest light, and is sufficient for its own explanation, especially in matters of faith and holiness, required to have the simplicity of its divine truths more fully developed, and placed in a more distinct view, by illustrations drawn from the abstrusest of human sciences, falsely so called.

It is only to those who perish that the Scriptures are obscure, especially in things necessary for salvation. Luke viii. 10:

'unto you it is given to know the mysteries of the kingdom of God, but to others in parables; that seeing they might not see, and hearing they might not understand.' 1 Cor. i. 18: 'the preaching of the cross is to them that perish foolishness; but unto us which are saved, it is the power of God.' ii. 14: 'the natural man receiveth not the things of the Spirit of God, for they are foolishness unto him; neither can he know them, because they are spiritually discerned.' 2 Cor. iv. 2, 3: 'by manifestation of the truth commending ourselves to every man's conscience in the sight of God: but if our gospel be hid, it is hid to them that are lost.' 2 Pet. iii. 16, speaking of the epistles of Paul, 'in which are some things hard to be understood, which they that are unlearned and unstable wrest, as they do also the other scriptures, unto their own destruction.'

No passage of Scripture is to be interpreted in more than one sense; in the Old Testament, however, this sense is sometimes a compound of the historical and typical, as in Hosea xi. 1, compared with Matt. ii. 15: 'out of Egypt have I called my son,' which may be explained in a double sense, as referring partly to the people of Israel, and partly to Christ in his infancy.

The custom of interpreting Scripture in the church is mentioned Nehem. viii. 8, 9: 'they read in the book in the law of God distinctly, and gave the sense, and caused them to understand the reading: and Nehemiah, which is the Tirshatha, and Ezra the priest the scribe, and the Levites that taught the people . . .' 2 Chron. xvii. 9: 'they taught in Judah, and had the book of the law of Jehovah with them, and went about throughout all the cities of Judah, and taught the people.' Luke iv. 17: 'then was delivered unto him the book of the prophet Esaias.' 1 Cor. xiv. 1: 'desire spiritual gifts, but rather that he may prophesy.'

The requisites for the public interpretation of Scripture have been laid down by divines with much attention to usefulness, although they have not been observed with equal fidelity. They consist in knowledge of languages; inspection of the originals; examination of the context; care in distinguishing between literal and figurative expressions; consideration of cause and circumstance, of antecedents and consequents; mutual comparison of texts; and regard to the analogy of faith. Attention must also be paid to the frequent anomalies of syntax; as for example, where the relative does not refer to the immediate antecedent, but to the principal word in the sentence, though more remote. See 2 Kings xvi. 2, compared with v. 1: 'twenty years old was Ahaz when he began to reign,' that is, Jotham the father of Ahaz, as appears by considering the age at which Hezekiah began his reign, xviii. 2. See also 2 Chron. xxxvi. 9: 'when he began to reign,' compared with 2 Kings xxiv. 8, Psal. xcix. 6: 'Moses and Aaron among his priests.' John viii. 44: 'he is a liar, and the father of it.' Lastly, no inferences from the text are to be admitted, but such as follow necessarily and plainly from the words themselves; lest we should be constrained to receive what is not written for what is written, the shadow for the substance, the fallacies of human reasoning for the doctrines of God: for it is by the declarations of Scripture, and not by the conclusions of the schools, that our consciences are bound.

Every believer has a right to interpret the Scriptures for himself, inasmuch as he has the Spirit for his guide, and the mind of Christ is in him; nay, the expositions of the public interpreter can be of no use to him, except so far as they are confirmed by his own conscience. More will be added on this subject in the next chapter, which treats of the members of particular churches. The right of public interpretation for the benefit of others is possessed by all whom God has appointed apostles, or prophets, or evangelists, or pastors, or teachers (1 Cor. xii. 8, 9, Eph. iv. 11–13), that is, by all who are endowed with the gift of teaching, 'every scribe which is instructed unto the kingdom of heaven' (Matt. xiii. 52), not by those whose sole commission is derived from human authority, or academical appointment; of whom it may too often be said in the words of Scripture, 'woe unto you, lawyers, for ye have taken away the key of knowledge; ye enter not yourselves, and them that were entering in ye hindered' (Luke xi. 52).

It is not therefore within the province of any visible church, much less of the civil magistrate, to impose their own interpretations on us as laws, or as binding on the conscience; in other words, as matter of implicit faith.

If, however, there be any difference among professed believers as to the sense of Scripture, it is their duty to tolerate such difference in each other, until God shall have revealed the truth to all. Philipp. iii. 15, 16: 'let us therefore, as many as be perfect, be thus minded; and if in anything ye be otherwise minded, God shall reveal even this unto you: nevertheless, whereto we have already attained, let us walk by the same rule, let us mind the same thing.' Rom. xiv. 4: 'to his own master he standeth or falleth: yea, he shall be holden up.'

The rule and canon of faith, therefore, is Scripture alone. Psal. xix. 9: 'the judgments of Jehovah are true and righteous altogether.' Scripture is the sole judge of controversies; or rather, every man is to decide for himself through its aid, under the guidance of the Spirit of God. For they who, on the authority of 1 Tim. iii. 15: 'the church of the living God, the pillar and ground of the truth,' claim for the visible church, however defined, the supreme right of interpreting Scripture and determining religious controversies, are confuted by a comparison of the words in question with the former part of the verse, and with that which precedes. What Paul here writes to Timothy, and which is intended to have the force of Scripture with him, is a direction by which he may know 'how he ought to behave himself in the house of God, which is the church'; that is, in any assembly of believers. It was not therefore 'the house of God,' or 'the church,' which was to be a rule to him 'that he might know,' but the Scripture which he had received from the hands of Paul. The church indeed is, or rather ought to be (for it is not always such in fact), the 'pillar and ground,' that is, the guardian, and repository, and support 'of the truth'; even where it is all this, however, it is not on that account to be considered as the rule or arbiter of truth and the Scripture; inasmuch as the house of God is not a rule to itself, but receives its rule from the word of God, which it is bound, at least, to observe scrupulously. Besides, the writings of the prophets and apostles, in other words the Scriptures themselves, are said to be the foundation of the church (Eph. ii. 20): 'built upon the foundation of the apostles and prophets, Jesus Christ himself being the chief corner-stone.' Now the church cannot be the rule or arbiter of that on which it is itself founded.

That some of the instructions of the apostles to the churches were not committed to writing, or that, if written, they have not come down to us, seems probable from 2 John 12: 'having many things to write unto you, I would not write with paper and ink.' See also 3 John 13, Col. iv. 16: 'that ye likewise read the epistle from Laodicea.' Seeing then that the lost particulars cannot be supposed to have contained anything necessary to salvation, but only matters profitable for doctrine, they are either to be collected from other passages of Scripture, or, if it be doubtful whether this is possible, they are to be supplied, not by the decrees of popes or councils, much less by the edicts of magistrates, but by the same Spirit which originally dictated them, enlightening us inwardly through the medium of faith and love. John xvi. 12, 13: 'I have yet many things to say unto you, but ye cannot bear them now; howbeit when he, the Spirit of truth is come, he shall guide you into all truth.' So also Peter admonishes us (2 Ep. i. 19): 'to take heed to the sure word of prophecy, until the day dawn, and the day-star arise in our hearts,' that is to say, the light of the gospel, which is not to be sought in written records alone, but in the heart. 2 Cor. iii. 3: 'ye are manifestly declared to be the epistle of Christ ministered by us, written not with ink, but with the Spirit of the living God; not in tables of stone, but in fleshy tables of the heart.' Eph. vi. 17: 'the sword of the Spirit, which is the word of God.' 1 John ii. 20: 'ye have an unction from the Holy One, and ye know all things.' v. 27: 'ye need not that any man teach you; but as the same anointing teacheth you of all things, and is truth, and is no lie, and even as it hath taught you, ye shall abide in him.' Thus when the Corinthians had made inquiry of Paul on certain subjects with regard to which there was no specific direction in Scripture, he answers them according to the natural dictates of Christianity, and the unction of the Spirit which he had received: 1 Cor. vii. 12: 'to the rest speak I, not the Lord.' v. 25: 'concerning virgins, I have no commandment of the Lord; yet I give my judgment as one that hath obtained mercy of the Lord to be faithful: I suppose therefore . . .' v. 40: 'she is happier if she so abide after my judgment; and I think also that I have the Spirit of God'; whence he reminds them that they are also able to give answer to themselves in such questions, v. 15: 'a brother or sister is not under bondage in such cases.' v. 36: 'if any man think that he behaveth himself uncomely towards his virgin, if she pass the flower of her age, and need so require, let him do what he will, he sinneth not.'

Under the gospel we possess, as it were, a twofold Scripture; one external, which is the written word, and the other internal, which is the Holy Spirit, written in the hearts of believers, according to the promise of God, and with the intent that it should by no means be neglected; as was shown above, chap. xxvii. on the gospel. Isai. lix. 21: 'as for me, this is my covenant with them, saith Jehovah; my Spirit which is upon thee, and my words which I have put in thy mouth, shall not depart out of thy mouth, nor out of the mouth of thy seed, nor out of the mouth of thy seed's seed, saith Jehovah, from henceforth and for ever.' See also Jer. xxxi. 33, 34. Acts v. 32: 'we are his witnesses of those things, and so is also the Holy Ghost, whom God hath given to them that obey him.' 1 Cor. ii. 12: 'we have received, not the spirit of the world, but the Spirit which is of God, that we might know the things that are freely given to us of God.'

Hence, although the external ground which we possess for our belief at the present day in the written word is highly important, and, in most instances at least, prior in point of reception, that which is internal, and the peculiar possession of each believer, is far superior to all, namely, the Spirit itself.

For the external Scripture, or written word, particularly of the New Testament (to say nothing of spurious books, with regard to which the apostle has long since cautioned us, 2 Thess. ii. 2: 'that ye be not shaken in mind . . . by letter as from us . . .'; iii. 17: 'the salutation of Paul with mine own hand, which is the token in every epistle:') the written word, I say, of the New Testament, has been liable to frequent corruption, and in some instances has been corrupted, through the number, and occasionally the bad faith of those by whom it has been handed down, the variety and discrepancy of the original manuscripts, and the additional diversity produced by subsequent transcripts and printed editions. But the Spirit which leads to truth cannot be corrupted, neither is it easy to deceive a man who is really spiritual, 1 Cor. ii. 15, 16: 'he that is spiritual judgeth all things, yet he himself is judged of no man: for who hath known the mind of the Lord, that he may instruct him? but we have the mind of Christ.' xii. 10: 'to another, discerning of spirits.' An instance of a corrupted text pervading nearly all the manuscripts occurs in Matt. xxvii. 9 where a quotation is attributed to Jeremiah, which belongs only to Zechariah; and similar instances are to be found in almost every page of Erasmus, Beza, and other editors of the New Testament.

Previously to the Babylonish captivity, the law of Moses was preserved in the sacred repository of the ark of the covenant; after that event, it was committed to the trust and guardianship of the priests and prophets, as Ezra, Zechariah, Malachi, and other men taught of God. There can be no doubt that these handed down the sacred volumes in an uncorrupted state to be preserved in the temple by the priests their successors, who were in all ages most scrupulous in preventing alterations, and who had themselves no grounds of suspicion to induce them to make any change. With regard to the remaining books, particularly the historical, although it be uncertain by whom and at what time they were written, and although they appear sometimes to contradict themselves on points of chronology, few or none have ever questioned the integrity of their doctrinal parts. The New Testament, on the contrary, has come down to us (as before observed) through the hands of a multitude of persons, subject to various temptations; nor have we in any instance the original copy in the author's handwriting, by which to correct the errors of the others. Hence Erasmus, Beza, and other learned men, have edited from the different manuscripts what in their judgment appeared most likely to be the authentic readings. It is difficult to conjecture the purpose of Providence in committing the writings of the New Testament to such uncertain and variable guardianship, unless it were to teach us by this very circumstance that the Spirit which is given to us is a more certain guide than Scripture, whom therefore it is our duty to follow.

For with regard to the visible church, which is also proposed as a criterion of faith, it is evident that, since the ascension of Christ, the 'pillar and ground of the truth' has not uniformly been the church, but the hearts of believers, which are properly 'the house and church of the living God,' 1 Tim. iii. 15. Certain it is, that the editors and interpreters of the New Testament (which is the chief authority for our faith) are accustomed to judge of the integrity of the text, not by its agreement with the visible church, but by the number and integrity of the manuscripts. Hence, where the manuscripts differ, the editors must necessarily be at a loss what to consider as the genuine word of God; as in the story of the woman taken in adultery, and some other passages.

The process of our belief in the Scriptures is, however, as follows: we set out with a general belief in their authenticity, founded on the testimony either of the visible church, or of the existing manuscripts; afterwards, by an inverse process, the authority of the church itself, and of the different books as contained in the manuscripts, are confirmed by the internal evidence implied in the uniform tenor of Scripture, considered as a whole; and, lastly, the truth of the entire volume is established by the inward persuasion of the Spirit working in the hearts of individual believers. So the belief of the Samaritans in Christ, though founded in the first instance on the word of the woman, derived its permanent establishment, less from her saying, than from the presence and discourses of Christ himself, John iv. 42. Thus, even on the authority of Scripture itself, everything is to be finally referred to the Spirit and the unwritten word.

Hence it follows, that when an acquiescence in human opinions or an obedience to human authority in matters of religion is exacted, in the name either of the church or of the Christian magistrate, from those who are themselves led individually by the Spirit of God, this is in effect to impose a yoke, not on man, but on the Holy Spirit itself. Certainly, if the apostles themselves, in a council governed by the inspiration of the Holy Spirit, determined that even the divinely instituted law was a yoke from which believers ought to be exempt, Acts xv. 10, 19, 28: 'why tempt ye God?' much less is any modern church, which cannot allege a similar claim to the presence of the Spirit, and least of all is the magistrate entitled to impose on believers a creed nowhere found in Scripture, or which is merely inferred from thence by human reasonings, carrying with them no certain conviction.

OF TRUE RELIGION, HERESY, SCHISM, TOLERATION;

AND WHAT BEST MEANS MAY BE USED

AGAINST THE GROWTH OF POPERY

Charles II had introduced a Declaration of Indulgence, which was intended to give freedom of worship to Roman Catholics rather than to Nonconformists. Milton was one of the more enlightened men of his time who wanted all forms of protestantism to be tolerated. He could not, however, endure the thought of tolerating catholicism, for he considered it the only truly heretical form of Christianity. The Declaration drove him to write this pamphlet in 1673, a year before his death.

Milton argued from two principles: first, the rule of truth in religion was only the word of God; secondly, this truth must be discovered by each believer for himself and not derived from any authority except that of Scripture—not even the church. On this basis, Protestants were bound to tolerate the religious views of other Protestants. No one holding these principles could be a heretic. He might err, but his endeavour was rightly directed, and he would be pardoned by God. Roman Catholics, who accepted their faith unquestioningly from the traditions of their church, were genuine heretics.

Sir Herbert Grierson blamed Milton for his intolerance of Catholics. It must be remembered, however, that he was in advance of a great many of his contemporaries, who would have preferred to impose their own brand of religion on all the rest of their countrymen.

It is unknown to no man, who knows aught of concernment among us, that the increase of popery is at this day no small trouble and offence to greatest part of the nation; and the rejoicing of all good men that it is so: the more their rejoicing, that God hath given a heart to the people, to remember still their great and happy deliverance from popish thraldom, and to esteem so highly the precious benefit of his gospel, so freely and so peaceably enjoyed among them. Since, therefore, some have already in public, with many considerable arguments, exhorted the people to beware the growth of this Romish weed, I thought it no less than a common duty to lend my hand, how unable soever, to so good a purpose. I will not now enter into

132

the labyrinth of councils and fathers, an entangled wood, which the papists love to fight in, not with hope of victory, but to obscure the shame of an open overthrow, which yet in that kind of combat many heretofore, and one of late, hath eminently given them. And such manner of dispute with them to learned men is useful and very commendable. But I shall insist now on what is plainer to common apprehension, and what I have to say without longer introduction.

True religion is the true worship and service of God, learned and believed from the word of God only. No man or angel can know how God would be worshipped and served unless God reveal it: he hath revealed and taught it us in the holy scriptures by inspired ministers, and in the gospel by his own Son and his apostles, with strictest command, to reject all other traditions or additions whatsoever: according to that of St Paul: 'Though we or an angel from heaven preach any other gospel unto you than that which we have preached unto you, let him be anathema, or accursed.' And Deut. iv. 2: 'Ye shall not add to the word which I command you, neither shall you diminish aught from it.' Rev. xxii. 18, 19: 'If any man shall add, etc. If any man shall take away from the words,' etc. With good and religious reason, therefore, all protestant churches with one consent, and particularly the church of England in her thirty-nine articles, article 6th, 19th, 20th, 21st, and elsewhere, maintain these two points, as the main principles of true religion—that the rule of true religion is the word of God only; and that their faith ought not to be an implicit faith, that is, to believe, though as the church believes, against or without express authority of scripture. And if all protestants, as universally as they hold these two principles, so attentively and religiously would observe them, they would avoid and cut off many debates and contentions, schisms, and persecutions, which too oft have been among them, and more firmly unite against the common adversary. For hence it directly follows, that no true protestant can persecute, or not tolerate, his fellow-protestant, though dissenting from him in some opinions, but he must flatly deny and renounce these two his own main principles, whereon true religion is founded; while he compels his brother from that which he believes as the manifest word of God, to an implicit faith (which he himself condemns) to the endangering of his brother's soul, whether by rash belief, or outward conformity: for 'whatsoever is not of faith is sin.'

I will now as briefly show what is false religion, or heresy, which will be done as easily; for, of contraries the definitions must needs be contrary. Heresy, therefore, is a religion taken up and believed from the traditions of men, and additions to the word of God. Whence also it follows clearly, that of all known sects, or pretended religions, at this day in Christendom, popery is the only or the greatest heresy; and he, who is so forward to brand all others for heretics, the obstinate papist, the only heretic. Hence one of their own famous writers found just cause to style the Romish church 'Mother of error, school of heresy.' And whereas the papist boasts himself to be a Roman Catholic, it is a mere contradiction, one of the pope's bulls, as if he should say, universal particular, a catholic schismatic. For catholic in Greek signifies universal; and the Christian church was so called, as consisting of all nations to whom the gospel was to be preached, in contradistinction to the Jewish church, which consisted for the most part of Jews only.

Sects may be in a true church as well as in a false, when men follow the doctrine too much for the teacher's sake, whom they think almost infallible; and this becomes, through infirmity, implicit faith; and the name sectary pertains to such a disciple.

Schism is a rent or division in the church, when it comes to the separating of congregations; and may also happen to a true church, as well as to a false; yet in the true needs not tend to the breaking of communion, if they can agree in the right administration of that wherein they communicate, keeping their other opinions to themselves, not being destructive to faith. The pharisees and sadducees were two sects, yet both met together in their common worship of God at Jerusalem. But here the papist will angrily demand, What! are Lutherans, Calvinists, Anabaptist, Socinians, Arminians, no heretics? I answer, All these may have some errors, but are no heretics. Heresy is in the will and choice professedly against scripture; error is against the will, in misunderstanding the scripture after all sincere endeavours to understand it rightly: hence it was said well by one of the ancients, 'Err I may, but a heretic I will not be.' It is a human frailty to err, and no man is infallible here on earth. But so long as all these profess to set the word of God only before them as the rule of faith and obedience; and use all diligence and sincerity of heart, by reading, by learning, by study, by prayer for illumination of the Holy Spirit, to understand the rule and obey it, they have done what man can do: God will assuredly pardon them, as he did the friends of Job; good and pious men, though much mistaken, as there it appears, in some points of doctrine. But some will say, with Christians it is otherwise, whom God hath promised by his Spirit to teach all things. True, all things absolutely necessary to salvation: but the hottest disputes among protestants, calmly and charitably inquired into, will be found less than such. The Lutheran holds consubstantiation; an error indeed, but not mortal. The Calvinist is taxed with predestination, and to make God the author of sin; not with any dishonourable thought of God, but it may be over-zealously asserting his absolute power, not without plea of scripture. The anabaptist is accused of denying infants their right to baptism; again they say, they deny nothing but what the scripture denies them. The Arian and Socinian are charged to dispute against the Trinity; they affirm to believe the Father, Son, and Holy Ghost, according to scripture and the apostolic creed; as for terms of trinity, triniunity, co-essentiality, tripersonality, and the like, they reject them as scholastic notions, not to be found in scripture, which by a general protestant maxim is plain and perspicuous abundantly to explain its own meaning in the properest words, belonging to so high a matter, and so necessary to be known; a mystery indeed in their sophistic subtilties, but in scripture a plain doctrine. Their other opinions are of less moment. They dispute the satisfaction of Christ, or rather the word 'satisfaction,' as not scriptural: but they acknowledge him both God and their Saviour. The Arminian, lastly, is condemned for setting up free will against free grace; but that imputation he disclaims in all his writings, and grounds himself largely upon scripture only. It cannot be denied, that the authors or late revivers of all these sects or opinions were learned, worthy, zealous, and religious men, as appears by their lives written, and the same of their many eminent and learned followers, perfect and powerful in the scriptures, holy and unblamable in their lives: and it cannot be imagined that God would desert such painful and zealous labourers in his church, and ofttimes great sufferers for their conscience, to damnable errors and a reprobate sense, who had so often implored the assistance of his Spirit; but rather, having made no man infallible, that he hath pardoned their errors, and accepts their pious endeavours, sincerely searching all things according to the rule of scripture, with such guidance and direction as they can obtain of God by prayer. What protestant then, who himself maintains the same principles, and disavows all implicit faith, would persecute, and not rather charitably tolerate, such men as these, unless he mean to abjure the principles of his own religion?

If it be asked, how far they should be tolerated; I answer, doubtless equally, as being all protestants; that is, on all occasions to give account of their faith, either by arguing, preaching in their several assemblies, public writing, and the freedom of printing. For if the French and Polonian protestants enjoy all this liberty among papists, much more may a protestant justly expect it among protestants; and yet sometimes here among us, the one persecutes the other upon every slight pretence.

But he is wont to say, he enjoins only things indifferent. Let them be so still; who gave him authority to change their nature by enjoining them? If by his own principles, as is proved, he ought to tolerate controverted points of doctrine not slightly grounded on scripture, much more ought he not impose things indifferent without scripture. In religion nothing is indifferent; but if it come to be imposed, is either a command or a prohibition, and so consequently an addition to the word of God, which he professes to disallow. Besides, how unequal, how uncharitable must it needs be, to impose that which his conscience cannot urge him to impose, upon him whose conscience forbids him to obey! What can it be but love of contention for things not necessary to be done, to molest the conscience of his brother, who holds them necessary to be not done? To conclude, let such a one but call to mind his own principles above mentioned, and he must necessarily grant, that neither he can impose, nor the other believe or obey, aught in religion, but from the word of God only. More amply to understand this, may be read the 14th and 15th chapters to the Romans, and the contents of the 14th, set forth no doubt but with full authority of the church of England: the gloss is this: 'Men may not contemn or condemn one the other for things indifferent.' And in the 6th article above mentioned: 'Whatsoever is not read in holy scripture, nor may be proved thereby, is not to be required of any man as an article of faith, or necessary to salvation.' And certainly what is not so, is not to be required at all, as being an addition to the word of God expressly forbidden.

Thus this long and hot contest, whether protestants ought to tolerate one another, if men will be but rational and not partial, may be ended without need of more words to compose it.

Let us now inquire whether popery be tolerable or no. Popery is a double thing to deal with, and claims a twofold power, ecclesiastical and political, both usurped, and the one supporting the other.

But ecclesiastical is ever pretended to political. The pope

by this mixed faculty pretends right to kingdoms and states, and especially to this of England, thrones and unthrones kings, and absolves the people from their obedience to them; sometimes interdicts to whole nations the public worship of God, shutting up their churches: and was wont to drain away greatest part of the wealth of this then miserable land, as part of his patrimony, to maintain the pride and luxury of his court and prelates; and now, since, through the infinite mercy and favour of God, we have shaken off his Babylonish yoke, hath not ceased by his spies and agents, bulls and emissaries, once to destroy both king and parliament; perpetually to seduce, corrupt, and pervert as many as they can of the people. Whether therefore it be fit or reasonable to tolerate men thus principled in religion towards the state, I submit it to the consideration of all magistrates, who are best able to provide for their own and the public safety. As for tolerating the exercise of their religion, supposing their state-activities not to be dangerous, I answer, that toleration is either public or private; and the exercise of their religion, as far as it is idolatrous, can be tolerated neither way: not publicly, without grievous and unsufferable scandal given to all conscientious beholders; not privately, without great offence to God, declared against all kind of idolatry, though secret. Ezek. viii. 7, 8: 'And he brought me to the door of the court; and when I looked, behold, a hole in the wall. Then said he unto me, Son of man, dig now in the wall: and when I had digged, behold a door; and he said unto me, Go in, and behold the wicked abominations that they do here.' And ver. 12: 'Then said he unto me, Son of man, hast thou seen what the ancients of the house of Israel do in the dark?' etc. And it appears by the whole chapter, that God was no less offended with these secret idolatries than with those in public; and no less provoked, than to bring on and hasten his judgments on the whole land for these also.

Having shown thus, that popery, as being idolatrous, is not to be tolerated either in public or in private; it must be now thought how to remove it, and hinder the growth thereof, I mean in our natives, and not foreigners, privileged by the law of nations. Are we to punish them by corporal punishment, or fines in their estates, upon account of their religion? I suppose it stands not with the clemency of the gospel, more than what appertains to the security of the state: but first we must remove their idolatry, and all the furniture thereof, whether idols or the mass wherein they adore their God under bread and wine: for the commandment forbids to adore, not only 'any graven image, but the likeness of anything in heaven above, or in the earth beneath, or in the water under the earth; thou shalt not bow down to them nor worship them, for I the Lord thy God am a jealous God.' If they say, that by removing their idols we violate their consciences, we have no warrant to regard conscience which is not grounded on scripture: and they themselves confess in their late defences, that they hold not their images necessary to salvation, but only as they are enjoined them by tradition.

Shall we condescend to dispute with them? The scripture is our only principle in religion; and by that only they will not be judged, but will add other principles of their own, which, forbidden by the word of God, we cannot assent to. And [in several places of the gospel] the common maxim also in logic is, 'against them who deny principles, we are not to dispute.' Let them bound their disputations on the scripture only, and an ordinary protestant, well read in the Bible, may turn and wind their doctors. They will not go about to prove their idolatries by the word of God, but turn to shifts and evasions, and frivolous distinctions; idols they say are laymen's books, and a great means to stir up pious thoughts and devotion in the learnedest. I say, they are no means of God's appointing, but plainly the contrary: let them hear the prophets. Jer. x. 8: 'The stock is a doctrine of vanities.' Hab. ii. 18: 'What profiteth the graven image, that the maker thereof hath graven it; the molten image and a teacher of lies?' But they allege in their late answers, that the laws of Moses, given only to the Jews, concern not us under the gospel; and remember not that idolatry is forbidden as expressly: but with these wiles and fallacies 'compassing sea and land, like the pharisees of old, to make one proselyte,' they lead away privily many simple and ignorant souls, men and women, 'and make them twofold more the children of hell than themselves' (Matt. xxiii. 15). But the apostle hath well warned us, I may say, from such deceivers as these, for their mystery was then working. 'I beseech you, brethren,' saith he, 'mark them which cause divisions and offences, contrary to the doctrine which ye have learned, and avoid them; for they that are such, serve not our Lord Jesus Christ, but their own belly, and by good words and fair speeches deceive the heart of the simple' (Rom. xvi. 17, 18).

The next means to hinder the growth of popery will be, to read duly and diligently the holy scriptures, which, as St Paul saith to Timothy, who had known them from a child, 'are able to make wise unto salvation.' And to the whole church of Colossi:

'Let the word of Christ dwell in you plentifully, with all wisdom' (Col. iii. 16). The papal antichristian church permits not her laity to read the Bible in their own tongue: our church, on the contrary, hath proposed it to all men, and to this end translated it into English, with profitable notes on what is met with obscure, though what is most necessary to be known be still plainest; that all sorts and degrees of men, not understanding the original, may read it in their mother tongue. Neither let the countryman, the tradesman, the lawyer, the physician, the statesman, excuse himself by his much business from the studious reading thereof. Our Saviour saith (Luke x. 41, 42): 'Thou art careful and troubled about many things; but one thing is needful.' If they were asked, they would be loath to set earthly things, wealth or honour, before the wisdom of salvation. Yet most men in the course and prac- tice of their lives are found to do so; and through unwillingness to take the pains of understanding their religion by their own diligent study, would fain be saved by a deputy. Hence comes implicit faith, ever learning and never taught, much hearing and small proficience, till want of fundamental knowledge easily turns to superstition or popery: therefore the apostle admonishes (Eph. iv. 14): 'That we henceforth be no more children, tossed to and fro and carried about with every wind of doctrine, by the sleight of men, and cunning craftiness whereby they lie in wait to deceive.' Every member of the church, at least of any breed- ing or capacity, so well ought to be grounded in spiritual know- ledge, as, if need be, to examine their teachers themselves. Acts xvii, 11: 'They searched the scriptures daily, whether those things were so.' Rev. ii. 2: 'Thou hast tried them which say they are apostles, and are not.' How should any private Christian try his teachers, unless he be well grounded himself in the rule of scripture, by which he is taught? As therefore among papists their ignorance in scripture chiefly upholds popery; so among protestant people, the frequent and serious reading thereof will soonest pull popery down.

Another means to abate popery arises from the constant read- ing of scripture, wherein believers, who agree in the main, are everywhere exhorted to mutual forbearance and charity one towards the other, though dissenting in some opinions. It is written that the coat of our Saviour was without seam; whence some would infer that there should be no division in the church of Christ. It should be so indeed; yet seams in the same cloth neither hurt the garment nor misbecome it; and not only seams, but schisms will be while men are fallible: but if they who dissent in matters not essential to belief, while the common adversary is in the field, shall stand jarring and pelting at one another, they will be soon routed and subdued. The papist with open mouth makes much advantage of our several opinions; not that he is able to confute the worst of them, but that we by our continual jangle among ourselves make them worse than they are indeed. To save ourselves, therefore, and resist the common enemy, it concerns us mainly to agree within ourselves, that with joint forces we may not only hold our own, but get ground: and why should we not? The gospel commands us to tolerate one another though of various opinions, and hath promised a good and happy event thereof. Phil. iii. 15: 'Let us therefore, as many as be perfect, be thus minded; and if in anything ye be otherwise minded, God shall reveal even this unto you.' And we are bid (1 Thess. v. 21): 'Prove all things, hold fast that which is good.' St Paul judged, that not only to tolerate, but to examine and prove all things, was no danger to our holding fast that which is good. How shall we prove all things, which includes all opinions at least founded on scripture, unless we not only tolerate them, but patiently hear them, and seriously read them? If he who thinks himself in the truth professes to have learnt it, not by implicit faith, but by attentive study of the scriptures, and full persuasion of heart, with what equity can he refuse to hear or read him who demonstrates to have gained his knowledge by the same way? Is it a fair course to assert truth, by arrogating to himself the only freedom of speech, and stopping the mouths of others equally gifted? This is the direct way to bring in that papistical implicit faith, which we all disclaim. They pretend it would unsettle the weaker sort; the same groundless fear is pretended by the Romish clergy. At least, then, let them have leave to write in Latin, which the common people understand not; that what they hold may be discussed among the learned only. We suffer the idolatrous books of papists, without this fear, to be sold and read as common as our own: why not much rather of Anabaptists, Arians, Arminians, and Socinians? There is no learned man but will confess he hath much profited by reading controversies, his senses awakened, his judgment sharpened, and the truth which he holds more firmly established. If then it be profitable for him to read, why should it not at least be tolerable and free for his adversary to write? In logic they teach, that contraries laid together more evidently appear: it follows, then, that all controversy being permitted, falsehood will appear more false, and truth the more true; which must needs conduce much, not only to the confounding of popery, but to the general confirmation of unimplicit truth.

The last means to avoid popery is, to amend our lives. It is a general complaint, that this nation of late years is grown more numerously and excessively vicious than heretofore; pride, luxury, drunkenness, whoredom, cursing, swearing, bold and open atheism everywhere abounding: where these grow, no wonder if popery also grow apace. There is no man so wicked but at sometimes his conscience will wring him with thoughts of another world, and the peril of his soul; the trouble and melancholy, which he conceives of true repentance and amendment, he endures not, but inclines rather to some carnal superstition, which may pacify and lull his conscience with some more pleasing doctrine. None more ready and officious to offer herself than the Romish, and opens wide her office, with all her faculties, to receive him; easy confession, easy absolution, pardons, indulgences, masses for him both quick and dead, Agnus Deis, relics, and the like: and he, instead of 'working out his salvation with fear and trembling,' straight thinks in his heart (like another kind of fool than he in the Psalms), to bribe God as a corrupt judge; and by his proctor, some priest, or friar, to buy out his peace with money, which he cannot with his repentance. For God, when men sin outrageously, and will not be admonished, gives over chastising them, perhaps by pestilence, fire, sword, or famine, which may all turn to their good, and takes up his severest punishments, hardness, besottedness of heart, and idolatry, to their final perdition. Idolatry brought the heathen to heinous transgressions (Rom. ii). And heinous transgressions ofttimes bring the slight professors of true religion to gross idolatry; 1 Thes. ii. 11, 12: 'For this cause God shall send them strong delusion, that they should believe a lie, that they all might be damned who believe not the truth, but had pleasure in unrighteousness.' And Isaiah xliv. 18, speaking of idolaters: 'They have not known nor understood, for he hath shut their eyes that they cannot see, and their hearts that they cannot understand.' Let us therefore, using this last means, last here spoken of, but first to be done, amend our lives with all speed; lest through impenitency we run into that stupidity which we now seek all means so warily to avoid, the worst of superstitions, and the heaviest of all God's judgments—popery.

On
CIVIL LIBERTY

AREOPAGITICA

Milton himself described the *Areopagitica* as a pamphlet written in defence of 'domestic or private liberty.' The modern reader, however, sees freedom of speech and freedom of the press as civil rather than personal liberties. In consequence it has been grouped with the political pamphlets.

There was no organized censorship of the press in England until the time of Queen Elizabeth I. The chief concern of her censors was to protect the monarchy and the established church. Control of the press was tightened in 1637 by a Decree of the Court of Star Chamber, and the scope of the censors was widened. Those pamphleteers who wrote for the Puritan cause suffered most. One of the first Acts of the Long Parliament was the abolition of the Court of Star Chamber. This Act destroyed the machinery of censorship, to the great satisfaction of Laud's opponents. When the Puritan element had the upper hand in Parliament, they discovered that the resulting flood of opposition pamphlets was as much of a thorn in the flesh to them as their own pamphlets had been to Laud. They departed from the principle of the freedom of the press, and passed an Ordinance for the regulation of printing in June 1643. (The terms of this Ordinance are summarized below.) This Ordinance seemed to Milton a piece of reactionary legislation, dictated by fears which were not only unworthy but unnecessary. Such men as William Walwyn, Henry Robinson, and Richard Overton were in full agreement with his plea for the removal of restrictions from the press.

Milton did his best to demonstrate that only tyrannies indulged in censorship of the press. He saw censorship as an insult to adult human beings, and worse than an insult to scholars and clergymen. In a state of tutelage, men had no chance to develop towards maturity. With a free press, men had scope for strenuous and virtuous action. Though men were fallen, they retained enough of the original gift of right reason to grow towards moral freedom. Milton was well aware that his theories would not work unless men were willing to take the responsibility of thinking and judging for themselves.

He felt sure that, in free controversy, truth would ultimately prevail. He despised men who talked in terms of a golden world near at hand, but he was certain that error would at length be defeated, however violent the means it employed in the struggle. The state had more to hope than to fear from free speech: the 'eluctation of truth' was worth the risks entailed.

Milton called the pamphlet *Areopagitica* because he was comparing the Parliament of England, to whom he was appealing, with the democratically elected supreme court of Athens in ancient Greece. This court was named after the hill Areopagus, on which it assembled.

The 'sage and severe judges' of Athens were much admired in seven-teenth-century Europe. Milton thought the English Parliament was made up of worthy representatives of the 'noble and puissant nation' whom they served. In the end they were to prove unequal to his trust.

ANALYSIS OF THE ORDER OF PARLIAMENT (JUNE 14, 1643), AGAINST WHICH THE AREOPAGITICA WAS DIRECTED

1. The Preamble recounts that 'many false ... scandalous, seditious, and libellous' works have lately been published, 'to the great defamation of Religion and government'; that many private printing-presses have been set up; and that 'divers of the Stationers' Company' have infringed the rights of the Company.

2. 'It is therefore ordered by the Lords and Commons in Parliament,' (1) that no Order 'of both or either House shall be printed' except by command; (2) *that no Book, etc.*, '*shall from henceforth be printed or put to sale, unless the same be first approved of and licensed by such person or persons as both or either of the said Houses shall appoint for the licensing of the same*'; (3) that no book, of which the copyright has been granted to the Company, 'for their relief and the maintenance of their poor,' be printed by any person or persons 'without the license and consent of the Master, Warden, and assistants of the said Company'; (4) that no book, 'formerly printed here,' he imported from beyond seas, 'upon pain of forfeiting the same to the Owner' of the Copyright, 'and such further punishment as shall be thought fit.'

3. The Stationers' Company and the officers of the two Houses are authorised to search for unlicensed Presses, and to break them up; to search for unlicensed Books, etc., and confiscate them; and to 'apprehend all authors, printers and others' concerned in publishing unlicensed books and to bring them before the Houses 'or the Committee of Examination' for 'further punishments,' such persons not to be released till they have given satisfaction and also 'sufficient caution not to offend in like sort for the future.'

4. 'All Justices of the Peace, Captains, Constables and other officers' are ordered to give aid in the execution of the above.

A SPEECH FOR THE LIBERTY OF UNLICENSED PRINTING, TO THE PARLIAMENT OF ENGLAND (1644)

THEY, who to states and governors of the Commonwealth direct their speech, High Court of Parliament, or, wanting such access in a private condition, write that which they foresee may advance the public good; I suppose them, as at the beginning of no mean endeavour, not a little altered and moved inwardly in their minds: some with doubt of what will be the success, others with fear of what will be the censure; some with hope, others with confidence of what they have to speak. And me perhaps each of these dispositions, as the subject was whereon I entered, may have at other times variously affected; and likely might in these foremost expressions now also disclose which of them swayed most, but that the very attempt of this address thus made, and the thought of whom it hath recourse to, hath got the power within me to a passion, far more welcome than incidental to a preface.

Which though I stay not to confess ere any ask, I shall be blameless, if it be no other than the joy and gratulation which it brings to all who wish and promote their country's liberty; whereof this whole discourse proposed will be a certain testimony, if not a trophy. For this is not the liberty which we can hope, that no grievance ever should arise in the Commonwealth —that let no man in this world expect; but when complaints are freely heard, deeply considered and speedily reformed, then is the utmost bound of civil liberty attained that wise men look for. To which if I now manifest by the very sound of this which I shall utter, that we are already in good part arrived, and yet from such a steep disadvantage of tyranny and superstition grounded into our principles as was beyond the manhood of a Roman recovery, it will be attributed first, as is most due, to the strong assistance of God our deliverer, next to your faithful guidance and undaunted wisdom, Lords and Commons of England. Neither is it in God's esteem the diminution of His glory, when honourable things are spoken of good men and worthy magistrates; which if I now first should begin to do, after so fair a progress of your laudable deeds, and such a long obligement upon the whole realm to your indefatigable virtues, I might be justly reckoned among the tardiest, and the unwillingest of them that praise ye.

Nevertheless there being three principal things, without which all praising is but courtship and flattery: First, when that only is praised which is solidly worth praise: next, when greatest likelihoods are brought that such things are truly and really in those persons to whom they are ascribed: the other, when he who praises, by showing that such his actual persuasion is of whom he writes, can demonstrate that he flatters not; the former two of these I have heretofore endeavoured, rescuing the employment from him who went about to impair your merits with a trivial and malignant encomium; the latter as belonging chiefly to mine own acquittal, that whom I so extolled I did not flatter, hath been reserved opportunely to this occasion.

For he who freely magnifies what hath been nobly done, and fears not to declare as freely what might be done better, gives ye the best covenant of his fidelity; and that his loyalist affection and his hope waits on your proceedings. His highest

praising is not flattery, and his plainest advice is a kind of praising. For though I should affirm and hold by argument, that
it would fare better with truth, with learning and the Commonwealth, if one of your published Orders, which I should name,
were called in; yet at the same time it could not but much redound to the lustre of your mild and equal government, whenas
private persons are hereby animated to think ye better pleased
with public advice, than other statists have been delighted heretofore with public flattery. And men will then see what difference there is between the magnanimity of a triennial Parliament,
and that jealous haughtiness of prelates and Cabin Counsellors
that usurped of late, whenas they shall observe ye in the midst
of your victories and successes more gently brooking written
exceptions against a voted Order than other Courts, which had
produced nothing worth memory but the weak ostentation of
wealth, would have endured the least signified dislike at any
sudden Proclamation.

If I should thus far presume upon the meek demeanour of
your civil and gentle greatness, Lords and Commons, as what
your published Order hath directly said, that to gainsay, I
might defend myself with ease, if any should accuse me of being
new or insolent, did they but know how much better I find ye
esteem it to imitate the old and elegant humanity of Greece,
than the barbaric pride of a Hunnish and Norwegian stateliness.
And out of those ages, to whose polite wisdom and letters we
owe that we are not yet Goths and Jutlanders, I could name
him who from his private house wrote that discourse to the
Parliament of Athens, that persuades them to change the form
of democracy which was then established. Such honour was
done in those days to men who professed the study of wisdom
and eloquence, not only in their own country, but in other lands,
that cities and signiories heard them gladly, and with great
respect, if they had aught in public to admonish the state. Thus
did Dion Prusaeus, a stranger and a private orator, counsel the
Rhodians against a former edict; and I abound with other like
examples, which to set here would be superfluous.

But if from the industry of a life wholly dedicated to studious
labours, and those natural endowments haply not the worse
for two and fifty degrees of northern latitude, so much must
be derogated, as to count me not equal to any of those who had
this privilege, I would obtain to be thought not so inferior, as
yourselves are superior to the most of them who received their
counsel: and how far you excel them, be assured, Lords and

Commons, there can no greater testimony appear, than when your prudent spirit acknowledges and obeys the voice of reason from what quarter soever it be heard speaking; and renders ye as willing to repeal any Act of your own setting forth, as any set forth by your predecessors.

If ye be thus resolved, as it were injury to think ye were not, I know not what should withhold me from presenting ye with a fit instance wherein to show both that love of truth which ye eminently profess, and that uprightness of your judgment which is not wont to be partial to yourselves; by judging over again that Order which ye have ordained to regulate Printing:—that no book, pamphlet, or paper shall be henceforth printed, unless the same be first approved and licensed by such, or at least one of such, as shall thereto be appointed. For that part which preserves justly every man's copy to himself, or provides for the poor, I touch not, only wish they be not made pretences to abuse and persecute honest and painful men, who offend not in either of these particulars. But that other clause of Licensing Books, which we thought had died with his brother quadragesimal and matrimonial when the prelates expired, I shall now attend with such a homily, as shall lay before ye, first the inventors of it to be those whom ye will be loth to own; next what is to be thought in general of reading, whatever sort the books be; and that this Order avails nothing to the suppressing of scandalous, seditious, and libellous books, which were mainly intended to be suppressed. Last, that it will be primely to the discouragement of all learning, and the stop of Truth, not only by disexercising and blunting our abilities in what we know already, but by hindering and cropping the discovery that might be yet further made both in religious and civil Wisdom.

I deny not, but that it is of greatest concernment in the Church and Commonwealth, to have a vigilant eye how books demean themselves as well as men; and thereafter to confine, imprison, and do sharpest justice on them as malefactors. For books are not absolutely dead things, but do contain a potency of life in them to be as active as that soul was whose progeny they are; nay, they do preserve as in a vial the purest efficacy and extraction of that living intellect that bred them. I know they are as lively, and as vigorously productive, as those fabulous dragon's teeth; and being sown up and down, may chance to spring up armed men. And yet, on the other hand, unless wariness be used, as good almost kill a man as kill a good book. Who kills a man kills a reasonable creature, God's image; but he who destroys a good book, kills reason itself, kills the image of God, as it were in the eye. Many a man lives a burden to the earth; but a good book is the precious life-blood of a master spirit, embalmed and treasured up on purpose to a life beyond life. 'Tis true, no age can restore a life, whereof perhaps there is no great loss; and revolutions of ages do not oft recover the loss of a rejected truth, for the want of which whole nations fare the worse.

We should be wary therefore what persecutions we raise against the living labours of public men, how we spill that seasoned life of man, preserved and stored up in books; since we see a kind of homicide may be thus committed, sometimes a martyrdom, and if it extend to the whole impression, a kind of massacre; whereof the execution ends not in the slaying of an elemental life, but strikes at that ethereal and fifth essence, the breath of reason itself, slays an immortality rather than a life. But lest I should be condemned of introducing licence, while I oppose licensing, I refuse not the pains to be so much historical, as will serve to show what hath been done by ancient and famous commonwealths against this disorder, till the very time that this project of licensing crept out of the inquisition, was catched up by our prelates, and hath caught some of our presbyters.

In Athens, where books and wits were ever busier than in any other part of Greece, I find but only two sorts of writings which the magistrate cared to take notice of; those either blasphemous and atheistical, or libellous. Thus the books of Protagoras were by the judges of Areopagus commanded to be burnt, and himself banished the territory for a discourse begun with his confessing not to know 'whether there were gods, or whether not.' And against defaming, it was agreed that none should be traduced by name, as was the manner of Vetus Comoedia, whereby we may guess how they censured libelling. And this course was quick enough, as Cicero writes, to quell both the desperate wits of other atheists, and the open way of defaming, as the event showed. Of other sects and opinions, though tending to voluptuousness, and the denying of Divine Providence, they took no heed.

Therefore we do not read that either Epicurus, or that libertine school of Cyrene, or what the Cynic impudence uttered, was ever questioned by the laws. Neither is it recorded that the writings of those old comedians were suppressed, though the acting of them were forbid; and that Plato commended the reading of Aristophanes, the loosest of them all, to his royal scholar

Dionysius, is commonly known, and may be excused, if holy Chrysostom, as is reported, nightly studied so much the same author and had the art to cleanse a scurrilous vehemence into the style of a rousing sermon.

That other leading city of Greece, Lacedaemon, considering that Lycurgus their lawgiver was so addicted to elegant learning, as to have been the first that brought out of Ionia the scattered works of Homer, and sent the poet Thales from Crete to prepare and mollify the Spartan surliness with his smooth songs and odes, the better to plant among them law and civility, it is to be wondered how museless and unbookish they were, minding nought but the feats of war. There needed no licensing of books among them, for they disliked all but their own laconic apothegms, and took a slight occasion to chase Archilochus out of their city, perhaps for composing in a higher strain than their own soldierly ballads and roundels could reach to. Or if it were for his broad verses, they were not therein so cautious but they were as dissolute in their promiscuous conversing; whence Euripides affirms in *Andromache*, that their women were all unchaste. Thus much may give us light after what sort of books were prohibited among the Greeks.

The Romans also, for many ages trained up only to a military roughness resembling most the Lacedaemonian guise, knew of learning little but what their twelve Tables, and the Pontific College with their augurs and flamens taught them in religion and law, so unacquainted with other learning, that when Carneades and Critolaus, with the Stoic Diogenes coming ambassadors to Rome, took thereby occasion to give the city a taste of their philosophy, they were suspected for seducers by no less a man than Cato the Censor, who moved it in the Senate to dismiss them speedily, and to banish all such Attic babblers out of Italy. But Scipio and others of the noblest senators withstood him and his old Sabine austerity; honoured and admired the men; and the censor himself at last, in his old age, fell to the study of what whereof before he was so scrupulous. And yet at the same time, Naevius and Plautus, the first Latin comedians, had filled the city with all the borrowed scenes of Menander and Philemon. Then began to be considered there also what was to be done to libellous books and authors; for Naevius was quickly cast into prison for his unbridled pen, and released by the tribunes upon his recantation; we read also that libels were burnt, and the makers punished by Augustus. The like severity, no doubt, was used, if aught were impiously written against their esteemed gods. Except in these two points, how the world went in books, the magistrate kept no reckoning.

And therefore Lucretius without impeachment versifies his Epicurism to Memmius, and had the honour to be set forth the second time by Cicero, so great a father of the commonwealth; although himself disputes against that opinion in his own writings. Nor was the satirical sharpness or naked plainness of Lucilius, or Catullus, or Flaccus, by any order prohibited. And for matters of state, the story of Titus Livius, though it extolled that part which Pompey held, was not therefore suppressed by Octavius Caesar of the other faction. But that Naso was by him banished in his old age, for the wanton poems of his youth, was but a mere covert of state over some secret cause: and besides, the books were neither banished nor called in. From hence we shall meet with little else but tyranny in the Roman empire, that we may not marvel, if not so often bad as good books were silenced. I shall therefore deem to have been large enough, in producing what among the ancients was punishable to write; save only which, all other arguments were free to treat on.

By this time the emperors were become Christians, whose discipline in this point I do not find to have been more severe than what was formerly in practice. The books of those whom they took to be grand heretics were examined, refuted, and condemned in the general Councils; and not till then were prohibited, or burnt, by authority of the emperor. As for the writings of heathen authors, unless they were plain invectives against Christianity, as those of Porphyrius and Proclus, they met with no interdict that can be cited, till about the year 400, in a Carthaginian Council, wherein bishops themselves were forbid to read the books of Gentiles, but heresies they might read: while others long before them, on the contrary, scrupled more the books of heretics than of Gentiles. And that the primitive Councils and bishops were wont only to declare what books were not commendable, passing no further, but leaving it to each one's conscience to read or to lay by, till after the year 800, is observed already by Padre Paolo, the great unmasker of the Trentine Council.

After which time the Popes of Rome, engrossing what they pleased of political rule into their own hands, extended their dominion over men's eyes, as they had before over their judgments, burning and prohibiting to be read what they fancied not; yet sparing in their censures, and the books not many

which they so dealt with: till Martin V, by his bull, not only
prohibited, but was the first that excommunicated the reading
of heretical books; for about that time Wickliffe and Huss,
growing terrible, were they who first drove the Papal Court to
a stricter policy of prohibiting. Which course Leo X and his
successors followed, until the Council of Trent and the Spanish
Inquisition engendering together brought forth, or perfected,
those Catalogues and expurging Indexes, that rake through the
entrails of many an old good author, with a violation worse
than any could be offered to his tomb. Nor did they stay in
matters heretical, but any subject that was not to their palate,
they either condemned in a Prohibition, or had it straight into
the new Purgatory of an Index.

To fill up the measure of encroachment, their last invention
was to ordain that no book, pamphlet, or paper should be
printed (as if St Peter had bequeathed them the keys of the
press also out of Paradise) unless it were approved and licensed
under the hands of two or three glutton friars. For example:

> Let the Chancellor Cini be pleased to see if in this present work
> be contained aught that may withstand the printing.
>> Vincent Rabbatta, Vicar of Florence.

> I have seen this present work, and find nothing athwart the
> Catholic faith and good manners: in witness whereof I have
> given, etc.   Nicolo Cini, Chancellor of Florence.

> Attending the precedent relation, it is allowed that this present
> work of Davanzati may be printed.
>> Vincent Rabbatta, etc.

> It may be printed, July 15.
>> Friar Simon Mompei d'Amelia, Chancellor of the holy
>> office in Florence.

Sure they have a conceit, if he of the bottomless pit had not
long since broke prison, that this quadruple exorcism would
bar him down. I fear their next design will be to get into their
custody the licensing of that which they say Claudius intended,
but went not through with. Vouchsafe to see another of their
forms, the Romans stamp:

> Imprimatur, If it seem good to the reverend master of the holy
> Palace.   Belcastro, Vicegerent.

> Imprimatur, Friar Nicolo Rodolphi, Master of the holy Palace.

Sometimes five Imprimaturs are seen together dialogue-wise

in the piazza of one title-page, complimenting and ducking each to other with their shaven reverences, whether the author, who stands by in perplexity at the foot of his epistle, shall to the press or to the sponge. These are the pretty responsories, these are the dear antiphonies, that so bewitched of late our Prelates and their chaplains with the goodly echo they made; and besotted us to the gay imitation of a lordly Imprimatur, one from Lambeth House, another from the west end of Pauls; so apishly romanizing, that the word of command still was set down in Latin; as if the learned grammatical pen that wrote it would cast no ink without Latin; or perhaps, as they thought, because no vulgar tongue was worthy to express the pure conceit of an Imprimatur; but rather, as I hope, for that our English, the language of men, ever famous and foremost in the achievements of liberty, will not easily find servile letters enow to spell such a dictatory presumption English.

And thus ye have the inventors and the original of book-licensing ripped up and drawn as lineally as any pedigree. We have it not, that can be heard of, from any ancient state, or polity or church; nor by any statute left us by our ancestors elder or later; nor from the modern custom of any reformed city or church abroad; but from the most antichristian council and the most tyrannous inquisition that ever inquired. Till then books were ever as freely admitted into the world as any other birth; the issue of the brain was no more stifled than the issue of the womb: no envious Juno sat cross-legged over the nativity of any man's intellectual offspring; but if it proved a monster, who denies, but that it was justly burnt, or sunk into the sea? But that a book, in worse condition than a peccant soul, should be to stand before a jury ere it be born to the world, and undergo yet in darkness the judgment of Radamanth and his colleagues, ere it can pass the ferry backward into light, was never heard before, till that mysterious iniquity, provoked and troubled at the first entrance of Reformation, sought out new limbos and new hells wherein they might include our books also within the number of their damned. And this was the rare morsel so officiously snatched up, and so ill-favouredly imitated by our inquisiturient bishops, and the attendant minorities their chaplains. That ye like not now these most certain authors of this licensing order, and that all sinister intention was far distant from your thoughts, when ye were importuned the passing it, all men who know the integrity of your actions, and how ye honour Truth, will clear ye readily.

But some will say, What though the inventors were bad, the thing for all that may be good? It may be so; yet if that thing be no such deep invention, but obvious, and easy for any man to light on, and yet best and wisest commonwealths through all ages and occasions have forborne to use it, and falsest seducers and oppressors of men were the first who took it up, and to no other purpose but to obstruct and hinder the first approach of Reformation; I am of those who believe it will be a harder alchymy than Lullius ever knew, to sublimate any good use out of such an invention. Yet this only is what I request to gain from this reason, that it may be held a dangerous and suspicious fruit, as certainly it deserves, for the tree that bore it, until I can dissect one by one the properties it has. But I have first to finish, as was propounded, what is to be thought in general of reading books, whatever sort they be, and whether be more the benefit or the harm that thence proceeds?

Not to insist upon the examples of Moses, Daniel, and Paul, who were skilful in all the learning of the Egyptians, Chaldeans, and Greeks, which could not probably be without reading their books of all sorts; in Paul especially, who thought it no defilement to insert into Holy Scripture the sentences of three Greek poets, and one of them a tragedian; the question was notwithstanding sometimes controverted among the primitive doctors, but with great odds on that side which affirmed it both lawful and profitable; as was then evidently perceived, when Julian the Apostate and subtlest enemy to our faith made a decree forbidding Christians the study of heathen learning: for, said he, they wound us with our own weapons, and with our own arts and sciences they overcome us. And indeed the Christians were put so to their shifts by this crafty means, and so much in danger to decline into all ignorance, that the two Apollinarii were fain, as a man may say, to coin all the seven liberal sciences out of the Bible, reducing it into divers forms of orations, poems, dialogues, even to the calculating of a new Christian grammar. But, saith the historian Socrates, the providence of God provided better than the industry of Apollinarius and his son, by taking away that illiterate law with the life of him who devised it. So great an injury they then held it to be deprived of Hellenic learning; and thought it a persecution more undermining, and secretly decaying the Church, than the open cruelty of Decius or Diocletian.

And perhaps it was the same politic drift that the devil whipped St Jerome in a Lenten dream, for reading Cicero; or else it was a phantasm bred by the fever which had then seized him. For had an angel been his discipliner, unless it were for dwelling too much upon Ciceronianisms, and had chastised the reading, not the vanity, it had been plainly partial; first to correct him for grave Cicero, and not for scurril Plautus, whom he confesses to have been reading, not long before; next to correct him only, and let so many more ancient fathers wax old in those pleasant and florid studies without the lash of such a tutoring apparition; insomuch that Basil teaches how some good use may be made of Margites, a sportful poem, not now extant, writ by Homer; and why not then of Morgante, an Italian romance much to the same purpose?

But if it be agreed we shall be tried by visions, there is a vision recorded by Eusebius, far ancienter than this tale of Jerome to the nun Eustochium, and, besides, has nothing of a fever in it. Dionysius Alexandrinus was about the year 240 a person of great name in the Church for piety and learning, who had wont to avail himself much against heretics by being conversant in their books; until a certain presbyter laid it scrupulously to his conscience, how he durst venture himself among those defiling volumes. The worthy man, loth to give offence; fell into a new debate with himself what was to be thought, when suddenly a vision sent from God (it is his own epistle that so avers it) confirmed him in these words: Read any books whatever come to thy hands, for thou art sufficient both to judge aright, and to examine each matter. To this revelation he assented the sooner, as he confesses, because it was answerable to that of the Apostle to the Thessalonians, Prove all things, hold fast that which is good. And he might have added another remarkable saying of the same author: To the pure, all things are pure; not only meats and drinks, but all kind of knowledge whether of good or evil; the knowledge cannot defile, nor consequently the books, if the will and conscience be not defiled.

For books are as meats and viands are; some of good, some of evil substance; and yet God, in that unapocryphal vision, said without exception, Rise, Peter, kill and eat, leaving the choice to each man's discretion. Wholesome meats to a vitiated stomach differ little or nothing from unwholesome; and best books to a naughty mind are not unappliable to occasions of evil. Bad meats will scarce breed good nourishment in the healthiest concoction; but herein the difference is of bad books, that they to a discreet and judicious reader serve in many respects to discover, to confute, to forewarn, and to illustrate. Whereof what better witness can ye expect I should produce, than one of your own now sitting in Parliament, the chief of learned men reputed in this land, Mr Selden; whose volume of natural and national laws proves, not only by great authorities brought together, but by exquisite reasons and theorems almost mathematically demonstrative, that all opinions, yea errors, known, read, and collated, are of main service and assistance toward the speedy attainment of what is truest. I conceive, therefore, that when God did enlarge the universal diet of man's body, saving ever the rules of temperance, He then also, as before, left arbitrary the dieting and repasting of our minds; as wherein every mature man might have to exercise his own leading capacity.

How great a virtue is temperance, how much of moment through the whole life of man! Yet God commits the managing so great a trust, without particular law or prescription, wholly to the demeanour of every grown man. And therefore when He Himself tabled the Jews from heaven, that omer, which was every man's daily portion of manna, is computed to have been more than might have well sufficed the heartiest feeder thrice as many meals. For those actions which enter into a man, rather than issue out of him, and therefore defile not, God uses not to captivate under a perpetual childhood of prescription, but trusts him with the gift of reason to be his own chooser; there were but little work left for preaching, if law and compulsion should grow so fast upon those things which heretofore were governed only by exhortation. Solomon informs us, that much reading is a weariness to the flesh; but neither he nor other inspired author tells us that such or such reading is unlawful: yet certainly had God thought good to limit us herein, it had been much more expedient to have told us what was unlawful than what was wearisome. As for the burning of those Ephesian books by St Paul's converts; 'tis replied the books were magic, the Syriac so renders them. It was a private act, a voluntary act, and leaves us to a voluntary imitation: the men in remorse burnt those books which were their own; the magistrate by this example is not appointed; these men practised the books, another might perhaps have read them in some sort usefully.

Good and evil we know in the field of this world grow up together almost inseparably; and the knowledge of good is so involved and interwoven with the knowledge of evil, and in so many cunning resemblances hardly to be discerned, that those confused seeds which were imposed upon Psyche as an incessant labour to cull out, and sort asunder, were not more intermixed. It was from out the rind of one apple tasted, that the knowledge of good and evil, as two twins cleaving together, leaped forth into the world. And perhaps this is that doom which Adam fell into of knowing good and evil, that is to say of knowing good by evil. As therefore the state of man now is; what wisdom can there be to choose, what continence to forbear without the knowledge of evil? He that can apprehend and consider vice with all her baits and seeming pleasures, and yet abstain, and yet distinguish, and yet prefer that which is truly better, he is the true wayfaring [1] Christian.

I cannot praise a fugitive and cloistered virtue, unexercised and unbreathed, that never sallies out and sees her adversary, but slinks out of the race, where that immortal garland is to be run for, not without dust and heat. Assuredly we bring not innocence into the world, we bring impurity much rather; that which purifies us is trial, and trial is by what is contrary. That virtue therefore which is but a youngling in the contemplation of evil, and knows not the utmost that vice promises to her followers, and rejects it, is but a blank virtue, not a pure; her whiteness is but an excremental whiteness. Which was the reason why our sage and serious poet Spenser, whom I dare be known to think a better teacher than Scotus or Aquinas, describing true temperance under the person of Guion, brings him in with his palmer through the cave of Mammon, and the bower of earthly bliss, that he might see and know, and yet abstain. Since therefore the knowledge and survey of vice is in this world so necessary to the constituting of human virtue, and the scanning of error to the confirmation of truth, how can we more safely, and with less danger, scout into the regions of sin and falsity than by reading all manner of tractates and hearing all manner of reason? And this is the benefit which may be had of books promiscuously read.

But of the harm that may result hence three kinds are usually reckoned. First, is feared the infection that may spread; but then all human learning and controversy in religious points must remove out of the world, yea the Bible itself; for that ofttimes relates blasphemy not nicely, it describes the carnal sense of

---

[1] In a copy presented by Milton to Mr Thomason, and now in the British Museum, 'wayfaring' is corrected, in a hand said to be contemporary, into 'warfaring.' If Milton really wrote 'wayfaring' he must have had in his mind the words of Isaiah xxxv. 8.

wicked men not unelegantly, it brings in holiest men passion-
ately murmuring against Providence through all the arguments
of Epicurus: in other great disputes it answers dubiously and
darkly to the common reader. And ask a Talmudist what ails
the modesty of his marginal Keri, that Moses and all the prophets
cannot persuade him to pronounce the textual Chetiv. For
these causes we all know the Bible itself put by the Papist into
the first rank of prohibited books. The ancientest fathers must
be next removed, as Clement of Alexandria, and that Eusebian
book of Evangelic preparation, transmitting our ears through
a hoard of heathenish obscenities to receive the Gospel. Who
finds not that Irenaeus, Epiphanius, Jerome, and others discover
more heresies than they well confute, and that oft for heresy
which is the truer opinion?

Nor boots it to say for these, and all the heathen writers of
greatest infection, if it must be thought so, with whom is bound
up the life of human learning, that they writ in an unknown
tongue, so long as we are sure those languages are known as well
to the worst of men, who are both most able, and most diligent
to instil the poison they suck, first into the courts of princes,
acquainting them with the choicest delights and criticisms of
sin. As perhaps did that Petronius whom Nero called his Arbiter,
the master of his revels; and the notorious ribald of Arezzo,
dreaded and yet dear to the Italian courtiers. I name not him
for posterity's sake, whom Henry VIII named in merriment
his Vicar of hell. By which compendious way all the contagion
that foreign books can infuse will find a passage to the people
far easier and shorter than an Indian voyage, though it could
be sailed either by the north of Cataio eastward, or of Canada
westward, while our Spanish licensing gags the English press
never so severely.

But on the other side that infection which is from books of
controversy in religion is more doubtful and dangerous to the
learned than to the ignorant; and yet those books must be
permitted untouched by the licenser. It will be hard to instance
where any ignorant man hath been ever seduced by papistical
book in English, unless it were commended and expounded to
him by some of that clergy: and indeed all such tractates,
whether false or true, are as the prophecy of Isaiah was to the
eunuch, not to be understood without a guide. But of our
priests and doctors how many have been corrupted by studying
the comments of Jesuits and Sorbonists, and how fast they could
transfuse that corruption into the people, our experience is both

late and sad. It is not forgot, since the acute and distinct Arminius was perverted merely by the perusing of a nameless discourse written at Delft, which at first he took in hand to confute.

Seeing, therefore, that those books, and those in great abundance, which are likeliest to taint both life and doctrine, cannot be suppressed without the fall of learning and of all ability in disputation, and that these books of either sort are most and soonest catching to the learned, from whom to the common people whatever is heretical or dissolute may quickly be conveyed, and that evil manners are as perfectly learnt without books a thousand other ways which cannot be stopped, and evil doctrine not with books can propagate, except a teacher guide, which he might also do without writing, and so beyond prohibiting, I am not able to unfold, how this cautelous enterprise of licensing can be exempted from the number of vain and impossible attempts. And he who were pleasantly disposed could not well avoid to liken it to the exploit of that gallant man who thought to pound up the crows by shutting his park gate.

Besides another inconvenience, if learned men be the first receivers out of books and dispreaders both of vice and error, how shall the licensers themselves be confided in, unless we can confer upon them, or they assume to themselves above all others in the land, the grace of infallibility and uncorruptedness? And again, if it be true that a wise man, like a good refiner, can gather gold out of the drossiest volume, and that a fool will be a fool with the best book, yea or without book; there is no reason that we should deprive a wise man of any advantage to his wisdom, while we seek to restrain from a fool, that which being restrained will be no hindrance to his folly. For if there should be so much exactness always used to keep that from him which is unfit for his reading, we should in the judgment of Aristotle not only, but of Solomon and of our Saviour, not vouchsafe him good precepts, and by consequence not willingly admit him to good books; as being certain that a wise man will make better use of an idle pamphlet, than a fool will do of sacred Scripture.

'Tis next alleged we must not expose ourselves to temptations without necessity, and next to that, not employ our time in vain things. To both these objections one answer will serve, out of the grounds already laid, that to all men such books are not temptations, nor vanities, but useful drugs and materials wherewith to temper and compare effective and strong medicines,

which man's life cannot want. The rest, as children and childish men, who have not the art to qualify and prepare these working minerals, well may be exhorted to forbear, but hindered
forcibly they cannot be by all the licensing that Sainted Inquisition
could ever yet contrive. Which is what I promised to deliver
next, That this order of licensing conduces nothing to the end
for which it was framed; and hath almost prevented me by being
clear already while thus much hath been explaining. See the
ingenuity of Truth, who, when she gets a free and willing hand,
opens herself faster than the pace of method and discourse can
overtake her.

It was the task which I began with, to show that no nation,
or well-instituted state, if they valued books at all, did ever use
this way of licensing; and it might be answered, that this is a
piece of prudence lately discovered. To which I return, that as
it was a thing slight and obvious to think on, so if it had been
difficult to find out, there wanted not among them long since
who suggested such a course; which they not following, leave
us a pattern of their judgment that it was not the not knowing, but the not approving, which was the cause of their not
using it.

Plato, a man of high authority, indeed, but least of all for his
commonwealth, in the book of his Laws, which no city ever yet
received, fed his fancy by making many edicts to his airy burgo-
masters, which they who otherwise admire him wish had been
rather buried and excused in the genial cups of an Academic
night sitting. By which laws he seems to tolerate no kind of
learning but by unalterable decree, consisting most of practical
traditions, to the attainment whereof a library of smaller bulk
than his own Dialogues would be abundant. And there also
enacts, that no poet should so much as read to any private
man what he had written, until the judges and law-keepers
had seen it, and allowed it. But that Plato meant this law
peculiarly to that commonwealth which he had imagined, and
to no other, is evident. Why was he not else a lawgiver to himself, but a transgressor, and to be expelled by his own magistrates;
both for the wanton epigrams and dialogues which he made,
and his perpetual reading of Sophron Mimus and Aristophanes,
books of grossest infamy, and also for commending the latter
of them, though he were the malicious libeller of his chief friends,
to be read by the tyrant Dionysius, who had little need of such
trash to spend his time on? But that he knew this licensing of
poems had reference and dependence to many other provisos

there set down in his fancied republic, which in this world could have no place: and so neither he himself, nor any magistrate, or city ever imitated that course, which, taken apart from those other collateral injunctions, must needs be vain and fruitless. For if they fell upon one kind of strictness, unless their care were equal to regulate all other things of like aptness to corrupt the mind, that single endeavour they knew would be but a fond labour; to shut and fortify one gate against corruption, and be necessitated to leave others round about wide open.

If we think to regulate printing, thereby to rectify manners, we must regulate all recreations and pastimes, all that is delightful to man. No music must be heard, no song be set or sung, but what is grave and Doric. There must be licensing dancers, that no gesture, motion, or deportment be taught our youth but what by their allowance shall be thought honest; for such Plato was provided of; it will ask more than the work of twenty licensers to examine all the lutes, the violins, and the guitars in every house; they must not be suffered to prattle as they do, but must be licensed what they may say. And who shall silence all the airs and madrigals that whisper softness in chambers? The windows also, and the balconies must be thought on; there are shrewd books, with dangerous frontispieces, set to sale; who shall prohibit them, shall twenty licensers? The villages also must have their visitors to inquire what lectures the bagpipe and the rebeck reads, even to the ballatry and the gamut of every municipal fiddler, for these are the countryman's Arcadias, and his Monte Mayors.

Next, what more national corruption, for which England hears ill abroad, than household gluttony: who shall be the rectors of our daily rioting? And what shall be done to inhibit the multitides that frequent those houses where drunkenness is sold and harboured? Our garments also should be referred to the licensing of some more sober workmasters to see them cut into a less wanton garb. Who shall regulate all the mixed conversation of our youth, male and female together, as is the fashion of this country? Who shall still appoint what shall be discoursed, what presumed, and no further? Lastly, who shall forbid and separate all idle resort, all evil company? These things will be, and must be; but how they shall be least hurtful, how least enticing, herein consists the grave and governing wisdom of a state.

To sequester out of the world into Atlantic and Utopian

polities which never can be drawn into use, will not mend our condition; but to ordain wisely as in this world of evil, in the midst whereof God hath placed us unavoidably. Nor is it Plato's licensing of books will do this, which necessarily pulls along with it so many other kinds of licensing, as will make us all both ridiculous and weary, and yet frustrate; but those unwritten, or at least unconstraining, laws of virtuous education, religious and civil nurture, which Plato there mentions as the bonds and ligaments of the commonwealth, the pillars and the sustainers of every written statute; these they be which will bear chief sway in such matters as these, when all licensing will be easily eluded. Impunity and remissness, for certain, are the bane of a commonwealth; but here the great art lies, to discern in what the law is to bid restraint and punishment, and in what things persuasion only is to work.

If every action, which is good or evil in man at ripe years, were to be under pittance and prescription and compulsion, what were virtue but a name, what praise could be then due to well-doing, what gramercy to be sober, just, or continent? Many there be that complain of Divine Providence for suffering Adam to transgress; foolish tongues! When God gave him reason, He gave him freedom to choose, for reason is but choosing; he had been else a mere artificial Adam, such an Adam as he is in the motions. We ourselves esteem not of that obedience, or love, or gift, which is of force: God therefore left him free, set before him a provoking object, ever almost in his eyes; herein consisted his merit, herein the right of his reward, the praise of his abstinence. Wherefore did He create passions within us, pleasures round about us, but that these rightly tempered are the very ingredients of virtue?

They are not skilful considerers of human things, who imagine to remove sin by removing the matter of sin; for, besides that it is a huge heap increasing under the very act of diminishing, though some part of it may for a time be withdrawn from some persons, it cannot from all, in such a universal thing as books are; and when this is done, yet the sin remains entire. Though ye take from a covetous man all his treasure, he has yet one jewel left, ye cannot bereave him of his covetousness. Banish all objects of lust, shut up all youth into the severest discipline that can be exercised in any hermitage, ye cannot make them chaste, that came not thither so: such great care and wisdom is required to the right managing of this point. Suppose we could expel sin by this means; look how much we thus expel of sin, so much we expel of virtue: for the matter of them both is the same; remove that, and ye remove them both alike.

This justifies the high providence of God, who, though He commands us temperance, justice, continence, yet pours out before us, even to a profuseness, all desirable things, and gives us minds that can wander beyond all limit and satiety. Why should we then affect a rigour contrary to the manner of God and of nature, by abridging or scanting those means, which books freely permitted are, both to the trial of virtue and the exercise of truth? It would be better done, to learn that the law must needs be frivolous, which goes to restrain things, uncertainly and yet equally working to good and to evil. And were I the chooser, a dram of well-doing should be preferred before many times as much the forcible hindrance of evil-doing. For God sure esteems the growth and completing of one virtuous person more than the restraint of ten vicious.

And albeit whatever thing we hear or see, sitting, walking, travelling, or conversing, may be fitly called our book, and is of the same effect that writings are, yet grant the thing to be prohibited were only books, it appears that this order hitherto is far insufficient to the end which it intends. Do we not see, not once or oftener, but weekly, that continued court-libel against the Parliament and City, printed, as the wet sheets can witness, and dispersed among us, for all that licensing can do? yet this is the prime service a man would think, wherein this Order should give proof of itself. If it were executed, you'll say. But certain, if execution be remiss or blindfold now, and in this particular, what will it be hereafter and in other books? If then the Order shall not be vain and frustrate, behold a new labour, Lords and Commons, ye must repeal and proscribe all scandalous and unlicensed books already printed and divulged; after ye have drawn them up into a list, that all may know which are condemned, and which not; and ordain that no foreign books be delivered out of custody, till they have been read over. This office will require the whole time of not a few overseers, and those no vulgar men. There be also books which are partly useful and excellent, partly culpable and pernicious; this work will ask as many more officials, to make expurgations and expunctions, that the Commonwealth of Learning be not damnified. In fine, when the multitude of books increase upon their hands, ye must be fain to catalogue all those printers who are found frequently offending, and forbid the importation of their whole suspected typography. In a word, that this your

Order may be exact and not deficient, ye must reform it perfectly according to the model of Trent and Seville, which I know ye abhor to do.

Yet though ye should condescend to this, which God forbid, the Order still would be but fruitless and defective to that end whereto ye meant it. If to prevent sects and schisms, who is so unread or so uncatechized in story, that hath not heard of many sects refusing books as a hindrance, and preserving their doctrine unmixed for many ages, only by unwritten traditions? The Christian faith, for that was once a schism, is not unknown to have spread all over Asia, ere any Gospel or Epistle was seen in writing. If the amendment of manners be aimed at, look into Italy and Spain, whether those places be one scruple the better, the honester, the wiser, the chaster, since all the inquisitional rigour that hath been executed upon books.

Another reason, whereby to make it plain that this Order will miss the end it seeks, consider by the quality which ought to be in every licenser. It cannot be denied but that he who is made judge to sit upon the birth or death of books, whether they may be wafted into this world or not, had need to be a man above the common measure, both studious, learned, and judicious; there may be else no mean mistakes in the censure of what is passable or not; which is also no mean injury. If he be of such worth as behoves him, there cannot be a more tedious and unpleasing journey-work, a greater loss of time levied upon his head, than to be made the perpetual reader of unchosen books and pamphlets, ofttimes huge volumes. There is no book that is acceptable unless at certain seasons; but to be enjoined the reading of that at all times, and in a hand scarce legible, whereof three pages would not down at any time in the fairest print, is an imposition which I cannot believe how he that values time and his own studies, or is but of a sensible nostril, should be able to endure. In this one thing I crave leave of the present licensers to be pardoned for so thinking; who doubtless took this office up, looking on it through their obedience to the Parliament, whose command perhaps made all things seem easy and unlaborious to them; but that this short trial hath wearied them out already, their own expressions and excuses to them who make so many journeys to solicit their licence are testimony enough. Seeing therefore those who now possess the employment by all evident signs wish themselves well rid of it; and that no man of worth, none that is not a plain unthrift of his own hours is ever likely to succeed them, except he mean to put himself to the salary of a press corrector; we may easily foresee what kind of licensers we are to expect hereafter, either ignorant, imperious, and remiss, or basely pecuniary. This is what I had to show, wherein this Order cannot conduce to that end whereof it bears the intention.

I lastly proceed from the no good it can do, to the manifest hurt it causes, in being first the greatest discouragement and affront that can be offered to learning, and to learned men.

It was the complaint and lamentation of prelates, upon every least breath of a motion to remove pluralities, and distribute more equally Church revenues, that then all learning would be for ever dashed and discouraged. But as for that opinion, I never found cause to think that the tenth part of learning stood or fell with the clergy: nor could I ever but hold it for a sordid and unworthy speech of any churchman who had a competency left him. If therefore ye be loth to dishearten heartily and dis-content, not the mercenary crew of false pretenders to learning, but the free and ingenuous sort of such as evidently were born to study, and love learning for itself, not for lucre or any other end but the service of God and of truth, and perhaps that lasting fame and perpetuity of praise which God and good men have consented shall be the reward of those whose published labours advance the good of mankind, then know that, so far to distrust the judgment and the honesty of one who hath but a common repute in learning, and never yet offended, as not to count him fit to print his mind without a tutor and examiner, lest he should drop a schism, or something of corruption, is the greatest displeasure and indignity to a free and knowing spirit that can be put upon him.

What advantage is it to be a man over it is to be a boy at school, if we have only escaped the ferula to come under the fescue of an Imprimatur, if serious and elaborate writings, as if they were no more than the theme of a grammar-lad under his pedagogue, must not be uttered without the cursory eyes of a temporizing and extemporizing licenser? He who is not trusted with his own actions, his drift not being known to be evil, and standing to the hazard of law and penalty, has no great argu-ment to think himself reputed in the Commonwealth, wherein he was born, for other than a fool or a foreigner. When a man writes to the world, he summons up all his reason and delibera-tion to assist him; he searches, meditates, is industrious, and likely consults and confers with his judicious friends; after all which done he takes himself to be informed in what he writes, as well as any that writ before him. If, in this the most consummate act of his fidelity and ripeness, no years, no industry, no former proof of his abilities can bring him to that state of maturity, as not to be still mistrusted and suspected, unless he carry all his considerate diligence, all his midnight watchings and expense of Palladian oil, to the hasty view of an unleisured licenser, perhaps much his younger, perhaps far his inferior in judgment, perhaps one who never knew the labour of book-writing, and if he be not repulsed or slighted, must appear in print like a puny with his guardian, and his censor's hand on the back of his title to be his bail and surety that he is no idiot or seducer, it cannot be but a dishonour and derogation to the author, to the book, to the privilege and dignity of Learning.

And what if the author shall be one so copious of fancy, as to have many things well worth the adding come into his mind after licensing, while the book is yet under the press, which not seldom happens to the best and diligentest writers; and that perhaps a dozen times in one book? The printer dares not go beyond his licensed copy; so often then must the author trudge to his leave-giver, that those his new insertions may be viewed; and many a jaunt will be made, ere that licenser, for it must be the same man, can either be found, or found at leisure; meanwhile either the press must stand still, which is no small damage, or the author lose his accuratest thoughts, and send the book forth worse than he had made it, which to a diligent writer is the greatest melancholy and vexation that can befall.

And how can a man teach with authority, which is the life of teaching, how can he be a doctor in his book as he ought to be, or else had better be silent, whenas all he teaches, all he delivers, is but under the tuition, under the correction of his patriarchal licenser to blot or alter what precisely accords not with the hidebound humour which he calls his judgment? When every acute reader, upon the first sight of a pedantic licence, will be ready with these like words to ding the book a quoit's distance from him: I hate a pupil teacher, I endure not an instructor that comes to me under the wardship of an overseeing fist. I know nothing of the licenser, but that I have his own hand here for his arrogance; who shall warrant me his judgment? The State, sir, replies the stationer, but has a quick return: The State shall be my governors, but not my critics; they may be mistaken in the choice of a licenser, as easily as this licenser may be mistaken in an author; this is some common stuff; and he might add from Sir Francis Bacon, That such

authorized books are but the language of the times.   For though
a licenser should happen to be judicious more than ordinary,
which will be a great jeopardy of the next succession, yet his
very office and his commission enjoins him to let pass nothing
but what is vulgarly received already.

Nay, which is more lamentable, if the work of any deceased
author, though never so famous in his lifetime and even to this
day, come to their hands for licence to be printed, or reprinted,
if there be found in his book one sentence of a venturous edge,
uttered in the height of zeal and who knows whether it might
not be the dictate of a divine spirit, yet not suiting with every
low decrepit humour of their own, though it were Knox himself,
the Reformer of a Kingdom, that spake it, they will not pardon
him their dash: the sense of that great man shall to all posterity
be lost, for the fearfulness or the presumptuous rashness of a
perfunctory licenser.   And to what an author this violence hath
been lately done, and in what book of greatest consequence to
be faithfully published, I could now instance, but shall forbear
till a more convenient season.

Yet if these things be not resented seriously and timely by
them who have the remedy in their power, but that such iron-
moulds as these shall have authority to gnaw out the choicest
periods of exquisitest books, and to commit such a treacherous
fraud against the orphan remainders of worthiest men after
death, the more sorrow will belong to that hapless race of men,
whose misfortune it is to have understanding.   Henceforth let
no man care to learn, or care to be more than worldly-wise; for
certainly in higher matters to be ignorant and slothful, to be a
common steadfast dunce, will be the only pleasant life, and only
in request.

And as it is a particular disesteem of every knowing person
alive, and most injurious to the written labours and monuments
of the dead, so to me it seems an undervaluing and vilifying of
the whole Nation.   I cannot set so light by all the invention, the
art, the wit, the grave and solid judgment which is in England,
as that it can be comprehended in any twenty capacities how
good soever, much less that it should not pass except their
superintendence be over it, except it be sifted and strained with
their strainers, that it should be uncurrent without their manual
stamp.   Truth and understanding are not such wares as to be
monopolized and traded in by tickets and statutes and standards.
We must not think to make a staple commodity of all the knowledge in the land, to mark and licence it like our broadcloth

and our woolpacks. What is it but a servitude like that imposed by the Philistines, not to be allowed the sharpening of our own axes and coulters, but we must repair from all quarters to twenty licensing forges? Had anyone written and divulged erroneous things and scandalous to honest life, misusing and forfeiting the esteem had of his reason among men, if after conviction this only censure were adjudged him that he should never henceforth write but what were first examined by an appointed officer, whose hand should be annexed to pass his credit for him that now he might be safely read; it could not be apprehended less than a disgraceful punishment. Whence to include the whole Nation, and those that never yet thus offended, under such a diffident and suspectful prohibition, may plainly be understood what a disparagement it is. So much the more, whenas debtors and delinquents may walk abroad without a keeper, but unoffensive books must not stir forth without a visible jailer in their title.

Nor is it to the common people less than a reproach; for if we be so jealous over them, as that we dare not trust them with an English pamphlet, what do we but censure them for a giddy, vicious, and ungrounded people; in such a sick and weak state of faith and discretion, as to be able to take nothing down but through the pipe of a licenser? That this is care or love of them, we cannot pretend, whenas, in those popish places where the laity are most hated and despised, the same strictness is used over them. Wisdom we cannot call it, because it stops but one breach of licence, nor that neither: whenas those corruptions, which it seeks to prevent, break in faster at other doors which cannot be shut.

And in conclusion it reflects to the disrepute of our Ministers also, of whose labours we should hope better, and of the proficiency which their flock reaps by them, than that after all this light of the Gospel which is, and is to be, and all this continual preaching, they should still be frequented with such an unprincipled, unedified and laic rabble, as that the whiff of every new pamphlet should stagger them out of their catechism, and Christian walking. This may have much reason to discourage the Ministers when such a low conceit is had of all their exhortations, and the benefiting of their hearers, as that they are not thought fit to be turned loose to three sheets of paper without a licenser; that all the sermons, all the lectures preached, printed, vented in such numbers, and such volumes, as have now well nigh made all other books unsaleable, should not be armour enough against one single Enchiridion, without the castle of St Angelo of an Imprimatur.

And lest some should persuade ye, Lords and Commons, that these arguments of learned men's discouragement at this your Order are mere flourishes, and not real, I could recount what I have seen and heard in other countries, where this kind of inquisition tyrannizes; when I have sat among their learned men, for that honour I had, and been counted happy to be born in such a place of philosophic freedom, as they supposed England was, while themselves did nothing but bemoan the servile condition into which learning amongst them was brought; that this was it which had damped the glory of Italian wits; that nothing had been there written now these many years but flattery and fustian. There it was that I found and visited the famous Galileo, grown old a prisoner to the Inquisition, for thinking in astronomy otherwise than the Franciscan and Dominican licensers thought.

And though I knew that England then was groaning loudest under the prelatical yoke, nevertheless I took it as a pledge of future happiness, that other nations were so persuaded of her liberty. Yet was it beyond my hope that those Worthies were then breathing in her air, who should be her leaders to such a deliverance, as shall never be forgotten by any revolution of time that this world hath to finish. When that was once begun, it was as little in my fear that, what words of complaint I heard among learned men of other parts uttered against the Inquisition, the same I should hear by as learned men at home uttered in time of Parliament against an order of licensing; and that so generally that, when I had disclosed myself a companion of their discontent, I might say, if without envy, that he whom an honest quaestorship had endeared to the Sicilians was not more by them importuned against Verres, than the favourable opinion which I had among many who honour ye, and are known and respected by ye, loaded me with entreaties and persuasions, that I would not despair to lay together that which just reason should bring into my mind, toward the removal of an undeserved thraldom upon learning. That this is not therefore the disburdening of a particular fancy, but the common grievance of all those who had prepared their minds and studies above the vulgar pitch to advance truth in others, and from others to entertain it, thus much may satisfy.

And in their name I shall for neither friend nor foe conceal what the general murmur is; that if it come to inquisitioning again and licensing, and that we are so timorous of ourselves, and so suspicious of all men, as to fear each book and the shaking of every leaf, before we know what the contents are; if some who but of late were little better than silenced from preaching shall come now to silence us from reading, except what they please, it cannot be guessed what is intended by some but a second tyranny over learning: and will soon put it out of controversy, that Bishops and Presbyters are the same to us, both name and thing. That those evils of Prelaty, which before from five to six and twenty sees were distributively charged upon the whole people, will now light wholly upon learning, is not obscure to us: whenas now the Pastor of a small unlearned Parish on the sudden shall be exalted Archbishop over a large diocese of books, and yet not remove, but keep his other cure too, a mystical pluralist. He who but of late cried down the sole ordination of every novice Bachelor of Art, and denied sole jurisdiction over the simplest parishioner, shall now at home in his private chair assume both these over worthiest and excellentest books and ablest authors that write them.

This is not, ye Covenants and Protestations that we have made! this is not to put down Prelaty; this is but to chop an Episcopacy; this is but to translate the Palace Metropolitan from one kind of dominion into another; this is but an old canonical sleight of commuting our penance. To startle thus betimes at a mere unlicensed pamphlet will after a while be afraid of every conventicle, and a while after will make a conventicle of every Christian meeting. But I am certain that a State governed by the rules of justice and fortitude, or a Church built and founded upon the rock of faith and true knowledge, cannot be so pusillanimous. While things are yet not constituted in Religion, that freedom of writing should be restrained by a discipline imitated from the Prelates and learnt by them from the Inquisition, to shut us all up again into the breast of a licenser, must needs give cause of doubt and discouragement to all learned and religious men.

Who cannot but discern the fineness of this politic drift, and who are the contrivers; that while Bishops were to be baited down, then all Presses might be open; it was the people's birthright and privilege in time of Parliament, it was the breaking forth of light? But now, the Bishops abrogated and voided out the Church, as if our Reformation sought no more but to make room for others into their seats under another name, the episcopal arts begin to bud again, the cruse of truth must run no more oil, liberty of Printing must be enthralled again under a prelatical commission of twenty, the privilege of the people nullified, and, which is worse, the freedom of learning must groan again, and to her old fetters: all this the Parliament yet sitting. Although their own late arguments and defences against the Prelates might remember them, that this obstructing violence meets for the most part with an event utterly opposite to the end which it drives at: instead of suppressing sects and schisms, it raises them and invests them with a reputation. 'The punishing of wits enhances their authority,' said the Viscount St Albans; 'and a forbidden writing is thought to be a certain spark of truth that flies up in the faces of them who seek to tread it out.' This Order, therefore, may prove a nursing-mother to sects, but I shall show how it will be a step-dame to Truth: and first by dis-enabling us to the maintenance of what is known already.

Well knows he who uses to consider, that our faith and know-ledge thrives by exercise, as well as our limbs and complexion. Truth is compared in Scripture to a streaming fountain; if her waters flow not in a perpetual progression, they sicken into a muddy pool of conformity and tradition. A man may be a heretic in the truth; and if he believe things only because his Pastor says so, or the Assembly so determines, without knowing other reason, though his belief be true, yet the very truth he holds becomes his heresy.

There is not any burden that some would gladier post off to another than the charge and care of their Religion. There be—who knows not that there be?—of Protestants and pro-fessors who live and die in as arrant an implicit faith as any lay Papist of Loretto. A wealthy man, addicted to his pleasure and to his profits, finds Religion to be a traffic so entangled, and of so many piddling accounts, that of all mysteries he cannot skill to keep a stock going upon that trade. What should he do? fain he would have the name to be religious, fain he would bear up with his neighbours in that. What does he therefore, but resolve to give over toiling, and to find himself out some factor, to whose care and credit he may commit the whole managing of his religious affairs? some Divine of note and estimation that must be. To him he adheres, resigns the whole warehouse of his religion, with all the locks and keys, into his custody; and indeed makes the very person of that man his religion; esteems his associating with him a sufficient evidence and commendatory of his own piety. So that a man may say his religion is now no more within himself, but is become a dividual movable, and goes and comes near him, according as that good man frequents the house. He entertains him, gives him gifts, feasts him, lodges him; his religion comes home at night, prays, is liberally supped, and sumptuously laid to sleep, rises, is saluted, and after the malmsey, or some well-spiced brewage, and better breakfasted than he whose morning appetite would have gladly fed on green figs between Bethany and Jerusalem, his Religion walks abroad at eight, and leaves his kind entertainer in the shop trading all day without his Religion.

Another sort there be who, when they hear that all things shall be ordered, all things regulated and settled, nothing written but what passes through the custom-house of certain Publicans that have the tonnaging and poundaging of all free-spoken truth, will straight give themselves up into your hands, make 'em and cut 'em out what religion ye please: there be delights, there be recreations and jolly pastimes that will fetch the day about from sun to sun, and rock the tedious year as in a delightful dream. What need they torture their heads with that which others have taken so strictly and so unalterably into their own purveying? These are the fruits which a dull ease and cessation of our knowledge will bring forth among the people. How goodly and how to be wished were such an obedient unanimity as this, what a fine conformity would it starch us all into! Doubtless a staunch and solid piece of framework, as any January could freeze together.

Nor much better will be the consequence even among the clergy themselves. It is no new thing never heard of before, for a parochial Minister, who has his reward and is at his Hercules' pillars in a warm benefice, to be easily inclinable, if he have nothing else that may rouse up his studies, to finish his circuit in an English Concordance and a topic folio, the gatherings and savings of a sober graduateship, a Harmony and a Catena; treading the constant round of certain common doctrinal heads, attended with the uses, motives, marks, and means, out of which, as out of an alphabet, or sol-fa, by forming and transforming, joining and disjoining variously, a little bookcraft, and two hours' meditation, might furnish him unspeakably to the performance of more than a weekly charge of sermoning: not to reckon up the infinite helps of interlinearies, breviaries, synopses, and other loitering gear. But as for the multitude of sermons ready printed and piled up, on every text that is not difficult, our London trading St Thomas in his vestry, and add to boot St Martin and St Hugh, have not within their hallowed limits more vendible ware of all sorts ready made: so that penury he never need fear of pulpit provision, having where so plenteously to refresh his magazine. But if his rear and flanks be not impaled, if his back door be not secured by the rigid licenser, but that a bold book may now and then issue forth and give the assault to some of his old collections in their trenches, it will concern him then to keep waking, to stand in watch, to set good guards and sentinels about his received opinions, to walk the round and counter-round with his fellow inspectors, fearing lest any of his flock be seduced, who also then would be better instructed, better exercised and disciplined.   And God send that the fear of this diligence, which must then be used, do not make us affect the laziness of a licensing Church.

For if we be sure we are in the right, and do not hold the truth guiltily, which becomes not, if we ourselves condemn not our own weak and frivolous teaching, and the people for an untaught and irreligious gadding rout, what can be more fair than when a man judicious, learned, and of a conscience, for aught we know, as good as theirs that taught us what we know, shall not privily from house to house, which is more dangerous, but openly by writing publish to the world what his opinion is, what his reasons, and wherefore that which is now thought cannot be sound?   Christ urged it as wherewith to justify himself, that he preached in public; yet writing is more public than preaching; and more easy to refutation, if need be, there being so many whose business and profession merely it is to be the champions of Truth; which if they neglect, what can be imputed but their sloth, or unability?

Thus much we are hindered and disinured by this course of licensing, toward the true knowledge of what we seem to know. For how much it hurts and hinders the licensers themselves in the calling of their ministry, more than any secular employment, if they will discharge that office as they ought, so that of necessity they must neglect either the one duty or the other, I insist not, because it is a particular, but leave it to their own conscience, how they will decide it there.

There is yet behind of what I proposed to lay open, the incredible loss and detriment that this plot of incensing puts us to; more than if some enemy at sea should stop up all our havens and ports and creeks, it hinders and retards the importation of our richest Merchandise, Truth; nay, it was first established and put in practise by Antichristian malice and mystery on set purpose to extinguish, if it were possible, the light of Reformation, and to settle falsehood; little differing from that policy wherewith the Turk upholds his Alcoran, by the pro-hibiting of Printing. 'Tis not denied, but gladly confessed, we are to send our thanks and vows to Heaven louder than most of nations, for that great measure of truth which we enjoy, especially in those main points between us and the Pope, with his appurtenances the Prelates: but he who thinks we are to pitch our tent here, and have attained the utmost prospect of reformation that the mortal glass wherein we contemplate can show us, till we come to beatific vision, that man by this very opinion declares that he is yet far short of Truth.

Trust indeed came once into the world with her Divine Master, and was a perfect shape most glorious to look on: but when He ascended, and His Apostles after Him were laid asleep, then straight arose a wicked race of deceivers, who, as that story goes of the Egyptian Typhoon with his conspirators, how they dealt with the good Osiris, took the virgin Truth, hewed her lovely form into a thousand pieces, and scattered them to the four winds. From that time ever since, the sad friends of Truth, such as durst appear, imitating the careful search that Isis made for the mangled body of Osiris, went up and down gathering up limb by limb, still as they could find them. We have not yet found them all, Lords and Commons, nor ever shall do, till her Master's second coming; He shall bring together every joint and member, and shall mould them into an immortal feature of loveli-ness and perfection. Suffer not these licensing prohibitions to stand at every place of opportunity, forbidding and disturbing them that continue seeking, that continue to do our obsequies to the torn body of our martyred saint.

We boast our light; but if we look not wisely on the Sun itself, it smites us into darkness. Who can discern those planets that are oft combust, and those stars of brightest magnitude that rise and set with the Sun, until the opposite motion of their orbs bring them to such a place in the firmament, where they may be seen evening or morning? The light which we have gained was given us, not to be ever staring on, but by it to discover onward things more remote from our knowledge. It is not the unfrocking of a priest, the unmitring of a bishop, and the re-moving him from off the presbyterian shoulders, that will make us a happy Nation. No, if other things as great in the Church, and in the rule of life both economical and political, be not looked into and reformed, we have looked so long upon the blaze that Zuinglius and Calvin hath beaconed up to us, that we are stark blind. There be who perpetually complain of schisms and sects, and make it such a calamity that any man dissents from their maxims. 'Tis their own pride and ignorance which causes the disturbing, who neither will hear with meekness, nor can convince; yet all must be suppressed which is not found in their Syntagma. They are the troublers, they are the dividers of unity, who neglect and permit not others to unite those disseuered pieces which are yet wanting to the body of Truth. To be still searching what we know not by what we know, still closing up truth to truth as we find it (for all her body is homogeneal and proportional), this is the golden rule in theology as well as in arithmetic, and makes up the best harmony in a Church; not the forced and outward union of cold and neutral, and inwardly divided minds.

Lords and Commons of England, consider what Nation it is whereof ye are, and whereof ye are the governors: a Nation not slow and dull, but of a quick, ingenious and piercing spirit, acute to invent, subtle and sinewy to discourse, not beneath the reach of any point, the highest that human capacity can soar to. Therefore the studies of Learning in her deepest sciences have been so ancient and so eminent among us, that writers of good antiquity and ablest judgment have been persuaded that even the school of Pythagoras and the Persian wisdom took beginning from the old philosophy of this island. And that wise and civil Roman, Julius Agricola, who governed once here for Caesar, preferred the natural wits of Britain before the laboured studies of the French. Nor is it for nothing that the grave and frugal Transylvanian sends out yearly from as far as the mountainous borders of Russia, and beyond the Hercynian wilderness, not their youth, but their staid men, to learn our language and our theologic arts.

Yet that which is above all this, the favour and the love of Heaven, we have great argument to think in a peculiar manner propitious and propending towards us. Why else was this Nation chosen before any other, that out of her, as out of Sion, should be proclaimed and sounded forth the first tidings and trumpet of Reformation to all Europe? And had it not been the obstinate perverseness of our prelates against the divine and admirable spirit of Wickliff, to suppress him as a schismatic and innovator, perhaps neither the Bohemian Huss and Jerome, no nor the name of Luther or of Calvin, had been ever known: the glory of reforming all our neighbours had been completely ours. But now, as our obdurate clergy have with violence demeaned the matter, we are become hitherto the latest and backwardest scholars, of whom God offered to have made us the teachers. Now once again by all concurrence of signs, and by the general instinct of holy and devout men, as they daily and solemnly express their thoughts, God is decreeing to begin some new and great period in His Church, even to the reforming of Reformation itself: what does He then but reveal Himself to His servants, and as His manner is, first to His Englishmen? I say, as His manner is, first to us, though we mark not the method of His counsels, and are unworthy.

Behold now this vast City: a city of refuge, the mansion house of liberty, encompassed and surrounded with His protection; the shop of war hath not there more anvils and hammers waking, to fashion out the plates and instruments of armed Justice in defence of beleaguered Truth, than there be pens and heads there, sitting by their studious lamps, musing, searching, revolving new notions and ideas wherewith to present, as with their homage and their fealty, the approaching Reformation: others as fast reading, trying all things, assenting to the force of reason and convincement. What could a man require more from a Nation so pliant and so prone to seek after knowledge? What wants there to such a towardly and pregnant soil, but wise and faithful labourers, to make a knowing people, a Nation of Prophets, of Sages, and of Worthies? We reckon more than five months yet to harvest; there need not be five weeks; had we but eyes to lift up, the fields are white already.

Where there is much desire to learn, there of necessity will be much arguing, much writing, many opinions; for opinion in good men is but knowledge in the making. Under these fantastic terrors of sect and schism, we wrong the earnest and zealous thirst after knowledge and understanding which God hath stirred up in this city. What some lament of, we rather should rejoice at, should rather praise this pious forwardness among men, to reassume the ill-reputed care of their Religion into their own hands again. A little generous prudence, a little forbearance of one another, and some grain of charity might win all these diligences to join, and unite in one general and brotherly search after Truth; could we but forgo this prelatical tradition of crowding free consciences and Christian liberties into canons and precepts of men. I doubt not, if some great and worthy stranger should come among us, wise to discern the mould and temper of a people, and how to govern it, observing the high hopes and aims, the diligent alacrity of our extended thoughts and reasonings in the pursuance of truth and freedom, but that he would cry out as Pyrrhus did, admiring the Roman docility and courage: If such were my Epirots, I would not despair the greatest design that could be attempted, to make a Church or Kingdom happy.

Yet these are the men cried out against for schismatics and sectaries; as if, while the temple of the Lord was building, some cutting, some squaring the marble, others hewing the cedars, there should be a sort of irrational men who could not consider there must be many schisms and many dissections made in the quarry and in the timber, ere the house of God can be built. And when every stone is laid artfully together, it cannot be united into a continuity, it can but be contiguous in this world; neither can every piece of the building be of one form; nay rather the perfection consists in this, that, out of many moderate varieties and brotherly dissimilitudes that are not vastly disproportional, arises the goodly and the graceful symmetry that commends the whole pile and structure.

Let us therefore be more considerate builders, more wise in spiritual architecture, when great reformation is expected. For now the time seems come, wherein Moses the great prophet may sit in heaven rejoicing to see that memorable and glorious wish of his fulfilled, when not only our seventy Elders, but all the Lord's people, are become prophets. No marvel then though some men, and some good men too perhaps, but young in goodness, as Joshua then was, envy them. They fret, and out of their own weakness are in agony, lest these divisions and subdivisions will undo us. The adversary again applauds, and waits the hour: When they have branched themselves out, saith he, small enough into parties and partitions, then will be our time. Fool! he sees not the firm root, out of which we all grow, though into branches: nor will be ware until he see our small divided maniples cutting through at every angle of his ill-united and unwieldy brigade. And that we are to hope better of all these supposed sects and schisms, and that we shall not need that solicitude, honest perhaps though over-timorous of them that vex in this behalf, but shall laugh in the end at those malicious applauders of our differences, I have these reasons to persuade me.

First, when a City shall be as it were besieged and blocked about, her navigable river infested, inroads and incursions round, defiance and battle oft rumoured to be marching up even to her walls and suburb trenches, that then the people, or the greater part, more than at other times, wholly taken up with the study of highest and most important matters to be reformed, should be disputing, reasoning, reading, inventing, discoursing, even to a rarity and admiration, things not before discoursed or written of, argues first a singular goodwill, contentedness and confidence in your prudent foresight and safe government, Lords and Commons; and from thence derives itself to a gallant bravery and well-grounded contempt of their enemies, as if there were no small number of as great spirits among us, as his was, who when Rome was nigh besieged by Hannibal, being in the city, bought that piece of ground at no cheap rate, whereon Hannibal himself encamped his own regiment.

Next, it is a lively and cheerful presage of our happy success and victory. For as in a body, when the blood is fresh, the spirits pure and vigorous, not only to vital but to rational faculties, and those in the acutest and the pertest operations of wit and subtlety, it argues in what good plight and constitution the body is so when the cheerfulness of the people is so sprightly up, as that it has not only wherewith to guard well its own free-dom and safety, but to spare, and to bestow upon the solidest and sublimest points of controversy and new invention, it be-tokens us not degenerated, nor drooping to a fatal decay, but casting off the old and wrinkled skin of corruption to outlive these pangs and wax young again, entering the glorious ways of truth and prosperous virtue, destined to become great and honourable in these latter ages. Methinks I see in my mind a noble and puissant nation rousing herself like a strong man after sleep, and shaking her invincible locks. Methinks I see her as an eagle mewing her mighty youth, and kindling her un-dazzled eyes at the full midday beam; purging and unscaling her long-abused sight at the fountain itself of heavenly radiance; while the whole noise of timorous and flocking birds, with those also that love the twilight, flutter about, amazed at what she means, and in their envious gabble would prognosticate a year of sects and schisms.

What would ye do then? should ye suppress all this flowery crop of knowledge and new light sprung up and yet springing daily in this city? should ye set an oligarchy of twenty engrossers over it, to bring a famine upon our minds again, when we shall know nothing but what is measured to us by their bushel? Believe it, Lords and Commons, they who counsel ye to such a suppressing do as good as bid ye suppress yourselves; and I will soon show how. If it be desired to know the immediate cause of all this free writing and free speaking, there cannot be assigned a truer than your own mild and free and humane government.   It is the liberty, Lords and Commons, which your own valorous and happy counsels have purchased us, liberty which is the nurse of all great wits; this is that which hath rarefied and enlightened our spirits like the influence of heaven; this is that which hath enfranchised, enlarged and lifted up our apprehensions degrees above themselves.

Ye cannot make us now less capable, less knowing, less eagerly pursuing of the truth, unless ye first make yourselves, that made us so, less the lovers, less the founders of our true liberty.   We can grow ignorant again, brutish, formal and slavish, as ye found us; but you then must first become that which ye cannot be, oppressive, arbitrary and tyrannous, as they were from whom ye have freed us.   That our hearts are now more capacious, our thoughts more erected to the search and expectation of greatest and exactest things, is the issue of your own virtue propagated in us; ye cannot suppress that, unless ye reinforce an abrogated and merciless law, that fathers may dispatch at will their own children.   And who shall then stick closest to ye, and excite others? not he who takes up arms for coat and conduct, and his four nobles of Danegelt.   Although I dispraise not the defence of just immunities, yet love my peace better, if that were all.   Give me the liberty to know, to utter, and to argue freely according to conscience, above all liberties.

What would be best advised, then, if it be found hurtful and so unequal to suppress opinions for the newness or the unsuitableness to a customary acceptance, will not be my task to say.   I only shall repeat what I have learned from one of your own honourable number, a right noble and pious lord, who, had he not sacrificed his life and fortunes to the Church and Commonwealth, we had not now missed and bewailed a worthy and undoubted patron of this argument.   Ye know him, I am sure; yet I for honour's sake, and may it be eternal to him, shall name him, the Lord Brook.   He writing of Episcopacy and by the way treating of sects and schisms, left ye his vote, or rather now the last words of his dying charge, which I know will ever be of dear and honoured regard with ye, so full of meekness and breathing charity, that next to His last testament, who bequeathed love and peace to His disciples, I cannot call to mind where I have read or heard words more mild and peaceful.   He there exhorts us to hear with patience and humility those, however they be miscalled, that desire to live purely, in such a use of God's ordinances, as the best guidance of their conscience gives them, and to tolerate them, though in some disconformity to ourselves.

The book itself will tell us more at large, being published to the world, and dedicated to the Parliament by him who, both for his life and for his death, deserves that what advice he left be not laid by without perusal.

And now the time in special is, by privilege to write and speak what may help to the further discussing of matters in agitation. The temple of Janus with his two controversial faces might now not unsignificantly be set open. And though all the winds of doctrine were let loose to play upon the earth, so Truth be in the field, we do injuriously, by licensing and prohibiting, to misdoubt her strength. Let her and Falsehood grapple; who ever knew Truth put to the worse, in a free and open encounter? Her confuting is the best and surest suppressing. He who hears what praying there is for light and clearer knowledge to be sent down among us, would think of other matters to be constituted beyond the discipline of Geneva, framed and fabricked already to our hands. Yet when the new light which we beg for shines in upon us, there be who envy and oppose, if it come not first in at their casements. What a collusion is this, whenas we are exhorted by the wise man to use diligence, to seek for wisdom as for hidden treasures early and late, that another order shall enjoin us to know nothing but by statute? When a man hath been labouring the hardest labour in the deep mines of knowledge; hath furnished out his findings in all their equipage; drawn forth his reasons as it were a battle ranged; scattered and defeated all objections in his way; calls out his adversary into the plain, offers him the advantage of wind and sun, if he please, only that he may try the matter by dint of argument: for his opponents then to skulk, to lay ambushments, to keep a narrow bridge of licensing where the challenger should pass, though it be valour enough in soldiership, is but weakness and cowardice in the wars of Truth.

For who knows not that Truth is strong, next to the Almighty? She needs no policies, nor stratagems, nor licensings to make her victorious; those are the shifts and the defences that error uses against her power. Give her but room, and do not bind her when she sleeps, for then she speaks not true, as the old Proteus did, who spake oracles only when he was caught and bound, but then rather she turns herself into all shapes, except her own, and perhaps tunes her voice according to the time, as Micaiah did before Ahab, until she be adjured into her own likeness. Yet is it not impossible that she may have more shapes than one. What else is all that rank of things indifferent, wherein Truth may be on this side or on the other, without being unlike herself? What but a vain shadow else is the abolition of those ordinances, that handwriting nailed to the cross? What great purchase is this Christian liberty which Paul so often boasts of? His doctrine is, that he who eats or eats not, regards a day or regards it not, may do either to the Lord. How many other things might be tolerated in peace, and left to conscience, had we but charity, and were it not the chief stronghold of our hypocrisy to be ever judging one another?

I fear yet this iron yoke of outward conformity hath left a slavish print upon our necks; the ghost of a linen decency yet haunts us. We stumble and are impatient at the least dividing of one visible congregation from another, though it be not in fundamentals; and through our forwardness to suppress, and our backwardness to recover any enthralled piece of truth out of the gripe of custom, we care not to keep truth separated from truth, which is the fiercest rent and disunion of all. We do not see that, while we still affect by all means a rigid external formality, we may as soon fall again into a gross conforming stupidity, a stark and dead congealment of wood and hay and stubble, forced and frozen together, which is more to the sudden degenerating of a Church than many subdichotomies of petty schisms.

Not that I can think well of every light separation, or that all in a Church is to be expected gold and silver and precious stones: it is not possible for man to sever the wheat from the tares, the good fish from the other fry; that must be the Angels' Ministry at the end of mortal things. Yet if all cannot be of one mind—as who looks they should be?—this doubtless is more wholesome, more prudent, and more Christian that many be tolerated, rather than all compelled. I mean not tolerated popery, and open superstition, which, as it extirpates all religions and civil supremacies, so itself should be extirpate, provided first that all charitable and compassionate means be used to win and regain the weak and the misled: that also which is impious or evil absolutely either against faith or manners no law can possibly permit, that intends not to unlaw itself: but those neighbouring differences, or rather indifferences, are what I speak of, whether in some point of doctrine or of discipline, which, though they may be many, yet need not interrupt the unity of Spirit, if we could but find among us the bond of peace.

In the meantime if any one would write, and bring his helpful hand to the slow-moving Reformation which we labour under, if Truth have spoken to him before others, or but seemed at

least to speak, who hath so bejesuited us that we should trouble
that man with asking licence to do so worthy a deed? and not
consider this, that if it come to prohibiting, there is not aught
more likely to be prohibited than truth itself; whose first appearance to our eyes, bleared and dimmed with prejudice and custom,
is more unsightly and unplausible than many errors, even as the
person is of many a great man slight and contemptible to see to.
And what do they tell us vainly of new opinions, when this very
opinion of theirs, that none must be heard, but whom they like,
is the worst and newest opinion of all others; and is the chief
cause why sects and schisms do so much abound, and true knowledge is kept at distance from us; besides yet a greater danger
which is in it?

For when God shakes a Kingdom with strong and healthful
commotions to a general reforming, 'tis not untrue that many
sectaries and false teachers are then busiest in seducing; but
yet more true it is, that God then raises to His own work men
of rare abilities, and more than common industry, not only
to look back and revise what hath been taught heretofore, but
to gain further and go on some new enlightened steps in the
discovery of truth. For such is the order of God's enlightening
His Church, to dispense and deal out by degrees His beam, so
as our earthly eyes may best sustain it.

Neither is God appointed and confined, where and out of what
place these His chosen shall be first heard to speak; for He
sees not as man sees, chooses not as man chooses, lest we should
devote ourselves again to set places, and assemblies, and outward callings of men; planting our faith one while in the old
Convocation house, and another while in the Chapel at West-
minister; when all the faith and religion that shall be there
canonized is not sufficient without plain convincement, and
the charity of patient instruction to supple the least bruise of
conscience, to edify the meanest Christian, who desires to walk
in the Spirit, and not in the letter of human trust, for all the
number of voices that can be there made; no, though Harry
VII himself there, with all his liege tombs about him, should
lend them voices from the dead, to swell their number.

And if the men be erroneous who appear to be the leading
schismatics, what withholds us but our sloth, our self-will,
and distrust in the right cause, that we do not give them gentle
meeting and gentle dismissions, that we debate not and examine
the matter thoroughly with liberal and frequent audience; if
not for their sakes, yet for our own? seeing no man who hath

tasted learning, but will confess the many ways of profiting by those who, not contented with stale receipts, are able to manage and set forth new positions to the world. And were they but as the dust and cinders of our feet, so long as in that notion they may yet serve to polish and brighten the armoury of Truth, even for that respect they were not utterly to be cast away. But if they be of those whom God hath fitted for the special use of these times with eminent and ample gifts, and those perhaps neither among the Priests nor among the Pharisees, and we in the haste of a precipitant zeal shall make no distinction, but resolve to stop their mouths, because we fear they come with new and dangerous opinions, as we commonly forejudge them ere we understand them, no less than woe to us, while, thinking thus to defend the Gospel, we are found the persecutors.

There have been not a few since the beginning of this Parliament, both of the Presbytery and others, who by their unlicensed books, to the contempt of an Imprimatur, first broke that triple ice clung about our hearts, and taught the people to see day: I hope that none of those were the persuaders to renew upon us this bondage which they themselves have wrought so much good by contemning. But if neither the check that Moses gave to young Joshua, nor the countermand which our Saviour gave to young John, who was so ready to prohibit those whom he thought unlicensed, be not enough to admonish our Elders how unacceptable to God their testy mood of prohibiting is, if neither their own remembrance what evil hath abounded in the Church by this let of licensing, and what good they themselves have begun by transgressing it, be not enough, but that they will persuade and execute the most Dominican part of the Inquisition over us, and are already with one foot in the stirrup so active at suppressing, it would be no unequal distribution in the first place to suppress the suppressors themselves: whom the change of their condition hath puffed up, more than their late experience of harder times hath made wise.

And as for regulating the Press, let no man think to have the honour of advising ye better than yourselves have done in that Order published next before this, 'that no book be Printed, unless the Printer's and the Author's name, or at least the Printer's, be registered.' Those which otherwise come forth, if they be found mischievous and libellous, the fire and the executioner, will be the timeliest and the most effectual remedy that man's prevention can use. For this authentic Spanish policy of licensing books, if I have said aught, will prove the most unlicensed book itself within a short while; and was the immediate image of a Star Chamber decree to that purpose made in those very times when that Court did the rest of those her pious works, for which she is now fallen from the stars with Lucifer. Whereby ye may guess what kind of state prudence, what love of the people, what care of Religion or good manners there was at the contriving, although with singular hypocrisy it pretended to bind books to their good behaviour. And how it got the upper hand of your precedent Order so well constituted before, if we may believe those men whose profession gives them cause to inquire most, it may be doubted there was in it the fraud of some old patentees and monopolizers in the trade of bookselling; who under pretence of the poor in their Company not to be defrauded, and the just retaining of each man his several copy, which God forbid should be gainsaid, brought divers glosing colours to the House, which were indeed but colours, and serving to no end except it to be exercise a superiority over their neighbours; men who do not therefore labour in an honest profession to which learning is indebted, that they should be made other men's vassals. Another end is thought was aimed at by some of them in procuring by petition this Order, that, having power in their hands, malignant books might the easier scape abroad, as the event shows.

But of these sophisms and elenchs of merchandise I skill not. This I know, that errors in a good government and in a bad are equally almost indicent; for what Magistrate may not be misinformed, and much the sooner, if Liberty of Printing be reduced into the power of a few? But to redress willingly and speedily what hath been erred, and in highest authority to esteem a plain advertisement more than others have done a sumptuous bribe, is a virtue (honoured Lords and Commons) answerable to your highest actions, and whereof none can participate but greatest and wisest men.

THE
TENURE OF KINGS AND MAGISTRATES:

PROVING

THAT IT IS LAWFUL, AND HATH BEEN HELD SO
THROUGH ALL AGES, FOR ANY WHO HAVE THE
POWER, TO CALL TO ACCOUNT A TYRANT, OR
WICKED KING, AND AFTER DUE CONVICTION, TO
DEPOSE, AND PUT HIM TO DEATH, IF THE ORDIN-
ARY MAGISTRATE HAVE NEGLECTED, OR DENIED
TO DO IT. AND THAT THEY WHO OF LATE SO MUCH
BLAME DEPOSING, ARE THE MEN THAT DID IT
THEMSELVES.

After the *Areopagitica*, Milton's political tracts were *ad hoc* pieces of persuasion, rather than philosophical discussions of principle. *The Tenure of Kings and Magistrates* was published in February 1649, a fortnight after the execution of Charles I. It was clearly intended to urge the justice of tyrannicide, and to show the Presbyterians how reprehensibly they had retreated from their earlier position. The passages specifically concerned with Milton's reproaches to the Presbyterians have been omitted from this selection.

Milton, in common with other Independents, believed that the people as represented in their Parliament had the right to create and alter their form of government. If the ruler broke the contract made between him and the people, to whom he was accountable, they had the right to punish him. Milton's theories had the backing of tradition, both Catholic and Calvinist. The doctrines of absolute monarchy were of relatively recent origin.

IF MEN within themselves would be governed by reason and not generally give up their understanding to a double tyranny, of custom from without and blind affections within, they would discern better what it is to favour and uphold the tyrant of a nation. But, being slaves within doors, no wonder that they strive so much to have the public state conformably governed to the inward vicious rule by which they govern themselves. For, indeed, none can love freedom heartily but good men. The rest love not freedom but licence, which never hath more scope or more indulgence than under tyrants. Hence is it that tyrants

are not oft offended, nor stand much in doubt of bad men, as
being all naturally servile, but in whom virtue and true worth
most is eminent, them they fear in earnest, as by right their
masters; against them lies all their hatred and suspicion.   Consequently, neither do bad men hate tyrants, but have been always
readiest with the falsified names of loyalty and obedience to
colour over their base compliances.

And although sometimes for shame, and when it comes
to their own grievances, of purse especially, they would seem
good patriots and side with the better cause, yet (when others
for the deliverance of their country, endued with fortitude and
heroic virtue to fear nothing but the curse written against those
'that do the work of the Lord negligently,' would go on to
remove not only the calamities and thraldoms of a people but
the roots and causes whence they spring) straight these men, and
sure helpers at need, as if they hated only the miseries but not the
mischiefs, after they have juggled and paltered with the world,
bandied and borne arms against their king, divested him, dis-
anointed him, nay, cursed him all over in their pulpits and their
pamphlets, to the engaging of sincere and real men beyond what
is possible or honest to retreat from, not only turn revolters from
those principles which only could at first move them, but lay the
stain of disloyalty and worse on those proceedings which are the
necessary consequences of their own former actions; nor disliked by themselves, were they managed to the entire advantages
of their own faction; not considering the while that he toward
whom they boasted their new fidelity, counted them accessory;
and by those statutes and laws which they so impotently brandish
against others, would have doomed them to a traitor's death for
what they have done already.

'Tis true that most men are apt enough to civil wars and
commotions as a novelty, and for a flash hot and active; but
through sloth or inconstancy, and weakness of spirit, either
fainting ere their own pretences, though never so just, be half
attained, or through an inbred falsehood and wickedness,
betray, ofttimes to destruction with themselves, men of noblest
temper joined with them for causes whereof they in their rash
undertakings were not capable.

If God and a good cause give them victory, the prosecution
whereof for the most part inevitably draws after it the alteration of laws, change of government, downfall of princes with
their families—then comes the task to those worthies which
are the soul of that enterprise, to be sweat and laboured out

amidst the throng and noises of vulgar and irrational men. Some contesting for privileges, customs, forms, and that old entanglement of iniquity, their gibberish laws, though the badge of their ancient slavery. Others, who have been fiercest against their prince under the notion of a tyrant, and no mean incendiaries of the war against him, when God out of his providence and high disposal hath delivered him into the hand of their brethren, on a sudden and in a new garb of allegiance, which their doings have long since cancelled, they plead for him, pity him, extol him, protest against those that talk of bringing him to the trial of justice, which is the sword of God, superior to all mortal things, in whose hand soever by apparent signs his testified will is to put it.

But certainly, if we consider who and what they are on a sudden grown so pitiful, we may conclude their pity can be no true and Christian commiseration, but either levity and shallowness of mind, or else a carnal admiring of that worldly pomp and greatness from whence they see him fallen; or rather, lastly, a dissembled and seditious pity, feigned of industry to beget new discord. As for mercy, if it be to a tyrant (under which name they themselves have cited him so oft in the hearing of God, of angels, and the holy church assembled, and there charged him with the spilling of more innocent blood be far than ever Nero did) undoubtedly the mercy which they pretend is the mercy of wicked men. And 'their mercies,' we read, 'are cruelties;' hazarding the welfare of a whole nation to have saved one whom so oft they have termed Agag, and vilifying the blood of many Jonathans that have saved Israel; insisting with much niceness on the unnecessariest clause of their covenant wrested, wherein the fear of change and the absurd contradiction of a flattering hostility had hampered them, but not scrupling to give away for compliments, to an implacable revenge, the heads of many thousand Christians more.

Another sort there is, who (coming in the course of these affairs to have their share in great actions above the form of law or custom, at least to give their voice and approbation) begin to swerve and almost shiver at the majesty and grandeur of some noble deed, as if they were newly entered into a great sin; disputing precedents, forms, and circumstances, when the commonwealth nigh perishes for want of deeds in substance, done with just and faithful expedition. To these I wish better instruction, and virtue equal to their calling; the former of which, that is to say, instruction, I shall endeavour, as my duty is, to bestow on them; and exhort them not to startle from the just and pious resolution of adhering with all their strength and assistance to the present parliament and army in the glorious way wherein justice and victory hath set them—the only warrants through all ages, next under immediate revelation, to exercise supreme power—in those proceedings, which hitherto appear equal to what hath been done in any age or nation heretofore justly or magnanimously.

Nor let them be discouraged or deterred by any new apostate scarecrows, who, under show of giving counsel, send out their barking monitories and mementoes, empty of aught else but the spleen of a frustrated faction. For how can that pretended counsel be either sound or faithful, when they that give it see not, for madness and vexation of their ends lost, that those statutes and scriptures which both falsely and scandalously they wrest against their friends and associates, would, by sentence of the common adversary, fall first and heaviest upon their own heads? Neither let mild and tender dispositions be foolishly softened from their duty and perseverance with the unmasculine rhetoric of any puling priest or chaplain, sent as a friendly letter of advice—for fashion sake in private—and forthwith published by the sender himself that we may know how much of friend there was in it, to cast an odious envy upon them to whom it was pretended to be sent in charity. Nor let any man be deluded by either the ignorance or the notorious hypocrisy and self-repugnance of our dancing divines, who have the conscience and the boldness to come with scripture in their mouths, glossed and fitted for their turns with a double contradictory sense, transforming the sacred verity of God to an idol with two faces, looking at once two several ways; and with the same quotations to charge others, which in the same case they made serve to justify themselves. For while the hope to be made classic and provincial lords led them on, while pluralities greased them thick and deep to the shame and scandal of religion more than all the sects and heresies they exclaim against—then to fight against the king's person, and no less a party of his lords and commons, or to put force upon both the houses, was good, was lawful, was no resisting of superior powers. They only were powers not to be resisted, who countenanced the good, and punished the evil.

But now that their censorious domineering is not suffered to be universal, truth and conscience to be freed, tithes and pluralities to be no more, though competent allowance provided and the warm experience of large gifts, and they so good at taking them—yet now to exclude and seize upon impeached members, to bring delinquents without exemption to a fair tribunal by the common national law against murder, is now to be no less than Korah, Dathan, and Abiram. He who but erewhile in the pulpits was a cursed tyrant, an enemy to God and saints, laden with all the innocent blood spilt in three kingdoms, and so to be fought against, is now, though nothing penitent or altered from his first principles, a lawful magistrate, a sovereign lord, the Lord's anointed, not to be touched, though by themselves imprisoned. As if this only were obedience, to preserve the mere useless bulk of his person, and that only in prison not in the field, and to disobey his commands, deny him his dignity and office, everywhere to resist his power but where they think it only surviving in their own faction.

But who in particular is a tyrant cannot be determined in a general discourse, otherwise than by supposition. His particular charge and the sufficient proof of it, must determine that; which I leave to magistrates, at least to the uprighter sort of them and of the people, though in number less by many, in whom faction least hath prevailed above the law of nature and right reason, to judge as they find cause. But this I dare own as part of my faith, that if such a one there be, by whose commission whole massacres have been committed on his faithful subjects, his provinces offered to pawn or alienation, as the hire of those whom he had solicited to come in and destroy whole cities and countries; be he king, or tyrant, or emperor, the sword of justice is above him, in whose hand soever is found sufficient power to avenge the effusion and so great a deluge of innocent blood. For if all human power to execute, not accidentally but intendedly, the wrath of God upon evildoers without exception, be of God, then that power, whether ordinary or, if that fail, extraordinary, so executing that intent of God, is lawful and not to be resisted.

But to unfold more at large this whole question, though with all expedient brevity, I shall here set down from first beginning, the original of kings; how and wherefore exalted to that dignity above their brethren; and from thence shall prove that, turning to tyranny, they may be as lawfully deposed and punished as they were at first elected. This I shall do by authorities and reasons, not learnt in corners among schisms and heresies, as our doubling divines are ready to calumniate, but fetched out of the minds of choicest and most authentic learning, and no prohibited authors, nor many heathen, but Mosaical, Christian, orthodoxal, and, which must needs be more convincing to our adversaries, presbyterial.

No man who knows aught, can be so stupid to deny that all men naturally were born free, being the image and resemblance of God himself, and were, by privilege above all the creatures, born to command, and not to obey; and that they lived so, till from the root of Adam's transgression falling among themselves to do wrong and violence, and foreseeing that such courses must needs tend to the destruction of them all, they agreed by common league to bind each other from mutual injury, and jointly to defend themselves against any that gave disturbance or opposition to such agreement. Hence came cities, towns, and commonwealths. And because no faith in all was found sufficiently binding, they saw it needful to ordain some authority that might restrain by force and punishment what was violated against peace and common right.

This authority and power of self-defence and preservation being originally and naturally in every one of them, and unitedly in them all, for ease, for order, and lest each man should be his own partial judge, they communicated and derived either to one whom for the eminence of his wisdom and integrity they chose above the rest, or to more than one whom they thought of equal deserving. The first was called a king, the other, magistrates: not to be their lords and masters (though afterwards those names in some places were given voluntarily to such as had been authors of inestimable good to the people), but to be their deputies and commissioners, to execute, by virtue of their intrusted power, that justice which else every man by the bond of nature and of covenant must have executed for himself, and for one another. And to him that shall consider well why among free persons one man by civil right should bear authority and jurisdiction over another, no other end or reason can be imaginable.

These for a while governed well and with much equity decided all things at their own arbitrement, till the temptation of such a power, left absolute in their hands, perverted them at length to injustice and partiality. Then did they who now by trial had found the danger and inconveniences of committing arbitrary power to any, invent laws, either framed or consented to by all, that should confine and limit the authority of whom they chose to govern them: that so man, of whose failing they had proof, might no more rule over them, but law and reason, abstracted as much as might be from personal errors and frailties: while, as the magistrate was set above the people, so the law was set above the magistrate. When this would not serve, but that the law was either not executed, or misapplied, they were constrained from that time, the only remedy left them, to put conditions and take oaths from all kings and magistrates at their first instalment to do impartial justice by law: who, upon those terms and no other, received allegiance from the people, that is to say, bond or covenant to obey them in execution of those laws which they, the people, had themselves made or assented to. And this oft-times with express warning, that if the king or magistrate proved unfaithful to his trust, the people would be disengaged.

They added also counsellors and parliaments, not to be only at his beck, but, with him or without him, at set times, or at all times when any danger threatened, to have care of the public safety. Therefore saith Claudius Sesell, a French statesman, 'The parliament was set as a bridle to the king'; which I instance rather, not because our English lawyers have not said the same long before, but because that French monarchy is granted by all to be a far more absolute than ours. That this and the rest of what hath hitherto been spoken is most true, might be copiously made appear throughout all stories, heathen and Christian; even of those nations where kings and emperors have sought means to abolish all ancient memory of the people's right by their en-croachments and usurpations. But I spare long insertions, appealing to the known constitutions of both the latest Christian empires in Europe, the Greek and the German, besides the French, Italian, Arragonian, English, and not least the Scottish histories: not forgetting this only by the way, that William the Norman, though a conqueror, and not unsworn at his coronation, was compelled the second time to take oath at St Albans ere the people would be brought to yield obedience.

It being thus manifest that the power of kings and magistrates is nothing else but what is only derivative, transferred, and committed to them in trust from the people to the common good of them all, in whom the power yet remains fundamentally and cannot be taken from them without a violation of their natural birthright, and seeing that from hence Aristotle, and the best of political writers, have defined a king, 'him who governs to the good and profit of his people, and not for his own ends'—it follows from necessary causes that the titles of sovereign lord, natural lord, and the like, are either arrogancies or flatteries, not admitted by emperors and kings of best note, and disliked by the church both of Jews (Isa. xxvi. 13) and ancient

Christians, as appears by Tertullian and others. Although generally the people of Asia, and with them the Jews also, especially since the time they chose a king against the advice and counsel of God, are noted by wise authors much inclinable to slavery.

Secondly, that to say, as is usual, the king hath as good right to his crown and dignity as any man to his inheritance, is to make the subject no better than the king's slave, his chattel, or his possession that may be bought and sold. And doubtless, if hereditary title were sufficiently inquired, the best foundation of it would be found either but in courtesy or convenience. But suppose it to be of right hereditary, what can be more just and legal, if a subject for certain crimes be to forfeit by law from himself and posterity all his inheritance to the king, than that a king, for crimes proportional, should forfeit all his title and inheritance to the people? Unless the people must be thought created all for him, he not for them, and they all in one body inferior to him single; which were a kind of treason against the dignity of mankind to affirm.

Thirdly, it follows that to say kings are accountable to none but God, is the overturning of all law and government. For if they may refuse to give account, then all covenants made with them at coronation, all oaths are in vain, and mere mockeries, all laws which they swear to keep, made to no purpose: for if the king fear not God (as how many of them do not?) we hold then our lives and estates by the tenure of his mere grace and mercy, as from a god, not a mortal magistrate—a position that none but court-parasites or men besotted would maintain. Aristotle, therefore, whom we commonly allow for one of the best interpreters of nature and morality, writes in the fourth of his *Politics*, chap. x., that 'monarchy unaccountable is the worst sort of tyranny, and least of all to be endured by free-born men.'

And surely no Christian prince, not drunk with high mind and prouder than those pagan Caesars that deified themselves, would arrogate so unreasonably above human condition, or derogate so basely from a whole nation of men, his brethren, as if for him only subsisting, and to serve his glory; valuing them in comparison of his own brute will and pleasure no more than so many beasts, or vermin under his feet, not to be reasoned with, but to be trod on; among whom there might be found so many thousand men for wisdom, virtue, nobleness of mind, and all other respects but the fortune of his dignity, far above him.

Yet some would persuade us that this absurd opinion was King
David's, because in the 51 Psalm he cries out to God, 'Against
thee only have I sinned'; as if David had imagined that to murder
Uriah and adulterate his wife had been no sin against his neigh-
bor, whenas that law of Moses was to the king expressly (Deut.
xvii), not to think so highly of himself above his brethren.
David, therefore, by those words could mean no other than either
that the depth of his guiltiness was known to God only, or to so
few as had not the will or power to question him, or that the sin
against God was greater beyond compare than against Uriah.
Whatever his meaning were, any wise man will see that the
pathetical words of a psalm can be no certain decision to a point
that hath abundantly more certain rules to go by.

How much more rationally spake the heathen king Demo-
phoön, in a tragedy of Euripides, than these interpreters would
put upon king David! 'I rule not my people by tyranny, as if
they were barbarians, but am myself liable, if I do unjustly, to
suffer justly.' Not unlike the speech of Trajan, the worthy
emperor, to one whom he made general of his praetorian forces:
'Take this drawn sword,' saith he, 'to use for me if I reign well;
if not, to use against me.' Thus Dion relates. And not Trajan
only, but Theodosius the younger, a Christian emperor and one
of the best, caused it to be enacted as a rule undeniable and fit to
be acknowledged by all kings and emperors, that a prince is
bound to the laws: that on the authority of law the authority
of a prince depends, and to the laws ought submit. Which
edict of his remains yet in the Code of Justinian (1. i. tit. 24) as
a sacred constitution to all the succeeding emperors. How
then can any king in Europe maintain and write himself accountable to none but God, when emperors in their own imperial
statutes have written and decreed themselves accountable to
law? And indeed where such account is not feared, he that
bids a man reign over him above law, may bid as well a savage
beast.

It follows, lastly, that since the king or magistrate holds his
authority of the people, both originally and naturally for their
good in the first place, and not his own, then may the people,
as oft as they shall judge it for the best, either choose him or
reject him, retain him or depose him, though no tyrant, merely
by the liberty and right of freeborn men to be governed as seems
to them best. This, though it cannot but stand with plain reason,
shall be made good also by Scripture (Deut. xvii. 14): 'When thou
art come into the land which the Lord thy God giveth thee, and

shalt say, I will set a king over me, like as all the nations about me.' These words confirm us that the right of choosing, yea of changing their own government, is by the grant of God himself in the people. And therefore when they desired a king, though then under another form of government, and though their changing displeased him, yet he that was himself their king and rejected by them, would not be a hindrance to what they intended, further than by persuasion, but that they might do therein as they saw good (1 Sam. viii), only he reserved to himself the nomination of who should reign over them. Neither did that exempt the king, as if he were to God only accountable, though by his especial command anointed. Therefore 'David first made a covenant with the elders of Israel, and so was by them anointed king' (2 Sam. v. 3; 1 Chron. xi). And Jehoiada the priest, making Jehoash king, made a covenant between him and the people (2 Kings xi. 17). Therefore when Roboam, at his coming to the crown, rejected those conditions which the Israelites brought him, hear what they answer him: 'What portion have we in David, or inheritance in the son of Jesse? See to thine own house, David.' And for the like conditions not performed, all Israel before that time deposed Samuel, not for his own default, but for the misgovernment of his sons.

But some will say to both these examples, it was evilly done. I answer that not the latter, because it was expressly allowed them in the law to set up a king if they pleased; and God himself joined with them in the work, though in some sort it was at that time displeasing to him, in respect of old Samuel, who had governed them uprightly. As Livy praises the Romans, who took occasion from Tarquinius, a wicked prince, to gain their liberty, which to have extorted, saith he, from Numa, or any of the good kings before, had not been seasonable. Nor was it in the former example done unlawfully; for when Roboam had prepared a huge army to reduce the Israelites, he was forbidden by the prophet (1 Kings xii. 24): 'Thus saith the Lord, ye shall not go up, nor fight against your brethren, for this thing is from me.' He calls them their brethren, not rebels, and forbids to be proceeded against them, owning the thing himself, not by single providence but by approbation, and that not only of the act, as in the former example, but of the fit season also. He had not otherwise forbid to molest them. And those grave and wise counsellors whom Rehoboam first advised with, spake no such thing as our old grey-headed flatterers now are wont: 'Stand upon your birthright, scorn to capitulate; you hold of

God, not of them.' For they knew no such matter, unless conditionally, but gave him politic counsel as in a civil transaction.

Therefore kingdom and magistracy, whether supreme or subordinate, is without difference called 'a human ordinance' (1 Pet. ii. 13, etc.), which we are taught is the will of God we should alike submit to, so far as for the punishment of evildoers and the encouragement of them that do well. 'Submit,' saith he, 'as free men.' But to any civil power unaccountable, unquestionable, and not to be resisted, no, not in wickedness and violent actions, how can we submit as free men? 'There is no power but of God,' saith Paul (Rom. xiii), as much as to say God put it into man's heart to find out that way at first for common peace and preservation, approving the exercise thereof; else it contradicts Peter, who calls the same authority an ordinance of man. It must be also understood of lawful and just power, else we read of great power in the affairs and kingdoms of the world permitted to the devil: for saith he to Christ (Luke, iv. 6): 'All this power will I give thee and the glory of them, for it is delivered to me, and to whomsoever I will, I give it'; neither did he lie, or Christ gainsay what he affirmed; for in the thirteenth of the Revelation, we read how the dragon gave to the beast 'his power, his seat, and great authority': which beast so authorized most expound to be the tyrannical powers and kingdoms of the earth. Therefore St Paul in the forecited chapter tells us that such magistrates he means as are not a terror to the good, but to the evil; such as bear not the sword in vain, but to punish offenders and to encourage the good.

If such only be mentioned here as powers to be obeyed, and our submission to them only required, then doubtless those powers that do the contrary are no powers ordained of God, and by consequence no obligation laid upon us to obey or not to resist them. And it may be well observed that both these apostles, whenever they give this precept, express it in terms not concrete but abstract, as logicians are wont to speak; that is, they mention the ordinance, the power, the authority, before the persons that execute it, and what that power is, lest we should be deceived they describe exactly. So that if the power be not such, or the person execute not such power, neither the one nor the other is of God, but of the devil, and by consequence to be resisted. From this exposition Chrysostom also, on the same place, dissents not, explaining that these words were not written in behalf of a tyrant. And this is verified by David, himself a king, and likeliest to be author of the Psalm (xciv. 20) which saith: 'Shall the throne of iniquity have fellowship with thee?' And it were worth the knowing, since kings in these days, and that by Scripture, boasts the justness of their title by holding it immediately of God, yet cannot show the time when God ever set on the throne them or their forefathers, but only when the people chose them; why by the same reason, since God ascribes as oft to himself the casting down of princes from the throne, it should not be thought as lawful and as much from God, when none are seen to do it but the people and that for just causes. For if it needs must be a sin in them to depose, it may as likely be a sin to have elected. And contrary, if the people's act in election be pleaded by a king as the act of God and the most just title to enthrone him, why may not the people's act of rejection be as well pleaded by the people as the act of God and the most just reason to depose him? So that we see the title and just right of reigning or deposing, in reference to God, is found in Scripture to be all one; visible only in the people, and depending merely upon justice and demerit. Thus far hath been considered briefly the power of kings and magistrates, how it was and is originally the people's, and by them conferred in trust only to be employed to the common peace and benefit; with liberty therefore and right remaining in them to reassure it to themselves, if by kings or magistrates it be abused, or to dispose of it by any alteration, as they shall judge most conducing to the public good.

We may from hence with more ease and force of argument determine what a tyrant is, and what the people may do against him. A tyrant, whether by wrong or by right coming to the crown, is he who, regarding neither law nor the common good, reigns only for himself and his faction: thus St Basil, among others, defines him. And because his power is great, his will boundless and exorbitant, the fulfilling whereof is for the most part accompanied with innumerable wrongs and oppressions of the people, murders, massacres, rapes, adulteries, desolation, and subversion of cities and whole provinces—look, how great a good and happiness a just king is, so great a mischief is a tyrant; as he the public father of his country, so this the common enemy. Against whom what the people lawfully may do, as against a common pest and destroyer of mankind, I suppose no man of clear judgment need go further to be guided than by the very principles of nature in him.

But because it is the vulgar folly of men to desert their own reason and shutting their eyes, to think they see best with other men's, I shall show by such examples as ought to have most weight with us, what hath been done in this case heretofore. The Greeks and Romans, as their prime authors witness, held it not only lawful, but a glorious and heroic deed rewarded publicly with statues and garlands, to kill an infamous tyrant at any time without trial—and but reason, that he who trod down all law, should not be vouchsafed the benefit of law. Insomuch that Seneca, the tragedian, brings in Hercules, the grand suppressor of tyrants, thus speaking:

> ———Victima haud ulla amplior
> Potest, magisque opima mactari Jovi
> Quam rex iniquus———

> ———There can be slain
> No sacrifice to God more acceptable
> Than an unjust and wicked king———.

But of these I name no more, lest it be objected they were heathen; and come to produce another sort of men that had the knowledge of true religion. Among the Jews this custom of tyrant-killing was not unusual. First, Ehud, a man whom God had raised to deliver Israel from Eglon King of Moab, who had conquered and ruled over them eighteen years, being sent to him as an ambassador with a present, slew him in his own house. But he was a foreign prince, an enemy, and Ehud besides had special warrant from God. To the first I answer, it imports not whether foreign or native. For no prince so native but professes to hold by law; which then he himself overturns, breaking all the covenants and oaths that gave him title to his dignity and were the bond and alliance between him and his people, what differs he from an outlandish king or from an enemy?

For look, how much right the King of Spain hath to govern us at all, so much right hath the King of England to govern us tyrannically. If he, though not bound to us by any league, coming from Spain in person to subdue us or to destroy us, might lawfully by the people of England either be slain in fight or put to death in captivity, what hath a native king to plead, bound by so many covenants, benefits, and honours, to the welfare of his people; why he (through the contempt of all laws and parliaments, the only tie of our obedience to him, for his own will's sake and a boasted prerogative unaccountable) after seven years' warring and destroying of his best subjects overcome and yielded prisoner, should think to scape unquestionable as a thing divine, in respect of whom so many thousand Christians destroyed should lie unaccounted for, polluting with their slaughtered carcasses all the land over, and crying for vengeance against the living that should have righted them? Who knows not that there is a mutual bond of amity and brotherhood between man and man over all the world, neither is it the English sea that can sever us from that duty and relation? A straiter bond yet there is between fellow-subjects, neighbours, and friends. But when any of these do one to another so as hostility could do no worse, what doth the law decree less against them than open enemies and invaders? Or if the law be not present or too weak, what doth it warrant us to less than single defence or civil war? And from that time forward the law of civil defensive war differs nothing from the law of foreign hostility. Nor is it distance of place that makes enmity, but enmity that makes distance. He, therefore, that keeps peace with me, near or remote, of whatsoever nation, is to me, as far as all civil and human offices, an Englishman and a neighbour. But if an Englishman, forgetting all laws, human, civil, and religious offend against life and liberty, to him offended and to the law in his behalf, though born in the same womb, he is no better than a Turk, a Saracen, a heathen.

This is gospel and this was ever law among equals; how much rather then in force against any king whatever, who in respect of the people is confessed inferior and not equal: to distinguish, therefore, of a tyrant by outlandish, or domestic, is a weak evasion. To the second, that he was an enemy, I answer, 'What tyrant is not?' Yet Eglon by the Jews had been acknowledged as their sovereign. They had served him eighteen years, as long almost as we our William the Conqueror, in all which time he could not be so unwise a statesman but to have taken of them oaths of fealty and allegiance, by which they made themselves his proper subjects, as their homage and present sent by Ehud testified. To the third, that he had special warrant to kill Eglon in that manner, it cannot be granted because not expressed. 'Tis plain that he was raised by God to be a deliverer, and went on just principles such as were then and ever held allowable to deal so by a tyrant that could no otherwise be dealt with.

Neither did Samuel, though a prophet, with his own hand abstain from Agag, a foreign enemy no doubt, but mark the reason: 'As thy sword hath made women childless,' a cause that by the sentence of law itself nullifies all relations. And as the law is between brother and brother, father and son, master and servant, wherefore not between king, or rather tyrant, and people?

And whereas Jehu had special command to slay Jehoram, a successive and hereditary tyrant, it seems not the less imitable for that. For where a thing grounded so much on natural reason hath the addition of a command from God, what does it but establish the lawfulness of such an act? Nor is it likely that God, who had so many ways of punishing the house of Ahab, would have sent a subject against his prince, if the fact in itself, as done to a tyrant had been of bad example. And if David refused to lift his hand against the Lord's anointed, the matter between them was not tyranny, but private enmity, and David, as a private person, had been his own revenger, not so much the people's: but when any tyrant at this day can show to be the Lord's anointed, the only mentioned reason why David withheld his hand, he may then, but not till then, presume on the same privilege.

We may pass, therefore, hence to Christian times. And first, our Saviour himself, how much he favoured tyrants and how much intended they should be found or honoured among Christians, declares his mind not obscurely; accounting their absolute authority no better than Gentilism, yea, though they flourished it over with the splendid name of benefactors; charging those that would be his disciples to usurp no such dominion; but that they who were to be of most authority among them, should esteem themselves ministers and servants to the public (Matt. xx. 25): 'The princes of the Gentiles exercise lordship over them,' and Mark x. 42. 'They that seem to rule,' saith he, either slighting or accounting them no lawful rulers; 'but ye shall not be so, but the greatest among you shall be your servant.' And although he himself were the meekest and came on earth to be so, yet to a tyrant we hear him not vouchsafe an humble word, but 'Tell that fox,' Luke xiii. So far we ought to be from thinking that Christ and his gospel should be made a sanctuary for tyrants from justice, to whom his law before never gave such protection. And wherefore did his mother, the Virgin Mary, give such praise to God in her prophetic song, that he had now, by the coming of Christ, 'cut down dynastas or proud monarchs from the throne,' if the church, when God manifests his power in them to do so, should rather choose all misery and vassalage to serve them, and let them sit on their potent seats to be adored for doing mischief?

Surely it is not for nothing that tyrants, by a kind of natural instinct, both hate and fear none more than the true church and saints of God, as the most dangerous enemies and subverters of monarchy, though indeed of tyranny. Hath not this been the perpetual cry of courtiers and court-prelates? Whereof no likelier cause can be alleged but that they well discerned the mind and principles of most devout and zealous men, and indeed the very discipline of church, tending to the dissolution of all tyranny. No marvel then if since the faith of Christ received, in purer or impurer times, to depose a king and put him to death for tyranny, hath been accounted so just and requisite that neighbour kings hath both upheld and taken part with subjects in the action. And Ludovicus Pius, himself an emperor, and son of Charles the Great, being made judge (du Haillan is my author) between Milegast, King of the Vultzes, and his subjects, who had deposed him, gave his verdict for the subjects and for him whom they had chosen in his room. Note here that the right of electing whom they please is, by the impartial testimony of an emperor, in the people: for, said he: 'A just prince ought to be preferred before an unjust, and the end of government before the prerogative.' And Constantinus Leo, another emperor, in the Byzantine laws saith: 'That the end of a king is for the general good, which he not performing, is but the counterfeit of a king.'

And to prove that some of our own monarchs have acknowledged that their high office exempted them not from punishment, they had the sword of St Edward borne before them by an officer, who was called earl of the palace, even at the times of their highest pomp and solemnities, to mind them, saith Matthew Paris, the best of our historians: 'that if they erred, the sword had power to restrain them.' And what restraint the sword comes to at length, having both edge and point, if any sceptic will doubt, let him feel. It is also affirmed from diligent search made in our ancient books of law that the peers and barons of England had a legal right to judge the king, which was the cause most likely (for it could be no slight cause) that they were called his peers or equals. This, however, may stand immovable, so long as man hath to deal with no better than man; that if our law judge all men to the lowest by their peers, it should in all equity ascend also and judge the highest.

* * * * *

For as to this question in hand, what the people by their just right may do in change of government or of governor, we see it cleared sufficiently, besides other ample authority even from the mouths of princes themselves. And surely they that shall boast, as we do, to be a free nation, and not have in themselves the power to remove or to abolish any governor supreme, or subordinate, with the government itself upon urgent causes, may please their fancy with a ridiculous and painted freedom, fit to cozen babies; but are indeed under tyranny and servitude, as wanting that power which is the root and source of all liberty, to dispose and economize in the land which God hath given them, as masters of family in their own house and free inheritance. Without which natural and essential power of a free nation, though bearing high their heads, they can in due esteem be thought no better than slaves and vassals born, in the tenure and occupation of another inheriting lord, whose government, though not illegal or intolerable, hangs over them as a lordly scourge, not as a free government—and therefore to be abrogated.

How much more justly then may they fling off tyranny, or tyrants, who being once deposed can be no more than private men, as subject to the reach of justice and arraignment as any other transgressors? And certainly if men, not to speak of heathen, both wise and religious, have done justice upon tyrants what way they could soonest, how much more mild and humane then is it to give them fair and open trial—to teach lawless kings and all who so much adore them, that not mortal man, or his imperious will, but justice, is the only true sovereign and supreme majesty upon earth? Let men cease therefore out of faction and hypocrisy to make outcries and horrid things of things so just and honourable.

Though perhaps till now no protestant state or kingdom can be alleged to have openly put to death their king, which lately some have written and imputed to their great glory, much mistaking the matter, it is not, neither ought to be, the glory of a protestant state never to have put their king to death; it is the glory of a protestant king never to have deserved death. And if the parliament and military council do what they do without precedent, if it appear their duty, it argues the more wisdom, virtue, and magnanimity, that they know themselves able to be a precedent to others; who perhaps in future ages, if they prove not too degenerate, will look up with honour and aspire towards these exemplary and matchless deeds of their ancestors, as to the highest top of their civil glory and emulation; which heretofore, in the pursuance of fame and foreign dominion, spent itself vaingloriously abroad, but henceforth may learn a better fortitude—to dare execute highest justice on them that shall by force of arms endeavour the oppressing and bereaving of religion and their liberty at home: that no unbridled potentate or tyrant, but to his sorrow, for the future may presume such high and irresponsible licence over mankind, to havoc and turn upside down whole kingdoms of men, as though they were no more in respect of his perverse will than a nation of pismires.

.   .   .   .   .

Gilby *de obedientia*, pp. 25 & 105.

'Kings have their authority of the people, who may upon occasion reassume it to themselves.'

England's Complaint against the Canons.

'The people may kill wicked princes as monsters and cruel beasts.'

Christopher Goodman, *Of Obedience.*

'When kings or rulers become blasphemers of God, oppressors and murderers of their subjects, they ought no more to be accounted kings or lawful magistrates, but as private men to be examined, accused, condemned, and punished by the law of God, and being convicted and punished by that law, it is not man's but God's doing.' (C. 10, p. 139.)

'By the civil laws a fool or idiot born, and so proved, shall lose the lands and inheritance whereto he is born, because he is not able to use them aright. And especially ought in no case be suffered to have the government of a whole nation; but there is no such evil can come to the commonwealth by fools and idiots as doth by the rage and fury of ungodly rulers; such therefore being without God ought to have no authority over God's people, who by his word requireth the contrary.' (C. 11, p. 143, 144.)

'No person is exempt by any law of God from this punishment, be he king, queen, or emperor, he must die the death, for God hath not placed them above others, to transgress his laws as they list, but to be subject to them as well as others, and if they be subject to his laws, then to the punishment also, so much the more as their example is more dangerous.' (C. 13, p. 184.)

'When magistrates cease to do their duty, the people are as it were without magistrates; yea worse, and then God giveth the sword into the people's hand, and he himself is become immediately their head.' p. 185.

'If princes do right and keep promise with you, then do you owe to them all humble obedience. If not, ye are discharged and your study ought to be in this case how ye may depose and punish according to the law such rebels against God and oppressors of their country.' (p. 190.)

This Goodman was a minister of the English church at Geneva, as Dudley Fenner was at Middleburgh, or some other place in that country. These were the pastors of those saints and confessors who, flying from the bloody persecution of Queen Mary, gathered up at length their scattered members into many congregations. Whereof some in upper, some in lower Germany, part of them settled at Geneva, where this author having preached on this subject to the great liking of certain learned and godly men who heard him, was by them sundry times and with much instance required to write more fully on that point. Who thereupon took it in hand, and conferring with the best learned in those parts (among whom Calvin was then living in the same city), with their special approbation he published this treatise, aiming principally, as is testified by Whittingham in the Preface, that his brethren of England, the protestants, might be persuaded in the truth of that doctrine concerning obedience to magistrates. (Whittingham in Prefat.)

These were the true protestant divines of England, our fathers in the faith we hold. This was their sense, who for so many years labouring under prelacy, through all storms and persecutions, kept religion from extinguishing; and delivered it pure to us, till there arose a covetous and ambitious generation of divines (for divines they call themselves) who, feigning on a sudden to be new converts and proselytes from episcopacy, under which they had long temporized, opened their mouths at length, in show against pluralities and prelacy, but with intent to swallow them down both; gorging themselves like harpies on those simonious places and preferments of their outed predecessors, as the quarry for which they hunted, not to plurality only but to multiplicity; for possessing which they had accused them, their brethren, and aspiring under another title to the same authority and usurpation over the consciences of all men.

Of this faction, divers reverend and learned divines (as they are styled in the phylactery of their own title-page) pleading the lawfulness of defensive arms against this king in a treatise called *Scripture and Reason*, seem in words to disclaim utterly the deposing of a king. But both the scripture and the reasons which they use draw consequences after them, which without their bidding, conclude it lawful. For if by scripture, and by that especially to the Romans which they most insist upon, kings, doing that which is contrary to St Paul's definition of a magistrate, may be resisted, they may altogether with as much force of consequence be deposed or punished. And if by reason the unjust authority of kings 'may be forfeited in part, and his power be reassumed in part, either by the parliament or people, for the case in hazard and the present necessity' (as they affirm, p. 34), there can no scripture be alleged, no imaginable reason given that necessity continuing—as it may always, and they in all prudence and their duty may take upon them to foresee it— why in such a case they may not finally amerce him with the loss of his kingdom, of whose amendment they have no hope. And if one wicked action persisted in against religion, laws, and liberties, may warrant us to thus much in part, why may not forty times as many tyrannies by him committed, warrant us to proceed on restraining him till the restraint become total? For the ways of justice are exactest proportion. If for one trespass of a king it require so much remedy or satisfaction, then for twenty more as heinous crimes, it requires of him twenty-fold, and so proportionably, till it come to what is utmost among men. If in these proceedings against their king they may not finish, by the usual course of justice, what they have begun, they could not lawfully begin at all. For this golden rule of justice and morality, as well as of arithmetic, out of three terms which they admit, will as certainly and unavoidably bring out the fourth as any problem that ever Euclid or Appollonius made good by demonstration.

And if the parliament, being undeposable but by themselves (as is affirmed, pp. 37, 38), might for his whole life, if they saw cause, take all power, authority, and the sword out of his hand, which in effect is to unmagistrate him, why might they not —being them themselves the sole magistrates in force—proceed to punish him, who, being lawfully deprived of all things that define a magistrate, can be now no magistrate to be degraded lower, but an offender to be punished. Lastly, whom they may defy and meet in battle, why may they not as well prosecute by justice? For lawful war is but the execution of justice against them who refuse law. Among whom if it be lawful (as they deny not, pp. 19, 20), to slay the king himself coming in front at his own peril, wherefore may not justice do that intendedly, which the chance of a defensive war might without blame have done casually, nay, purposely, if there it find him among the rest? They ask (p. 19): 'By what rule of conscience or God a state is bound to sacrifice religion, laws, and liberties, rather than a prince, defending such as subvert them, should come in hazard of his life.' And I ask by what conscience, or divinity, or law, or reason, a state is bound to leave all these sacred concernments under a perpetual hazard and extremity of danger rather than cut off a wicked prince, who sits plotting day and night to subvert them.

They tell us that the law of nature justifies any man to defend himself, even against the king in person. Let them show us then why the same law may not justify much more a state or whole people, to do justice upon him against whom each private man may lawfully defend himself; seeing all kind of justice done is a defence to good men, as well as a punishment to bad, and justice done upon a tyrant is no more but the necessary self-defence of a whole commonwealth. To war upon a king that his instruments may be brought to condign punishment, and thereafter to punish them the instruments, and not to spare only, but to defend and honour him the author, is the strangest piece of justice to be called Christian, and the strangest piece of reason to be called human, that by men of reverence and learning, as their style imports them, ever yet was vented. They maintain in the third and fourth section that a judge or inferior magistrate is anointed of God, is his minister, hath the sword in his hand, is to be obeyed by St Peter's rule, as well as the supreme, and without difference anywhere expressed: and yet will have us fight against the supreme till he remove and punish the inferior magistrate (for such were greatest delinquents); whenas by scripture and by reason there can no more authority be shown to resist the one than the other; and altogether as much, to punish or depose the supreme himself, as to make war upon him, till he punish or deliver up his inferior magistrates, whom in the same terms we are commanded to obey and not to resist.

EIKONOKLASTES

Some few days after the execution of Charles I a book was published entitled *Eikon Basilike*. It purported to have been written by the dead king, defending the course he had taken. In all probability it was the work of the Anglican bishop, John Gauden. The author was a persuasive writer, able to evoke admiration and arouse feelings of pity and indignation in his readers. Following on the shock of the actual execution, the book stirred up a great deal of resentment against Cromwell and the remainder of the Rump Parliament. It was necessary to compose an official answer. Milton's *Eikonoklastes*, published in October 1649, stated the Parliamentary view: Charles I had deserved his punishment.

IT might well be thought by him who reads no further than the title of this last essay, that it required no answer. For all other human things are disputed, and will be variously thought of to the world's end. But this business of death is a plain case, and admits no controversy: in that centre all opinions meet. Nevertheless, since out of those few mortifying hours that should have been entirest to themselves, and most at peace from all passion and disquiet, he can afford spare time to inveigh bitterly against that justice which was done upon him; it will be needful to say something in defence of those proceedings, though briefly, in regard so much on this subject hath been written lately.

It happened once, as we find in Esdras and Josephus, authors not less believed than any under sacred, to be a great and solemn debate in the court of Darius, what thing was to be counted strongest of all other. He that could resolve this, in reward of his excellent wisdom, should be clad in purple, drink in gold, sleep on a bed of gold, and sit next Darius. None but they, doubtless, who were reputed wise had the question propounded to them; who after some respite given them by the king to consider, in full assembly of all his lords and gravest counsellors, returned severally what they thought. The first held that wine was strongest; another, that the king was strongest; but Zorobabel, prince of the captive Jews, and heir to the crown of Judah, being one of them, proved women to be stronger than the king, for that he himself had seen a concubine take his crown from off his head to set it upon her own; and others beside him have likewise seen the like feat done, and not in jest.   Yet he proved on, and it was so yielded by the king himself, and all his sages, that neither wine, nor women, nor the king, but truth of all other things was the strongest.

For me, though neither asked, nor in a nation that gives such rewards to wisdom, I shall pronounce my sentence somewhat different from Zorobabel; and shall defend that either truth and justice are all one (for truth is but justice in our knowledge, and justice is but truth in our practice); and he indeed so explains himself, in saying that with truth is no accepting of persons, which is the property of justice, or else if there be any odds, that justice, though not stronger than truth, yet by her office is to put forth and exhibit more strength in the affairs of mankind. For truth is properly no more than contemplation; and her utmost efficiency is but teaching: but justice in her very essence is all strength and activity; and hath a sword put into her hand, to use against all violence and oppression on the earth.   She it is most truly, who accepts no person, and exempts none from the severity of her stroke.   She never suffers injury to prevail, but when falsehood first prevails over truth; and that also is a kind of justice done on them who are so deluded.   Though wicked kings and tyrants counterfeit her sword, as some did that buckler fabled to fall from heaven into the capital, yet she communicates her power to none but such as, like herself, are just, or at least will do justice.   For it were extreme partiality and injustice, the flat denial and overthrow of herself, to put her own authentic sword into the hand of an unjust and wicked man, or so far to accept and exalt one mortal person above his equals, that he alone shall have the punishing of all other men transgressing, and not receive like punishment from men, when he himself shall be found the highest transgressor.

We may conclude, therefore, that justice, above all other things, is and ought to be the strongest; she is the strength, the kingdom, the power, and majesty of all ages.   Truth herself would subscribe to this, though Darius and all the monarchs of the world should deny.   And if by sentence thus written it were my happiness to set free the minds of Englishmen from longing to return poorly under that captivity of kings from which the strength and supreme sword of justice hath delivered them, I shall have done a work not much inferior to that of Zorobabel; who, by well-praising and extolling the force of truth, in that contemplative strength conquered Darius, and freed his country and the people of God from the captivity of Babylon.   Which I shall yet not despair to do, if they in this land, whose minds are yet captive, be but as ingenuous to acknowledge the strength and supremacy of justice, as that heathen king was to confess the strength of truth: or let them but, as he did, grant that, and they will soon perceive that truth resigns all her outward strength to justice: justice therefore must needs be strongest, both in her own, and in the strength of truth. But if a king may do among men whatsoever is his will and pleasure, and notwithstanding be unaccountable to men, then, contrary to his magnified wisdom of Zorobabel, neither truth nor justice, but the king, is strongest of all other things, which that Persian monarch himself, in the midst of all his pride and glory, durst not assume.

Let us see, therefore, what this king hath to affirm, why the sentence of justice, and the weight of that sword, which she delivers into the hands of men, should be more partial to him offending, than to all others of human race. First, he pleads that 'no law of God or man gives to subjects any power of judicature without or against him.' Which assertion shall be proved in every part to be most untrue. The first express law of God given to mankind was that to Noah, as a law, in general, to all the sons of men. And by that most ancient and universal law, 'Whosoever sheddeth man's blood, by man shall his blood be shed,' we find here no exception. If a king therefore do this, to a king, and that by men also, the same shall be done. This in the law of Moses, which came next, several times is repeated, and in one place remarkably, Numb. xxxv, 'Ye shall take no satisfaction for the like of a murderer, but he shall surely be put to death: the land cannot be cleansed of the blood that is shed therein, but by the blood of him that shed it.' This is so spoken as that which concerned all Israel, not one man alone, to see performed; and if no satisfaction were to be taken, then certainly no exception. Nay, the king, when they should set up any, was to observe the whole law, and not only to see it done, but to 'do it; that his heart might not be lifted up above his brethren'; to dream of vain and useless prerogatives or exemptions, whereby the law itself must needs be founded in unrighteousness.

And were that true, which is most false, that all kings are the Lord's anointed, it were yet absurd to think that the anointment of God should be, as it were, a charm against law, and give them privilege, who punish others, to sin themselves unpunishably. The high-priest was the Lord's anointed as well as any king, and with the same consecrated oil; yet Solomon had put to death Abiathar, had it not been for other respects than that anointed. If God himself say to kings, 'Touch not mine anointed,' meaning his chosen people, as is evident in that Psalm, yet no man will argue thence, that he protects them from civil laws if they offend; then certainly, though David, as a private man, and in his own cause, feared to lift his hand against the Lord's anointed, much less can this forbid the law, or disarm justice from having legal power against any king. No other supreme magistrate, in what kind of government soever, lays claim to any such enormous privilege; wherefore then should any king, who is but one kind of magistrate, and set over the people for no other end than they?

Next in order of time to the laws of Moses are those of Christ, who declares professedly his judicature to be spiritual, abstract from civil managements, and therefore leaves all nations to their own particular laws and way of government. Yet because the church hath a kind of jurisdiction within her own bounds, and that also, though in process of time much corrupted and plainly turned into a corporal judicature, yet much approved by this king; it will be firm enough and valid against him, if subjects, by the laws of church also, be 'invested with a power of judicature' both without and against their king, though pretending, and by them acknowledged, 'next and immediately under Christ supreme head and governor.' Theodosius, one of the best Christian emperors, having made a slaughter of the Thessalonians for sedition, but too cruelly, was excommunicated to his face by St Ambrose, who was his subject; and excommunion is the utmost of ecclesiastical judicature, a spiritual putting to death.

But this, ye will say, was only an example. Read then the story; and it will appear, both that Ambrose avouched it for the law of God, and Theodosius confessed it of his own accord to be so; 'and that the law of God was not to be made void in him, for any reverence to his imperial power.' From hence, not to be tedious, I shall pass into our own land of Britain; and show that subjects here have exercised the utmost of spiritual judicature, and more than spiritual, against their kings, his predecessors. Vortiger, for committing incest with his daughter, was by St German, at that time his subject, cursed and condemned in a British council, about the year 448; and thereupon soon after was deposed. Mauricus, a king in Wales, for breach of oath and murder of Cynetus, was excommunicated and cursed, with all his offspring, by Oudoceus, Bishop of Llandaff, in full synod, about the year 560, and not restored till he had repented. Morcant, another king in Wales, having slain Frioc his uncle, was fain to come in person and receive judgment from the same bishop and his clergy; who upon his penitence acquitted him, for no other cause than lest the kingdom should be destitute of a successor in the royal line.

These examples are of the primitive, British, and episcopal church; long ere they had any commerce or communion with the church of Rome. What power afterwards of deposed kings, and so consequently of putting them to death, was assumed and practised by the canon law, I omit, as a thing generally known. Certainly, if whole councils of the Romish church have in the midst of their dimness discerned so much of truth, as to decree at Constance, and at Basil, and many of them to avouch at Trent also, that a council is above the pope, and may judge him, though by them not denied to be the vicar of Christ; we in our clearer light may be ashamed not to discern further, that a parliament is by all equity and right above a king, and may judge him, whose reasons and pretensions to hold of God only, as his immediate vicegerent, we know how far-fetched they are, and insufficient.

As for the laws of man, it would ask a volume to repeat all that might be cited in this point against him from all antiquity. In Greece, Orestes, the son of Agamemnon, and by succession King of Argos, was in that country judged and condemned to death for killing his mother; whence escaping, he was judged again, though a stranger, before the great council of Areopagus in Athens. And this memorable act of judicature was the first that brought the justice of that grave senate into fame and high estimation over all Greece for many ages after. And in the same city tyrants were to undergo legal sentence by the laws of Solon.

The kings of Sparta, though descended lineally from Hercules, esteemed a god among them, were often judged, and sometimes put to death, by the most just and renowned laws of Lycurgus; who, though a king, thought it most unequal to bind his subjects by any law to which he bound not himself. In Rome, the laws made by Valerius Publicola, soon after the expelling of Tarquin and his race, expelled without a written law, the law being afterward written; and what the senate decreed against Nero, that he should be judged and punished according to the laws of their ancestors, and what in like manner was decreed against other emperors, is vulgarly known; as it was known to those heathen, and found just by nature ere any law mentioned it.

And that the Christian civil law warrants like power of judicature to subjects against tyrants, is written clearly by the best and famousest civilians. For if it was decreed by Theodosius, and stands yet firm in the code of Justinian, that the law is above the emperor, then certainly the emperor being under law, the law may judge him; and if judge him, may punish him, proving tyrannous: how else is the law above him, or to what purpose? These are necessary deductions; and thereafter hath been done in all ages and kingdoms, oftener than to be here recited.

But what need we any further search after the law of other lands, for that which is so fully and so plainly set down lawful in our own? Where ancient books tell us, Bracton, Fleta, and others, that the king is under law, and inferior to his court of parliament; that although his place 'to do juctice' be highest, yet that he stands as liable 'to receive justice' as the meanest of his kingdom. Nay, Alfred, the most worthy king, and by some accounted first absolute monarch of the Saxons here, so ordained; as is cited out of an ancient law-book called *The Mirror*; in *Rights of the Kingdom*, p. 31, where it is complained of, 'as the sovereign abuse of all,' that the king should be deemed above the law, whereas he ought to be subject to it by his oath. Of which oath anciently it was the last clause, that the king 'should be as liable, and obedient to suffer right, as others of his people.' And indeed it were but fond and senseless, that the king should be accountable to every petty suit in lesser courts as we all know he was, and not be subject to the judicature of parliament in the main matters of our common safety or destruction; that he should be answerable in the ordinary course of law for any wrong done to a private person, and not answerable in court of parliament for destroying the whole kingdom.

By all this, and much more that might be added, as in an argument over-copious rather than barren, we see it manifest that all laws, both of God and man, are made without exemption of any person whomsoever; and that if kings presume to overtop the law by which they reign for the public good, they are by law to be reduced into order; and that can no way be more justly, than by those who exalt them to that high place.   For who should better understand their own laws, and when they are transgressed, than they who are governed by them, and whose consent first made them? And who can have more right to take knowledge of things done within a free nation than they within themselves?

Those objected oaths of allegiance and supremacy we swore,

not to his person, but as it was invested with his authority; and his authority was by the people first given him conditionally, in law, and under law, and under oath also for the kingdom's good, and not otherwise; the oaths then were interchanged, and mutual; stood and fell together; he swore fidelity to his trust (not as a deluding ceremony, but as a real condition of their admitting him for king; and the Conqueror himself swore it oftener than at his crowning); they swore homage and fealty to his person in that trust. There was no reason why the kingdom should be further bound by oaths to him, than he by his coronation oath to us, which he hath every way broken: and having broken, the ancient crown oath of Alfred above mentioned conceals not his penalty.

As for the covenant, if that be meant, certainly no discreet person can imagine it should bind us to him in any stricter sense than those oaths formerly. The acts of hostility, which we received from him, were no such dear obligements, that we should owe him more fealty and defence for being our enemy, than we could before when we took him only for a king. They were accused by him and his party, to pretend liberty and reformation, but to have no other end than to make themselves great, and to destroy the king's person and authority. For which reason they added that third article, testifying to the world, that as they were resolved to endeavour first a reformation in the church, to extirpate prelacy, to preserve the rights of parliament, and the liberties of the kingdom, so they intended, so far as it might consist with the preservation and defence of these, to preserve the king's person and authority; but not otherwise. As far as this comes to, they covenant and swear in the sixth article to preserve and defend the persons and authority of one another, and all those that enter into that league; so that this covenant gives no unlimitable exemption to the king's person, but gives to all as much defence and preservation as to him, and to him as much as to their own persons, and no more; that is to say, in order and subordination to those main ends for which we live and are a nation of men joined in society either Christian, or, at least, human.

But if the covenant were made absolute, to preserve and defend any one whomsoever, without respect had, either to the true religion, or those other superior things to be defended and preserved however, it cannot then be doubted, but that the covenant was rather a most foolish, hasty, and unlawful vow, than a deliberate and well-weighed covenant; swearing us into labyrinths and repugnances, no way to be solved or reconciled, and therefore no way to be kept; as first offending against the law of God, to vow the absolute preservation, defence, and maintaining of one man, though in his sins and offences never so great and heinous against God or his neighbour; and to except a person from justice, whereas his law excepts none.   Secondly, it offends against the law of this nation, wherein, as hath been proved, kings in receiving justice, and undergoing due trial, are not differenced from the meanest subject.

Lastly, it contradicts and offends against the covenant itself, which vows in the fourth article to bring to open trial and condign punishment all those that shall be found guilty of such crimes and delinquencies, whereof the king, by his own letters, and other undeniable testimonies not brought to light till afterward, was found and convicted to be chief actor in what they thought him, at the time of taking that covenant, to be overruled only by evil counsellors; and those, or whomsoever they should discover to be principal, they vowed to try, either by their own 'supreme judicatories' (for so even then they called them), 'or by others having power from them to that effect.' So that to have brought the king to condign punishment hath not broke the covenant, but it would have broke the covenant to have saved him from those judicatories, which both nations declared in that covenant to be supreme against any person whatsoever.

And besides all this, to swear in covenant the bringing of his evil counsellors and accomplices to condign punishment, and not only to leave unpunished and untouched the grand offender, but to receive him back again from the accomplishment of so many violences and mischiefs, dipped from head to foot and stained over with the blood of thousands that were his faithful subjects, forced to their own defence against a civil war by him first raised upon them; and to receive him thus, in this gory pickle, to all his dignities and honours, covering the ignominious and horrid purple robe of innocent blood, that sat so close about him, with the glorious purple of royalty and supreme rule, the reward of highest excellence and virtue here on earth, were not only to swear and covenant the performance of an unjust vow, the strangest and most impious to the face of God, but were the most unwise and unprudential act as to civil government.

For so long as a king shall find by experience that, do the worst he can, his subjects, overawed by the religion of their own covenant, will only prosecute his evil instruments, nor dare to touch his person; and that whatever hath been on his part offended or transgressed, he shall come off at last with the same reverence to his person, and the same honour as for well doing, he will not fail to find them work; seeking far and near, and inviting to his court all the concourse of evil counsellors, or agents, that may be found: who, tempted with preferments and his promise to uphold them, will hazard easily their own heads, and the chance of ten to one but they shall prevail at last over men so quelled and fitted to be slaves by the false conceit of a religious covenant. And they in that superstition neither wholly yielding, nor to the utmost resisting, at the upshot of all their foolish war and expense, will find to have done no more but fetched a compass only of their miseries, ending at the same point of slavery, and in the same distractions wherein they first began.

But when kings themselves are made as liable to punishment as their evil counsellors, it will be both as dangerous from the king himself as from his parliament, to those that evil counsel him: and they, who else would be his readiest agents in evil, will then not fear to dissuade or to disobey him, not only in respect of themselves and their own lives, which for his sake they would not seem to value, but in respect of that danger which the king himself may incur, whom they would seem to love and serve with greatest fidelity. On all these grounds therefore of the covenant itself, whether religious or political, it appears likeliest, that both the English parliament and the Scotch commissioners, thus interpreting the covenant (as indeed at that time they were the best and most authentical interpreters joined together), answered the king unanimously, in their letter dated 13th January, 1645, that till security and satisfaction first given to both kingdoms for the blood spilled, for the Irish rebels brought over, and for the war in Ireland by him fomented, they could in nowise yield their consent to his return.

Here was satisfaction, full two years and upward after the covenant taken, demanded of the king by both nations in parliament for crimes at least capital, wherewith they charged him. And what satisfaction could be given for so much blood, but justice upon him that spilled it? till which done, they neither took themselves bound to grant him the exercise of his regal office by any meaning of the covenant which they then declared (though other meanings have been since contrived), nor so much regarded the safety of his person, as to admit of his return among them from the midst of those whom they declared to be his greatest enemies; nay, from himself as from an actual enemy, not as from a king, they demanded security. But if the covenant, all this notwithstanding, swore otherwise to preserve him than in the preservation of true religion and our liberties, against which he fought, if not in arms, yet in resolution, to his dying day, and now after death still fights again in this his book, the covenant was better broken, than he saved. And God hath testified by all propitious and the most evident signs, whereby in these latter times he is wont to testify what pleases him, that such a solemn and for many ages unexampled act of due punishment was no mockery of justice, but a most grateful and well-pleasing sacrifice. Neither was it to cover their perjury, as he accuses, but to uncover his perjury to the oath of his coronation.

The rest of his discourse quite forgets the title; and turns his meditations upon death into obloquy and bitter vehemence against his 'judges and accusers'; imitating therein, not our Saviour, but his grandmother, Mary Queen of Scots, as also in the most of his other scruples, exceptions, and evasions; and from whom he seems to have learnt, as it were by heart, or else by kind, that which is thought by his admirers to be the most virtuous, most manly, most Christian, and most martyr-like, both of his words and speeches here, and of his answers and behaviour at his trial.

'It is a sad fate,' he saith, 'to have his enemies both accusers, parties, and judges.' Sad indeed, but no sufficient plea to acquit him from being so judged. For what malefactor might not sometimes plead the like? If his own crimes have made all men his enemies, who else can judge him? They of the powder-plot against his father might as well have pleaded the same. Nay, at the resurrection it may as well be pleaded, that the saints, who then shall judge the world, are 'both enemies, judges, parties, and accusers.'

So much he thinks to abound in his own defence, that he undertakes an unmeasurable task, to bespeak 'the singular care and protection of God over all kings,' as being the greatest patrons of law, justice, order, and religion on earth. But what patrons they be, God in the Scripture oft enough hath expressed; and the earth itself hath too long groaned under the burden of their injustice, disorder, and irreligion. Therefore 'to bind their kings in chains, and their nobles with links of iron,' is an honour belonging to his saints; not to build Babel (which was Nimrod's work, the first king, and the beginning of his kingdom was

Babel) but to destroy it, especially that spiritual Babel: and first to overcome those European kings, which receive their power, not from God, but from the beast; and are counted no better than his ten horns. 'These shall hate the great whore,' and yet 'shall give their kingdoms to the beast that carries her; they shall commit fornication with her,' and yet 'shall burn her with fire,' and yet 'shall lament the fall of Babylon,' where they fornicated with her. Rev. xvii, xviii.

Thus shall they be to and fro, doubtful and ambiguous in all their doings, until at last, 'joining their armies with the beast,' whose power first raised them, they shall perish with him by the 'King of kings,' against whom they have rebelled; and 'the fowls shall eat their flesh.' This is their doom written, Rev. xix, and the utmost that we find concerning them in these latter days; which we have much more cause to believe, than his unwarranted revelation here, prophesying what shall follow after his death, with the spirit of enmity, not of St John.

He would fain bring us out of conceit with the good success which God vouchsafed us. We measure not our cause by our success, but our success by our cause. Yet certainly in a good cause success is a good confirmation; for God hath promised it to good men almost in every leaf of scripture. If it argue not for us, we are sure it argues not against us; but as much more or for us, than ill success argues for them; for to the wicked God hath denounced ill success in all they take in hand.

He hopes much of those 'softer tempers,' as he calls them, and 'less advantaged by his ruin, that their consciences do already' gripe them. It is true, there be a sort of moody, hotbrained, and always unedified consciences; apt to engage their leaders into great and dangerous affairs past retirement, and then upon a sudden qualm and swimming of their conscience, to betray them basely in the midst of what was chiefly undertaken for their sakes. Let such men never meet with any faithful parliament to hazard for them; never with any noble spirit to conduct and lead them out: but let them live and die in servile condition and their scrupulous queasiness, if no instruction will confirm them! Others there be, in whose consciences the loss of gain, and those advantages they hoped for, hath sprung a sudden leak. These are they that cry out, 'The covenant broken!' and, to keep it better, slide back into neutrality, or join actually with incendiaries and malignants. But God hath eminently begun to punish those, first in Scotland, then in Ulster, who have provoked him with the most hateful kind of mockery, to break his covenant under pretence of strictest keeping it; and hath subjected them to those malignants with whom they scrupled not to be associates. In God therefore we shall not fear what their false fraternity can do against us.

He seeks again with cunning words to turn our success into our sin: but might call to mind, that the scripture speaks of those also, who 'when God slew them, then sought him'; yet did but 'flatter him with their mouth, and lied to him with their tongues; for their heart was not right with him.' And there was one who in the time of his affliction trespassed more against God. This was that king Ahaz.

He glories much in the forgiveness of his enemies; so did his grandmother at her death. Wise men would sooner have believed him, had he not so often told us so. But he hopes to erect 'the trophies of his charity over us.' And trophies of charity no doubt will be as glorious as trumpets before the alms of hypocrites; and more especially the trophies of such an aspiring charity, as offers in his prayer to share victory with God's compassion, which is over all his works. Such prayers as these may haply catch the people, as was intended: but how they please God is to be much doubted, though prayed in secret, much less written to be divulged. Which perhaps may gain him after death a short, contemptible, and soon fading reward; not what he aims at, to stir the constancy and solid firmness of any wise man, or to unsettle the conscience of any knowing Christian (if he could ever aim at a thing so hopeless, and above the genius of his cleric elocution), but to catch the worthless approbation of an inconstant, irrational, and image-doting rabble; that like a credulous and hapless herd, begotten to servility, and enchanted with these popular institutes of tyranny, subscribed with a new device of the king's picture at his prayers, hold out both their ears with such delight and ravishment to be stigmatized and bored through, in witness of their own voluntary and beloved baseness. The rest, whom perhaps ignorance without malice, or some error, less than fatal, hath for the time misled, on this side sorcery or obduration, may find the grace and good guidance to bethink themselves and recover.

THE READY AND EASY WAY

TO ESTABLISH

A FREE COMMONWEALTH

AND THE EXCELLENCE THEREOF

COMPARED WITH THE INCONVENIENCES AND DANGERS

OF RE-ADMITTING KINGSHIP IN THIS NATION

————————Et nos
Consilium dedimus Syllae, demus populo nunc.

In February 1660 General Monk forced the Rump Parliament to readmit those Members who had been 'purged' by Colonel Pride in 1648. It was clear to Milton that there was grave danger of a restoration of the monarchy in the person of Charles II. In spite of the possible consequences to himself, Milton published in March a political pamphlet advocating the setting up of a perpetual grand council to rule England as a republic. The preservation of the commonwealth achieved by years of civil war seemed to Milton of the first importance, since a free commonwealth was the surest means of promoting 'due liberty . . . both human, civil, and Christian.' In his commonwealth, the elective council was to consist of the ablest men in the country. A check on the council was to be provided by local assemblies federated to the main council. 'To make the people fittest to choose, and the chosen fittest to govern, will be to mend our corrupt and faulty education, to teach the people faith, not without virtue, temperance, modesty, sobriety, parsimony, justice; not to admire wealth or honour; to hate turbulence and ambition; to place every one his private welfare and happiness in the public peace, liberty, and safety.' Milton's commonwealth was intended to breed citizens who were complete and integrated human beings, living in a Christian society.

The text of the pamphlet is taken from the second edition, revised by Milton to meet criticisms of the first. It was published in April, only a month before the return of Charles II to England.

ALTHOUGH, since the writing of this treatise, the face of things hath had some change, writs for new elections have been recalled, and the members at first chosen readmitted from exclusion; yet not a little rejoicing to hear declared the resolution of those who are in power, tending to the establishment of a free commonwealth, and to remove, if it be possible, this noxious humour of returning to bondage, instilled of late by some deceivers, and nourished from bad principles and false apprehensions among too many of the people; I thought best not to suppress what I had written, hoping that it may now be of much more use and concernment to be freely published, in the midst of our elections to a free parliament, or their sitting to consider freely of the government; whom it behoves it have all things represented to them that may direct their judgment therein; and I never read of any state, scarce of any tyrant, grown so incurable, as to refuse counsel from any in a time of public deliberation, much less to be offended. If their absolute determination be to enthral us, before so long a Lent of servitude, they may permit us a little shroving-time first, wherein to speak freely, and take our leaves of liberty. And because in the former edition, through haste, many faults escaped, and many books were suddenly dispersed, ere the note to mend them could be sent, I took the opportunity from this occasion to revise and somewhat to enlarge the whole discourse, especially that part which argues for a perpetual senate. The treatise thus revised and enlarged, is as follows:

The Parliament of England, assisted by a great number of the people who appeared and stuck to them faithfulest in defence of religion and their civil liberties, judging kingship by long experience a government unnecessary, burdensome, and dangerous, justly and magnanimously abolished it, turning regal bondage into a free commonwealth, to the admiration and terror of our emulous neighbours. They took themselves not bound by the light of nature or religion to any former covenant, from which the king himself, by many forfeitures of a latter date or discovery, and our own longer consideration thereon, had more and more unbound us, both to himself and his posterity; as hath been ever the justice and the prudence of all wise nations that have ejected tyranny. They covenanted 'to preserve the king's person and authority, in the preservation of the true religion, and our liberties'; not in his endeavouring to bring in upon our consciences a popish religion; upon our liberties, thraldom; upon our lives, destruction, by his occasioning, if not complotting, as was after discovered, the Irish massacre; his fomenting and arming the rebellion; his covert leaguing with the rebels against us; his refusing, more than seven times, propositions most just and necessary to the true religion and our liberties, tendered him by the parliament both of England

and Scotland. They made not their covenant concerning him with no difference between a king and a God; or promised him, as Job did to the Almighty, 'to trust in him though he slay us': they understood that the solemn engagement, wherein we all forswore kingship, was no more a breach of the covenant, than the covenant was of the protestation before, but a faithful and prudent going on both in words well weighed, and in the true sense of the covenant 'without respect of persons,' when we could not serve two contrary masters, God and the king, or the king and that more supreme law, sworn in the first place to maintain our safety and our liberty. They knew the people of England to be a free people, themselves the representers of that freedom; and although many were excluded, and as many fled (so they pretended) from tumults to Oxford, yet they were left a sufficient number to act in parliament, therefore not bound by any statute of preceding parliaments, but by the law of nature only, which is the only law of laws truly and properly to all mankind fundamental; the beginning and the end of all government; to which no parliament or people that will throughly reform, but may and must have recourse, as they had, and must yet have, in church reformation (if they throughly intend it) to evangelic rules; not to ecclesiastical canons, though never so ancient, so ratified and established in the land by statutes which for the most part are mere positive laws, neither natural nor moral: and so by any parliament, for just and serious consideration, without scruple to be at any time repealed.

If others of their number in these things were under force, they were not, but under free conscience; if others were excluded by a power which they could not resist, they were not therefore to leave the helm of government in no hands, to discontinue their care of the public peace and safety, to desert the people in anarchy and confusion, no more than when so many of their members left them, as made up in outward formality a more legal parliament of three estates against them. The best affected also, and best principled of the people, stood not numbering or computing, on which side were most voices in parliament, but on which side appeared to them most reason, most safety, when the house divided upon main matters. What was well mentioned and advised, they examined not whether fear or persuasion carried it in the vote, neither did they measure votes and counsels by the intentions of them that voted; knowing that intentions either are but guessed at, or not soon enough known; and although good, can neither make the deed such, nor prevent the consequence from being bad. Suppose bad intentions in things otherwise well done; what was well done, was by them who so thought, not the less obeyed or followed in the state; since in the church, who had not rather follow Iscariot or Simon, the magician, though to covetous ends, preaching, than Saul, though in the uprightness of his heart persecuting the gospel?

Safer they, therefore, judged what they thought the better counsels, though carried on by some perhaps to bad ends, than the worse by others, though endeavoured with best intentions. And yet they were not to learn that a greater number might be corrupt within the walls of a parliament, as well as of a city; whereof in matters of nearest concernment all men will be judges; nor easily permit that the odds of voices in their greatest council shall more endanger them by corrupt or credulous votes, than the odds of enemies by open assaults; judging that most voices ought not always to prevail, where main matters are in question. If others hence will pretend to disturb all counsels; what is that to them who pretend not, but are in real danger; not they only so judging, but a great, though not the greatest number of their chosen patriots, who might be more in weight than the others in numbers: there being in number little virtue, but by weight and measure wisdom working all things, and the dangers on either side they seriously thus weighed?

From the treaty, short fruits of long labours, and seven years' war; security for twenty years, if we can hold it; reformation in the church for three years: then put to shift again with our vanquished master. His justice, his honour, his conscience declared quite contrary to ours which would have furnished him with many such evasions, as in a book entitled *An Inquisition for Blood*, soon after were not concealed: bishops not totally removed, but left, as it were, in ambush, a reserve, with ordination in their sole power; their lands already sold, not to be alienated, but rented, and the sale of them called 'sacrilege'; delinquents, few of many brought to condign punishment; accessories punished, the chief author, above pardon, though, after utmost resistance, vanquished; not to give, but to receive, laws; yet besought, treated with, and to be thanked for his gracious concessions, to be honoured, worshipped, glorified.

If this we swore to do, with what righteousness in the sight of God, with what assurance that we bring by such an oath, the whole sea of blood-guiltiness upon our heads? If on the other side we prefer a free government, though for the present not obtained, yet all those suggested fears and difficulties, as the event will prove, easily overcome, we remain finally secure from the exasperated regal power, and out of snares; shall retain the best part of our liberty, which is our religion, and the civil part will be from these who defer us, much more easily recovered, being neither so subtle nor so awful as a king re-inthroned.   Nor were their actions less both at home and abroad, than might become the hopes of a glorious rising commonwealth: nor were the expressions both of army and people, whether in their public declarations or several writings, other than such as testified a spirit in this nation, no less noble and well-fitted to the liberty of a commonwealth, than in the ancient Greeks or Romans.   Nor was the heroic cause unsuccessfully defended to all Christendom, against the tongue of a famous and thought invincible adversary; nor the constancy and fortitude, that so nobly vindicated our liberty, our victory at once against two the most prevailing usurpers over mankind, superstition and tyranny, unpraised or uncelebrated in a written monument, likely to outlive detraction, as it hath hitherto convinced or silenced not a few of our detractors, especially in parts abroad.

After our liberty and religion thus prosperously fought for, gained, and many years possessed, except in those unhappy interruptions, which God hath removed; now that nothing remains, but in all reason the certain hopes of a speedy and immediate settlement for ever in a firm and free common-wealth, for this extolled and magnified nation, regardless both of honour won, or deliverances vouchsafed from heaven, to fall back, or rather to creep back so poorly, as it seems the multitude would, to their once abjured and detested thraldom of kingship, to be ourselves the slanderers of our own just and religious deeds, though done by some to covetous and ambitious ends, yet not therefore to be stained with their infamy, or they to asperse the integrity of others; and yet these now by revolting from the conscience of deeds well done, both in church and state, to throw away and forsake, or rather to betray a just and noble cause for the mixture of bad men who have ill-managed and abused it (which had our fathers done heretofore, and on the same pretence deserted true religion, what had long ere this become of our gospel, and all protestant reformation so much intermixed with the avarice and ambition of some reformers?), and by thus relapsing, to verify all the bitter predictions, of our triumphing enemies, who will now think they wisely discerned and justly

censured both us and all our actions as rash, rebellious, hypocritical, and impious; not only argues a strange, degenerate
contagion suddenly spread among us, fitted and prepared for
new slavery, but will render us a scorn and derision to all our
neighbours.

And what will they at best say of us, and of the whole English
name, but scoffingly, as of that foolish builder mentioned by
our Saviour, who began to build a tower, and was not able to
finish it? Where is this goodly tower of a commonwealth, which
the English boasted they would build to overthrow kings, and
be another Rome in the west? The foundation indeed they lay
gallantly, but fell into a worse confusion, not of tongues, but of
factions, than those at the tower of Babel; and have left no
memorial of their work behind them remaining but in the common laughter of Europe. Which must needs redound the more
to our shame, if we but look on our neighbours the United
Provinces, to us inferior in all outward advantages; who notwithstanding, in the midst of greater difficulties, courageously,
wisely, constantly, went through with the same work, and are
settled in all the happy enjoyments of a potent and flourishing
republic to this day.

Besides this, if we return to kingship, and soon repent (as
undoubtedly we shall, when we begin to find the old encroachment coming on by little and little upon our consciences, which
must necessarily proceed from king and bishop united inseparably in one interest), we may be forced perhaps to fight over
again all that we have fought, and spend over again all that we
have spent. but are never like to attain thus far as we are now
advanced to the recovery of our freedom, never to have it in
possession as we now have it, never to be vouchsafed hereafter the like mercies and signal assistances from Heaven in our
cause, if by our ingrateful backsliding we make these fruitless;
flying now to regal concessions from his divine condescensions
and gracious answers to our once importuning prayers against
the tyranny which we then groaned under; making vain and
viler than dirt the blood of so many thousand faithful and
valiant Englishmen, who left us in this liberty, bought with
their lives; losing by a strange after-game of folly all the battles
we have won, together with all Scotland as to our conquest,
hereby lost, which never any of our kings could conquer, all the
treasure we have spent, not that corruptible treasure only, but
that far more precious of all our late miraculous deliverances;
treading back again with lost labour all our happy steps in the

progress of reformation, and most pitifully depriving ourselves the instant fruition of that free government, which we have so dearly purchased, a free commonwealth, not only held by wisest men in all ages the noblest, the manliest, the equallest, the justest government, the most agreeable to all due liberty and proportioned equality, both human, civil, and Christian, most cherishing to virtue and true religion, but also (I may say it with greatest probability) plainly commended, or rather enjoined by our Saviour himself, to all Christians, not without remarkable disallowance, and the brand of Gentilism upon kingship.

God in much displeasure gave a king to the Israelites, and imputed it a sin to them that they sought one; but Christ apparently forbids his disciples to admit of any such heathenish government: 'The kings of the Gentiles,' saith he, 'exercise lordship over them,' and they that 'exercise authority upon them are called benefactors: but ye shall not be so; but he that is greatest among you, let him be as the younger; and he that is chief, as he that serveth.' The occasion of these his words was the ambitious desire of Zebedee's two sons to be exalted above their brethren in his kingdom, which they thought was to be ere long upon earth. That he speaks of civil government, is manifest by the former part of the comparison, which infers the other part to be always in the same kind. And what government comes nearer to this precept of Christ, than a free commonwealth; wherein they who are the greatest, are perpetual servants and drudges to the public at their own cost and charges, neglect their own affairs, yet are not elevated above their brethren; live soberly in their families, walk the street as other men, may be spoken to freely, familiarly, friendly, without adoration? Whereas a king must be adored like a demigod, with a dissolute and haughty court about him, of vast expense and luxury, masks and revels, to the debauching of our prime gentry, both male and female; not in their pastimes only, but in earnest, by the loose employments of court-service, which will be then thought honourable. There will be a queen of no less charge; in most likelihood outlandish and a papist; besides a queen-mother such already; together with both their courts and numerous train: then a royal issue, and ere long severally their sumptuous courts; to the multiplying of a servile crew, not of servants only, but of nobility and gentry, bred up then to the hopes not of public, but of court offices, to be stewards, chamberlains, ushers, grooms even of the close-stool; and the lower their minds debased with court-opinions, contrary to all virtue and reformation, the haughtier will be their pride and profuseness. We may well remember this not long since at home; nor need but look at present into the French court, where enticements and preferments daily draw away and pervert the protestant nobility.

As to the burden of expense, to our cost we shall soon know it; for any good to us deserving to be termed no better than the vast and lavish price of our subjection, and their debauchery, which we are now so greedily cheapening, and would so fain be paying most inconsiderately to a single person: who, for anything wherein the public really needs him, will have little else to do, but to bestow the eating and drinking of excessive dainties, to set a pompous face upon the superficial actings of state, to pageant himself up and down in progress among the perpetual bowings and cringings of an abject people, on either side deifying and adoring him for nothing done that can deserve it. For what can he more than another man? who, even in the expression of a late court-poet, sits only like a great cipher set to no purpose before a long row of other significant figures. Nay, it is well and happy for the people, if their king be but a cipher, being ofttimes a mischief, a pest, a scourge of the nation, and, which is worse, not to be removed, not to be controlled, much less accused or brought to punishment, without the danger of a common ruin, without the shaking and almost subversion of the whole land: whereas in a free commonwealth, any governor or chief counsellor offending may be removed and punished, without the least commotion.

Certainly then that people must needs be mad or strangely infatuated, that build the chief hope of their common happiness or safety on a single person; who, if he happen to be good, can do no more than another man; if to be bad, hath in his hands to do more evil without check, than millions of other men. The happiness of a nation must needs be firmest and certainest in full and free council of their own electing, where no single person, but reason only, sways. And what madness is it for them who might manage nobly their own affairs themselves, sluggishly and weakly to devolve all on a single person; and, more like boys under age than men, to commit all to his patronage and disposal, who neither can perform what he undertakes; and yet for undertaking it, though royally paid, will not be their servant, but their lord! How unmanly must it needs be, to count such a one the breath of our nostrils, to hang all our felicity on him, all our safety, our well-bring, for which if we were aught else but sluggards or babies, we need depend on none but God and our own counsels, our own active virtue and industry! 'Go to the ant, thou sluggard,' saith Solomon; 'consider her ways, and be wise; which having no prince, ruler, or lord, provides her meat in the summer, and gathers her food in the harvest': which evidently shows us, that they who think the nation undone without a king, though they look grave or haughty, have not so much true spirit and understanding in them as a pismire; neither are these diligent creatures hence concluded to live in lawless anarchy, or that commended; but are set the examples to imprudent and ungoverned men, of a frugal and self-governing democracy or commonwealth: safer and more thriving in the joint providence and counsel of many industrious equals than under the single domination of one imperious lord.

It may be well wondered that any nation, styling themselves free, can suffer any man to pretend hereditary right over them as their lord; whenas, by acknowledging that right, they conclude themselves his servants and his vassals, and so renounce their own freedom. Which how a people and their leaders especially can do, who have fought so gloriously for liberty; how they can change their noble words and actions, heretofore so becoming the majesty of a free people, into the base necessity of court flatteries and prostrations, is not only strange and admirable, but lamentable to think on. That a nation should be so valorous and courageous to win their liberty in the field, and when they have won it, should be so heartless and unwise in their counsels, as not to know how to use it, value it, what to do with it, or with themselves; but after ten or twelve years' prosperous war and contestation with tyranny, basely and besottedly to run their necks again into the yoke which they have broken, and prostrate all the fruits of their victory for nought at the feet of the vanquished, besides our loss of glory, and such an example as kings or tyrants never yet had the like to boast of, will be an ignominy if it befall us, that never yet befell any nation possessed of their liberty; worthy indeed themselves, whatsoever they be, to be for ever slaves, but that part of the nation which consents not with them, as I persuade me of a great number, far worthier than by their means to be brought into the same bondage.

Considering these things so plain, so rational, I cannot but yet further admire on the other side, how any man, who hath the true principles of justice and religion in him, can presume or take upon him to be a king and lord over his brethren, whom he cannot but know, whether as men or Christians, to be for the most part every way equal or superior to himself: how he can display with such vanity and ostentation his regal splendour, so supereminently above other mortal men; or, being a Christian, can assume such extraordinary honour and worship to himself, while the kingdom of Christ, our common king and lord, is hid to this world, and such gentilish imitation forbid in express words by himself to all his disciples. All protestants hold that Christ in his church hath left no vicegerent of his power; but himself, without deputy, is the only head thereof governing it from heaven: how then can any Christian man derive his king-ship from Christ, but with worse usurpation than the pope his headship over the church, since Christ not only hath not left the least shadow of a command for any such vicegerence from him in the state, as the pope pretends for his in the church, but hath expressly declared that such regal dominion is from the gentiles, not from him, and hath strictly charged us not to imitate them therein?

I doubt not but all ingenuous and knowing men will easily agree with me, that a free commonwealth without single person or house of lords is by far the best government, if it can be had; but we have all this while, say they, been expecting it, and cannot yet attain it. It is true, indeed, when monarchy was dissolved, the form of a commonwealth should have forthwith been framed, and the practice thereof immediately begun; that the people might have soon been satisfied and delighted with the decent order, ease, and benefit thereof; we had been then by this time firmly rooted, past fear of commotions or mutations, and now flourishing; this care of timely settling a new government instead of the old, too much neglected, hath been our mischief. Yet the cause thereof may be ascribed with most reason to the frequent disturbances, interruptions, and dissolutions, which the parliament hath had, partly from the impatient or disaffected people, partly from some ambitious leaders in the army; much contrary, I believe, to the mind and approbation of the army itself, and their other commanders, once undeceived, or in their own power.

Now is the opportunity, now the very season, wherein we may obtain a free commonwealth, and establish it for ever in the land, without difficulty or much delay. Writs are sent out for elections, and, which is worth observing, in the name, not of any king, but of the keepers of our liberty, to summon a free parliament: which then only will indeed be free; and deserve the true honour of that supreme title, if they preserve us a free people. Which never parliament was more free to do, being now called not as heretofore, by the summons of a king, but by the voice of liberty. And if the people, laying aside prejudice and impatience, will seriously and calmly now consider their own good, both religious and civil, their own liberty and the only means thereof, as shall be here laid down before them, and will elect their knights and burgesses able men, and according to the just and necessary qualifications (which, for aught I hear, remain yet in force unrepealed, as they were formerly decreed in parliament), men not addicted to a single person or house of lords, the work is done; at least the foundation firmly laid of a free commonwealth, and good part also erected of the main structure. For the ground and basis of every just and free government (since men have smarted so oft for committing all to one person), is a general council of ablest men, chosen by the people to consult of public affairs from time to time for the common good. In this grand council must the sovereignty, not transferred, but delegated only, and as it were deposited, reside; with this caution, they must have the forces by sea and land committed to them for preservation of the common peace and liberty; must raise and manage the public revenue, at least with some inspectors deputed for satisfaction of the people, how it is employed; must make or propose, as more expressly shall be said anon, civil laws, treat of commerce, peace or war with foreign nations; and, for the carrying on some particular affairs with more secrecy and expedition, must elect, as they have already out of their own number and others, a council of state.

And, although it may seem strange at first hearing, by reason that men's minds are prepossessed with the notion of successive parliaments, I affirm, that the grand or general council, being well chosen, should be perpetual: for so their business is or may be, and ofttimes urgent; the opportunity of affairs gained or lost in a moment. The day of council cannot be set as the day of a festival; but must be ready always to prevent or answer all occasions. By this continuance they will become every way skilfullest, best provided of intelligence from abroad, best acquainted with the people at home, and the people with them. The ship of the commonwealth is always under sail; they sit at the stern, and if they steer well, what need is there to change them, it being rather dangerous? Add to this, that the grand council is both foundation and main pillar of the whole state;

and to move pillars and foundations, not faulty, cannot be safe for the building.

I see not, therefore, how we can be advantaged by successive and transitory parliaments; but that they are much likelier continually to unsettle rather than to settle a free government, to breed commotions, changes, novelties, and uncertainties, to bring neglect upon present affairs and opportunities, while all minds are in suspense with expectation of a new assembly, and the assembly, for a good space, taken up with the new settling of itself. After which, if they find no great work to do, they will make it, by altering or repealing former acts, or making and multiplying new; that they may seem to see what their predecessors saw not, and not to have assembled for nothing; till all law be lost in the multitude of clashing statutes. But if the ambition of such as think themselves injured, that they also partake not of the government, and are impatient till they be chosen, cannot brook the perpetuity of others chosen before them; or if it be feared, that long continuance of power may corrupt sincerest men, the known expedient is, and by some lately propounded, that annually (or if the space be longer, so much perhaps the better) the third part of senators may go out according to the precedence of their election, and the like number be chosen in their places, to prevent their settling of too absolute a power, if it should be perpetual: and this they call 'partial rotation.'

But I could wish, that this wheel, or partial wheel in state, if it be possible, might be avoided, as having too much affinity with the wheel of Fortune. For it appears not how this can be done, without danger and mischance of putting out a great number of the best and ablest: in whose stead new elections may bring in as many raw, unexperienced, and otherwise affected, to the weakening and much altering for the worse of public transactions. Neither do I think a perpetual senate, especially chosen or entrusted by the people, much in this land to be feared, where the well-affected, either in a standing army, or in a settled militia, have their arms in their own hands. Safest therefore to me it seems, and of least hazard or interruption to affairs, that none of the grand council be moved, unless by death, or just conviction of some crime: for what can be expected firm or steadfast from a floating foundation? However, I forejudge not any probable expedient, any temperament that can be found in things of this nature, so disputable on either side.

Yet lest this which I affirm be thought my single opinion, I shall add sufficient testimony. Kingship itself is therefore counted the more safe and durable because the king, and for the most part his council, is not changed during life. But a commonwealth is held immortal, and therein firmest, safest, and most above fortune; for the death of a king causeth oft-times many dangerous alterations; but the death now and then of a senator is not felt, the main body of them still continuing permanent in greatest and noblest commonwealths and as it were eternal. Therefore among the Jews, the supreme council of seventy, called the Sanhedrim, founded by Moses, in Athens that of Areopagus, in Sparta that of the ancients, in Rome the senate, consisted of members chosen for term of life; and by that means remained as it were still the same to generations. In Venice they change indeed oftener than every year some particular council of state, as that of six, or such other: but the true senate, which upholds and sustains the government, is the whole aristocracy immovable. So in the United Provinces, the states-general, which are indeed but a council of state deputed by the whole union, are not usually the same persons for above three or six years; but the states of every city, in whom the sovereignty hath been placed time out of mind, are a standing senate, without succession, and accounted chiefly in that regard the main prop of their liberty. And why they should be so in every well-ordered commonwealth, they who write of policy give these reasons: That to make the senate successive, not only impairs the dignity and lustre of the senate, but weakens the whole commonwealth, and brings it into manifest danger; while by this means the secrets of state are frequently divulged, and matters of greatest consequence committed to inexpert and novice counsellors, utterly to seek in the full and intimate knowledge of affairs past.

I know not therefore what should be peculiar in England, to make successive parliament thought safest or convenient here more than in other nations, unless it be the fickleness which is attributed to us as we are islanders. But good education and acquisite wisdom ought to correct the fluxible fault, if any such be, of our watery situation. It will be objected, that in those places where they had perpetual senates, they had also popular remedies against their growing too imperious: as in Athens, besides Areopagus, another senate of four or five hundred; in Sparta, the Ephori; in Rome, the tribunes of the people. But the event tells us, that these remedies either little availed the people, or brought them to such a licentious and unbridled democracy, as in fine ruined themselves with their own excessive power. So that the main reason urged why popular assemblies are to be trusted with the people's liberty, rather than a senate of principal men, because great men will be still endeavouring to enlarge their power, but the common sort will be contented to maintain their own liberty, is by experience found false; none being more immoderate and ambitious to amplify their power, than such popularities which were seen in the people of Rome; who, at first contented to have their tribunes, at length contended with the senate that one consul, then both; soon after, that the censors and praetors also should be created plebeian, and the whole empire put into their hands; adoring lastly those who most were adverse to the senate, till Marius, by fulfilling their inordinate desires, quite lost them all the power for which they had so long been striving, and left them under the tyranny of Sylla. The balance therefore must be exactly so set, as to preserve and keep up due authority on either side, as well in the senate as in the people. And this annual rotation of a senate to consist of three hundred, as is lately propounded, requires also another popular assembly upward of a thousand, with an answerable rotation. Which, besides that it will be liable to all those inconveniences found in the aforesaid remedies, cannot but be troublesome and chargeable, both in their motion and their session, to the whole land, unwieldy with their own bulk, unable in so great a number to mature their consultations as they ought, if any be allotted them, and that they meet not from so many parts remote to sit a whole year lieger in one place, only now and then to hold up a forest of fingers, or to convey each man his bean or ballot into the box, without reason shown or common deliberation; incontinent of secrets, if any be imparted to them; emulous and always jarring with the other senate. The much better way doubtless will be, in this wavering condition of our affairs, to defer the changing or circumscribing of our senate, more than may be done with ease, till the commonwealth be thoroughly settled in peace and safety, and they themselves give us the occasion.

Military men hold it dangerous to change the form of battle in view of an enemy: neither did the people of Rome bandy with their senate, while any of the Tarquins lived, the enemies of their liberty; nor sought, by creating tribunes, to defend themselves against the fear of their patricians, till, sixteen years after the expulsion of their kings, and in full security of their state, they had or thought they had just cause given them by the senate. Another way will be, to well qualify and refine elections: not committing all to the noise and shouting of a rude multitude, but permitting only those of them who are rightly qualified, to nominate as many as they will; and out of that number others of a better breeding, to choose a less number more judiciously, till after a third or fourth sifting and refining of exactest choice, they only be left chosen who are the due number, and seem by most voices the worthiest.

To make the people fittest to choose, and the chosen fittest to govern, will be to mend our corrupt and faulty education, to teach the people faith, not without virtue, temperance, modesty, sobriety, parsimony, justice; not to admire wealth or honour; to hate turbulence and ambition; to place every one his private welfare and happiness in the public peace, liberty, and safety. They shall not then need to be much mistrustful of their chosen patriots in the grand council; who will be then rightly called the true keepers of our liberty, though the most of their business will be in foreign affairs. But to prevent all mistrust, the people then will have their several ordinary assemblies (which will henceforth quite annihilate the odious power and name of committees) in the chief towns of every county, without the trouble, charge, or time lost of summoning and assembling from far in so great a number, and so long residing from their own houses, or removing of their families, to do as much at home in their several shires, entire or subdivided toward the securing of their liberty, as a numerous assembly of them all formed and convened on purpose with the wariest rotation. Whereof I shall speak more ere the end of this discourse; for it may be referred to time, so we be still going on by degrees to perfection. The people well weighing and performing these things, I suppose would have no cause to fear, though the parliament abolishing that name, as originally signifying but the parley of our lords and commons with the Norman king when he pleased to call them, should, with certain limitations of their power, sit perpetual, if their ends be faithful and for a free commonwealth, under the name of a grand or general council.

Till this be done, I am in doubt whether our state will be ever certainly and throughly settled; never likely till then to see an end of our troubles and continual changes, or at least never the true settlement and assurance of our liberty. The grand council being thus firmly constituted to perpetuity, and still, upon the death or default of any member, supplied and kept in full number, there can be no cause alleged, why peace, justice, plentiful trade, and all prosperity should not thereupon ensue throughout the whole land; with as much assurance as can be of human things, that they shall so continue (if God favour us, and our wilful sins provoke him not) even to the coming of our true and rightful, and only to be expected King, only worthy as he is our only Saviour, the Messiah, the Christ, the only heir of his eternal Father, the only by him anointed and ordained since the work of our redemption finished, universal Lord of all mankind.

The way propounded is plain, easy, and open before us; without intricacies, without the introducement of new or absolute forms or terms, or exotic models; ideas that would effect nothing; but with a number of new injunctions to manacle the native liberty of mankind; turning all virtue into prescription, servitude, and necessity, to the great inpairing and frustrating of Christian liberty. I say again, this way lies free and smooth before us; is not tangled with inconveniences; invents no new incumbrances, requires no perilous, no injurious alteration or circumscription of men's lands and properties; secure, that in this commonwealth, temporal and spiritual lords removed, no man or number of men can attain to such wealth or vast possession, as will need the hedge of an agrarian law (never successful, but the cause rather of sedition, save only where it began seasonably with first possession) to confine them from endangering our public liberty. To conclude, it can have no considerable objection made against it, that it is not practicable; lest it be said hereafter, that we gave up our liberty for want of a ready way or distinct form proposed of a free commonwealth. And this facility we shall have above our next neighbouring commonwealth (if we can keep us from the fond conceit of something like a duke of Venice, put lately into many men's heads, by some one or other subtly driving on under that notion his own ambitious ends to lurch a crown), that our liberty shall not be hampered or hovered over by any engagement to such a potent family as the house of Nassau, of whom to stand in perpetual doubt and suspicion, but we shall live the clearest and absolutest free nation in the world.

On the contrary, if there be a king, which the inconsiderate multitude are now so mad upon, mark how far short we are like to come of all those happinesses which in a free state we shall immediately be possessed of. First, the grand council, which, as I showed before, should sit perpetually (unless their

leisure give them now and then some intermissions or vaca-
tions, easily manageable by the council of state left sitting),
shall be called, by the king's good will and utmost endeavour,
as seldom as may be.   For it is only the king's right, he will say,
to call a parliament; and this he will do most commonly about
his own affairs rather than the kingdom's, as will appear plainly
as soon as they are called.   For what will their business then be,
and the chief expense of their time, but an endless tugging
between petition of right and royal prerogative, especially
about the negative voice, militia, or subsidies, demanded and
ofttimes extorted without reasonable cause appearing to the
commons, who are the only true representatives of the people
and their liberty, but will be then mingled with a court-faction;
besides which, within their own walls, the sincere part of them
who stand faithful to the people will again have to deal with
two troublesome counter-working adversaries from without,
mere creatures of the king, spiritual, and the greater part, as
is likeliest, of temporal lords, nothing concerned with the
people's liberty.

If these prevail not in what they please, though never so
much against the people's interest, the parliament shall be
soon dissolved, or sit and do nothing; not suffered to remedy
the least grievance, or enact aught advantageous to the people.
Next, the council of state shall not be chosen by the parliament,
but by the king, still his own creatures, courtiers, and favourers;
who will be sure in all their counsels to set their master's grandeur
and absolute power, in what they are able, far above the people's
liberty.   I deny not but that there may be such a king, who may
regard the common good before his own, may have no vicious
favourite, may hearken only to the wisest and incorruptest
of his parliament: but this rarely happens in a monarchy not
elective; and it behoves not a wise nation to commit the sum of
their well-being, the whole state of their safety to fortune.   What
need they? and how absurd would it be, whenas they themselves,
to whom his chief virtue will be but to hearken, may with
much better management and dispatch, with much more com-
mendation of their own worth and magnanimity, govern without
a master?   Can the folly be paralleled, to adore and be slaves of
a single person, for doing that which it is ten thousand to one
whether he can or will do, and we without him might do more
easily, more effectually, more laudably ourselves?   Shall we never
grow old enough to be wise, to make seasonable use of gravest
authorities, experiences, examples?   Is it such an unspeakable

joy to serve, such felicity to wear a yoke? to clink our shackles, locked on by pretended law of subjection, more intolerable and hopeless to be ever shaken off, than those which are knocked on by illegal injury and violence?

Aristotle, our chief instructor in the universities, lest this doctrine be thought sectarian, as the royalist would have it thought, tells us in the third of his Politics, that certain men at first, for the matchless excellence of their virtue above others, or some great public benefit, were created kings by the people, in small cities and territories, and in the scarcity of others to be found like them; but when they abused their power, and governments grew larger, and the number of prudent men increased, that then the people, soon deposing their tyrants, betook them, in all civilest places, to the form of a free commonwealth. And why should we thus disparage and prejudicate our own nation, as to fear a scarcity of able and worthy men united in counsel to govern us, if we will but use diligence and impartiality, to find them out and choose them, rather yoking ourselves to a single person, the natural adversary and oppressor of liberty; though good, yet far easier corruptible by the excess of his single power and exaltation, or at best, not comparably sufficient to bear the weight of government, nor equally disposed to make us happy in the enjoyment of our liberty under him?

But admit that monarchy of itself may be convenient to some nations; yet to us who have thrown it out, received back again, it cannot but prove pernicious. For kings to come, never forgetting their former ejection, will be sure to fortify and arm themselves sufficiently for the future against all such attempts hereafter from the people; who shall be then so narrowly watched and kept so low, that though they would never so fain, and at the same rate of their blood and treasure, they never shall be able to regain what they now have purchased and may enjoy, or to free themselves from any yoke imposed upon them. Nor will they dare to go about it; utterly disheartened for the future, if these their highest attempts prove unsuccessful; which will be the triumph of all tyrants hereafter over any people that shall resist oppression; and their song will then be, to others, How sped the rebellious English? to our posterity, How sped the rebels, your fathers?

This is not my conjecture, but drawn from God's known denouncement against the gentilising Israelites, who, though they were governed in a commonwealth of God's own ordaining, he only their king, they his peculiar people, yet affecting rather to resemble heathen, but pretending the misgovernment of Samuel's sons, no more a reason to dislike their commonwealth, than the violence of Eli's sons was imputable to that priesthood or religion, clamoured for a king.   They had their longing, but with this testimony of God's wrath: 'Ye shall cry out in that day, because of your king whom ye shall have chosen, and the Lord will not hear you in that day.'   Us if he shall hear now, how much less will he hear when we cry hereafter, who once delivered by him from a king, and not without wondrous acts of his providence, insensible and unworthy of those high mercies, are returning precipitantly, if he withhold us not, back to the captivity from whence he freed us!

Yet neither shall we obtain or buy at an easy rate this new gilded yoke, which thus transports us: a new royal revenue must be found, a new episcopal; for those are individual: both which being wholly dissipated, or bought by private persons, or assigned for service done, and especially to the army, cannot be recovered without general detriment and confusion to men's estates, or a heavy imposition on all men's purses; benefit to none but to the worst and ignoblest sort of men, whose hope is to be either the ministers of court riot and excess, or the gainers by it.   But not to speak more of losses and extraordinary levies on our estates, what will then be the revenges and offences remembered and returned, not only by the chief person, but by all his adherents; accounts and reparations that will be required, suits, indictments, inquiries, discoveries, complaints, informations, who knows against whom or how many, though perhaps neuters, if not to utmost infliction, yet to imprisonment, fines, banishment, or molestation? if not these, yet disfavour, discountenance, disregard, and contempt on all but the known royalist, or whom he favours, will be plenteous.

Nor let the new royalized presbyterians persuade themselves, that their old doings, though now recanted, will be forgotten; whatever conditions be contrived or trusted on.   Will they not believe this; nor remember the pacification, how it was kept to the Scots; how other solemn promises many a time to us? Let them but now read the diabolical forerunning libels, the faces, the gestures, that now appear foremost and briskest in all public places, as the harbingers of those that are in expectation to reign over us; let them but hear the insolencies, the menaces, the insultings, of our newly animated common enemies, crept lately out of their holes, their hell I might say, by the language of their infernal pamphlets, the spew of every drunkard, every ribald; nameless, yet not for want of licence, but for very shame of their own vile persons, not daring to name themselves, while they traduce others by name; and give us to foresee, that they intend to second their wicked words, if ever they have power, with more wicked deeds.

Let our zealous backsliders forethink now with themselves how their necks yoked with these tigers of Bacchus, these new fanatics of not the preaching, but the sweating tub, inspired with nothing holier than the venereal pox, can draw one way under monarchy to the establishing of church discipline with these new disgorged atheisms. Yet shall they not have the honour to yoke with these, but shall be yoked under them; these shall plough on their backs. And do they among them, who are so forward to bring in the single person, think to be by him trusted or long regarded? So trusted they shall be, and so regarded, as by kings are wont reconciled enemies; neglected, and soon after discarded, if not persecuted for old traitors; the first inciters, beginners, and more than to the third part actors, of all that followed.

It will be found also, that there must be then, as necessarily as now (for the contrary part will be still feared), a standing army; which for certain shall not be this, but of the fiercest cavaliers, of no less expense, and perhaps again under Rupert. But let this army be sure they shall be soon disbanded, and likeliest without arrear of pay; and being disbanded, not be sure but they may as soon be questioned for being in arms against their king. The same let them fear who have contributed money; which will amount to no small number; that must then take their turn to be made delinquents and compounders. They who past reason and recovery are devoted to kingship perhaps will answer, that a greater part by far of the nation will have it so, the rest therefore must yield.

Not so much to convince these, which I little hope, as to confirm them who yield not, I reply, that this greatest part have both in reason, and the trial of just battle, lost the right of their election what the government shall be. Of them who have not lost that right, whether they for kingship be the greater number, who can certainly determine? Suppose they be, yet of freedom they partake all alike, one main end of government; which if the greater part value not, but will degenerately forgo, is it just or reasonable, that most voices against the main end of government should enslave the less number that would be free? More just it is, doubtless, if it come to force, that a less number compel a greater to retain, which can be no wrong to them, their liberty, than that a greater number, for the pleasure of their baseness, compel a less most injuriously to be their fellow-slaves. They who seek nothing but their own just liberty, have always right to win it and to keep it, whenever they have power, be the voices never so numerous that oppose it. And how much we above others are concerned to defend it from kingship, and from them who in pursuance thereof so perniciously would betray us and themselves to most certain misery and thraldom, will be needless to repeat.

Having thus far shown with what ease we may now obtain a free commonwealth, and by it, with as much ease, all the freedom, peace, justice, plenty, that we can desire; on the other side, the difficulties, troubles, uncertainties, nay, rather impossibilities, to enjoy these things constantly under a monarch; I will now proceed to show more particularly wherein our freedom and flourishing condition will be more ample and secure to us under a free commonwealth, than under kingship.

The whole freedom of man consists either in spiritual or civil liberty. As for spiritual, who can be at rest, who can enjoy anything in this world with contentment, who hath not liberty to serve God, and to save his own soul, according to the best light which God hath planted in him to that purpose, by the reading of his revealed will, and the guidance of his Holy Spirit? That this is best pleasing to God, and that the whole protestant church allows no supreme judge or rule in matters of religion, but the Scriptures; and these to be interpreted by the Scriptures themselves, which necessarily infers liberty of conscience, I have heretofore proved at large in another treatise; and might yet further, by the public declarations, confessions, and admonitions of whole churches and states, obvious in all histories since the reformation.

This liberty of conscience, which above all other things ought to be to all men dearest and most precious, no government more inclinable not to favour only, but to protect, than a free commonwealth; as being most magnanimous, most fearless, and confident of its own fair proceedings. Whereas kingship, though looking big, yet indeed most pusillanimous, full of fears, full of jealousies, startled at every umbrage, as it hath been observed of old to have ever suspected most and mistrusted them who were in most esteem for virtue and generosity of mind, so it is now known to have most in doubt and suspicion them who are most reputed to be religious. Queen Elizabeth, though herself accounted so good a protestant, so moderate, so confident of her subjects' love, would never give way so much as to presbyterian reformation in this land, though once and again besought, as Camden relates; but imprisoned and persecuted the very proposers thereof, alleging it as her mind and maxim unalterable, that such reformation would diminish regal authority.

What liberty of conscience can we then expect of others, far worse principled from the cradle, trained up and governed by popish and Spanish counsels, and on such depending hitherto for subsistence? Especially what can this last parliament expect, who having revived lately and published the covenant, have re-engaged themselves, never to readmit episcopacy? Which no son of Charles returning but will most certainly bring back with him, if he regard the last and strictest charge of his father, 'to persevere in, not the doctrine only, but government of the church of England, not to neglect the speedy and effectual suppressing of errors and schisms'; among which he accounted presbytery one of the chief.

Or, if notwithstanding that charge of his father, he submit to the covenant, how will he keep faith to us, with disobedience to him; or regard that faith given, which must be founded on the breach of that last and solemnest paternal charge, and the reluctance, I may say the antipathy, which is in all kings, against presbyterian and independent discipline? For they hear the gospel speaking much of liberty; a word which monarchy and her bishops both fear and hate, but a free commonwealth both favours and promotes; and not the word only, but the thing itself. But let our governors beware in time, lest their hard measure to liberty of conscience be found the rock whereon they shipwreck themselves, as others have now done before them in the course wherein God was directing their steerage to a free commonwealth; and the abandoning of all those whom they call sectaries, for the detected falsehood and ambition of some, be a wilful rejection of their own chief strength and interest in the freedom of all protestant religion, under what abusive name soever calumniated.

The other part of our freedom consists in the civil rights and advancements of every person according to his merit: the enjoyment of those never more certain, and the access to these never more open, than in a free commonwealth. Both which, in my opinion, may be best and soonest obtained, if every county in the land were made a kind of subordinate commonalty or commonwealth, and one chief town or more, according as the shire is in circuit, made cities, if they be not so called already; where the nobility and chief gentry, from a proportionable compass of territory annexed to each city, may build houses or palaces befitting their quality; may bear part in the government, make their own judicial laws, or use those that are, and execute them by their own elected judicatures and judges without appeal, in all things of civil government between man and man. So they shall have justice in their own hands, law executed fully and finally in their own counties and precincts, long wished and spoken of, but never yet obtained. They shall have none then to blame but themselves, if it be not well administered; and fewer laws to expect or fear from the supreme authority; or to those that shall be made, of any great concernment to public liberty, they may, without much trouble in these commonalties, or in more general assemblies called to their cities from the whole territory on such occasion, declare and publish their assent or dissent by deputies, within a time limited, sent to the grand council; yet so as this their judgment declared shall submit to the greater number of other counties or commonalties, and not avail them to any exemption of themselves, or refusal of agreement with the rest, as it may in any of the United Provinces, being sovereign within itself, ofttimes to the great disadvantage of that union.

In these employments they may, much better than they do now, exercise and fit themselves till their lot fall to be chosen into the grand council, according as their worth and merit shall be taken notice of by the people. As for controversies that shall happen between men of several counties, they may repair, as they do now, to the capital city, or any other more commodious, indifferent place, and equal judges. And this I find to have been practised in the old Athenian commonwealth, reputed the first and ancientest place of civility in all Greece; that they had in their several cities a peculiar, in Athens a common government; and their right, as it befell them, to the administration of both.

They should have here also schools and academies at their own choice, wherein their children may be bred up in their own sight to all learning and noble education; not in grammar only, but in all liberal arts and exercises. This would soon spread much more knowledge and civility, yea, religion, through all parts of the land, by communicating the natural heat of government and culture more distributively to all extreme parts, which now lie numb and neglected; would soon make the whole nation more industrious, more ingenious at home, more potent, more honourable abroad. To this a free commonwealth will easily assent (nay, the parliament hath had already some such thing in design); for of all governments a commonwealth aims most to make the people flourishing, virtuous, noble, and high-spirited. Monarchs will never permit; whose aim is to make the people wealthy indeed perhaps, and well fleeced, for their own shearing, and the supply of regal prodigality; but otherwise softest, basest, viciousest, servilest, easiest to be kept under. And not only in fleece, but in mind also sheepishest; and will have all the benches of judicature annexed to the throne, as a gift of royal grace, that we have justice done us; whenas nothing can be more essential to the freedom of a people, than to have the administration of justice, and all public ornaments, in their own election, and within their own bounds, without long travelling or depending upon remote places to obtain their right, or any civil accomplishment; so it be not supreme, but subordinate to the general power and union of the whole republic.

In which happy firmness, as in the particular above-mentioned, we shall also far exceed the United Provinces, by having not as they (to the retarding and distracting ofttimes of their counsels or urgentest occasions), many sovereignties united in one commonwealth, but many commonwealths under one united and intrusted sovereignty. And when we have our forces by sea and land either of a faithful army, or a settled militia, in our own hands, to the firm establishing of a free commonwealth, public accounts under our own inspection, general laws and taxes, with their causes in our own domestic suffrages, judicial laws, offices, and ornaments at home in our own ordering and administration, all distinction of lords and commoners, that may any way divide or sever the public interest, removed; what can a perpetual senate have then, wherein to grow corrupt, wherein to encroach upon us, or usurp? Or if they do, wherein to be formidable? Yet if all this avail not to remove the fear or envy of a perpetual sitting, it may be easily provided, to change a third part of them yearly, or every two or three years, as was above mentioned; or that it be at those times in the people's choice, whether they will change them, or renew their power, as they shall find cause.

I have no more to say at present: few words will save us, well considered; few and easy things, now seasonably done. But if the people be so affected as to prostitute religion and liberty to the vain and groundless apprehension, that nothing but kingship can restore trade, not remembering the frequent plagues and pestilences that then wasted this city, such as through God's mercy we never have felt since; and that trade flourishes nowhere more than in the free commonwealths of Italy, Germany, and the Low Countries, before their eyes at this day; yet if trade be grown so craving and importunate through the profuse living of tradesmen, that nothing can support it but the luxurious expenses of a nation upon trifles or superfluities; so as if the people generally should betake themselves to frugality, it might prove a dangerous matter, lest tradesmen should mutiny for want of trading; and that therefore we must forgo and set to sale religion, liberty, honour, safety, all concernments divine or human, to keep up trading: if, lastly, after all this light among us, the same reason shall pass for current, to put our necks again under kingship, as was made use of by the Jews to return back to Egypt, and to the worship of their idol queen, because they falsely imagined that they then lived in more plenty and prosperity; our condition is not sound, but rotten, both in religion and all civil prudence; and will bring us soon, the way we are marching, to those calamities, which attend always and unavoidably on luxury, all national judgments under foreign and domestic slavery: so far we shall be from mending our condition by monarchizing our government, whatever new conceit now possesses us.

However, with all hazard I have ventured what I thought my duty to speak in season, and to forewarn my country in time; wherein I doubt not but there be many wise men in all places and degrees, but am sorry the effects of wisdom are so little seen among us. Many circumstances and particulars I could have added in those things whereof I have spoken: but a few main matters now put speedily in execution, will suffice to recover us, and set all right: and there will want at no time who are good at circumstances; but men who set their minds on main matters, and sufficiently urge them, in these most difficult times I find not many.

What I have spoken, is the language of that which is not called amiss 'The good old Cause': if it seem strange to any, it will not seem more strange, I hope, than convincing to backsliders. Thus much I should perhaps have said, though I was sure I should have spoken only to trees and stones; and had none to cry to, but with the prophet, 'O earth, earth, earth!' to tell the very soil itself, what her perverse inhabitants are deaf to. Nay, though what I have spoke should happen (which thou suffer not, who didst create mankind free! nor thou next, who didst redeem us from being servants of men!) to be the last words of our expiring liberty. But I trust I shall have spoken persuasion to abundance of sensible and ingenuous men; to some, perhaps, whom God may raise from these stones to become children of reviving liberty; and may reclaim, though they seem now choosing them a captain back for Egypt, to bethink themselves a little, and consider whither they are rushing; to exhort this torrent also of the people, not to be so impetuous, but to keep their due channel; and at length recovering and uniting their better resolutions, now that they see already how open and unbounded the insolence and rage is of our common enemies, to stay these ruinous proceedings, justly and timely fearing to what a precipice of destruction the deluge of this epidemic madness would hurry us, through the general defection of a misguided and abused multitude.

On
DOMESTIC LIBERTY

THE DOCTRINE AND DISCIPLINE
OF DIVORCE

RESTORED TO THE GOOD OF BOTH SEXES, FROM THE
BONDAGE OF CANON LAW, AND OTHER MISTAKES,
TO THE TRUE MEANING OF SCRIPTURE IN THE LAW
AND GOSPEL COMPARED

WHEREIN ALSO ARE SET DOWN THE BAD CONSE-
QUENCES OF ABOLISHING, OR CONDEMNING AS SIN,
THAT WHICH THE LAW OF GOD ALLOWS, AND
CHRIST ABOLISHED NOT

NOW THE SECOND TIME REVISED AND MUCH
AUGMENTED IN TWO BOOKS

TO THE PARLIAMENT OF ENGLAND WITH THE
ASSEMBLY

MATT. xiii. 52. 'Every scribe instructed in the kingdom of heaven is
like the master of a house, which bringeth out of his treasury things new
and old.'

PROV. xviii. 13. 'He that answereth a matter before he heareth it, it
is folly and shame unto him.'

Milton published *The Doctrine and Discipline of Divorce* in August
1643, to further the general cause of liberty. He considered that no
one could enjoy real and substantial liberty in his work and worship
if he were indissolubly tied to a wife who would not or could not be
to him the helpmeet intended by God. 'Farewell all hope of true
reformation in the state, while such an evil as this lies undiscerned or
unregarded in the house: on the redress whereof depends not only
the spiritual and orderly life of our grown men, but the willing and
careful education of our children.' He was convinced that matrimony,
as an ordinance, must not be preferred 'before the good of man and the
plain exigence of charity.'

In the first book, Milton tried to reconcile the pronouncements
of Moses and Christ on the causes for which divorce could be permitted.
In the second, he emphasized that both their views must be interpreted
in the light of the Christian rule of charity.

His interest in the subject of divorce was no doubt made more
personal by the unsatisfactory nature of his own first marriage, but
it is misleading to suggest that Mary Powell's behaviour occasioned
the composition of the Divorce pamphlets. Milton was writing in a
tradition revived by Erasmus, and carried on by such men as Grotius
and Selden. His views would have seemed neither revolutionary nor
shocking to the more learned of his contemporaries.

The strong feeling expressed in this pamphlet had much of its origin in Milton's sensitive appreciation of the value of a true marriage —a human society based on the companionship of mind and mind. When God, and no mere ceremony, had joined two human beings, they formed a society of peace and love which glorified God and promoted their own happiness.   When two human beings had been improperly yoked, 'chained unnaturally together,' the union was displeasing to God.   Milton was incensed by divorce laws which exalted the body above the soul of man, by making adultery the sole pretext of divorce.

The text is taken from the revised edition, published in 1644.

TO THE PARLIAMENT OF ENGLAND, WITH THE ASSEMBLY

If it were seriously asked (and it would be no untimely question), renowned parliament, select assembly! who of all teachers and masters, that have ever taught, hath drawn the most disciples after him, both in religion and in manners? it might be not untruly answered, custom.   Though virtue be commended for the most persuasive in her theory, and conscience in the plain demonstration of the spirit finds most evincing; yet whether it be the secret of divine will, or the original blindness we are born in, so it happens for the most part that custom still is silently received for the best instructor.   Except it be, because her method is so glib and easy, in some manner like to that vision of Ezekiel rolling up her sudden book of implicit knowledge, for him that will to take and swallow down at pleasure; which proving but of bad nourishment in the concoction, as it was heedless in the devouring, puffs up unhealthily a certain big face of pretended learning, mistaken among credulous men for the wholesome habit of soundness and good constitution, but is indeed no other than that swoln visage of counterfeit knowledge and literature, which not only in private mars our education, but also in public is the common climber into every chair, where either religion is preached, or law reported; filling each estate of life and profession with abject and servile principles, depressing the high and heaven-born spirit of man far beneath the condition wherein either God created him, or sin hath sunk him. To pursue the allegory, custom being but a mere face, as echo is a mere voice, rests not in her unaccomplishment, until by secret inclination she accorporate herself with error, who being a blind and serpentine body without a head, willingly accepts what he wants, and supplies what her incompleteness went seeking.   Hence it is, that error supports custom, custom countenances error; and these two between them would persecute and chase away all truth and solid wisdom out of human life, were it not that God, rather than man, once in many ages calls together the prudent and religious counsels of men, deputed to repress the incroachments, and to work off the inveterate blots and obscurities wrought upon our minds by the subtle insinuating of error and custom; who, with the numerous and vulgar train of their followers, make it their chief design to envy and cry down the industry of free reasoning, under the terms of humour and innovation; as if the womb of teeming truth were to be closed up, if she presume to bring forth aught that sorts not with their unchewed notions and suppositions, against which notorious injury and abuse of man's free soul, to testify and oppose the utmost that study and true labour can attain, heretofore the incitement of men reputed grave hath led me among others; and now the duty and the right of an instructed Christian calls me through the chance of good or evil report, to be the sole advocate of a discountenanced truth: a high enterprise, lords and commons! a high enterprise and a hard, and such as every seventh son of a seventh son does not venture on. Nor have I amidst the clamour of so much envy and impertinence whither to appeal, but to the concourse of so much piety and wisdom here assembled. Bringing in my hands an ancient and most necessary, most charitable, and yet most injured statute of Moses: not repealed ever by him who only had the authority, but thrown aside with much inconsiderate neglect, under the rubbish of canonical ignorance; as once the whole law was by some such like conveyance in Josiah's time. And he who shall endeavour the amendment of any old neglected grievance in church or state, or in the daily course of life, if he be gifted with abilities of mind, that may raise him to so high an undertaking, I grant he hath already much whereof not to repent him; yet let me aread him, not to be the foreman of any misjudged opinion, unless his resolutions be firmly seated in a square and constant mind, not conscious to itself of any deserved blame, and regardless of ungrounded suspicions. For this let him be sure, he shall be boarded presently by the ruder sort, but not by discreet and well-nurtured men, with a thousand idle descants and surmises. Who when they cannot confute the least joint or sinew of any passage in the book; yet God forbid that truth should be truth, because they have a boisterous conceit of some pretences in the writer. But were they not more busy and inquisitive than the apostle commends, they would hear him at least, 'rejoicing so the truth be preached, whether of envy or other pretence whatsoever': for truth is an impossible to be soiled by any outward touch, as the sunbeam; though this ill hap wait on her nativity, that she never comes into the world, but like a bastard, to the ignominy of him that brought her forth; till time, the midwife rather than the mother of truth, have washed and salted the infant, declared her legitimate, and churched the father of his young Minerva, from the needless causes of his purgation. Yourselves can best witness this, worthy patriots! and better will, no doubt, hereafter: for who among ye of the foremost that have travailed in her behalf to the good of church or state, hath not been often traduced to be the agent of his own by-ends, under pretext of reformation? So much the more I shall not be unjust to hope, that however infamy or envy may work in other men to do her fretful will against this discourse, yet that the experience of your own uprightness misinterpreted will put ye in

mind to give it free audience and generous construction. What
though the brood of Belial, the draff of men, to whom no liberty is
pleasing, but unbridled and vagabond lust without pale or partition,
will laugh broad perhaps, to see so great a strength of scripture muster-
ing up in favour, as they suppose, of their debaucheries; they will know
better when they shall hence learn, that honest liberty is the greatest
foe to dishonest licence.   And what though others, out of a waterish
and queasy conscience, because ever crazy and never yet sound, will
rail and fancy to themselves that injury and licence is the best of this
book?   Did not the distemper of their own stomachs affect them with a
dizzy megrim, they would soon tie up their tongues and discern themselves like that Assyrian blasphemer, all this while reproaching not
man, but the Almighty, the Holy One of Israel, whom they do not deny
to have belawgiven his own sacred people with this very allowance,
which they now call injury and licence, and dare cry shame on, and
will do yet a while, till they get a little cordial sobriety to settle their
qualming zeal.   But this question concerns not us perhaps: indeed
man's disposition, though prone to search after vain curiosities, yet
when points of difficulty are to be discussed, appertaining to the
removal of unreasonable wrong and burden from the perplexed life of
our brother, it is incredible how cold, how dull, and far from all fellow-
feeling we are, without the spur of self-concernment.   Yet if the
wisdom, the justice, the purity of God be to be cleared from foulest
imputations, which are not yet avoided; if charity be not to be degraded
and trodden down under a civil ordinance; if matrimony be not to be
advanced like that exalted perdition written of to the Thessalonians,
'above all that is called God,' or goodness, nay, against them both;
then I dare affirm, there will be found in the contents of this book that
which may concern us all.   You it concerns chiefly, worthies in
parliament! on whom, as on our deliverers, all our grievances and
cares, by the merit of your eminence and fortitude, are devolved.   Me
it concerns next, having with much labour and faithful diligence first
found out, or at least with a fearless and communicative candour first
published, to the manifest good of Christendom, that which, calling
to witness everything mortal and immortal, I believe unfeignedly to
be true.   Let not other men think their consciences bound to search
continually after truth, to pray for enlightening from above, to publish
what they think they have so obtained, and debar me from con-
ceiving myself tied by the same duties. Ye have now, doubtless,
by the favour and appointment of God, ye have now in your hands a
great and populous nation to reform; from what corruption, what
blindness in religion, ye know well; in what a degenerate and fallen
spirit from the apprehension of native liberty, and true manliness, I
am sure ye find; with what unbounded licence rushing to whoredoms
and adulteries, needs not long inquiry: insomuch that the fears, which
men have of too strict a discipline, perhaps exceed the hopes that can
be in others of ever introducing it with any great success.   What if
I should tell ye now of dispensations and indulgences, to give a little
the reins, to let them play and nibble with the bait awhile; a people as

hard of heart as that Egyptian colony that went to Canaan. This is the common doctrine that adulterous and injurious divorces were not connived only, but with eye open allowed of old for hardness of heart. But that opinion, I trust, by then this following argument hath been well read, will be left for one of the mysteries of an indulgent Antichrist to farm out incest by, and those his other tributary pollutions. What middle way can be taken then, may some interrupt, if we must neither turn to the right, nor to the left, and that the people hate to be reformed? Mark then, judges and lawgivers, and ye whose office it is to be our teachers, for I will utter now a doctrine, if ever any other, though neglected or not understood, yet of great and powerful importance to the governing of mankind. He who wisely would restrain the reasonable soul of man within due bounds, must first himself know perfectly, how far the territory and dominion extends of just and honest liberty. As little must he offer to bind that which God hath loosened, as to loosen that which he hath bound. The ignorance and mistake of this high point hath heaped up one huge half of all the misery that hath been since Adam. In the gospel we shall read a supercilious crew of masters, whose holiness, or rather whose evil eye, grieving that God should be so facile to man, was to set straighter limits to obedience than God hath set, to enslave the dignity of man, to put a garrison upon his neck of empty and over-dignified precepts: and we shall read our Saviour never more grieved and troubled than to meet with such a peevish madness among men against their own freedom. How can we expect him to be less offended with us, when much of the same folly shall be found yet remaining where it least ought, to the perishing of thousands? The greatest burden in the world is superstition, not only of ceremonies in the church, but of imaginary and scarecrow sins at home. What greater weakening, what more subtle stratagem against our Christian warfare, when besides the gross body of real transgressions to encounter, we shall be terrified by a vain and shadowy menacing of faults that are not? When things indifferent shall be set to overfront us under the banners of sin, what wonder if we be routed, and by this art of our adversary, fall into the subjection of worst and deadliest offences? The superstition of the papist is, 'Touch not, taste not,' when God bids both; and ours is, 'Part not, separate not,' when God and charity both permits and commands. 'Let all your things be done with charity,' saith St Paul; and his master saith, 'She is the fulfilling of the law.' Yet now a civil, an indifferent, a sometime dissuaded law of marriage, must be forced upon us to fulfil, not only without charity but against her. No place in heaven or earth, except hell, where charity may not enter: yet marriage, the ordinance of our solace and contentment, the remedy of our loneliness, will not admit now either of charity or mercy, to come in and mediate, or pacify the fierceness of this gentle ordinance, the unremedied loneliness of this remedy. Advise ye well, supreme senate, if charity be thus excluded and expulsed, how ye will defend the untainted honour of your own actions and proceedings. He who marries, intends as little to conspire his own ruin, as he that swears allegiance: and as a whole people is in proportion to an ill government, so is one man to an ill marriage. If they, against any authority, covenant, or statute, may, by the sovereign edict of charity, save not only their lives but honest liberties from unworthy bondage, as well may he against any private covenant, which he never entered to his mischief, redeem himself from unsupportable disturbances to honest peace and just contentment. And much the rather, for that to resist the highest magistrate though tyrannizing, God never gave us express allowance, only he gave us reason, charity, nature, and good example to bear us out; but in this economical misfortune thus to demean ourselves, besides the warrant of those four great directors, which doth as justly belong hither, we have an express law of God, and such a law, as whereof our Saviour with a solemn threat forbade the abrogating. For no effect of tyranny can sit more heavy on the commonwealth, than this household unhappiness on the family. And farewell all hope of true reformation in the state, while such an evil as this lies undiscerned or unregarded in the house: on the redress whereof depends not only the spiritful and orderly life of our grown men, but the willing and careful education of our children. Let this therefore be new examined, this tenure and freehold of mankind, this native and domestic charter given us by a greater lord than that Saxon king the Confessor. Let the statutes of God be turned over, be scanned anew, and considered not altogether by the narrow intellectuals of quotationists and common places, but (as was the ancient right of councils) by men of what liberal profession soever, of eminent spirit and breeding, joined with a diffuse and various knowledge of divine and human things; able to balance and define good and evil, right and wrong, throughout every state of life; able to show us the ways of the Lord straight and faithful as they are, not full of cranks and contradictions, and pitfalling dispenses, but with divine insight and benignity measured out to the proportion of each mind and spirit, each temper and disposition created so different each from other, and yet by the skill of wise conducting, all to become uniform in virtue. To expedite these knots were worthy a learned and memorable synod; while our enemies expect to see the expectation of the church tired out with dependencies and independencies, how they will compound and in what calends. Doubt not, worthy senators! to vindicate the sacred honour and judgment of Moses your predecessor, from the shallow commenting of scholastics and canonists. Doubt not after him to reach out your steady hands to the misinformed and wearied life of man; to restore this his lost heritage into the household state; wherewith be sure that peace and love, the best subsistence of a Christian family, will return home from whence they are now banished; places of prostitution will be less haunted, the neighbour's bed less attempted, the yoke of prudent and manly discipline will be generally submitted to; sober and well-ordered living will soon spring up in the commonwealth. Ye have an author great beyond exception, Moses; and one yet greater, he who hedged in from abolishing every smallest jot and tittle of precious equity contained in that law, with a more accurate and lasting Masoreth, than either the synagogue of Ezra or the Galilaean school at Tiberias hath left us. Whatever else ye can enact, will scarce concern a third part of the British name: but the benefit and good of this your magnanimous example will easily spread far beyond the banks of Tweed and the Norman isles. It would not be the first or second time, since our ancient druids, by whom this island was the cathedral of philosophy to France, left off their pagan rights, that England hath had this honour vouchsafed from heaven, to give out reformation to the world. Who was it but our English Constantine that baptized the Roman empire? Who but the Northumbrian Willibrode, and Winifride of Devon, with their followers, were the first apostles of Germany? Who but Alcuin and Wickliff, our countrymen, opened the eyes of Europe, the one in arts, the other in religion? Let not England forget her precedence of teaching nations how to live.

Know, worthies! and exercise the privilege of your honoured country. A greater title I here bring ye than is either in the power or in the policy of Rome to give her monarchs; this glorious act will style ye the defenders of charity. Nor is this yet the highest inscription that will adorn so religious and so holy a defence as this; behold here the pure and sacred law of God, and his yet purer and more sacred name, offering themselves to you, first of all, Christian reformers, to be acquitted from the long-suffered ungodly attribute of patronizing adultery. Defer not to wipe off instantly these imputative blurs and stains cast by rude fancies upon the throne and beauty itself of inviolable holiness: lest some other people more devout and wise than we bereave us this offered immortal glory, our wonted prerogative, of being the first asserters in every great vindication. For me, as far as my part leads me, I have already my greatest gain, assurance and inward satisfaction to have done in this nothing unworthy of an honest life, and studies well employed. With what event, among the wise and right understanding handful of men, I am secure. But how among the drove of custom and prejudice this will be relished by such whose capacity, since their youth run ahead into the easy creek of a system or a medulla, sails there at will under the blown physiognomy of their unlaboured rudiments; for them, what their taste will be, I have also surety sufficient, from the entire league that hath ever been between formal ignorance and grave obstinacy. Yet when I remember the little that our Saviour could prevail about this doctrine of charity against the crabbed textuists of his time, I make no wonder, but rest confident, that whoso prefers either matrimony or other ordinance before the good of man and the plain exigence of charity, let him profess papist, or protestant, or what he will, he is no better than a pharisee, and understands not the gospel: whom as a misinterpreter of Christ I openly protest against; and provoke him to the trial of this truth before all the world: and let him bethink him withal how he will sodder up the shifting flaws of his ungirt permissions, his venial and unvenial dispenses, wherewith the law of God pardoning and unpardoning hath been shamefully branded for want of heed in glossing, to have eluded and baffled out all faith and chastity from the marriage-bed of that holy seed, with politic and judicial adulteries. I seek not to seduce the simple and illiterate; my errand is to find out the choicest and the learnedest, who have this high gift of wisdom to answer solidly, or to be convinced. I crave it from the piety, the learning, and the prudence which is housed in this place. It might perhaps more fitly have been written in another tongue: and I had done so, but that the esteem I have of my country's judgment, and the love I bear to my native language to serve it first with what I endeavour, make me speak it thus, ere I assay the verdict of outlandish readers. And perhaps also here I might have ended nameless, but that the address of these lines chiefly to the parliament of England might have seemed ingrateful not to acknowledge by whose religious care, unwearied watchfulness, courageous and heroic resolutions, I enjoy the peace and studious leisure to remain,

The Honourer and Attendant of their
noble Worth and Virtues,

JOHN MILTON.

BOOK I

THE PREFACE

That Man is the Occasion of his own Miseries in most of those Evils which he imputes to God's inflicting—The Absurdity of our Canonists in their Decrees about Divorce—The Christian imperial Laws framed with more Equity—The opinion of Hugo Grotius and Paulus Fagius: And the Purpose in General of this Discourse.

MANY men, whether it be their fate or fond opinion, easily persuade themselves, if God would but be pleased a while to withdraw his just punishments from us, and to restrain what power either the devil or any earthly enemy hath to work us wo, that then man's nature would find immediate rest and releasement from all evils. But verily they who think so, if they be such as have a mind large enough to take into their thoughts a general survey of human things, would soon prove themselves in that opinion far deceived. For though it were granted us by divine indulgence to be exempt from all that can be harmful to us from without, yet the perverseness of our folly is so bent, that we should never cease hammering out of our own hearts, as it were out of a flint, the seeds and sparkles of new misery to ourselves, till all were in a blaze again. And no marvel if out of our own hearts, for they are evil; but even out of those things which God meant us, either for a principal good, or a pure contentment, we are still hatching and contriving upon ourselves matter of continual sorrow and perplexity.

What greater good to man than that revealed rule, whereby God vouchsafes to show us how he would be worshipped? And yet that not rightly understood became the cause, that once a famous man in Israel could not but oblige his conscience to be the sacrificer; or if not, the jailer of his innocent and only daughter; and was the cause ofttimes that armies of valiant men have given up their throats to a heathenish enemy on the sabbath day; fondly thinking their defensive resistance to be as then a work unlawful. What thing more instituted to the solace and delight of man than marriage? And yet the misinterpreting of some scripture, directed mainly against the abusers of the law for divorce given by Moses, hath changed the blessing of matrimony not seldom into a familiar and coinhabiting mischief; at least into a drooping and disconsolate household captivity, without refuge or redemption. So ungoverned and so wild a race doth superstition run us, from one extreme of abused liberty into the other of unmerciful restraint. For although God in the first ordaining of marriage taught us to what end he did it, in words expressly implying the apt and cheerful conversation of man with woman, to comfort and refresh him against the evil of solitary life, not mentioning the purpose of generation till afterwards, as being but a secondary end in dignity, though not in necessity: yet now, if any two be but once handed in the church, and have tasted in any sort the nuptial bed, let them find themselves never so mistaken in their dispositions through any error, concealment, or misadventure, that through their different tempers, thoughts and constitutions, they can neither be to one another a remedy against loneliness, nor live in any union or contentment all their days; yet they shall, so they be but found suitably weaponed to the least possibility of sensual enjoyment, be made, spite of antipathy, to fadge together, and combine as they may to their unspeakable wearisomeness, and despair of all sociable delight in the ordinance which God established to that very end. What a calamity is this? and, as the wise man, if he were alive, would sigh out in his own phrase, what a 'sore evil is this under the sun!' All which we can refer justly to no other author than the canon law and her adherents, not consulting with charity, the interpreter and guide of our faith, but resting in the mere element of the text; doubtless by the policy of the devil to make that gracious ordinance become unsupportable, that what with men not daring to venture upon wedlock, and what with men wearied out of it, all inordinate licence might abound. It was for many ages that marriage lay in disgrace with most of the ancient doctors, as a work of the flesh, almost a defilement, wholly denied to priests, and the second time dissuaded to all, as he that reads Tertullian or Jerome may see at large. Afterwards it was thought so sacramental, that no adultery or desertion could dissolve it; and this is the sense of our canon courts in England to this day, but in no other reformed church else: yet there remains in them also a burden on it as heavy as the other two were disgraceful or superstitious, and of as much iniquity, crossing a law not only written by Moses, but charactered in us by nature, of more antiquity and deeper ground than marriage itself; which law is to force nothing against the faultless proprieties of nature, yet that this may be colourably done, our Saviour's words touching divorce are as it were congealed into a stony rigour, inconsistent both with his doctrine and his office; and that which he preached only to the conscience is by canonical tyranny snatched into the compulsive censure of a judicial court; where laws are imposed even against the venerable and secret power of nature's impression, to love, whatever cause be found to loathe: which is a heinous barbarism both against the honour of marriage, the dignity of man and his soul, the goodness of Christianity, and all the human respects of civility. Notwithstanding that some the wisest and gravest among the Christian emperors, who had about them, to consult with, those of the fathers then living, who for their learning and holiness of life are still with us in great renown, have made their statutes and edicts concerning this debate far more easy and relenting in many necessary cases, wherein the canon is inflexible. And Hugo Grotius, a man of these times, one of the best learned, seems not obscurely to adhere in his persuasion to the equity of those imperial decrees, in his notes upon the Evangelists; much allaying the outward roughness of the text, which hath for the most part been too immoderately expounded; and excites the diligence of others to inquire further into this question, as containing many points that have not yet been explained. Which ever likely to remain intricate and hopeless upon the suppositions commonly stuck to, the authority of Paulus Fagius, one so learned and so eminent in England once, if it might persuade, would straight acquaint us with a solution of these differences no less prudent than compendious. He, in his comment on the Pentateuch, doubted not to maintain that divorces might be as lawfully permitted by the magistrates to Christians, as they were to the Jews. But because he is but brief, and these things of great consequence not to be kept obscure, I shall conceive it nothing above my duty, either for the difficulty or the censure that may pass thereon, to communicate such thoughts as I also have had, and do offer them now in this general labour of reformation to the candid view both of church and magistrate: especially because I see it the hope of good men, that those irregular and unspiritual courts have spun their utmost date in this land, and some better course must now be constituted. This therefore shall be the task and period of this discourse to prove, first, that other reasons of divorce, besides adultery, were by the law of Moses, and are yet to be allowed by the Christian magistrate as a piece of justice, and that the words of Christ are not hereby contraried. Next, that to prohibit absolutely any divorce whatsoever, except those which Moses excepted, is against the reason of law, as in due place I shall show out of Fagius, with many additions. He therefore who by adventuring shall be so happy as with success to light the way of such an expedient liberty and truth as this, shall restore the much-wronged and over-sorrowed state of matrimony, not only to those merciful and life-giving remedies of Moses, but, as much as may be, to that serene and blissful condition it was in at the beginning, and shall deserve of all apprehensive men (considering the troubles and distempers, which, for want of this in sight, have been so oft in kingdoms, in states, and families), shall deserve to be reckoned among the public benefactors of civil and human life, above the inventors of wine and oil; for this is a far dearer, far nobler, and more desirable cherishing to man's life, unworthily exposed to sadness and mistake, which he shall vindicate. Not that licence, and levity, and unconsented breach of faith should herein be countenanced, but that some conscionable and tender pity might be had of those who have unwarily, in a thing they never practised before, made themselves the bondmen of a luckless and helpless matrimony. In which argument, he whose courage can serve him to give the first onset, must look for two several oppositions: the one from those who having sworn themselves to long custom, and the letter of the text, will not out of the road; the other from those whose gross and vulgar apprehensions conceit but low of matrimonial purposes, and in the work of male and female think they have all. Nevertheless, it shall be here sought by due ways to be made appear, that those words of God in the institution, promising a meet help against loneliness, and those words of Christ, that 'his yoke is easy, and his burden light,' were not spoken in vain: for if the knot of marriage may in no case be dissolved but for adultery, all the burdens and services of the law are not so intolerable. This only is desired of them who are minded to judge hardly of thus maintaining, that they would be still, and hear all out, nor think it equal to answer deliberate reason with sudden heat and noise; remembering this, that many truths now of reverend esteem and credit, had their birth and beginning once from singular and private thoughts, while the most of men were otherwise possessed; and had the fate at first to be generally exploded and exclaimed on by many violent opposers: yet I may err perhaps in soothing myself, that this present truth revived will deserve on all hands to be not sinisterly received, in that it undertakes the cure of an inveterate disease crept into the best part of human society; and to do this with no smarting corrosive, but a smooth and pleasing lesson, which received both the virtue to soften and dispel rooted and knotty sorrows, and without enchantment, if that be feared, or spell used, hath regard at once both to serious pity and upright honesty; that tends to the redeeming and restoring of none but such as are the object of compassion, having in an ill hour hampered themselves, to the utter dispatch of all their most beloved comforts and repose for this life's term. But if we shall obstinately dislike this new overture of unexpected ease and recovery, what remains but to deplore the frowardness of our hopeless condition, which neither can endure the estate we are in, nor admit of remedy either sharp or sweet? Sharp we ourselves distaste; and sweet, under whose hands we are, is scrupled and suspected as too luscious. In such a posture Christ found the Jews, who were neither won with the austerity of John the Baptist, and thought it too much licence to follow freely the charming pipe of him who sounded and proclaimed liberty and relief to all distresses: yet truth in some age or other will find her witness, and shall be justified at last by her own children.

CHAPTER I

The Position proved by the Law of Moses—That Law expounded and asserted to a moral and charitable Use, first by Paulus Fagius, next with other Additions.

To remove therefore, if it be possible, this great and sad oppression, which through the strictness of a literal interpreting hath invaded and disturbed the dearest and most peaceable estate of household society, to the overburdening, if not the overwhelming of many Christians better worth than to be so deserted of the church's considerate care, this position shall be laid down, first proving, then answering what may be objected either from scripture or light of reason.

'That indisposition, unfitness, or contrariety of mind, arising from a cause in nature unchangeable, hindering, and ever likely to hinder the main benefits of conjugal society, which are solace and peace; is a greater reason of divorce than natural frigidity, especially if there be no children, and that there be mutual consent.'

This I gather from the law in Deut. xxiv. 1: 'When a man hath taken a wife and married her, and it come to pass that she find no favour in his eyes, because he hath found some uncleanness in her, let him write her a bill of divorcement, and give it in her hand, and send her out of his house,' etc. This law, if the words of Christ may be admitted into our belief, shall never, while the world stands, for him be abrogated. First therefore I here set down what learned Fagius hath observed on this law: 'The law of God,' saith he, 'permitted divorce for the help of human weakness. For every one that of necessity separates, cannot live single. That Christ denied divorce to his own, hinders not; for what is that to the unregenerate, who hath not attained such perfection? Let not the remedy be despised, which was given to weakness. And when Christ saith, who marries the divorced commits adultery, it is to be understood if he had any plot in the divorce.' The rest I reserve until it be disputed, how the magistrate is to do herein. From hence we may plainly discern a twofold consideration in this law: first, the end of the law-giver, and the proper act of the law, to command or to allow something just and honest, or indifferent. Secondly, his sufferance from some accidental result of evil by this allowance, which the law cannot remedy. For if this law have no other end or act but only the allowance of sin, though never to so good intention, that law is no law, but sin muffled in the robe of law, or law disguised in the loose garment of sin. Both which are too foul hypotheses, to save the phenomenon of our Saviour's answer to the pharisees about this matter. And I trust anon, by the help of an infallible guide, to perfect such Prutenic tables, as shall mend the astronomy of our wide expositors.

The cause of divorce mentioned in the law is translated 'some uncleanness,' but in the Hebrew it sounds, 'nakedness of aught, or any real nakedness'; which by all the learned interpreters is referred to the mind as well as to the body. And what greater nakedness or unfitness of mind than that which hinders ever the solace and peaceful society of the married couple? And what hinders that more than the unfitness and defectiveness of an unconjugal mind? The cause therefore of divorce expressed in the position cannot but agree with that described in the best and equallest sense of Moses's law. Which being a matter of pure charity, is plainly moral, and more now in force than ever; therefore surely lawful. For if under the law such was God's gracious indulgence, as not to suffer the ordinance of his goodness and favour through any error to be seared and stigmatized upon his servants to their misery and thraldom; much less will he suffer it now under the covenant of grace, by abrogating his former grant of remedy and relief. But the first institution will be objected to have ordained marriage inseparable. To that a little patience until this first part have amply discoursed the grave and pious reasons of this divorcive law; and then I doubt not but with one gentle stroking to wipe away ten thousand tears out of the life of man. Yet thus much I shall now insist on, that whatever the institution were, it could not be so enormous, nor so rebellious against both nature and reason, as to exalt itself above the end and person for whom it was instituted.

CHAPTER II

The first Reason of the Law grounded on the prime Reason of Matrimony—That no Covenant whatsoever obliges against the main End both of itself, and of the parties covenanting.

For all sense and equity reclaims, that any law or covenant, how solemn or strait soever, either between God and man, or man and man, though of God's joining, should bind against a prime and principal scope of its own institution, and of both or either party covenanting; neither can it be of force to engage a blameless creature to his own perpetual sorrow, mistaken for his expected solace, without suffering charity to step in and do a confessed good work of parting those whom nothing holds together but this God's joining, falsely supposed against the express end of his own ordinance. And what his chief end was of creating woman to be joined with man, his own instituting words declare, and are infallible to inform us what is marriage, and what is no marriage; unless we can think them set there to no purpose: 'It is not good,' saith he, 'that man should be alone.

I will make him a help meet for him.' From which words, so plain, less cannot be concluded, nor is by any learned interpreter, than that in God's intention a meet and happy conversation is the chiefest and the noblest end of marriage: for we find here no expression so necessarily implying carnal knowledge, as this prevention of loneliness to the mind and spirit of man. To this Fagius, Calvin, Pareus, Rivetus, as willingly and largely assent as can be wished. And indeed it is a greater blessing from God, more worthy so excellent a creature as man is, and a higher end to honour and sanctify the league of marriage, whenas the solace and satisfaction of the mind is regarded and provided for before the sensitive pleasing of the body. And with all generous persons married thus it is, that where the mind and person pleases aptly, there some unaccomplishment of the body's delight may be better borne with, than when the mind hangs off in an unclosing disproportion, though the body be as it ought; for there all corporal delight will soon become unsavoury and contemptible. And the solitariness of man, which God had namely and principally ordered to prevent by marriage, hath no remedy, but lies under a worse condition than the loneliest single life: for in single life the absence and remoteness of a helper might inure him to expect his own comforts out of himself, or to seek with hope; but here the continual sight of his deluded thoughts, without cure, must needs be to him, if especially his complexion incline him to melancholy, a daily trouble and pain of loss, in some degree like that which reprobates feel. Lest therefore so noble a creature as man should be shut up incurably under a worse evil by an easy mistake in that ordinance which God gave him to remedy a less evil, reaping to himself sorrow while he went to rid away solitariness, it cannot avoid to be concluded, that if the woman be naturally so of disposition, as will not help to remove, but help to increase that same God-forbidden loneliness, which in time draws on with it a general discomfort and dejection of mind, not beseeming either Christian profession or moral conversation, unprofitable and dangerous to the commonwealth, when the household estate, out of which must flourish forth the vigour and spirit of all public enterprises, is so ill-contented and procured at home, and cannot be supported; such a marriage can be no marriage, whereto the most honest end is wanting; and the aggrieved person shall do more manly, to be extraordinary and singular in claiming the due right whereof he is frustrated, than to piece up his lost contentment by visiting the stews, or stepping to his neighbour's bed, which is the common shift in this misfortune; or else by suffering his useful life to waste away, and be lost under a secret affliction of an unconscionable size to human strength. Against all which evils the mercy of this Mosaic law was graciously exhibited.

CHAPTER III

The Ignorance and Iniquity of Canon-law, providing for the Right of the Body in Marriage, but nothing for the Wrongs and Grievances of the Mind. An Objection, that the Mind should be better looked to before contract, answered.

How vain, therefore, is it and how preposterous in the canon law, to have made such careful provision against the impediment of carnal performance, and to have had no care about the unconversing inability of mind so defective to the purest and most sacred end of matrimony; and that the vessel of voluptuous enjoyment must be made good to him that has taken it upon trust, without any caution; whenas the mind, from whence must flow the acts of peace and love, a far more precious mixture than the quintessence of an excrement, though it be found never so deficient and unable to perform the best duty of marriage in a cheerful and agreeable conversation, shall be thought good enough, however flat and melancholious it be, and must serve, though to the eternal disturbance and languishing of him that complains! Yet wisdom and charity, weighing God's own institution, would think that the pining of a sad spirit wedded to loneliness should deserve to be freed, as well as the impatience of a sensual desire so providently relieved. It is read to us in the liturgy, that 'we must not marry to satisfy the fleshly appetite, like brute beasts, that have no understanding'; but the canon so runs, as if it dreamed of no other matter than such an appetite to be satisfied; for if it happen that nature hath stopped or extinguished the veins of sensuality, that marriage is annulled. But though all the faculties of the understanding and conversing part after trial appear to be so ill and so aversely met through nature's unalterable working, as that neither peace, nor any sociable contentment can follow, it is as nothing; the contract shall stand firm as ever, betide what will. What is this but secretly to instruct us, that however many grave reasons are pretended to the married life, yet nothing indeed is thought worth regard therein, but the prescribed satisfaction of an irrational heat? Which cannot be but ignominious to the state of marriage, dishonourable to the undervalued soul of man, and even to Christian doctrine itself: while it seems more moved at the disappointing of an impetuous nerve, than at the ingenuous grievance of a mind unreasonably yoked; and to place more of marriage in the channel of concupiscence, than in the pure influence of peace and love, whereof the soul's lawful contentment is the only fountain.

But some are ready to object, that the disposition ought seriously to be considered before. But let them know again, that for all the wariness can be used, it may yet befall a discreet man to be mistaken in his choice: and we have plenty of examples. The soberest and best-governed men are least practised in these affairs; and who knows not that the bashful muteness of a virgin may ofttimes hide all the unliveliness and natural sloth which is really unfit for conversation? Nor is there that freedom of access granted or presumed, as may suffice to a perfect discerning till too late; and where any indisposition is suspected, what more usual than the persuasion of friends, that acquaintance, as it increases, will amend all? And lastly, it is not strange though many, who have spent their youth chastely, are in some things not so quick-sighted, while they haste too eagerly to light the nuptial torch; nor is it, therefore, that for a modest error a man should forfeit so great a happiness, and no charitable means to release him, since they who have lived most loosely, by reason of their bold accustoming, prove most successful in their matches, because their wild affections, unsettling at will have been as so many divorces to teach them experience. Whenas the sober man honouring the appearance of modesty, and hoping well of every social virtue under that veil, may easily chance to meet, if not with a body impenetrable, yet often with a mind to all other due conversation inaccessible, and to all the more estimable and superior purposes of matrimony useless and almost lifeless; and what a solace, what a fit help such a consort would be through the whole life of a man, is less pain to conjecture than to have experience.

CHAPTER IV

The second Reason of this Law, because without it Marriage, as it happens oft, is not a Remedy of that which it promises, as any rational Creature would expect—That Marriage, if we pattern from the Beginning, as our Saviour bids, was not properly the Remedy of Lust, but the fulfilling of conjugal Love and Helpfulness.

And that we may further see that a violent cruel thing it is to force the continuing of those together whom God and nature in the gentlest end of marriage never joined; divers evils and extremities, that follow upon such a compulsion, shall here be set in view. Of evils, the first and greatest is, that hereby a most absurb and rash imputation is fixed upon God and his holy laws, of conniving and dispensing with open and common adultery among his chosen people; a thing which the rankest politician would think it shame and disworship that his laws should countenance: how and in what manner that comes to pass I shall reserve till the course of method brings on the unfolding of many scriptures. Next, the law and gospel are hereby made liable to more than one contradiction, which I refer also thither. Lastly, the supreme dictate of charity is hereby many ways neglected and violated; which I shall forthwith address to prove. First, we know St Paul saith, 'It is better to marry than to burn.' Marriage, therefore, was given as a remedy of that trouble: but what might this burning mean? Certainly not the mere motion of carnal lust, not the mere goad of a sensitive desire: God does not principally take care of such cattle. What is it then but that desire which God put into Adam in Paradise, before he knew the sin of incontinence; that desire which God saw it was not good that man should be left alone to burn in; the desire and longing to put off an unkindly solitariness by uniting another body, but not without a fit soul to his, in the cheerful society of wedlock? Which if it were so needful before the fall, when man was much more perfect in himself, how much more is it needful now against all the sorrows and casualties of this life, to have an intimate and speaking help, a ready and reviving associate in marriage? Whereof who misses, by chancing on a mute and spiritless mate, remains more alone than before, and in a burning less to be contained than that which is fleshly, and more to be considered; as being more deeply rooted even in the faultless innocence of nature. As for that other burning, which is but as it were the venom of a lusty and over-abounding concoction, strict life and labour, with the abatement of a full diet, may keep that low and obedient enough; but this pure and more inbred desire of joining to itself in conjugal fellowship a fit conversing soul (which desire is properly called love) 'is stronger than death,' as the spouse of Christ thought; 'many waters cannot quench it, neither can the floods drown it.' This is that rational burning that marriage is to remedy, not to be allayed with fasting, nor with any penance to be subdued: which how can he assuage who by mishap hath met the most unmeet and unsuitable mind? Who hath the power to struggle with an intelligible flame, not in Paradise to be resisted, become now more ardent by being failed of what in reason it looked for and even then most unquenched, when the importunity of a provender burning is well enough appeased; and yet the soul hath obtained nothing of what it justly desires. Certainly such a one forbidden to divorce, is in effect forbidden to marry, and compelled to greater difficulties than in a single life; for if there be not a more humane burning which marriage must satisfy, or else may be dissolved, than that of copulation, marriage cannot be honourable for the meet reducing and terminating lust between two; seeing many beasts in voluntary and chosen couples live together as unadulterously, and are as truly married in that respect. But all ingenuous men will see that the dignity and blessing of marriage is placed rather in the mutual enjoyment of that which the wanting soul needfully seeks, than of that which the plenteous body would joyfully give away. Hence it is that Plato in his festival discourse brings in Socrates relating what he feigned to have learned from the prophetess Diotima, how Love was the son of Penury, begot of Plenty, in the garden of Jupiter. Which divinely sorts with that which in effect Moses tells us, that Love was the son of Loneliness, begot in Paradise by that sociable and helpful aptitude which God implanted between man and woman toward each other. The same, also, is that burning mentioned by St Paul, whereof marriage ought to be the remedy: the flesh hath other mutual and easy curbs which are in the power of any temperate man. When, therefore, this original and sinless penury, or loneliness of the soul, cannot lay itself down by the side of such a meet and acceptable union as God ordained in marriage, at least in some proportion, it cannot conceive and bring forth love, but remains utterly unmarried under a formal wedlock, and still burns in the proper meaning of St Paul. Then enters Hate; not that hate that sins, but that which only is natural dissatisfaction, and the turning aside from a mistaken object: if that mistake have done injury, it fails not to dismiss with recompense; for to retain still, and not be able to love, is to heap up more injury. Thence this wise and pious law of dismission now defended took beginning: he, therefore, who lacking of his due in the most native and humane end of marriage, thinks it better to part than to live sadly and injuriously to that cheerful covenant (for not to be behoved, and yet retained, is the greatest injury to a gentle spirit), he, I say, who therefore seeks to part, is one who highly honours the married life and would not stain it: and the reasons which now move him to divorce are equal to the best of those that should first warrant him to marry; for, as was plainly shown, both the hate which now diverts him, and the loneliness which leads him still powerfully to seek a fit help, hath not the least grain of a sin in it, if he be worthy to understand himself.

CHAPTER V

The third Reason of this Law, because without it, he who has happened where he finds nothing but remediless Offences and Discontents, is in more and greater Temptations than ever before.

Thirdly, yet it is next to be feared, if he must be still bound without reason by a deaf rigour, that when he perceives the just expectance of his mind defeated, he will begin even against law to cast about where he may find his satisfaction more complete, unless he be a thing heroically virtuous; and that are not the common lump of men, for whom chiefly the laws ought to be made; though not to their sins, yet to their unsinning weaknesses, it being above their strength to endure the lonely estate, which while they shunned they are fallen into. And yet there follows upon this a worse temptation: for if he be such as hath spent his youth unblamably, and laid up his chiefest earthly comforts in the enjoyments of a contented marriage, nor did neglect that furtherance which was to be obtained therein by constant prayers; when he shall find himself bound fast to an uncomplying discord of nature, or, as it oft happens, to an image of earth and phlegm, with whom he looked to be the co-partner of a sweet and gladsome society, and sees withal that his bondage is now inevitable; though he be almost the strongest Christian, he will be ready to despair in virtue, and mutiny against Divine Providence: and this doubtless is the reason of those lapses, and that melancholy despair, which we see in many wedded persons, though they understand it not, or pretend other causes, becauses they know no remedy; and is of extreme danger: therefore when human frailty surcharged is at such a loss, charity ought to venture much, and use bold physic, lest an overtossed faith endanger to shipwreck.

CHAPTER VI

The fourth Reason of this Law, that God regards Love and Peace in the Family, more than a compulsive Performance of Marriage, which is more broke by a grievous Continuance, than by a needful Divorce.

Fourthly, marriage is a covenant, the very being whereof consists not in a forced cohabitation, and counterfeit performance of duties, but in unfeigned love and peace: and of matrimonial love, no doubt but that was chiefly meant, which by the ancient sages was thus parabled; that Love, if he be not twin born, yet hath a brother wondrous like him, called Anteros; whom while he seeks all about, his chance is to meet with many false and feigning desires, that wander singly up and down in his likeness: by them in their borrowed garb, Love, though not wholly blind, as poets wrong him, yet having but one eye, as being born an archer aiming, and that eye not the quickest in this dark region here below, which is not Love's proper sphere, partly out of the simplicity and credulity which is native to him, often deceived, embraces and consorts him with these obvious and suborned striplings, as if they were his mother's own sons; for so he thinks them, while they subtilly keep themselves most on his blind side. But after a while, as his manner is, when soaring up into the high tower of his Apogaeum, above the shadow of the earth, he darts out the direct rays of his then most piercing eyesight upon the impostures and trim disguises that were used with him, and discerns that this is not his genuine brother, as he imagined; he has no longer the power to hold fellowship with such a personated mate: for straight his arrows lose their golden heads, and shed their purple feathers, his silken braids untwine, and slip their knots, and that original and fiery virtue given him by fate all on a sudden goes out, and leaves him undeified and despoiled of all his force; till finding Anteros at last, he kindles and repairs the almost-faded ammunition of his deity by the reflection of a coequal and homogeneal fire. Thus mine author sung it to me: and by the leave of those who would be counted the only grave ones, this is no mere amatorious novel (though to be wise and skilful in these matters, men heretofore of greatest name in virtue have esteemed it one of the highest arcs that human contemplation circling upwards can make from the globy sea whereon she stands); but this is a deep and serious verity, showing us that love in marriage cannot live nor subsist unless it be mutual; and where love cannot be, there can be left of wedlock nothing but the empty husk of an outside matrimony, as undelightful and unpleasing to God as any other kind of hypocrisy. So far is his command from tying men to the observance of duties which there is no help for, but they must be dissembled. If Solomon's advice be not over-frolic, 'Live joyfully,' saith he, 'with the wife whom thou lovest, all thy days, for that is thy portion': how then, where we find it impossible to rejoice or to love, can we obey this precept? How miserably do we defraud ourselves of that comfortable portion, which God gives us, by striving vainly to glue an error together, which God and nature will not join, adding but more vexation and violence to that blissful society by our importunate superstition, that will not hearken to St Paul, 1 Cor. vii, who, speaking of a marriage and divorce, determines plain enough in general, that God therein 'hath called us to peace, and not to bondage'! Yea, God himself commands in his law more than once, and by his prophet Malachi, as Calvin and the best translations read, that 'he who hates, let him divorce,' that is, he who cannot love. Hence it is that the rabbins, and Maimonides, famous among the rest, in a book of his set forth by Buxtorfius, tells us, that 'divorce was permitted by Moses to preserve peace in marriage, and quiet in the family.' Surely the Jews had their saving peace about them as well as we; yet care was taken that this wholesome provision for household peace should also be allowed them: and must this be denied to Christians? O perverseness! that the law should be made more provident of peace-making than the gospel! that the gospel should be put to beg a most necessary help of mercy from the law, but must not have it! and that to grind in the mill of an undelighted and servile copulation, must be the only forced work of a Christian marriage, ofttimes with such a yoke-fellow, from whom both love and peace, both nature and religion mourns to be separated. I cannot therefore be so diffident as not securely to conclude, that he who can receive nothing of the most important helps in marriage, being thereby disenabled to return that duty which is his, with a clear and hearty countenance, and thus continues to grieve whom he would not, and is no less grieved; that man ought even for love's sake and peace to move divorce upon good and liberal conditions to the divorced. And it is a less breach of wedlock to part with wise and quiet consent betimes, than still to foil and profane that mystery of joy and union with a polluting sadness and perpetual distemper: for it is not the outward continuing of marriage that keeps whole that covenant, but whatsoever does most according to peace and love, whether in marriage or in divorce, he it is that breaks marriage least; it being so often written, that 'Love only is the fulfilling of every commandment.'

CHAPTER VII

The fifth Reason, that nothing more hinders and disturbs the whole Life of a Christian, than a Matrimony found to be incurably unfit, and doth the same in effect that an idolatrous Match.

Fifthly, as those priests of old were not to be long in sorrow, or if they were, they could not rightly execute their function; so every true Christian in a higher order of priesthood, is a person dedicate to joy and peace, offering himself a lively sacrifice of praise and thanksgiving, and there is no Christian duty that is not to be seasoned and set off with cheerishness; which in a thousand outward and intermitting crosses may yet be done well, as in this vale of tears: but in such a bosom affliction as this, crushing the very foundation of his inmost nature, when he shall be forced to love against a possibility, and to use a dissimulation against his soul in the perpetual and ceaseless duties of a husband; doubtless his whole duty of serving God must needs be blurred and tainted with a sad unpreparedness and dejection of spirit, wherein God has no delight. Who sees not therefore how much more Christianity it would be to break by divorce that which is more broken by undue and forcible keeping, rather than 'to cover the altar of the Lord with continual tears, so that he regardeth not the offering any more,' rather than that the whole worship of a Christian man's life should languish and fade away beneath the weight of an immeasurable grief and discouragement? And because some think the children of a second matrimony succeeding a divorce would not be a holy seed, it hindered not the Jews from being so; and why should we not think them more holy than the offspring of a former ill-twisted wedlock, begotten only out of a bestial necessity, without any true love or contentment, or joy to their parents?

So that in some sense we may call them the 'children of wrath' and anguish, which will as little conduce to their sanctifying, as if they had been bastards: for nothing more than disturbance of mind suspends us from approaching to God; such a disturbance especially, as both assaults our faith and trust in God's providence, and ends, if there be not a miracle of virtue on either side, not only in bitterness and wrath, the canker of devotion, but in a desperate and vicious carelessness, when he sees himself, without fault of his, trained by a deceitful bait into a snare of misery, betrayed by an alluring ordinance, and then made the thrall of heaviness and discomfort by an undivorcing law of God, as he erroneously thinks, but of man's iniquity, as the truth is; for that God prefers the free and cheerful worship of a Christian, before the grievance and exacted observance of an unhappy marriage, besides that the general maxims of religion assure us, will be more manifest by drawing a parallel argument from the ground of divorcing an idolatress, which was, lest he should alienate his heart from the true worship of God: and, what difference is there whether she pervert him to superstition by her enticing sorcery, or disenable him in the whole service of God through the disturbance of her unhelpful and unfit society; and so drive him at last, through murmuring and despair, to thoughts of atheism? Neither doth it lessen the cause of separating, in that the one willingly allures him from the faith, the other perhaps unwillingly drives him; for in the account of God it comes all to one, that the wife loses him a servant: and therefore by all the united force of the Decalogue she ought to be disbanded, unless we must set marriage above God and charity, which is the doctrine of devils, no less than forbidding to marry.

CHAPTER VIII

That an idolatrous Heretic ought to be divorced, after a convenient Space given to hope of Conversion—That Place of 1 Cor. vii. restored from a twofold erroneous Exposition; and that the common Expositors flatly contradict the moral Law.

And here by the way, to illustrate the whole question of divorce, ere this treatise end, I shall not be loath to spend a few lines, in hope to give a full resolve of that which is yet so much controverted: whether an idolatrous heretic ought to be divorced. To the resolving whereof we must first know, that the Jews were commanded to divorce an unbelieving Gentile for two causes: First, because all other nations, especially the Canaanites, were to them unclean. Secondly, to avoid seducement. That other nations were to the Jews impure, even to the separating of marriage, will appear out of Exod. xxxiv. 16, Deut. vii. 3, 6, compared with Ezra ix. 2, also chap. x. 10, 11, Neh. xiii. 30. This was the ground of that doubt raised among the Corinthians by some of the circumcision, whether an unbeliever were not still to be counted an unclean thing, so as that they ought to divorce from such a person. This doubt of theirs St Pauls removes by an evangelical reason, having respect to that vision of St Peter, wherein the distinction of clean and unclean being abolished, all living creatures were sanctified to a pure and Christian use, and mankind especially, now invited by a general call to the covenant of grace. Therefore, saith St Paul, 'The unbelieving wife is sanctified by the husband'; that is, made pure and lawful to his use, so that he need not put her away for fear lest her unbelief should defile him; but that if he found her love still towards him, he might rather hope to win her. The second reason of that divorce was to avoid seducement, as is proved by comparing those two places of the law to that which Ezra and Nehemiah did by divine warrant in compelling the Jews to forgo their wives. And this reason is moral and perpetual in the rule of Christian faith without evasion; therefore, saith the apostle, 2 Cor. vi, 'Misyoke not together with infidels,' which is interpreted of marriage in the first place. And although the former legal pollution be now done off, yet there is a spiritual contagion in idolatry as much to be shunned; and though seducement were not to be feared, yet where there is no hope of converting, there always ought to be a certain religious aversation and abhorring, which can no way sort with marriage: therefore saith St Paul, 'What fellowship hath righteousness with unrighteousness? What communion hath light with darkness? What concord hath Christ with Belial? What part hath he that believeth with an infidel?' And in the next verse but one he moralizes, and makes us liable to that command of Isaiah, 'Wherefore come out from among them, and be ye separate, saith the Lord; touch not the unclean thing, and I will receive ye.' And this command thus gospelized to us, hath the same force with that whereon Ezra grounded the pious necessity of divorcing. Neither had he other commission for what he did, than such a general command in Deuteronomy as this, nay, not so direct, for he is bid there not to marry, but not bid to divorce; and yet we see with what a zeal and confidence he was the author of a general divorce between the faithful and the unfaithful seed. The gospel is more plainly on his side, according to three of the evangelists, than the words of the law; for where the case of divorce is handled with such severity, as was fittest to aggravate the fault of unbounded licence; yet still in the same chapter, when it comes into question afterwards, whether any civil respect, or natural relation which is dearest, may be our plea to divide, or hinder or but delay our duty to religion, we hear it determined that father, and mother, and wife also, is not only to be hated, but forsaken, if we mean to inherit the great reward there promised. Nor will it suffice to be put off by saying we must forsake them only by not consenting or not complying with them, for that were to be done, and roundly too, though being of the same faith, they should but seek out of a fleshly tenderness to weaken our Christian fortitude with worldly persuasions, or but to unsettle our constancy with timorous and softening suggestions; as we may read with what a vehemence Job, the patientest of men, rejected the desperate counsels of his wife; and Moses, the meekest, being thoroughly offended with the profane speeches of Zippora, sent her back to her father. But if they shall perpetually, at our elbow, seduce us from the true worship of God, or defile and daily scandalize our conscience by their hopeless continuance in misbelief; then even in the due progress of reason, and that ever equal proportion which justice proceeds by, it cannot be imagined that his cited place commands less than a total and final separation from such an adherent; at least that no force should be used to keep them together; while we remember that God commanded Abraham to send away his irreligious wife and her son for the offences which they gave in a pious family. And it may be guessed that David for the like cause disposed of Michal in such a sort, as little differed from a dismission. Therefore, against reiterated scandals and seducements, which never cease, much more can no other remedy or retirement be found but absolute departure. For what kind of matrimony can that remain to be, what one duty between such can be performed as it should be from the heart, when their thoughts and spirits fly asunder as far as heaven from hell; especially if the time that hope should send forth her expected blossoms, be past in vain? It will easily be true, that a father or a brother may be hated zealously, and loved civilly or naturally; for those duties may be performed at distance, and do admit of any long absence:

but how the peace and perpetual cohabitation of marriage can be kept, how that benevolent and intimate communion of body can be held, with one that must be hated with a most operative hatred, must be forsaken and yet continually dwelt with and accompanied; he who can distinguish, hath the gift of an affection very oddly divided and contrived: while others both just and wise, and Solomon among the rest, if they may not hate and forsake as Moses enjoins, and the gospel imports, will find it impossible not to love otherwise than will sort with the love of God, whose jealousy brooks no corrival. And whether is more likely, that Christ bidding to forsake wife for religion, meant it by divorce as Moses meant it, whose law, grounded on moral reason, was both his office and his essence to maintain; or that he should bring a new morality into religion, not only new, but contrary to an unchangeable command, and dangerously derogating from our love and worship of God? As if when Moses had bid divorce absolutely, and Christ had said, hate and forsake, and his apostle had said, no communication with Christ and Belial; yet that Christ after all this could be understood to say, Divorce not; no, not for religion, seduce, or seduce not. What mighty and invisible remora is this in matrimony, able to demur and to contemn all the divorcive engines in heaven or earth! both which may now pass away, if this be true; for more than many jots or tittles, a whole moral law is abolished. But if we dare believe it is not, then in the method of religion, and to save the honour and dignity of our faith, we are to retreat and gather up ourselves from the observance of an inferior and civil ordinance, to the strict maintaining of a general and religious command, which is written, 'Thou shalt make no covenant with them,' Deut. vii. 2, 3: and that covenant which cannot be lawfully made, we have directions and examples lawfully to dissolve. Also 2 Chron. ii. 19, 'Shouldest thou love them that hate the Lord?' No, doubtless; for there is a certain scale of duties, there is a certain hierarchy of upper and lower commands, which for want of studying in right order, all the world is in confusion.

Upon these principles I answer, that a right believer ought to divorce an idolatrous heretic, unless upon better hopes: however, that it is in the believer's choice to divorce or not.

The former part will be manifest thus first, that an apostate idolater, whether husband or wife seducing, was to die by the decree of God, Deut. xiii. 6, 9; that marriage, therefore, God himself disjoins: for others born idolaters, the moral reason of their dangerous keeping, and the incommunicable antagony that is between Christ and Belial, will be sufficient to enforce the commandment of those two inspired reformers, Ezra and Nehemiah, to put an idolater away as well under the gospel.

The latter part, that although there be no seducement feared, yet if there be no hope given, the divorce is lawful, will appear by this; that idolatrous marriage is still hateful to God, therefore still it may be divorced by the pattern of that warrant that Ezra had, and by the same everlasting reason: neither can any man give an account wherefore, if those whom God joins no man can separate, it should not follow, that whom he joins not, but hates to join, those men ought to separate. But saith the lawyer, 'That which ought not to have been done, once done, avails.' I answer, 'This is but a crotchet of the law, but that brought against it is plain scripture.' As for what Christ spake concerning divorce, it is confessed by all knowing men, he meant only between them of the same faith. But what shall we say then to St Paul, who seems to bid us not divorce an infidel willing to stay? We may safely say thus, that wrong collections have been hitherto made out of those words by modern divines. His drift, as was heard before, is plain; not to command our stay in marriage with an infidel, that had been a flat renouncing of the religious and moral law; but to inform the Corinthians that the body of an unbeliever was not defiling, if his desire to live in Christian wedlock showed any likelihood that his heart was opening to the faith; and therefore advises to forbear departure so long till nothing have been neglected to set forward a conversion: this, I say, he advises, and that with certain cautions, not commands, if we can take up so much credit for him, as to get him believed upon his own word: for what is this else but his counsel in a thing indifferent, 'To the rest speak I, not the Lord'? for though it be true that the Lord never spake it, yet from St Paul's mouth we should have took it as a command, had not himself forewarned us, and disclaimed; which notwithstanding if we shall still avouch to be a command, he palpably denying it, this is not to expound St Paul, but to outface him. Neither doth it follow that the apostle may interpose his judgment in a case of Christian liberty, without the guilt of adding to God's word. How do we know marriage or single life to be of choice, but by such like words as these, 'I speak this by permission, not of commandment; I have no command of the Lord, yet I give my judgment'? Why shall not the like words have leave to signify a freedom in this our present question, though Beza deny? Neither is the scripture hereby less inspired, because St Paul confesses to have written therein what he had not of command: for we grant that the Spirit of God led him thus to express himself to Christian prudence, in a matter which God thought best to leave uncommanded. Beza, therefore, must be warily read, when he taxes St Austin of blasphemy, for holding that St Paul spake here as of a thing indifferent. But if it must be a command, I shall yet the more evince it to be a command that we should herein be left free; and that out of the Greek word used in the 12th verse, which instructs us plainly, there must be a joint assent and good liking on both sides: he that will not deprave the text must thus render it: 'If a brother have an unbelieving wife, and she join in consent to dwell with him' (which cannot utter less to us than a mutual agreement), let him not put her away from the mere surmise of Judaical uncleanness: and the reason follows, for the body of an infidel is not polluted, neither to benevolence, nor to procreation. Moreover, this note of mutual complacency forbids all offer of seducement, which to a person of zeal cannot be attempted without great offence: if, therefore, seducement be feared, this place hinders not divorce. Another caution was put in this supposed command, of not bringing the believer into 'bondage' hereby, which doubtless might prove extreme, if Christian liberty and conscience were left to the humour of a pagan staying at pleasure to play with, and to vex and wound with a thousand scandals and burdens, above strength to bear. If, therefore, the conceived hope of gaining a soul come to nothing, then charity commands that the believer be not wearied out with endless waiting under many grievances sore to his spirit; but that respect be had rather to the present suffering of a true Christian, than the uncertain winning of an obdured heretic. The counsel we have from St Paul to hope, cannot countermand the moral and evangelic charge we have from God to fear seducement, to separate from the misbeliever, the unclean, the obdurate. The apostle wisheth us to hope; but does not send us a wool-gathering after vain hope; he saith, 'How knowest thou, O man, whether thou shalt save thy wife?' that is, till he try all due means, and set some reasonable time to himself, after which he may give over washing an Ethiop, if he will hear the advice of the gospel; 'Cast not pearls before swine,' saith Christ himself. 'Let him be to thee as a heathen.' 'Shake the dust off thy feet.' If this be not enough, 'hate and forsake' what relation soever. And this also that follows must appertain to the precept, 'Let every man wherein he is called, therein abide with God,' v. 24, that is, so walking in his inferior calling of marriage, as not, by dangerous subjection to that ordinance, to hinder and disturb the higher calling of his Christianity. Last, and never too oft remembered, whether this be a command or an advice, we must look that it be so understood as not to contradict the least point of moral religion that God hath formerly commanded; otherwise what do we but set the moral law and the gospel at civil war together? and who then shall be able to serve these two masters?

CHAPTER IX

That Adultery is not the greatest Breach of Matrimony: that there may be other Violations as great.

Now whether idolatry or adultery be the greatest violation of marriage, if any demand let him thus consider; that among Christian writers touching matrimony, there be three chief ends thereof agreed on: godly society; next, civil; and thirdly, that of the marriage bed. Of these the first in name to be the highest and most excellent, no baptized man can deny, nor that idolatry smites directly against this prime end; nor that such as the violated end is, such is the violation: but he who affirms adultery to be the highest breach, affirms the bed to be the highest of marriage, which is in truth a gross and boorish opinion, how common soever; so far from the countenance of scripture, as from the light of all clean philosophy or civil nature. And out of question the cheerful help that may be in marriage toward sanctity of life, is the purest, and so the noblest end of that contract: but if the particular of each person be considered, then of those three ends which God appointed, that to him is greatest which is most necessary; and marriage is then most broken to him when he utterly wants the fruition of that which he most sought therein, whether it were religious, civil, or corporal society. Of which wants to do him right by divorce only for the last and meanest is a perverse injury, and the pretended reason of it as frigid as frigidity itself, which the code and canon are only sensible of. Thus much of this controversy. I now return to the former argument. And having shown that disproportion, contrariety, or numbness of mind may justly be divorced, by proving already the prohibition thereof opposes the express end of God's institution, suffers not marriage to satisfy that intellectual and innocent desire which God himself kindled in man to be the bond of wedlock, but only to remedy a sublunary and bestial burning, which frugal diet, without marriage, would easily chasten. Next, that it drives many to transgress the conjugal bed, while the soul wanders after that satisfaction which it had hope to find at home, but hath missed; or else it sits repining, even to atheism, finding itself hardly dealt with, but misdeeming the cause to be in God's law, which is in man's unrighteous ignorance. I have shown also how it unties the inward knot of marriage, which is peace and love (if that can be untied which was never knit), while it aims to keep fast the outward formality: how it lets perish the Christian man, to compel impossibly the married man.

CHAPTER X

The sixth Reason of this Law; that to prohibit Divorce sought for natural Causes, is against Nature.

The sixth place declares this prohibition to be as respectless of human nature as it is of religion, and therefore is not of God. He teaches, that an unlawful marriage may be lawfully divorced; and that those who have thoroughly discerned each other's disposition, which ofttimes cannot be till after matrimony, shall then find a powerful reluctance and recoil of nature on either side, blasting all the content of their mutual society, that such persons are not lawfully married (to use the apostle's words), 'Say I these things as a man; or saith not the law also the same? For it is written, Deut. xxii, "Thou shalt not sow thy vineyard with different seeds, lest thou defile both. Thou shalt not plough with an ox and an ass together"'; and the like. I follow the pattern of St Paul's reasoning: 'Doth God care for asses and oxen,' how ill they yoke together? 'or is it not said altogether for our sakes? For our sakes no doubt this is written.' Yea, the apostle himself, in the forecited 2 Cor. vi. 14, alludes from that place of Deut. to forbid misyoking marriage, as by the Greek word is evident; though he instance but in one example of mismatching with an infidel, yet next to that, what can be a fouler incongruity, a greater violence to the reverend secret of nature, than to force a mixture of minds that cannot unite, and to sow the sorrow of man's nativity with seed of

too incoherent and incombining dispositions? which act being
kindly and voluntary, as it ought, the apostle in the language
he wrote called 'eunoia,' and the Latins 'benevolence,' intimat-
ing the original thereof to be in the understanding and the will;
if not, surely there is nothing which might more properly be called
a malevolence rather; and is the most injurious and unnatural
tribute that can be extorted from a person endued with reason,
to be made pay out the best substance of his body, and of his
soul too, as some think, when either for just and powerful causes
he cannot like, or from unequal causes finds not recompense.
And that there is a hidden efficacy of love and hatred in man as
well as in other kinds, not moral but natural, which though not
always in the choice, yet in the success of marriage, will ever be
most predominant: besides daily experience, the author of
Ecclesiasticus, whose wisdom hath set him next the Bible,
acknowledges, xiii. 16: 'A man,' saith he, 'will cleave to his
like.' But what might be the cause, whether each one's allotted
genius or proper star, or whether the supernal[1] influence of
schemes and angular aspects, or this elemental crasis here
below; whether all these jointly or singly meeting friendly or
unfriendly in either party, I dare not, with the men I am like
to clash, appear so much a philosopher as to conjecture. The
ancient proverb in Homer, less abstruse, entitles this work of
leading each like person to his like, peculiarly to God himself:
which is plain enough also by his naming of a meet or like help
in the first espousal instituted; and that every woman is meet
for every man, none so absurd as to affirm. Seeing then there
is a twofold seminary or stock in nature, from whence are
derived the issues of love and hatred, distinctly flowing through
the whole mass of created things, and that God's doing ever is
to bring the due likenesses and harmonies of his works together,
except when out of two contraries, met to their own destruction,
he moulds a third existence; and that it is error, or some evil
angel which either blindly or maliciously hath drawn together,
in two persons ill embarked in wedlock, the sleeping discords
and enmities of nature, lulled on purpose with some false bait,
that they may wake to agony and strife, later than prevention
could have wished, if from the bent of just and honest intentions beginning what was begun and so continuing, all that is
equal, all that is fair and possible hath been tried, and no
accommodation likely to succeed; what folly is it still to stand
combating and battering against invincible causes and effects,

[1] The first edition has *supernatural*.

with evil upon evil, till either the best of our days be lingered out, or ended with some speeding sorrow! The wise Ecclesiasticus advises rather (xxxvii. 27): 'My son, prove thy soul in thy life; see what is evil for it, and give not that unto it.' Reason he had to say so; for if the noisomeness or disfigurement of body can soon destroy the sympathy of mind to wedlock duties, much more will the annoyance and trouble of mind infuse itself into all the faculties and acts of the body, to render them invalid, unkindly, and even unholy against the fundamental law-book of nature, which Moses never thwarts but reverences; therefore he commands us to force nothing against sympathy or natural order, no, not upon the most abject creatures; to show that such an indignity cannot be offered to man without an impious crime. And certainly those divine meditating words of finding out a meet and like help to man, have in them a consideration of more than the indefinite likeness of womanhood; nor are they to be made waste paper on, for the dulness of canon divinity: no, nor those other allegoric precepts of beneficence fetched out of the closet of nature, to teach us goodness and compassion in not compelling together unmatchable societies; or if they meet through mischance, by all consequence to disjoin them, as God and nature signifies, and lectures to us not only by those recited decrees, but even by the first and last of all his visible works; when by his divorcing command the world first rose out of chaos, nor can be renewed again out of confusion, but by the separating of unmeet consorts.

CHAPTER XI

The seventh Reason, that sometimes Continuance in Marriage may be evidently the Shortening or Endangering of Life to either Party; both Law and Divinity concluding, that Life is to be preferred before Marriage, the intended Solace of Life.

Seventhly, the canon law and divines consent, that if either party be found contriving against another's life, they may be severed by divorce: for a sin against the life of marriage is greater than a sin against the bed; the one destroys, the other but defiles. The same may be said touching those persons who being of a pensive nature and course of life, have summed up all their solace in that free and lightsome conversation which God and man intends in marriage; whereof when they see themselves deprived by meeting an unsociable consort, they ofttimes resent

one another's mistake so deeply, that long it is not ere grief end
one of them. When therefore this danger is foreseen, that the
life is in peril by living together, what matter is it whether
helpless grief or wilful practice be the cause? This is certain,
that the preservation of life is more worth than the compulsory
keeping of marriage; and it is no less than cruelty to force a
man to remain in that state as the solace of his life, which he
and his friends know will be either the undoing or the disheartening of his life. And what is life without the vigour and
spiritual exercise of life? How can it be useful to private
or public employment? Shall it therefore be quite dejected,
though never so valuable, and left to moulder away in heaviness,
for the superstitious and impossible performance of an ill-driven
bargain? Nothing more inviolable than vows made to God;
yet we read in Numbers, that if a wife had made such a vow, the
mere will and authority of her husband might break it: how
much more then may he break the error of his own bonds with
an unfit and mistaken wife, to the saving of his welfare, his
life, yea, his faith and virtue, from the hazard of overstrung
temptations! For if man be lord of the sabbath, to the curing
of a fever, can he be less than lord of marriage in such important
causes as these?

CHAPTER XII

The eighth Reason, It is probable, or rather certain, that every one who
happens to marry hath not the Calling; and therefore upon Unfitness
found and considered, Force ought not to be used.

Eighthly, it is most sure that some even of those who are not
plainly defective in body, yet are destitute of all other marriage-
able gifts, and consequently have not the calling to marry unless
nothing be requisite thereto but a mere instrumental body;
which to affirm, is to that unanimous covenant a reproach:
yet it is as sure that many such, not of their own desire, but by
the persuasion of friends, or not knowing themselves, do often
enter into wedlock; where finding the difference at length
between the duties of a married life, and the gifts of a single life,
what fitness of mind, what wearisomeness, scruples, and doubts,
to an incredible offence and displeasure, are like to follow
between, may be soon imagined; whom thus to shut up, and
immure, and shut up together, the one with a mischosen mate,
the other in a mistaken calling, is not a course that Christian

wisdom and tenderness ought to use. As for the custom that some parents and guardians have of forcing marriages, it will be better to say nothing of such a savage inhumanity, but only thus; that the law which gives not all freedom of divorce to any creature endued with reason so assassinated, is next in cruelty.

CHAPTER XIII

The ninth Reason; because Marriage is not a mere carnal Coition, but a human Society: where that cannot reasonably be had, there can be no true Matrimony. Marriage compared with all other Covenants and Vows warrantably broken for the good of Man. Marriage the Papists' Sacrament, and unfit Marriage the Protestants' Idol.

Ninthly, I suppose it will be allowed us that marriage is a human society, and that all human society must proceed from the mind rather than the body, else it would be but a kind of animal or beastish meeting: if the mind therefore cannot have that due company by marriage that it may reasonably and humanly desire, that marriage can be no human society, but a certain formality; or gilding over of little better than a brutish congress, and so in very wisdom and pureness to be dissolved.

But marriage is more than human, 'the covenant of God,' Prov. ii. 17; therefore man cannot dissolve it. I answer, if it be more than human, so much the more it argues the chief society thereof to be in the soul rather than in the body, and the greatest breach thereof to be unfitness of mind rather than defect of body: for the body can have least affinity in a covenant more than human, so that the reason of dissolving holds good the rather. Again, I answer, that the sabbath is a higher institution, a command of the first table, for the breach whereof God hath far more and oftener testified his anger than for divorces, which from Moses to Malachi he never took displeasure at, nor then neither if we mark the text; and yet as oft as the good of man is concerned, he not only permits, but commands to break the sabbath. What covenant more contracted with God and less in man's power, than the vow which hath once passed his lips? yet if it be found rash, if offensive, if unfruitful either to God's glory or the good of man, our doctrine forces not error and unwillingness irksomely to keep it, but counsels wisdom and better thoughts boldly to break it; therefore to enjoin the indissoluble keeping of a marriage found unfit against the good of man both soul and body, as hath been evidenced, is to make an idol of marriage, to advance it above the worship of God and the good of man, to make it a transcendent command, above both the second and first table; which is a most prodigious doctrine.

Next, whereas they cite out the Proverbs, that it is the covenant of God, and therefore more than human, that consequence is manifestly false; for so the covenant which Zedekiah made with the infidel king of Babel is called the covenant of God, Ezek. xvii. 19, which would be strange to hear counted more than a human covenant. So every covenant between man and man, bound by oath, may be called the covenant of God, because God therein is attested. So of marriage he is the author and the witness; yet hence will not follow any divine astriction more than what is subordinate to the glory of God, and the main good of either party: for as the glory of God and their esteemed fitness one for the other, was the motive which led them both at first to think without other revelation that God had joined them together; so when it shall be found by their apparent unfitness, that their continuing to be man and wife is against the glory of God and their mutual happiness, it may assure them that God never joined them, who hath revealed his gracious will not to set the ordinance above the man for whom it was ordained; not to canonize marriage either as a tyranness or a goddess over the enfranchised life and soul of man; for wherein can God delight, wherein be worshipped, wherein be glorified by the forcible continuing of an improper and ill-yoking couple? He that loved not to see the disparity of several cattle at the plough, cannot be pleased with vast unmeetness in marriage. Where can be the peace and love which must invite God to such a house? May it not be feared that the not divorcing of such a helpless disagreement will be the divorcing of God finally from such a place? But it is a trial of our patience, say they: I grant it; but which of Job's afflictions were sent him with that law, that he might not use means to remove any of them if he could? And what if it subvert our patience and our faith too? Who shall answer for the perishing of all those souls, perishing by stubborn expositions of particular and inferior precepts against the general and supreme rule of charity? They dare not affirm that marriage is either a sacrament or a mystery, though all those sacred things give place to man; and yet they invest it with such an awful sanctity, and give it such adamantine chains to bind with, as if it were to be worshipped like some Indian deity, when it can confer no blessing upon us, but works more and more to our misery. To such teachers the saying of St

Peter at the council of Jerusalem will do well to be applied: 'Why tempt ye God to put a yoke upon the necks of' Christian men, which neither the Jews, God's ancient people, 'not we are able to bear'; and nothing but unwary expounding hath brought upon us?

CHAPTER XIV

Considerations concerning Familism, Antinomianism; and why it may be thought that such Opinions may proceed from the undue Restraint of some just Liberty, than which no greater Cause to contemn Discipline.

To these considerations this also may be added as no improbable conjecture, seeing that sort of men who follow Anabaptism, Familism, Antinomianism, and other fanatic dreams (if we understand them not amiss), be such most commonly as are by nature addicted to religion, of life also not debauched, and that their opinions having full swing, do end in satisfaction of the flesh; it may be come with reason into the thoughts of a wise man, whether all this proceed not partly, if not chiefly, from the restraint of some lawful liberty, which ought to be given men, and is denied them? As by physic we learn in menstruous bodies, where nature's current hath been stopped, that the suffocation and upward forcing of some lower part affects the head and inward sense with dotage and idle fancies. And on the other hand, whether the rest of vulgar men not so religiously professing, do not give themselves much the more to whoredom and adulteries, loving the corrupt and venial discipline of clergy-courts, but hating to hear of perfect reformation; whenas they foresee that then fornication shall be austerely censured, adultery punished, and marriage, the appointed refuge of nature, though it hap to be never so incongruous and displeasing, must yet of force be worn out, when it can be to no other purpose but of strife and hatred, a thing odious to God? This may be worth the study of skilful men in theology, and the reason of things. And lastly, to examine whether some undue and ill-grounded strictness upon the blameless nature of man, be not the cause in those places where already reformation is, that the discipline of the church, so often and so unavoidably broken, is brought into contempt and derision? And if it be thus, let those who are still bent to hold this obstinate literality, so prepare themselves, as to share in the account for all these transgressions, when it shall be demanded at the last day, by one who will scan and sift things with more than a literal wisdom of equity: for if these reasons be duly pondered, and that the gospel is more jealous of laying on excessive burdens than ever the law was, lest the soul of a Christian, which is inestimable, should be overtempted and cast away; considering also that many properties of nature, which the power of regeneration itself never alters, may cause dislike of conversing, even between the most sanctified; which continually grating in harsh tone together, may breed some jar and discord, and that end in rancour and strife, a thing so opposite both to marriage and to Christianity, it would perhaps be less scandal to divorce a natural disparity, than to link violently together an unchristian dissension, committing two insnared souls inevitably to kindle one another, not with the fire of love, but with hatred irreconcilable; who, were they dissevered, would be straight friends in any other relation.   But if an alphabetical servility must be still urged, it may so fall out, that the true church may unwittingly use as much cruelty in forbidding to divorce, as the church of antichrist doth wilfully in forbidding to marry.

Book II

CHAPTER I

The Ordinance of Sabbath and Marriage compared—Hyperbole no unfrequent Figure in the Gospel—Excess cured by contrary Excess— Christ neither did nor could abrogate the Law of Divorce, but only reprieve the Abuse thereof.

HITHERTO the position undertaken has been declared, and proved by a law of God, that law proved to be moral and unabolishable, for many reasons equal, honest, charitable, just, annexed thereto.   It follows now, that those places of scripture, which have a seeming to revoke the prudence of Moses, or rather that merciful decree of God, be forthwith explained and reconciled.   For what are all these reasonings worth, will some reply, whenas the words of Christ are plainly against all divorce, 'except in case of fornication'? to whom he whose mind were to answer no more but this, 'except also in case of charity,' might safely appeal to the more plain words of Christ in defence of so excepting.   'Thou shalt do no manner of work,' saith the

commandment of the sabbath. Yes, saith Christ, works of
charity. And shall we be more severe in paraphrasing the
considerate and tender gospel, than he was in expounding the
rigid and peremptory law? What was ever in all appearance
less made for man, and more for God alone, than the sabbath?
Yet when the good of man comes into the scales, we hear that
voice of infinite goodness and benignity, that 'sabbath was
made for man, not man for sabbath.' What thing ever was more
made for man alone, and less for God, than marriage? And
shall we load it with a cruel and senseless bondage utterly
against both the good of man, and the glory of God? Let whoso
will now listen, I want neither pall nor mitre, I stay neither for
ordination nor induction; but in the firm faith of a knowing
Christian, which is the best and truest endowment of the keys,
I pronounce, the man, who shall bind so cruelly a good and
gracious ordinance of God, hath not in that the spirit of Christ.
Yet that every text of scripture seeming opposite may be attended
with a due exposition, this other part ensues, and makes account
to find no slender arguments for this assertion, out of those very
scriptures which are commonly urged against it.

First therefore let us remember, as a thing not to be denied,
that all places of scripture, wherein just reason of doubt arises
from the letter, are to be expounded by considering upon what
occasion everything is set down, and by comparing other texts.
The occasion, which induced our Saviour to speak of divorce,
was either to convince the extravagance of the pharisees in
that point, or to give a sharp and vehement answer to a tempting
question. And in such cases, that we are not to repose all upon
the literal terms of so many words, many instances will teach
us: wherein we may plainly discover how Christ meant not
to be taken word for word, but like a wise physician, administering one excess against another to reduce us to a permiss; where
they were too remiss, he saw it needful to seem most severe:
in one place he censures an unchaste look to be adultery already
committed; another time he passes over actual adultery with
less reproof than for an unchaste look; not so heavily condemning secret weakness, as open malice: so here he may be
justly thought to have given this rigid sentence against divorce,
not to cut off all remedy from a good man, who finds himself
consuming away in a disconsolate and unenjoined matrimony,
but to lay a bridle upon the bold abuses of those overweening
rabbins; which he could not more effectually do, than by a
counter-sway of restraint curbing their wild exorbitance almost

in the other extreme; as when we bow things the contrary way, to make them come to their natural straightness. And that this was the only intention of Christ is most evident if we attend but to his own words and protestation made in the same sermon, not many verses before he treats of divorcing, that he came not to abrogate from the law 'one jot or tittle,' and denounces against them that shall so teach.

But St Luke, the verse immediately foregoing that of divorce, inserts the same caveat, as if the latter could not be understood without the former; and as a witness to produce against this our wilful mistake of abrogating, which must needs confirm us, that whatever else in the political law of more special relation to the Jews might cease to us; yet that of those precepts concerning divorce, not one of them was repealed by the doctrine of Christ, unless we have vowed not to believe his own cautious and immediate profession; for if these our Saviour's words inveigh against all divorce, and condemn it as adultery, except it be for adultery, and be not rather understood against the abuse of those divorces permitted in the law, then is that law of Moses, Deut. xxiv. 1, not only repealed and wholly annulled against the promise of Christ, and his known profession not to meddle in matters judicial; but that which is more strange, the very substance and purpose of that law is contradicted, and convinced both of injustice and impurity, as having authorised and maintained legal adultery by statute. Moses also cannot scape to be guilty of unequal and unwise decrees, punishing one act of secret adultery by death, and permitting a whole life of open adultery by law. And albeit lawyers write, that some political edicts, though not approved, are yet allowed to the scum of the people, and the necessity of the times; these excuses have but a weak pulse: for first, we read, not that the scoundrel people, but the choicest, the wisest, the holiest of that nation have frequently used these laws, or such as these, in the best and holiest times. Secondly, be it yielded, that in matters not very bad or impure, a human lawgiver may slacken something of that which is exactly good, to the disposition of the people and the times: but if the perfect, the pure, the righteous law of God (for so are all his statutes and his judgments), be found to have allowed smoothly, without any certain reprehension, that which Christ afterward declares to be adultery, how can we free this law from the horrible indictment of being both impure, unjust, and fallacious?

CHAPTER II

How Divorce was permitted for Hardness of Heart, cannot be understood by the common Exposition—That the Law cannot permit, much less enact a Permission of Sin.

Neither will it serve to say this was permitted for the hardness of their hearts, in that sense as it is usually explained; for the law were then but a corrupt and erroneous schoolmaster, teaching us to dash against a vital maxim of religion, by doing foul evil in hope of some certain good.

This only text is not to be matched again throughout the whole scripture, whereby God in his perfect law should seem to have granted to the hard hearts of his holy people, under his own hand, a civil immunity and free charter to live and die in a long successive adultery, under a covenant of works, till the Messiah, and then that indulgent permission to be strictly denied by a covenant of grace; besides, the incoherence of such a doctrine cannot, must not be thus interpreted, to the raising of a paradox never known till then, only hanging by the twined thread of one doubtful scripture, against so many other rules and leading principles of religion, of justice, and purity of life. For what could be granted more either to the fear, or to the lust of any tyrant or politician, than this authority of Moses thus expounded; which opens him a way at will to dam up justice, and not only to admit of any Romish or Austrian dispenses, but to enact a statute of that which he dares not seem to approve, even to legitimate vice, to make sin itself, the ever alien and vassal sin, a free citizen of the commonwealth, pretending only these or these plausible reasons?   And well he might, all the while that Moses shall be alleged to have done as much without showing any reason at all.   Yet this could not enter into the heart of David, Psalm xciv. 20, how any such authority, as endeavours to 'fashion wickedness by a law,' should derive itself from God.   And Isaiah says, 'Wo upon them that decree unrighteous decrees,' chap. x. 1.   Now which of these two is the better lawgiver, and which deserves most a wo, he that gives out an edict singly unjust, or he that confirms to generations a fixed and unmolested impunity of that which is not only held to be unjust, but also unclean, and both in a high degree; not only as they themselves affirm, an injurious expulsion of one wife, but also an unclean freedom by more than a patent to wed another

adulterously? How can we therefore with safety thus dangerously confine the free simplicity of our Saviour's meaning to
that which merely amounts from so many letters, whenas it
can consist neither with its former and cautionary words, nor
with other more pure and holy principles, nor finally with a
scope of charity, commanding by his express commission in a
higher strain? But all rather of necessity must be understood as
only against the abuse of that wise and ingenuous liberty which
Moses gave, and to terrify a roving conscience from sinning under
that pretext.

CHAPTER III

That to allow Sin by Law, is against the Nature of Law, the End of the
Lawgiver, and the Good of the People—Impossible therefore in the Law of
God—That is makes God the Author of Sin more than anything objected
by the Jesuits or Arminians against Predestination.

But let us yet further examine upon what consideration a
law of licence could be thus given to a holy people for their
hardness of heart. I suppose all will answer, that for some good
end or other. But here the contrary shall be proved. First,
that many ill effects, but no good end of such a sufferance can
be shown; next, that a thing unlawful can, for no good end
whatever, be either done or allowed by a positive law. If there
were any good end aimed at, that end was then good either to
the law or to the lawgiver licensing; or as to the person licensed.
That it could not be the end of the law, whether moral or judicial,
to licence a sin, I prove easily out of Rom. v. 20: 'The law
entered, that the offence might abound'; that is, that sin might
be made abundantly manifest to be heinous and displeasing to
God, that so his offered grace might be the more esteemed. Now
if the law, instead of aggravating and terrifying sin, shall give
out licence, it foils itself and turns recreant from its own end:
it forestalls the pure grace of Christ, which is through righteousness, with impure indulgences, which are through sin. And
instead of discovering sin, for 'by the law is the knowledge
thereof,' saith St Paul, and that by certain and true light for
men to walk in safety, it holds out false and dazzling fires to
stumble men; or, like those miserable flies, to run into with
delight and be burnt: for how many souls might easily think
that to be lawful which the law and magistrate allowed them?
Again, we read (1 Tim. i. 5): 'The end of the commandment is

charity out of a pure heart, and of a good conscience, and of faith unfeigned.' But never could that be charity, to allow a people what they could not use with a pure heart, but with conscience and faith both deceived, or else despised. The more particular end of the judicial law is set forth to us clearly, Rom. xiii. That God hath given to that law 'a sword not in vain, but to be a terror to evil works, a revenge to execute wrath upon him that doth evil.' If this terrible commission should but forbear to punish wickedness, were it other to be accounted than partial and unjust? But if it begin to write indulgence to vulgar uncleanness, can it do more to corrupt and shame the end of its own being? Lastly, if the law allow sin, it enters into a kind of covenant with sin; and if it do, there is not a greater sinner in the world than the law itself. The law, to use an allegory something different from that in Philo-Judaeus concerning Amalek, though haply more significant, the law is the Israelite, and hath this absolute charge given it (Deut. xxv): 'To blot out the memory of sin, the Amalekite, from under heaven, not to forget it.' Again, the law is the Israelite, and hath this express repeated command, 'to make no covenant with sin, the Canaanite,' but to expel him, lest he prove a snare. And to say truth, it were too rigid and reasonless to proclaim such an enmity between man and man, were it not the type of a greater enmity between law and sin. I speak even now, as if sin were condemned in a perpetual villanage never to be free by law never to be manumitted: but sure sin can have no tenure by law at all, but is rather an eternal outlaw, and in hostility with law past all atonement: both diagonal contraries, as much allowing one another, as day and night together in one hemisphere. Or if it be possible, that sin with his darkness may come to composition, it cannot be without a foul eclipse and twilight to the law, whose brightness ought to surpass the noon. Thus we see how this unclean permittance defeats the sacred and glorious end both of the moral and judicial law.

As little good can the lawgiver propose to equity by such a lavish remissness as this: if to remedy hardness of heart, Paraeus and other divines confess it more increases by this liberty, than is lessened: and how is it probable that their hearts were more hard in this, that it should be yielded to, than in any other crime? Their hearts were set upon usury, and are to this day, no nation more; yet that which was the endamaging only of their estates was narrowly forbid: this, which is thought the extreme injury and dishonour of their wives and daughters, with the defilement also of themselves is bounteously allowed. Their hearts were as hard under their best kings to offer in high places, though to the true God: yet that, but a small thing, it strictly forewarned; this, accounted a high offence against one of the greatest moral duties, is calmly permitted and established. How can it be evaded, but that the heavy censure of Christ should fall worse upon this lawgiver of theirs, than upon all the scribes and pharisees? For they did but omit judgment and mercy to trifle in mint and cummin, yet all according to law; but this their lawgiver, altogether as punctual in such niceties, goes marching on to adulteries, through the violence of divorce by law against law. If it were such a cursed act of Pilate, a subordinate judge to Caesar, overswayed by those hard hearts, with much ado to suffer one transgression of law but once, what is it then with less ado to publish a law of transgression for many ages? Did God for this come down and cover the mount of Sinai with his glory, uttering in thunder those his sacred ordinances out of the bottomless treasures of his wisdom and infinite pureness, to patch up an ulcerous and rotten commonwealth with strict and stern injunctions, to wash the skin and garments for every unclean touch; and such easy permission given to pollute the soul with adulteries by public authority, without disgrace or question? No; it had been better that man had never known law or matrimony, than that such foul iniquity should be fastened upon the Holy One of Israel, the Judge of all the earth; and such a piece of folly as Belzebub would not commit, to divide against himself, and prevent his own ends: or if he, to compass more certain mischief, might yield perhaps to feign some good deed, yet that God should enact a licence of certain evil for uncertain good against his own glory and pureness, is abominable to conceive. And as it is destructive to the end of law, and blasphemous to the honour of the lawgiver licensing, so it is as pernicious to the person licensed. If a private friend admonish not, the scripture saith, 'He hates his brother, and lets him perish'; but if he soothe him and allow him in his faults, the Proverbs teach us: 'He spreads a net for his neighbour's feet, and worketh ruin.' If the magistrate or prince forget to administer due justice, and restrain not sin, Eli himself could say: 'It made the Lord's people to transgress.' But if he countenance them against law by his own example, what havoc it makes both in religion and virtue among the people may be guessed, by the anger it brought upon Hophni and Phineas not to be appeased 'with sacrifice nor offering for ever.' If the law be silent to declare sin, the people must needs generally go astray, for the apostle himself saith, 'he had not known lust but by the law': and surely a nation seems not to be under the illuminating guidance of God's law, but under the horrible doom rather of such as despise the gospel: 'He that is filthy, let him be filthy still.' But where the law itself gives a warrant for sin, I know not what condition of misery to imagine miserable enough for such a people, unless that portion of the wicked, or rather of the damned, on whom God threatens, in Psalm xi, 'to rain snares'; but that questionless cannot be by any law, which the apostle saith is 'a ministry ordained of God for our good,' and not so many ways and in so high a degree to our destruction, as we have now been graduating. And this is all the good can come to the person licensed in his hardness of heart.

I am next to mention that, which because it is a ground in divinity, Rom. iii, will save the labour of demonstrating, unless her given axioms be more doubted than in other hearts (although it be no less firm in the precepts of philosophy), that a thing unlawful can for no good whatsoever be done, much less allowed by a positive law. And this is the matter why interpreters upon that passage in Hosea will not consent it to be a true story, that the prophet took a harlot to wife: because God, being a pure spirit, could not command a thing repugnant to his own nature, no, not for so good an end as to exhibit more to the life a wholesome and perhaps a converting parable to many an Israelite. Yet that he commanded the allowance of adulterous and injurious divorces for hardness of heart, a reason obscure and in a wrong sense, they can very favourably persuade themselves; so tenacious is the leaven of an old conceit. But they shift it: he permitted only. Yet silence in the law is consent, and consent is accessory: why then is not the law, being silent, or not active against a crime, accessory to its own conviction, itself judging? For though we should grant, that it approves not, yet it wills: and the lawyers' maxim is, that 'the will compelled is yet the will.' And though Aristotle in his Ethics call this 'a mixed action,' yet he concludes it to be voluntary and inexcusable, if it be evil. How justly, then, might human law and philosophy rise up against the righteousness of Moses, if this be true, while our vulgar divinity fathers upon him, yea, upon God himself, not silently, and only negatively to permit, but in his law to divulge a written and general privilege to commit and persist in unlawful divorces with a high hand, with security and no ill fame? For this is more than permitting and

contriving, this is maintaining: this is warranting, this is protecting, yea, this is doing evil, and such an evil as that reprobate
lawgiver did, whose lasting infamy is engraven upon him like
a surname, 'he who made Israel to sin.' This is the lowest pitch
contrary to God that public fraud and injustice can descend.

If it be affirmed, that God, as being Lord, may do what he
will, yet we must know, that God hath not two wills, but one
will, much less two contrary. If he once willed adultery should
be sinful, and to be punished with death, all his omnipotence
will not allow him to will the allowance that his holiest people
might, as it were, by his own antinomy, or counterstatute, live
unreproved in the same fact as he himself esteemed it, according
to our own common explainers. The hidden ways of his providence we adore and search not, but the law is his revealed will,
his complete, his evident and certain will: herein he appears to
us, as it were, in human shape, enters into covenant with us,
swears to keep it, binds himself like a just lawgiver to his own
prescriptions, gives himself to be understood by men, judges
and is judged, measures and is commensurate to right reason;
cannot require less of us in one cantle of his law than in another,
his legal justice cannot be so fickle and so variable, sometimes
like a devouring fire, and by and by connivant in the embers,
or, if I may so say, oscitant and supine. The vigour of his law
could no more remit, than the hallowed fire upon his altar
could be let go out. The lamps that burned before him might
need snuffing, but the light of his law never. Of this also more
beneath, in discussing a solution of Rivetus.

The Jesuits, and that sect among us which is named of
Arminius, are wont to charge us of making God the author of
sin, in two degrees especially, not to speak of his permission:
1. Because we hold, that he hath decreed some to damnation,
and consequently to sin, say they; next, Because those means,
which are of saving knowledge to others, he makes to them an
occasion of greater sin. Yet considering the perfection wherein
man was created, and might have stood, no degree necessitating
his freewill, but subsequent, though not in time, yet in order to
causes, which were in his own power; they might methinks be
persuaded to absolve both God and us. Whenas the doctrine of
Plato and Chrysippus, with their followers, the academics and
the stoics, who knew not what a consummate and most adorned
Pandora was bestowed upon Adam, to be the nurse and guide
of his arbitrary happiness and perseverance, I mean, his native
innocence and perfection, which might have kept him from being

our true Epimetheus; and though they taught of virtue and vice to be both the gift of divine destiny, they could yet give reasons not invalid, to justify the councils of God and fate from the insulsity of mortal tongues: that man's own freewill self-corrupted, is the adequate and sufficient cause of his disobedience besides fate; as Homer also wanted not to express, both in his Iliad and Odyssee. And Manilius the poet, although in his fourth book he tells of some 'created both to sin and punishment'; yet without murmuring, and with an industrious cheerfulness, he acquits the Deity. They were not ignorant in their heathen lore, that it is most godlike to punish those who of his creatures became his enemies with the greatest punishment; and they could attain also to think that the greatest, when God himself throws a man furthest from him: which then they held he did, when he blinded, hardened, and stirred up his offenders, to finish and pile up their desperate work since they had undertaken it. To banish for ever into a local hell, whether in the air or in the centre, or in that uttermost and bottomless gulf of chaos, deeper from holy bliss than the world's diameter multiplied; they thought not a punishing so proper and proportionate for God to inflict, as to punish sin with sin. Thus were the common sort of Gentiles wont to think, without any wry thoughts cast upon divine governance. And therefore Cicero, not in his Tusculan or Campanian retirements among the learned wits of that age, but even in the senate to a mixed auditory (though he were sparing otherwise to broach his philosophy among statists and lawyers), yet as to this point, both in his Oration against Piso, and in that which is about the answers of the soothsayers against Clodius, he declares it publicly as no paradox to common ears, that God cannot punish man more, nor make him more miserable, than still making him more sinful. Thus we see how in this controversy the justice of God stood upright even among heathen disputers. But if any one be truly, and not pretendedly zealous for God's honour, here I call him forth, before men and angels, to use his best and most advised skill, lest God more unavoidably than ever yet, and in the guiltiest manner, be made the author of sin: if he shall not only deliver over and incite his enemies by rebuke so sin as a punishment, but shall be patent under his own broad seal allow his friends whom he would sanctify and save, whom he would unite to himself and not disjoin, whom he would correct by wholesome chastening, and not punish as he doth the damned be lewd sinning; if he shall allow these in his law, the perfect rule of his own purest will, and our most edified conscience, the perpetrating of an odious and manifold sin without the least contesting. It is wondered how there can be in God a secret and revealed will; and yet what wonder, if there be in man two answerable causes? But here there must be two revealed wills grappling in a fraternal war with one another without any reasonable cause apprehended. This cannot be less than to engraft sin into the substance of the law, which law is to provoke sin by crossing and forbidding, not by complying with it. Nay, this is, which I tremble in uttering, to incarnate sin into the unpunishing and well-pleased will of God. To avoid these dreadful consequences, that tread upon the heels of those allowances to sin, will be a task of far more difficulty than to appease those minds, which perhaps out of a vigilant and wary conscience except against predestination. Thus finally we may conclude, that a law wholly giving licence cannot upon any good consideration be given to a holy people, for hardness of heart in the vulgar sense.

CHAPTER IV

That if Divorce be no Command, no more is Marriage—That Divorce could be no Dispensation, if it were sinful—The Solution of Rivetus, that God dispensed by some unknown Way, ought not to satisfy a Christian Mind.

Others think to evade the matter by not granting any law of divorce, but only a dispensation which is contrary to the words of Christ, who himself calls it a 'law,' Mark x. 5: or if we speak of a command in the strictest definition, then marriage itself is no more a command than divorce, but only a free permission to him who cannot contain. But as to dispensation, I affirm the same as before of the law, that it can never be given to the allowance of sin: God cannot give it, neither in respect of himself, nor in respect of man; not in respect of himself, being a most pure essence, the just avenger of sin; neither can he make that cease to be a sin, which is in itself unjust and impure, as all divorces, they say, were, which were not for adultery. Not in respect of man, for then it must be either to his good, or to his evil. Not to his good; for how can that be imagined any good to a sinner, whom nothing but rebuke and due correction can save, to hear the determinate oracle of divine law louder than any reproof dispensing and providing for the impunity and convenience of sin; to make that doubtful, or rather lawful, which the end of the law was to make most evidently hateful? Nor to the evil of man can dispense be given; for if 'the law were ordained unto life,' Rom. vii. 10, how can the same God publish dispenses against that law, which must needs be unto death? Absurd and monstrous would that dispense be, if any judge or law should give it a man to cut his own throat, or to damn himself. Dispense, therefore, presupposes full pardon, or else it is not a dispense, but a most baneful and bloody snare. And why should God enter covenant with a people to be holy, as 'the command is holy, and just, and good,' Rom. vii. 12, and yet suffer an impure and treacherous dispense to mislead and betray them under the vizard of law to a legitimate practice of uncleanness? God is no covenant-breaker; he cannot do this.

Rivetus, a diligent and learned writer, having well weighed what hath been written by those founders of dispense, and finding the small agreement among them, would fain work himself aloof these rocks and quicksands, and thinks it best to conclude that God certainly did dispense, but by some way to us unknown, and so to leave it. But to this I oppose that a Christian by no means ought to rest himself in such an ignorance; whereby so many absurdities will straight reflect both against the purity, justice, and wisdom of God, the end also both of law and gospel, and the comparison of them both together. God indeed in some ways of his providence is high and secret, past finding out: but in the delivery and execution of his law, especially in the managing of a duty so daily and so familiar as this is whereof we reason, hath plain enough revealed himself, and requires the observance thereof not otherwise, than to the law of nature and equity imprinted in us seems correspondent. And he hath taught us to love and extol his laws, not only as they are his, but as they are just and good to every wise and sober understanding. Therefore Abraham, even to the face of God himself, seemed to doubt of divine justice, if it should swerve from the irradiation wherewith it had enlightened the mind of man, and bound itself to observe its own rule: 'Wilt thou destroy the righteous with the wicked? that be far from thee; shall not the judge of the earth do right?' Thereby declaring that God hath created a righteousness in right itself, against which he cannot do. So David (Psalm cxix): 'The testimonies which thou hast commanded are righteous and very faithful; thy word is very pure, therefore thy servant loveth it.' Not only then for the author's sake, but for its own purity. 'He is faithful,' saith

St Paul, 'he cannot deny himself'; that is, cannot deny his own
promises, cannot but be true to his own rules.   He often pleads
with men the uprightness of his ways by their own principles.
How should we imitate him else, to 'be perfect as he is perfect'?
If at pleasure he can dispense with golden poetic ages of such
pleasing licence, as in the fabled reign of old Saturn, and this
perhaps before the law might have some covert; but under such
an undispensing covenant as Moses made with them, and not
to tell us why and wherefore indulgence cannot give quiet to the
breast of an intelligent man?   We must be resolved how the law
can be pure and perspicuous, and yet throw a polluted skirt over
these Eleusinian mysteries, that no man can utter what they
mean: worse in this than the worst obscenities of heathen superstition; for their filthiness was hid, but the mystic reason thereof
known to their sages.   But this Jewish imputed filthiness was
daily and open, but the reason of it is not known to our divines.
We know of no design the gospel can have to impose new righteousness upon works, but to remit the old by faith without works,
if we mean justifying works: we know no mystery our Saviour
could have to lay new bonds upon marriage in the covenant of
grace which himself had loosened to the severity of law.   So
that Rivetus may pardon us, if we cannot be contented with his
non-solution, to remain in such a peck of uncertainties and
doubts, so dangerous and ghastly to the fundamentals of our
faith.

·   ·   ·   ·   ·

CHAPTER XVI

How to be understood, that they must be one Flesh; and how that those
whom God hath joined, Man should not sunder.

Next he saith, 'They must be one flesh,' which when all
conjecturing is done, will be found to import no more but to
make legitimate and good the carnal act, which else might
seem to have something of pollution in it; and infers thus much
over, that the fit union of their souls be such as may even incorporate them to love and amity: but that can never be where
no correspondence is of the mind; nay, instead of being one
flesh, they will be rather two carcasses chained unnaturally
together; or, as it may happen, a living soul bound to a dead
corpse; a punishment too like that inflicted by the tyrant Mezen-
tius, so little worthy to be received as that remedy of loneliness

which God meant us: Since we know it is not the joining of another body will remove loneliness, but the uniting of another compliable mind; and that it is no blessing but a torment, nay, a base and brutish condition to be one flesh, unless where nature can in some measure fix a unity of disposition. The meaning therefore of these words, 'For this cause shall a man leave his father and his mother, and shall cleave to his wife,' was first to show us the dear affection which naturally grows in every not unnatural marriage, even to the leaving of parents, or other familiarity whatsoever. Next, it justifies a man in so doing, that nothing is done undutifully to father or mother. But he that should be here sternly commanded to cleave to his error, a disposition which to his he finds will never cement, a quotidian of sorrow and discontent in his house; let us be excused to pause a little, and bethink us every way round ere we lay such a flat solecism upon the gracious, and certainly not inexorable, not ruthless and flinty ordinance of marriage. For if the meaning of these words must be thus blocked up within their own letters from all equity and fair deduction, they will serve then well indeed their turn, who affirm divorce to have been granted only for wives; whenas we see no word of this text binds women, but men only, what it binds. No marvel then if Salomith (sister to Herod) sent a writ of ease to Costobarus her husband, which (as Josephus there attests) was lawful only to men. No marvel though Placidia, the sister of Honorius, threatened the like to earl Constantius for a trivial cause, as Photius relates from Olympiodorus. No marvel anything, if letters must be turned into palisadoes, to stake out all requisite sense from entering to their due enlargement.

Lastly, Christ himself tells who should not be put asunder, namely, those whom God hath joined. A plain solution of this great controversy, if men would but use their eyes. For when is it that God may be said to join? when the parties and their friends consent? No, surely; for that may concur to lewdest ends. Or is it when church rites are finished? Neither; for the efficacy of those depends upon the presupposed fitness of either party. Perhaps after carnal knowledge. Least of all; for that may join persons whom neither law no nature dares join. It is left, that only then when the minds are fitly disposed and enabled to maintain a cheerful conversation, to the solace and love of each other, according as God intended and promised in the very first foundation of matrimony, 'I will make him a helpmeet for him'; for surely what God intended and promised, that only can be thought to be his joining, and not the contrary. So likewise the apostle witnesseth, 1 Cor. vii. 15, that in marriage 'God hath called us to peace.' And doubtless in what respect he hath called us to marriage, in that also he hath joined us. The rest, whom either disproportion, or deadness of spirit, or something distasteful and averse in the immutable bent of nature renders conjugal, error may have joined, but God never joined against the meaning of his own ordinance. And if he joined them not, then is there no power above their own consent to hinder them from unjoining, when they cannot reap the soberest ends of being together in any tolerable sort. Neither can it be said properly that such twain were ever divorced, but only parted from each other, as two persons unconjunctive are unmarriable together. But if, whom God hath made a fit help, frowardness or private injuries hath made unfit, that being the secret of marriage, God can better judge than man, neither is man indeed fit or able to decide this matter: however it be, undoubtedly a peaceful divorce is a less evil, and less in scandal than hateful, hard-hearted, and destructive continuance of marriage in the judgment of Moses and of Christ, that justifies him in choosing the less evil: which if it were an honest and civil prudence in the law, what is there in the gospel forbidding such a kind of legal wisdom, though we should admit the common expositors?

CHAPTER XVII

The Sentence of Christ concerning Divorce how to be expounded. What Grotius hath observed—Other Additions.

Having thus unfolded those ambiguous reasons, wherewith Christ (as his wont was) gave to the pharisees that came to sound him, such an answer as they deserved, it will not be uneasy to explain the sentence itself that now follows: 'Whosoever shall put away his wife, except it be for fornication, and shall marry another, committeth adultery.' First therefore I will set down what is observed by Grotius upon this point, a man of general learning. Next, I produce what mine own thoughts gave me before I had seen his annotations. Origen, saith he, notes that Christ named adultery rather as one example of other like cases, than as one only exception; and that is frequent not only in human but in divine laws, to express one kind of fact, whereby other causes of like nature may have the like plea, as Exod. xxi. 18, 19, 20, 26; Deut. xix. 5. And from the maxims of civil law he shows, that even in sharpest penal laws the same reason hath the same right; and in gentler laws, that from like causes to like the law interprets rightly. But it may be objected, saith he, that nothing destroys the end of wedlock so much as adultery. To which he answers, that marriage was not ordained only for copulation, but for mutual help and comfort of life: and if we mark diligently the nature of our Saviour's commands, we shall find that both their beginning and their end consists in charity: whose will is that we should so be good to others, as that we be not cruel to ourselves: and hence it appears why Mark, and Luke, and St Paul to the Corinthians, mentioning this precept of Christ, add no exception, because exceptions that arise from natural equity are included silently under general terms: it would be considered therefore, whether the same equity may not have place in other cases less frequent. Thus far he. From hence is what I add: First, that this saying of Christ, as it is usually expounded, can be no law at all, that a man for no cause should separate but for adultery, except it be a supernatural law, not binding us as we now are. Had it been the law of nature, either the Jews, or some other wise and civil nation, would have pressed it: or let it be so, yet that law, Deut. xxiv. 1, whereby a man hath leave to part, whenas for just and natural cause discovered he cannot love, is a law ancienter and deeper engraven in blameless nature than the other: therefore the inspired lawgiver Moses took care that this should be specified and allowed; the other he let vanish in silence, not once repeated in the volume of his law, even as the reason of it vanished with Paradise. Secondly, this can be no new command, for the gospel enjoins no new morality, save only the infinite enlargement of charity, which in this respect is called the new commandment by St John, as being the accomplishment of every command. Thirdly, it is no command of perfection further than it partakes of charity, which is 'the bond of perfection.' Those commands, therefore, which compel us to self-cruelty above our strength, so hardly will help forward to perfection, that they hinder and set backward in all the common rudiments of Christianity, as was proved. It being thus clear, that the words of Christ can be no kind of command as they are vulgarly taken, we shall now see in what sense they may be a command, and that an excellent one, the same with that of Moses and no other. Moses had granted, that only for a natural annoyance, defect, or dislike, whether in body or mind (for so the Hebrew word plainly notes), which a man could not force himself to live with, he might give a bill of divorce, thereby forbidding any other cause, wherein amendment or reconciliation might have place. This law the pharisees depraving extended to any slight contentious cause whatsoever. Christ therefore seeing where they halted, urges the negative part of the law, which is necessarily understood (for the determinate permission of Moses binds them from further licence), and checking their supercilious drift, declares that no accidental, temporary, or reconcilable offence (except fornication) can justify a divorce. He touches not here those natural and perpetual hinderances of society, whether in body or mind, which are not to be removed; for such as they are aptest to cause an unchangeable offence, so are they not capable of reconcilement, because not of amendment: they do not break indeed, but they annihilate the bands of marriage more than adultery. For that fault committed argues not always a hatred either natural or incidental against who it is committed; neither does it infer a disability of all future helpfulness, or loyalty, or loving agreement, being once past and pardoned, where it can be pardoned: but that which naturally distastes, and 'finds no favour in the eyes' of matrimony, can never be concealed, never appeased, never intermitted, but proves a perpetual nullity of love and contentment, a solitude and dead vacation of all acceptable conversing. Moses therefore permits divorce, but in cases only that have no hands to join, and more need separating than adultery. Christ forbids it, but in matters only that may accord, and those less than fornication. Thus in Moses's law here plainly confirmed, and those causes which he permitted not a jot gainsaid. And that this is the true meaning of this place, I prove by no less an author than St Paul himself, 1 Cor. vii. 10, 11; upon which text interpreters agree, that the apostle only repeats the precept of Christ: where while he speaks of the 'wife's reconcilement to her husband,' he puts it out of controversy, that our Saviour meant chiefly matters of strife and reconcilement; of which sort he would not that any difference should be the occasion of divorce, except fornication. And that we may learn better how to value a grave and prudent law of Moses, and how unadvisedly we smatter with our lips, when we talk of Christ's abolishing any judicial law of his great Father, except in some circumstances which are judaical rather than judicial, and need no abolishing, but cease of themselves; I say again, that this recited law of Moses contains a cause of divorce greater beyond compare than that for adultery: and whoso cannot so conceive it, errs and wrongs exceedingly a law of deep wisdom for want of well fathoming. For let him mark, no man urges the just divorcing for adultery as it is a sin, but as it is an injury to marriage; and though it be but once committed, and that without malice, whether through importunity or opportunity, the gospel does not therefore dissuade him who would therefore divorce; but that natural hatred whenever it arises, is a greater evil in marriage than the accident of adultery, a greater defrauding, a greater injustice, and yet not blameable, he who understands not after all this representing, I doubt his will, like a hard spleen, draws faster than his understanding can well sanguify: nor did that man ever know or feel what it is to love truly, not ever yet comprehend in his thoughts what the true intent of marriage is. And this also will be somewhat above his reach, but yet no less a truth for lack of his perspective, that as no man apprehends what vice is so well as he who is truly virtuous, no man knows hell like him who converses most in heaven; so there is none that can estimate the evil and the affliction of a natural hatred in matrimony, unless he have a soul gentle enough and spacious enough to contemplate what is true love.

And the reason why men so disesteem this wise judging law of God, and count hate, or 'the not finding of favour,' as it is there termed, a humorous, a dishonest, and slight cause of divorce, is because themselves apprehend so little of what true concord means: for if they did, they would be juster in their balancing between natural hatred and casual adultery; this being but a transient injury, and soon amended, I mean as to the party against whom the trespass is: but that other being an unspeakable and unremitting sorrow and offence, whereof no amends can be made, no cure, no ceasing but by divorce, which like a divine touch in one moment heals all, and (like the word of God) in one instant hushes outrageous tempests into a sudden stillness and peaceful calm. Yet all this so great a good of God's own enlarging to us is, by the hard reins of them that sit us, wholly diverted and embezzled from us. Maligners of mankind! But who hath taught you to mangle thus, and make more gashes in the miseries of a blameless creature, with the leaden daggers of your literal decrees, to whose ease you cannot add the tithe of one small atom, but by letting alone your unhelpful surgery? As for such as think wandering concupiscence to be here newly and more precisely forbidden than it was before; if the apostle can convince them, we know that we are to 'know lust by the law,' and not by any new discovery of the gospel. The law of Moses knew what it permitted, and the gospel knew what it forbid; he that under a peevish conceit of debarring concupiscence shall go about to make a novice of Moses (not to say a worse thing, for reverence sake), and such a one of God himself, as is a horror to think, to bind our Saviour in the default of a downright promise-breaking; and to bind the disunions of complaining nature in chains together, and curb them with a canon bit; it is he that commits all the whoredom and adultery which himself adjudges, besides the former guilt so manifold that lies upon him. And if none of these considerations, with all their weight and gravity, can avail to the dispossessing him of his precious literalism, let some one or other entreat him but to read on in the same 19th of Matt. till he comes to that place that says: 'Some make themselves eunuchs for the kingdom of heaven's sake.' And if then he please to make use of Origen's knife, he may do well to be his own carver.

CHAPTER XVIII

Whether the Words of our Saviour be rightly expounded only of actual Fornication to be the Cause of Divorce—The Opinion of Grotius, with other Reasons.

But because we know that Christ never gave a judicial law, and that the word fornication is variously significant in scripture, it will be much right done to our Saviour's words, to consider diligently whether it be meant here, that nothing but actual fornication, proved by witness, can warrant a divorce; for so our canon law judges. Nevertheless, as I find that Grotius on this place hath observed the Christian emperors, Theodosius the Second and Justinian, men of high wisdom and reputed piety, decreed it to be a divorcive fornication, if the wife attempted either against the knowledge, or obstinately against the will of her husband, such things as gave open suspicion of adulterizing, as the wilful haunting of feasts, and invitations with men not of her near kindred, the lying forth of her house without probable cause, the frequenting of theatres against her husband's mind, her endeavour to prevent or destroy conception. Hence that of Jerome, 'Where fornication is suspected, the wife may lawfully be divorced': not that every motion of a jealous mind should be regarded; but that it should not be exacted to prove all things by the visibility of law witnessing, or else to hookwink the mind: for the law is not able to judge of these things but by the rule of equity, and by permitting a wise man to walk the middle way of prudent circumspection, neither wretchedly jealous, nor stupidly and tamely patient.   To this purpose hath Grotius in his notes. He shows also, that fornication is taken in scripture for such a continual headstrong behaviour, as tends to plain contempt of the husband, and proves it out of Judges xix. 2, where the Levite's wife is said to have played the whore against him; which Josephus and the Septuagint, with the Chaldean, interpret only of stubbornness and rebellion against her husband: and to this I add, that Kimchi, and the two other rabbins who gloss the text, are in the same opinion.   Ben Gersom reasons, that had it been whoredom, a Jew and a Levite would have disdained to fetch her again.   And this I shall contribute, that had it been whoredom, she would have chosen any other place to run to than to her father's house, it being so infamous for a Hebrew woman to play the harlot, and so opprobrious to the parents.   Fornication then in this place of the Judges is understood for stubborn disobedience against the husband, and not for adultery.   A sin of that sudden activity, as to be already committed when no more is done, but only looked unchastely: which yet I should be loath to judge worthy a divorce, though in our Saviour's language it be called adultery.   Nevertheless when palpable and frequent signs are given, the law of God, Numb. v, so far gave way to the jealously of a man, as that the woman, set before the sanctuary with her head uncovered, was adjured by the priest to swear whether she were false or no, and constrained to drink that 'bitter water,' with an undoubted 'curse of rottenness and tympany' to follow, unless she were innocent.   And the jealous man had not been guiltless before God, as seems by the last verse, if having such a suspicion in his head, he should neglect his trial; which if to this day it be not to be used, or be thought as uncertain of effect as our antiquated law of Ordalium, yet all equity will judge, that many adulterous demeanours, which are of lewd suspicion and example, may be held sufficient to incur a divorce, though the act itself hath not been proved.   And seeing the generosity of our nation is so, as to account no reproach more abominable than to be nicknamed the husband of an adulteress; that our law should not be as ample as the law of God, to vindicate a man from that ignoble sufferance, is our barbarous unskilfulness, not considering that the law should be exasperated according to our estimation of the injury.   And if it must be suffered till the act be visibly proved, Solomon himself, whose judgment will be granted to surpass the acuteness of any canonist, confesses, Prov. xxx. 19, 20, that for the act of adultery it is as difficult to be found as the 'track of an eagle in the air, or the way of a ship in the sea'; so that a man may be put to unmanly indignities ere it be found out.   This therefore may be enough to inform us that divorcive adultery is not limited by our Saviour to the utmost act, and that to be attested always by eyewitness, but may be extended also to divers obvious actions, which either plainly lead to adultery, or give such presumption whereby sensible men may suspect the deed to be already done.   And this the rather may be thought in that our Saviour chose to use the word fornication, which word is found to signify other matrimonial transgressions of main breach to that covenant besides actual adultery.   For that sin needed not the riddance of divorce, but of death by the law, which was active even till then by the example of the woman taken in adultery; or if the law had been dormant, our Saviour was more likely to have told them of their neglect, than to have let a capital crime silently scape into a divorce: or if it be said, his business was not to tell them what was criminal in the civil courts, but what was sinful at the bar of conscience, how dare they then, having no other ground than these our Saviour's words, draw that into the trial of law, which both by Moses and our Saviour was left to the jurisdiction of conscience?   But we take from our Saviour, say they, only that it was adultery, and our law of itself applies the punishment. but by their leave that so argue, the great Lawgiver of all the world, who knew best what was adultery, both to the Jew and to the Gentile, appointed no such applying, and never likes when mortal men will be vainly presuming to outstrip his justice.

CHAPTER XIX

Christ's manner of teaching—St Paul adds to this matter of Divorce without command, to show the matter to be of Equity, not of Rigour— That the Bondage of a Christian may be as much, and his Peace as little, in some other Marriages besides idolatrous—If those Arguments, therefore, be good in that one Case, why not in those other?   Therefore the Apostle himself adds, ἐν τοῖς τοιούτοις.

Thus at length we see, both by this and other places, that there is scarce any one saying in the gospel but must be read with limitations and distinctions to be rightly understood;

for Christ gives no full comments or continued discourses, but (as Demetrius the rhetorician phrases it) speaks oft in mono-syllables, like a master scattering the heavenly grain of his doctrine like pearls here and there, which requires a skilful and laborious gatherer, who must compare the words he finds with other precepts, with the end of every ordinance, and with the general analogy of evangelic doctrine: otherwise many particular sayings would be but strange repugnant riddles, and the church would offend in granting divorce for frigidity, which is not here excepted with adultery, but by them added. And this was it undoubtedly which gave reason to St Paul of his own authority, as he professes and without command from the Lord, to enlarge the seeming construction of those places in the gospel, by adding a case wherein a person deserted (which is some-thing less than divorced) may lawfully marry again. And having declared his opinions in one case, he leaves a further liberty for Christian prudence to determine in cases of like importance, using words so plain as not to be shifted off, 'that a brother or a sister is not under bondage in such cases'; adding also, that 'God hath called us to peace' in marriage.

Now if it be plain that a Christian may be brought into un-worthy bondage, and his religious peace not only interrupted now and then, but perpetually and finally hindered in wedlock, by misyoking with a diversity of nature as well as of religion, the reasons of St Paul cannot be made special to that one case of infidelity, but are of equal moment to a divorce, wherever Christian liberty and peace are without fault equally obstructed: that the ordinance which God gave to our comfort may not be pinned upon us to our undeserved thraldom, to be cooped up, as it were, in mockery of wedlock, to a perpetual betrothed loneliness and discontent, if nothing worse ensue. There being nought else of marriage left between such but a displeasing and forced remedy against the sting of a brute desire; which fleshly accustoming without the soul's union and commixture of in-tellectual delight, as it is rather a soiling than a fulfilling of marriage rites, so is it enough to abase the mettle of a generous spirit, and sinks him to a low and vulgar pitch of endeavour in all his actions; or, which is worse, leaves him in a despairing plight of abject and hardened thoughts: which condition rather than a good man should fall into, a man useful in the service of God and mankind, Christ himself hath taught us to dispense with the most sacred ordinance of his worship, even for a bodily healing to dispense with that holy and speculative rest of sabbath, much more than with the erroneous observance of an ill-knotted marriage, for the sustaining of an overcharged faith and perseverance.

CHAPTER XX

The Meaning of St Paul, that 'Charity believeth all Things'—What is to be said to the Licence which is vainly feared will grow hereby—What to those who never have done prescribing Patience in this Case—The Papist most severe against Divorce, yet most easy to all Licence—Of all the Miseries in Marriage God is to be cleared, and the Faults to be laid on Man's unjust Laws.

And though bad causes would take licence by this pretext, if that cannot be remedied, upon their conscience be it who shall so do. This was that hardness of heart, and abuse of a good law, which Moses was content to suffer, rather than good men should not have it at all to use needfully. And he who, to run after one lost sheep, left ninety-nine of his own flock at random in the wilderness, would little perplex his thoughts for the obduring of nine hundred and ninety such as will daily take worse liberties, whether they have permission or not. To conclude, as without charity God hath given no commandment to men, so without it neither can men rightly believe any commandment given. For every act of true faith, as well that whereby we believe the law as that whereby we endeavour the law, is wrought in us by charity, according to that in the divine hymn of St Paul, 1 Cor. xiii, 'Charity believeth all things'; not as if she were so credulous, which is the exposition hitherto current, for that were a trivial praise, but to teach us that charity is the high governess of our belief, and that we cannot safely assent to any precept written in the Bible, but as charity commends it to us. Which agrees with that of the same apostle to the Eph. iv. 14, 15; where he tells us, that the way to get a sure undoubted knowledge of things, is to hold that for truth which accords most with charity. Whose unerring guidance and conduct having followed as a loadstar, with all diligence and fidelity, in this question, I trust, through the help of that illuminating Spirit which hath favoured me, to have done no every day's work, in asserting, after many the words of Christ, with other scriptures of great concernment, from burdensome and remorseless obscurity, tangled with manifold repugnances, to their native lustre and consent between each other; hereby also dissolving tedious and Gordian difficulties; which have hitherto molested the church of God, and are now decided, not with the sword of Alexander, but with the immaculate hands of charity, to the unspeakable good of Christendom. And let the extreme literalist sit down now, and revolve whether this in all necessity be not the due result of our Saviour's words; or if he persist to be otherwise opinioned, let him well advice, lest thinking to gripe fast the gospel, he be found instead with the canon law in his fist; whose boisterous edicts tyrannizing the blessed ordinance of marriage into the quality of a most unnatural and unchristianly yoke, hath given the flesh this advantage to hate it, and turn aside, ofttimes unwillingly, to all dissolute uncleanness, even till punishment itself is weary of and overcome by the incredible frequency of trading lust and uncontrolled adulteries. Yet men whose creed is custom, I doubt not will be still endeavouring to hide the sloth of their own timorous capacities with this pretext, that for all this it is better to endure with patience and silence this affliction which God hath sent. And I agree it is true, if this be exhorted and not enjoined; but withal it will be wisely done to be as sure as may be, that what man's iniquity hath laid on be not imputed to God's sending, lest under the colour of an affected patience we detain ourselves at the gulf's mouth of many hideous temptations, not to be withstood without proper gifts, which, as Perkins well notes, God gives not ordinarily, no, not to most earnest prayers. Therefore we pray, 'Lead us not into temptation'; a vain prayer, if, having led ourselves thither, we love to stay in that perilous condition. God sends remedies as well as evils, under which he who lies and groans, that may lawfully acquit himself, is accessory to his own ruin; nor will it excuse him though he suffer through a sluggish fearfulness to search thoroughly what is lawful, for fear of disquieting the secure falsity of an old opinion. Who doubts not but that it may be piously said, to him who would dismiss his frigidity, Bear your trial; take it as if God would have you live this life of continence? If he exhort this, I hear him as an angel, though he speak without warrant; but if he would compel me, I know him for Satan. To him who divorces an adulteress, piety might say, Pardon her; you may show much mercy, you may win a soul: yet the law both of God and man leaves it freely to him; for God loves not to plough out the heart of our endeavours with overhard and sad tasks. God delights not to make a drudge of virtue, whose actions must be all elective and unconstrained. Forced virtue is as a bolt overshot, it goes neither forward nor backward, and does no good as it stands. Seeing, therefore, that neither scripture nor reason hath laid this unjust austerity upon divorce, we may resolve that nothing else hath wrought it but that letter-bound servility of the canon doctors, supposing marriage to be a sacrament, and out of the art they have to lay unnecessary burdens upon all men, to make a fair show in the fleshly observance of matrimony, though peace and love, with all other conjugal respects, fare never so ill. And, indeed, the papists, who are the strictest forbidders of divorce, are the easiest libertines to admit of grossest uncleanness; as if they had a design by making wedlock a supportless yoke, to violate it most, under colour of preserving it most inviolable; and withal delighting (as their mystery is) to make men the day labourers of their own afflictions, as if there were such a scarcity of miseries from abroad, that we should be made to melt our choicest home blessings, and coin them into crosses, for want whereby to hold commerce with patience. If any, therefore, who shall hap to read this discourse, hath been through misadventure ill engaged in this contracted evil here complained of, and finds the fits and workings of a high impatience frequently upon him; of all those wild words which men in misery think to ease themselves by uttering, let him not open his lips against the providence of Heaven, or tax the ways of God and his divine truth; for they are equal, easy, and not burdensome; nor do they ever cross the just and reasonable desires of men, nor involve this our portion of mortal life into a necessity of sadness and malcontent, by laws commanding over the unreducible antipathies of nature, sooner or later found, but allow us to remedy and shake off these evils into which human error hath led us through the midst of our best intentions, and to support our incident extremities by that authentic precept of sovereign charity, whose grand commission is to do and to dispose over all the ordinances of God to man, that love and truth may advance each other to everlasting. While we, literally superstitious, through customary faintness of heart, not venturing to pierce with our free thoughts into the full latitude of nature and religion, abandon ourselves to serve under the tyranny of usurped opinions; suffering those ordinances which were allotted to our solace and reviving, to trample over us, and hale us into a multitude of sorrows, which God never meant us. And where he sets us in a fair allowance of way, with honest liberty and prudence to our guard, we never leave subtilizing and casuisting till we have straitened and pared that liberal path into a razor's edge to walk on; between a precipice of unnecessary mischief on either side, and starting at every false alarm, we do not know which way to set a foot forward with manly confidence and Christian resolution, through the confused ringing in our ears of panic scruples and amazements.

CHAPTER XXI

That the Matter of Divorce is not to be tried by Law, but by Conscience, as many other Sins are—The Magistrate can only see that the Condition of the Divorce be just and equal—The Opinion of Fagius, and the Reasons of the Assertion.

Another act of papal encroachment it was to pluck the power and arbitrement of divorce from the master of the family, into whose hands God and the law of all nations had put it, and Christ so left it, preaching only to the conscience, and not authorizing a judicial court to toss about and divulge the unaccountable and secret reason of disaffection between man and wife, as a thing most improperly answerable to any such kind of trial. But the popes of Rome, perceiving the great revenue and high authority it would give them even over princes, to have the judging and deciding of such a main consequence in the life of man as was divorce; wrought so upon the superstition of those ages, as to divest them of that right, which God from the beginning had entrusted to the husband: by which means they subjected that ancient and naturally domestic prerogative to an external and unbefitting judicature. For although differences in divorce about dowries, jointures, and the like, besides the punishing of adultery, ought not to pass without referring, if need be, to the magistrate; yet that the absolute and final hindering of divorce cannot belong to any civil or earthly power, against the will and consent of both parties, or of the husband alone, some reasons will be here urged as shall not need to decline the touch. But first I shall recite what hath been already yielded by others in favour of this opinion. Grotius and many more agree, that notwithstanding what Christ spake therein to the conscience, the magistrate is not thereby enjoined aught against the preservation of civil peace, of equity, and of convenience. And among these Fagius is most remarkable, and gives the same liberty of pronouncing divorce to the Christian magistrate as the Mosaic had. 'For whatever,' saith he, 'Christ spake to the regenerate, the judge hath to deal with the vulgar: if therefore any through hardness of heart will not be a tolerable wife to her busband, it will be lawful as well now as of old to pass the bill of divorce, not by private but by public authority. Nor doth man separate them then, but God by his law of divorce given by Moses. What can hinder the magistrate from so doing, to whose government all outward things are subject, to separate and remove from perpetual vexation, and no small danger, those bodies whose minds are already separate; it being his office to procure peaceable and convenient living in the commonwealth; and being as certain also, that they so necessarily separated cannot all receive a single life?' And this I observe, that our divines do generally condemn separation of bed and board, without the liberty of second choice: if that therefore in some cases be most purely necessary (as who so blockish to deny?), then is this also as needful. Thus far by others is already well stepped, to inform us that divorce is not a matter of law, but of charity; if there remain a furlong yet to end the question, these following reasons may serve to gain it with any apprehension not too unlearned or too wayward. First, because ofttimes the causes of seeking divorce reside so deeply in the radical and innocent affections of nature, as is not within the diocese of law to tamper with. Other relations may aptly enough be held together by a civil and virtuous love: but the duties of man and wife are such as are chiefly conversant in that love which is most ancient and merely natural, whose two prime statutes are to join itself to that which is good, and acceptable, and friendly; and to turn aside and depart from what is disagreeable, displeasing, and unlike: of the two this latter is the strongest, and most equal to be regarded; for although a man many often be unjust in seeking that which he loves, yet he can never be unjust or blameable in retiring from his endless trouble and distaste, whenas his tarrying can redound to no true content on either side. Hate is of all things the mightiest divider; nay, is division itself. To couple hatred therefore, though wedlock try all her golden links, and borrow to her aid all the iron manacles and fetters of law, it does but seek to twist a rope of sand, which was a task they say that posed the devil: and that sluggish fiend in hell, Ocnus, whom the poems tell of, brought his idle cordage to as good effect, which never served to bind with, but to feed the ass that stood at his elbow. And that the restrictive law against divorce attains as little to bind anything truly in a disjointed marriage, or to keep it bound, but serves only to feed the ignorance and definitive impertinence of a doltish canon, were no absurd allusion. To hinder therefore those deep and serious regresses of nature in a reasonable soul, parting from that mistaken help which he justly seeks in a person created for him, recollecting himself from an unmeet help which was never meant, and to detain him by compulsion in such an unpredestined misery as this, is in diameter against both nature and institution: but to interpose a jurisdictive power over the inward and irremediable disposition of man, to command love and sympathy, to forbid dislike against the guiltless instinct of nature, is not within the province of any law to reach; and were indeed an uncommodious rudeness, not a just power: for that law may bandy with nature, and traverse her sage motions, was an error in Callicles the rhetorician, whom Socrates from high principles confutes in Plato's Gorgias. If therefore divorce may be so natural, and that law and nature are not to go contrary; then to forbid divorce compulsively, is not only against nature but against law.

Next, it must be remembered, that all law is for some good, that may be frequently attained without the admixture of a worse inconvenience; and therefore many gross faults, as ingratitude and the like, which are too far within the soul to be cured by constraint of law, are left only to be wrought on by conscience and persuasion. Which made Aristotle, in the 10th of his Ethics to Nicomachus, aim at a kind of division of law into private or persuasive, and public or compulsive. Hence it is, that the law forbidding divorce never attains to any good end of such prohibition, but rather multiplies evil. For if nature's resistless sway in love or hate be once compelled, it grows careless of itself, vicious, useless to friends, unserviceable and spiritless to the commonwealth. Which Moses rightly foresaw, and all wise lawgivers that ever knew man, what kind of creature he was. The parliament also and clergy of England were not ignorant of this, when they consented that Henry VIII might put away his queen Anne of Cleve, whom he could not like after he had been wedded half a year; unless it were that, contrary to the proverb, they made a necessity of that which might have been a virtue in them to do; for even the freedom and eminence of man's creation gives him to be a law in this matter to himself, being the head of the other sex which was made for him: whom therefore though he ought not to injure, yet neither should he be forced to retain in society to his own overthrow, nor to hear any judge therein above himself: it being also an unseemly affront to the sequestered and veiled modesty of that sex, to have her unpleasingness and other concealments bandied up and down, and aggravated in open court by those hired masters of tongue-fence. Such uncomely exigencies it befell no less a majesty than Henry VIII to be reduced to, who, finding just reason in his conscience to forego his brother's wife, after many indignities of being deluded and made a boy of by those his two cardinal judges, was constrained at last, for want of other proof that she had been carnally known by prince Arthur, even to uncover the nakedness of that virtuous lady, and to recite openly the obscene evidence of his brother's chamberlain. Yet it pleased God to make him see all the tyranny of Rome, by discovering this which they exercised over divorce, and to make him the beginner of a reformation to this whole kingdom, by first asserting into his familiary power the right of just divorce. It is true, an adulteress cannot be shamed enough by any public proceeding; but the woman whose honour is not appeached is less injured by a silent dismission, being otherwise not illiberally dealt with, than to endure a clamouring debate of utterless things, in a business of that civil secrecy and difficult discerning, as not to be overmuch questioned by nearest friends. Which drew that answer from the greatest and worthiest Roman of his time, Paulus Emilius, being demanded why he would put away his wife for no visible reason? 'This shoe,' said he, and held it out on his foot, 'is a neat shoe, a new shoe, and yet none of you know where it wrings me': much less by the unfamiliar cognizance of a feed gamester can such a private difference be examined, neither ought it.

Again, if law aim at the firm establishment and preservation of matrimonial faith, we know that cannot thrive under violent means, but is the more violated. It is not when two unfortunately met are by the canon forced to draw in that yoke an unmerciful day's work of sorrow till death unharness them, that then the law keeps marriage most inviolated and unbroken; but when the law takes order that marriage be accountant and responsible to perform that society, whether it be religious, civil, or corporal, which may be consciably required and claimed therein, or else to be dissolved if it cannot be undergone. This is to make marriage most indissoluble, by making it a just and equal dealer, a performer of those due helps which instituted the covenant; being otherwise a most unjust contract, and no more to be maintained under tuition of law, than the vilest fraud, or cheat, or theft, that may be committed. But because this is such a secret kind of fraud or theft, as cannot be discerned by law but only by the plaintiff himself; therefore to divorce

was never counted a political or civil offence, neither to Jew nor
Gentile, nor by any judicial intendment of Christ, further than
could be discerned to transgress the allowance of Moses, which
was of necessity so large, that it doth all one as if it sent back
the matter undeterminable at law, and intractable by rough
dealing, to have instructions and admonitions bestowed about
it by them whose spiritual office is to adjure and to denounce,
and so left to the conscience.   The law can only appoint the just
and equal conditions of divorce; and is to look how it is an injury
to the divorced, which in truth it can be none, as a mere separation; for if she consent, wherein has the law to right her? or
consent not, then is it either just, and so deserved; or if unjust,
such in all likelihood was the divorcer: and to part from an
unjust man is a happiness, and no injury to be lamented.   But
suppose it be to an injury, the law is not able to amend it, unless
she think it other than a miserable redress, to return back from
whence she was expelled, or but entreated to be gone, or else
to live apart still married without marriage, a married widow.
Last, if it be to chasten the divorcer, what law punishes a deed
which is not moral but natural, a deed which cannot certainly
be found to be an injury; or how can it be punished by prohibiting the divorce, but that the innocent must equally partake
both in the shame and in the smart?   So that which way soever
we look, the law can to no rational purpose forbid divorce, it
can only take care that the conditions of divorce be not injurious.   Thus then we see the trial of law, how impertinent it is
to the question of divorce, how helpless next, and then how
hurtful.

CHAPTER XXII

The last Reason why Divorce is not to be restrained by Law, it being
against the Law of Nature and of Nations—The larger Proof whereof
referred to Mr Selden's Book, *De Jure Naturali et Gentium*—An Objection
of Paraeus answered—How it ought to be ordered by the Church—That
this will not breed any worse Inconvenience, nor so bad as is now suffered.

Therefore the last reason why it should not be, is the example
we have, not only from the noblest and wisest commonwealths,
guided by the clearest light of human knowledge, but also from
the divine testimonies of God himself, lawgiving in person to a
sanctified people.   That all this is true, whoso desires to know at
large with least pains, and expects not here overlong rehearsals

of that which is by others already so judiciously gathered, let him hasten to be acquainted with that noble volume written by our learned Selden, 'Of the Law of Nature and of Nations,' a work more useful and more worthy to be perused by whosoever studies to be a great man in wisdom, equity, and justice, than all those 'decretals and sumless sums,' which the pontifical clerks have doted on ever since that unfortunate mother famously sinned thrice, and died impenitent of her bringing into the world those two misbegotten infants, and for ever infants, Lombard and Gratian, him the compiler of canon iniquity, the other the Tubalcain of scholastic sophistry, whose overspreading barbarism hath not only infused their own bastardy upon the fruitfullest part of human learning, not only dissipated and dejected the clear light of nature in us, and of nations, but hath tainted also the fountains of divine doctrine, and rendered the pure and solid law of God unbeneficial to us by their calumnious dunceries. Yet this law, which their unskilfulness hath made liable to all ignominy, the purity and wisdom of this law shall be the buckler of our dispute. Liberty of divorce we claim not, we think not but from this law; the dignity, the faith, the authority thereof is now grown among Christians, O astonishment! a labour of no mean difficulty and envy to defend. That it should not be counted a faltering dispense, a flattering permission of sin, the bill of adultery, a snare, is the expense of all this apology. And all that we solicit is, that it may be suffered to stand in the place where God set it, amidst the firmament of his holy laws, to shine, as it was wont, upon the weaknesses and errors of men, perishing else in the sincerity of their honest purposes: for certain there is no memory of whoredoms and adulteries left among us now, when this warranted freedom of God's own giving is made dangerous and discarded for a scroll of licence. It must be your suffrages and votes, O English men, that this exploded decree of God and Moses may scape and come off fair, without the censure of a shameful abrogating: which, if yonder sun ride sure, and means not to break word with us to-morrow, was never yet abrogated by our Saviour. Give sentence if you please, that the frivolous canon may reverse the infallible judgment of Moses and his great director. Or if it be the reformed writers, whose doctrine persuades this rather, their reasons I dare affirm are all silenced, unless it be only this. Paraeus, on the Corinthians, would prove that hardness of heart in divorce is no more now to be permitted, but to be amerced with fine and imprisonment. I am not willing to discover the forgettings of reverend men, yet here I must: what article or clause of the whole new covenant can Paraeus bring, to exasperate the judicial law upon any infirmity under the gospel? I say infirmity, for if it were the high hand of sin, the law as little would have endured it as the gospel; it would not stretch to the dividing of an inheritance; it refused to condemn adultery, not that these things should not be done at law, but to show that the gospel hath not the least influence upon judicial courts, much less to make them sharper and more heavy, least of all to arraign before a temporal judge that which the law without summons acquitted. 'But,' saith he, 'the law was the time of youth, under violent affections; the gospel in us is mature age, and ought to subdue affections.' True, and so ought the law too, if they be found inordinate, and not merely natural and blameless. Next I distinguish, that the time of the law is compared to youth and pupilage in respect of the ceremonial part, which led the Jews as children through corporal and garish rudiments, until the fulness of time should reveal to them the higher lessons of faith and redemption. This is not meant of the moral part; therein it soberly concerned them not to be babies, but to be men in good earnest: the sad and awful majesty of that law was not to be jested with: to bring a bearded nonage with lascivious dispensations before that throne, had been a lewd affront, as it is now a gross mistake. But what discipline is this, Paraeus, to nourish violent affections in youth, by cockering and wanton indulgencies, and to chastise them in mature age with a boyish rod of correction? How much more coherent is it to scripture, that the law, as a strict schoolmaster, should have punished every trespass without indulgence so baneful to youth, and that the gospel should now correct that by admonition and reproof only, in free and mature age, which was punished with stripes in the childhood and bondage of the law? What, therefore, it allowed then so fairly, much less is to be whipped now, especially in penal courts: and if it ought now to trouble the conscience, why did that angry accuser and condemner law reprieve it? So then, neither from Moses nor from Christ hath the magistrate any authority to proceed against it. But what, shall then the disposal of that power return again to the master of a family? Wherefore not, since God there put it, and the presumptuous canon thence bereft it? This only must be provided, that the ancient manner be observed in the presence of the minister and other grave selected elders, who after they shall have admonished and pressed upon him the words of our Saviour, and he shall have protested in the faith of the eternal gospel, and the hope he has of happy resurrection, that otherwise than thus he cannot do, and thinks himself and this his case not contained in that prohibition of divorce which Christ pronounced, the matter not being of malice, but of nature, and so not capable of reconciling; to constrain him further were to unchristian him, to unman him, to throw the mountain of Sinai upon him, with the weight of the whole law to boot, flat against the liberty and essence of the gospel; and yet nothing available either to the sanctity of marriage, the good of husband, wife, or children, nothing profitable either to church or commonwealth, but hurtful and pernicious in all these respects. But this will bring in confusion: yet these cautious mistrusters might consider, that what they thus object lights not upon this book, but upon that which I engage against them, the book of God and Moses, with all the wisdom and providence which had forecast the worst of confusion that could succeed, and yet thought fit of such a permission. But let them be of good cheer, it wrought so little disorder among the Jews, that from Moses till after the captivity, not one of the prophets thought it worth the rebuking; for that of Malachi well looked into will appear to be not against divorcing, but rather against keeping strange concubines, to the vexation of their Hebrew wives. If, therefore, we Christians may be thought as good and tractable as the Jews were (and certainly the prohibitors of divorce presume us to be better), then less confusion is to be feared for this among us than was among them. If we be worse, or but as bad, which lamentable examples confirm we are, then have we more, or at least as much, need of this permitted law, as they to whom God therefore gave it (as they say) under a harsher covenant. Let not, therefore, the frailty of man go on thus inventing needless troubles to itself, to groan under the false imagination of a strictness never imposed from above; enjoining that for duty which is an impossible and vain supererogating. 'Be not righteous overmuch,' is the counsel of Ecclesiastes; 'why shouldst thou destroy thyself?' Let us not be thus over-curious to strain at atoms, and yet to stop every vent and cranny of permissive liberty, lest nature, wanting those needful pores and breathing-places which God hath not debarred our weakness, either suddenly break out into some wide rupture of open vice and frantic heresy, or else inwardly fester with repining and blasphemous thoughts, under an unreasonable and fruitless rigour of unwarranted law. Against which evils nothing can more beseem the religion of the church, or the wisdom of the state, than to consider timely and provide. And in so doing let them not doubt but they shall vindicate the misreputed honour of God and his great lawgiver, by suffering him to give his own laws according to the condition of man's nature best known to him, without the unsufferable imputation of dispensing legally with many ages of ratified adultery. They shall recover the misattended words of Christ to the sincerity of their true sense from manifold contradictions, and shall open them with the key of charity. Many helpless Christians they shall raise from the depth of sadness and distress, utterly unfitted as they are to serve God or man: many they shall reclaim from obscure and giddy sects, many regain from dissolute and brutish licence, many from desperate hardness, if ever that were justly pleaded. They shall set free many daughters of Israel not wanting much of her sad plight whom 'Satan had bound eighteen years.' Man they shall restore to his just dignity and prerogative in nature, preferring the soul's free peace before the promiscuous draining of a carnal rage. Marriage, from a perilous hazard and snare, they shall reduce to be a more certain haven and retirement of happy society; when they shall judge according to God and Moses (and how not then according to Christ), when they shall judge it more wisdom and goodness to break that covenant seemingly, and keep it really, than by compulsion of law to keep it seemingly, and by compulsion of blameless nature to break it really, at least if it were ever truly joined. The vigour of discipline they may then turn with better success upon the prostitute looseness of the times, when men, finding in themselves the infirmities of former ages, shall not be constrained above the gift of God in them to unprofitable and impossible observances, never required from the civilest, the wisest, the holiest nations, whose other excellencies in moral virtue they never yet could equal. Last of all, to those whose mind is still to maintain textual restrictions, whereof the bare sound cannot consist sometimes with humanity, much less with charity; I would ever answer, by putting them in remembrance of a command above all commands, which they seem to have forgot, and who spake it: in comparison whereof, this which they so exalt is but a petty and subordinate precept. 'Let them go,' therefore, with whom I am loath to couple them, yet they will needs run into the same blindness with the pharisees; 'let them go, therefore,' and consider well what this lesson means, 'I will have mercy and no sacrifice': for on that 'saying all the law and prophets depend'; much more the gospel, whose end and excellence is mercy and peace. Or if they cannot learn that, how will they hear this? which yet I shall not doubt to leave with them as a conclusion, that God the Son hath put all other things under his own feet, but his commandments he hath left all under the feet of charity.

OF EDUCATION

Milton's pamphlet *Of Education*, published in June 1644, was one of several open letters on education addressed to the Prussian exile, Samuel Hartlib. These were occasioned by the publication of Hartlib's own book, *A Reformation of Schools*, in 1642.

Above all, Milton wanted schools to train character. Education was to endow men with that power of right thinking that was the only foundation of right action. Those who were at school must 'repair the ruins of our first parents by regaining to know God aright.' They must learn how to take responsibility within the community, how to guide and lead others in any civil conflict that might arise.

Milton has been blamed for grossly overestimating the capacity for learning in young boys. Professor Merritt Hughes has reminded Milton's critics that similar schemes of study had been in operation for more than a hundred years at famous continental schools, including Vittorino da Feltre's Giocosa, near Venice. Nor was he, as has been suggested, a classical antiquarian recommending a return to a culture which had no bearing on modern life. He was speaking of Latin textbooks on agriculture that were used by farmers in his own day, and of a treatise on geography that, according to Robert Boyle, was still capable of stimulating men to explore the world of natural science.

Milton acknowledged in his *Defensio Secunda* that *Of Education* was written in the cause of liberty. Those who learned to value virtue and hard work had the essentials of moral freedom.

Letter to Mr Hartlib (1644)

Master Hartlib,

I am long since persuaded that to say and do aught worth memory and imitation, no purpose or respect should sooner move us than simply the love of God and of mankind. Nevertheless, to write now the reforming of education, though it be one of the greatest and noblest designs that can be thought on, and for the want whereof this nation perishes, I had not yet at this time been induced but by your earnest entreaties and serious conjurements; as having my mind diverted for the present in the pursuance of some other assertions, the knowledge and the use of which cannot but be a great furtherance both to the enlargement of truth and honest living with much more peace.

Nor should the laws of any private friendship have prevailed with me to divide thus or transpose my former thoughts; but that I see those aims, those actions which have won you with me the esteem of a person sent hither by some good providence from a far country to be the occasion and incitement of great good to this island, and (as I hear) you have obtained the same repute with men of most approved wisdom and some of the highest authority among us; not to mention the learned correspondence which you hold in foreign parts, and the extraordinary pains and diligence which you have used in this matter both here and beyond the seas, either by the definite will of God so ruling, or the peculiar sway of nature, which also is God's working.

Neither can I think that, so reputed and so valued as you are, you would, to the forfeit of your own discerning ability, impose upon me an unfit and over-ponderous argument; but that the satisfaction, which you profess to have received from those incidental discourses which we have wandered into, hath pressed and almost constrained you into a persuasion, that what you require from me in this point I neither ought nor can in conscience defer beyond this time, both of so much need at once, and so much opportunity to try what God hath determined.

I will not resist, therefore, whatever it is either of divine or human obligement that you lay upon me; but will forthwith set down in writing, as you request me, that voluntary idea, which hath long in silence presented itself to me, of a better education, in extent and comprehension far more large, and yet of time far shorter and of attainment far more certain, than hath been yet in practice. Brief I shall endeavour to be; for that which I have to say assuredly this nation hath extreme need should be done sooner than spoken. To tell you, therefore, that I have benefited herein among old renowned authors I shall spare; and to search what many modern Januas and Didactics more than ever I shall read have projected, my inclination leads me not. But if you can accept of these few observations which have flowered off, and are, as it were, the burnishing of many contemplative years altogether spent in the search of religious and civil knowledge, and such as pleased you so well in the relating, I here give you them to dispose of.

The end, then, of learning is, to repair the ruins of our first parents by regaining to know God aright, and out of that knowledge to love him, to imitate him, to be like him, as we may the nearest, by possessing our souls of true virtue, which, being united to the heavenly grace of faith, makes up the highest perfection. But because our understanding cannot in this body found itself but on sensible things, nor arrive so clearly to the knowledge of God and things invisible as by orderly conning over the visible and inferior creature, the same method is necessarily to be followed in all discreet teaching.

And seeing every nation affords not experience and tradition enough for all kind of learning, therefore we are chiefly taught the languages of those people who have at any time been most industrious after wisdom; so that language is but the instrument conveying to us things useful to be known. And though a linguist should pride himself to have all the tongues that Babel cleft the world into, yet if he have not studied the solid things in them as well as the words and lexicons, he were nothing so much to be esteemed a learned man as any yeoman or tradesman competently wise in his mother-dialect only.

Hence appear the many mistakes which have made learning generally so unpleasing and so unsuccessful. First, we do amiss to spend seven or eight years merely in scraping together so much miserable Latin and Greek as might be learned otherwise easily and delightfully in one year. And that which casts our proficiency therein so much behind is our time lost in too oft idle vacancies given both to schools and universities; partly in a preposterous exaction, forcing the empty wits of children to compose themes, verses, and orations, which are the acts of ripest judgment, and the final work of a head filled, by long reading and observing, with elegant maxims and copious invention.

These are not matters to be wrung from poor striplings, like blood out of the nose, or the plucking of untimely fruit; besides the ill habit which they get of wretched barbarizing against the Latin and Greek idiom with their untutored Anglicisms, odious to be read, yet not to be avoided without a well-continued and judicious conversing among pure authors, digested, which they scarce taste. Whereas, if after some preparatory grounds of speech by their certain forms got into memory they were led to the praxis hereof in some chosen short book lessoned thoroughly to them, they might then forthwith proceed to learn the substance of good things and arts in due order, which would bring the whole language quickly into their power. This I take to be the most rational and most profitable way of learning languages, and whereby we may best hope to give account to God of our youth spent herein.

And for the usual method of teaching arts, I deem it to be an old error of universities, not yet well recovered from the scholastic grossness of barbarous ages, that, instead of beginning with arts most easy (and those be such as are most obvious to the sense), they present their young unmatriculated novices at first coming with the most intellective abstractions of logic and metaphysics; so that they, having but newly left those grammatic flats and shallows where they stuck unreasonably to learn a few words with lamentable construction, and now on the sudden transported under another climate, to be tossed and turmoiled with their unballasted wits in fathomless and unquiet deeps of controversy, do, for the most part, grow into hatred and contempt of learning, mocked and deluded all this while with ragged notions and babblements, while they expected worthy and delightful knowledge; till poverty or youthful years call them importunately their several ways, and hasten them, with the sway of friends, either to an ambitious and mercenary, or ignorantly zealous divinity: some allured to the trade of law, grounding their purposes not on the prudent and heavenly contemplation of justice and equity, which was never taught them, but on the promising and pleasing thoughts of litigious terms, fat contentions, and flowing fees. Others betake them to state affairs with souls so unprincipled in virtue and true generous breeding, that flattery, and court-shifts, and tyrannous aphorisms appear to them the highest points of wisdom, instilling their barren hearts with a conscientious slavery, if, as I rather think, it be not feigned. Others, lastly, of a more delicious and airy spirit, retire themselves, knowing no better, to the enjoyments of ease and luxury, living out their days in feast and jollity; which, indeed, is the wisest and safest course of all these, unless they were with more integrity undertaken. And these are the errors, and these are the fruits of mis-spending our prime youth at the schools and universities, as we do, either in learning mere words, or such things chiefly as were better unlearnt.

I shall detain you no longer in the demonstration of what we should not do, but straight conduct you to a hillside, where I will point you out the right path of a virtuous and noble education; laborious indeed at the first ascent, but else so smooth, so green, so full of goodly prospect and melodious sounds on every side, that the harp of Orpheus was not more charming. I doubt not but ye shall have more ado to drive our dullest and laziest youth, our stocks and stubs, from the infinite desire of such a happy nurture, than we have now to haul and drag

our choicest and hopefullest wits to that asinine feast of sow-
thistles and brambles which is commonly set before them as
all the food and entertainment of their tenderest and most
docible age. I call, therefore, a complete and generous education, that which fits a man to perform justly, skilfully, and magnanimously all the offices, both private and public, of peace and
war.   And how all this may be done between twelve and one-and-
twenty, less time than is now bestowed in pure trifling at grammar
and sophistry, is to be thus ordered:

First, to find out a spacious house and ground about it fit
for an academy, and big enough to lodge one hundred and fifty
persons, whereof twenty or thereabout may be attendants, all
under the government of one who shall be thought of desert
sufficient, and ability either to do all, or wisely to direct and
oversee it done. This place should be at once both school and
university, not needing a remove to any other house of scholar-
ship, except it be some peculiar college of law or physic, where
they mean to be practitioners; but as for those general studies
which take up all our time from Lilly to the commencing, as
they term it, master of art, it should be absolute. After this
pattern, as many edifices may be converted to this use as shall
be needful in every city throughout this land, which would tend
much to the increase of learning and civility everywhere. This
number, less or more, thus collected, to the convenience of a
foot-company or interchangeably two troops of cavalry, should
divide their day's work into three parts as it lies orderly—their
studies, their exercise, and their diet.

For their studies: first, they should begin with the chief and
necessary rules of some good grammar, either that now used,
or any better; and while this is doing, their speech is to be
fashioned to a distinct and clear pronunciation, as near as may
be to the Italian, especially in the vowels. For we Englishmen,
being far northerly, do not open our mouths in the cold air
wide enough to grace a southern tongue, but are observed by
all other nations to speak exceeding close and inward; so that
to smatter Latin with an English mouth is as ill hearing as
law French.

Next, to make them expert in the usefullest points of grammar,
and withal to season them and win them early to the love of
virtue and true labour, ere any flattering seducement or vain
principle seize them wandering, some easy and delightful book
of education should be read to them, whereof the Greeks have
store, as Cebes, Plutarch, and other Socratic discourses; but in

Latin we have none of classic authority extant, except the two or three first books of Quintilian and some select pieces elsewhere.

But here the main skill and groundwork will be to temper them such lectures and explanations upon every opportunity, as may lead and draw them in willing obedience, inflamed with the study of learning and the admiration of virtue, stirred up with high hopes of living to be brave men and worthy patriots, dear to God and famous to all ages: that they may despise and scorn all their childish and ill-taught qualities, to delight in manly and liberal exercises; which he who hath the art and proper eloquence to catch them with, what with mild and effectual persuasions, and what with the intimation of some fear, if need be, but chiefly by his own example, might in a short space gain them to an incredible diligence and courage, infusing into their young breasts such an ingenuous and noble ardour as would not fail to make many of them renowned and matchless men.

At the same time, some other hour of the day might be taught them the rules of arithmetic, and, soon after, the elements of geometry, even playing, as the old manner was. After evening repast till bed-time their thoughts would be best taken up in the easy grounds of religion and the story of Scripture.

The next step would be to the authors of agriculture, Cato, Varro, and Columella, for the matter is most easy; and if the language is difficult, so much the better; it is not a difficulty above their years. And here will be an occasion of inciting and enabling them hereafter to improve the tillage of their country, to recover the bad soil, and to remedy the waste that is made of good; for this was one of Hercules' praises.

Ere half these authors be read (which will soon be with plying hard and daily) they cannot choose but be masters of an ordinary prose: so that it will be then seasonable for them to learn in any modern author the use of the globes and all the maps, first with the old names and then with the new; or they might then be capable to read any compendious method of natural philosophy; and, at the same time, might be entering into the Greek tongue, after the same manner as was before prescibed for the Latin; whereby the difficulties of grammar being soon overcome, all the historical physiology of Aristotle and Theophrastus are open before them and, as I may say, under contribution. The like access will be to Vitruvius, to Seneca's *Natural Questions*, to Mela, Celsus, Pliny, or Solinus. And having thus past the principles of arithmetic, geometry, astronomy, and geography, with a general compact of physics, they may descend in mathematics to the instrumental science of trigonometry, and from thence to fortification, architecture, enginery, or navigation. And in natural philosophy they may proceed leisurely from the history of meteors, minerals, plants, and living creatures, as far as anatomy.

Then also in course might be read to them out of some not tedious writer the institution of physics; that they may know the tempers, the humours, the seasons, and how to manage a crudity; which he who can wisely and timely do is not only a great physician to himself and to his friends, but also may at some time or other save an army by this frugal and expenseless means only, and not let the healthy and stout bodies of young men rot away under him for want of this discipline, which is a great pity, and no less a shame to the commander.

To set forward all these proceedings in nature and mathematics, what hinders but that they may procure, as oft as shall be needful, the helpful experiences of hunters, fowlers, fishermen, shepherds, gardeners, apothecaries; and in other sciences, architects, engineers, mariners, anatomists, who, doubtless, would be ready, some for reward and some to favour such a hopeful seminary. And this would give them such a real tincture of natural knowledge as they shall never forget, but daily augment with delight. Then also those poets which are now counted most hard will be both facile and pleasant, Orpheus, Hesiod, Theocritus, Aratus, Nicander, Oppian, Dionysius; and, in Latin, Lucretius, Manilius, and the rural part of Virgil.

By this time years and good general precepts will have furnished them more distinctly with that act of reason which in ethics is called proairesis, that they may with some judgment contemplate upon moral good and evil. Then will be required a special reinforcement of constant and sound endoctrinating to set them right and firm, instructing them more amply in the knowledge of virtue and the hatred of vice, while their young and pliant affections are led through all the moral works of Plato, Xenophon, Cicero, Plutarch, Laertius, and those Locrian remnants; but still to be reduced in their nightward studies, wherewith they close the day's work, under the determinate sentence of David or Solomon, or the evangels and apostolic scriptures.

Being perfect in the knowledge of personal duty, they may then begin the study of economics. And either now or before this they may have easily learned at any odd hour the Italian tongue. And soon after, but with wariness and good antidote, it would be wholesome enough to let them taste some choice comedies, Greek, Latin, or Italian; those tragedies also that treat of household matters, as Trachiniae, Alcestis, and the like.

The next move must be to the study of politics; to know the beginning, end, and reasons of political societies, that they may not, in a dangerous fit of the commonwealth, be such poor shaken uncertain reeds, of such a tottering conscience as many of our great councillors have lately shown themselves, but steadfast pillars of the State. After this they are to dive into the grounds of law and legal justice, delivered first and with best warrant by Moses, and, as far as human prudence can be trusted, in those extolled remains of Grecian Law-givers, Lycurgus, Solon, Zaleucus, Charondas; and thence to all the Roman edicts and tables, with their Justinian; and so down to the Saxon and common laws of England and the statutes.

Sundays also and every evening may now be understandingly spent in the highest matters of theology and church history, ancient and modern: and ere this time at a set hour the Hebrew tongue might have been gained, that the Scriptures may be now read in their own original; whereto it would be no impossibility to add the Chaldee and the Syrian dialect.

When all these employments are well conquered, then will the choice histories, heroic poems, and Attic tragedies of stateliest and most regal argument, with all the famous political orations, offer themselves; which, if they were not only read, but some of them got by memory, and solemnly pronounced with right accent and grace, as might be taught, would endue them even with the spirit and vigour of Demosthenes or Cicero, Euripides or Sophocles.

And now, lastly, will be the time to read with them those organic arts which enable men to discourse and write perspicuously, elegantly, and according to the fitted style of lofty, mean or lowly. Logic, therefore, so much as is useful, is to be referred to this due place, with all her well-couched heads and topics, until it be time to open her contracted palm into a graceful and ornate rhetoric taught out of the rule of Plato, Aristotle, Phalereus, Cicero, Hermogenes, Longinus.

To which poetry would be made subsequent, or, indeed, rather precedent, as being less subtile and fine, but more simple, sensuous, and passionate; I mean not here the prosody of a verse which they could not but have hit on before among the rudiments of grammar, but that sublime art which in Aristotle's

Poetics, in Horace, and the Italian commentaries of Castlevetro, Tasso, Mazzoni, and others, teaches what the laws are of a true epic poem, what of a dramatic, what of a lyric, what decorum is, which is the grand masterpiece to observe. This would make them soon perceive what despicable creatures our common rhymers and playwriters be; and show them what religious, what glorious and magnificent use might be made of poetry, both in divine and human things.

From hence, and not till now, will be the right season of forming them to be able writers and composers in every excellent matter, when they shall be thus fraught with an universal insight into things: or whether they be to speak in parliament or council, honour and attention would be waiting on their lips. There would then appear in pulpits other visages, other gestures, and stuff otherwise wrought, than we now sit under, ofttimes to as great a trial of our patience as any other that they preach to us.

These are the studies wherein our noble and our gentle youth ought to bestow their time in a disciplinary way from twelve to one-and-twenty, unless they rely more upon their ancestors dead than upon themselves living. In which methodical course it so is supposed they must proceed by the steady pace of learning onward, as at convenient times for memory's sake to retire back into the middle ward, and sometimes into the rear, of what they have been taught, until they have confirmed and solidly united the whole body of their perfected knowledge, like the last embattling of a Roman legion. Now will be worth the seeing what exercises and recreations may best agree and become those studies.

The course of study hitherto briefly described is, what I can guess by reading, likest to those ancient and famous schools of Pythagoras, Plato, Isocrates, Aristotle, and such others, out of which were bred such a number of renowned philosophers, orators, historians, poets, and princes all over Greece, Italy, and Asia, besides the flourishing studies of Cyrene and Alexandria. But herein it shall exceed them, and supply a defect as great as that which Plato noted in the commonwealth of Sparta. Whereas that city trained up their youth most for war, and these in their academies and Lycaeum all for the gown, this institution of breeding which I here delineate shall be equally good both for peace and war. Therefore, about an hour and a half ere they eat at noon should be allowed them for exercise, and due rest afterwards; but the time for this may be enlarged at pleasure, according as their rising in the morning shall be early. The exercise which I command first is the exact use of their weapon, to guard, and to strike safely with edge or point. This will keep them healthy, nimble, strong, and well in breath; is also the likeliest means to make them grow large and tall, and to inspire them with a gallant and fearless courage; which, being tempered with seasonable lectures and precepts to make them of true fortitude and patience, will turn into a native and heroic valour, and make them hate the cowardice of doing wrong. They must be also practised in all the locks and gripes of wrestling, wherein Englishmen are wont to excel, as need may often be in fight to tug, to grapple, and to close. And this, perhaps, will be enough wherein to prove and heat their single strength.

The interim of unsweating themselves regularly, and convenient rest before meat, may both with profit and delight be taken up in recreating and composing their travailed spirits with the solemn and divine harmonies of music heard or learned either whilst the skilful organist plies his grave and fancied descant in lofty fugues, or the whole symphony with artful and unimaginable touches adorn and grace the well-studied chords of some choice composer; sometimes the lute or soft organ-stop, waiting on elegant voices either to religious, martial, or civil ditties, which, if wise men and prophets be not extremely out, have a great power over dispositions and manners to smooth and make them gentle from rustic harshness and distempered passions. The like also would not be unexpedient after meat, to assist and cherish nature in her first concoction, and send their minds back to study in good tune and satisfaction.

Where having followed it under vigilant eyes until about two hours before supper, they are, by a sudden alarum or watchword, to be called out on their military motions, under sky or covert, according to the season, as was the Roman wont; first on foot, then, as their age permits, on horseback to all the art of cavalry; that having in sport, but with much exactness and daily muster, served out the rudiments of their soldiership in all the skill of embattling, marching, encamping, fortifying, besieging, and battering, with all the helps of ancient and modern stratagems, tactics, and warlike maxims, they may, as it were out of a long war, come forth renowned and perfect commanders in the service of their country.

They would not then, if they were trusted with fair and hopeful armies, suffer them for want of just and wise discipline to shed away from about them like sick feathers, though they be never so oft supplied; they would not suffer their empty and unrecruitable colonels of twenty men in a company to quaff out or convey into secret hoards the wages of a delusive list and miserable remnant; yet in the meanwhile to be overmastered with a score or two of drunkards, the only soldiery left about them, or else to comply with all rapines and violences. No, certainly, if they knew aught of that knowledge which belongs to good men or good governors, they would not suffer these things.

But to return to our own institute. Besides these constant exercises at home, there is another opportunity of gaining experience to be won from pleasure itself abroad: in those vernal seasons of the year, when the air is calm and pleasant, it were an injury and sullenness against nature not to go out and see her riches and partake in her rejoicing with heaven and earth. I should not, therefore, be a persuader to them of studying much then, after two or three years that they have well laid their grounds, but to ride out in companies with prudent and staid guides to all the quarters of the land, learning and observing all places of strength, all commodities of building and of soil for towns and tillage, harbours, and ports for trade. Sometimes taking sea as far as to our navy, to learn there also what they can in the practical knowledge of sailing and sea-fight.

These ways would try all their peculiar gifts of nature, and if there were any secret excellence among them, would fetch it out and give it fair opportunity to advance itself by, which could not but mightily redound to the good of this nation, and bring into fashion again those old admired virtues and excellences, with far more advantage now in this purity of Christian knowledge.

Nor shall we then need the monsieurs of Paris to take our hopeful youth into their slight and prodigal custodies, and send them over back again transformed into mimics, apes, and keks-hose. But if they desire to see other countries at three or four and twenty years of age, not to learn principles, but to enlarge experience and make wise observation, they will by that time be such as shall deserve the regard and honour of all men where they pass, and the society and friendship of those in all places who are best and most eminent. And perhaps then other nations will be glad to visit us for their breeding, or else to imitate us in their own country.

Now, lastly, for their diet there cannot be much to say, save only that it would be best in the same house; for much time else would be lost abroad, and many ill habits got; and that it should be plain, healthful, and moderate, I suppose is out of controversy.

Thus, Mr Hartlib, you have a general view in writing, as your desire was, of that which at several times I had discoursed with you concerning the best and noblest way of education; not beginning, as some have done, from the cradle, which yet might be worth many considerations, if brevity had not been my scope. Many other circumstances also I could have mentioned; but this, to such as have the worth in them to make trial, for light and direction may be enough. Only I believe that this is not a bow for every men to shoot in that counts himself a teacher, but will require sinews almost equal to those which Homer gave Ulysses. Yet I am withal persuaded that it may prove much more easy in the assay than it now seems at distance, and much more illustrious: howbeit not more difficult than I imagine; and that imagination presents me with nothing but very happy and very possible according to best wishes, if God have so decreed, and this age have spirit and capacity enough to apprehend.

TETRACHORDON:

EXPOSITIONS

ON

Gen. 1, 27, 28, compared and explained by Gen. ii. 18, 23, 24. Deut. xxiv. 1, 2. Matt. v. 31, 32, with Matt. xix. from ver. 3 to 11. 1 Cor. vii. from ver. 10 to 16.

Wherein the doctrine and discipline of divorce, as was lately published, is confirmed by explanation of scripture: by testimony of ancient fathers; of civil laws in the primitive church; of famousest reformed divines; and lastly, by an intended act of the parliament and church of England in the last year of Edward the Sixth.

Σκαιοῖσι καινὰ προσφέρων σοφὰ
Δόξεις ἀχρεῖος, κοὐ σοφὸς πεφυκέναι
Τῶν δ' αὐδοκούντων εἰδέναι τι ποικίλον,
Κρείσσων νομισθεὶς ἐν πόλει, λυπρὸς φανῇ—Euripid. Medea.

After revising the *Doctrine and Discipline of Divorce* for its second edition in February 1644, Milton published an endorsement of his views by Martin Bucer in the following July. He subsequently collected material for two further treatises on the problem of divorce, *Tetrachordon* and *Colasterion*, both published in March 1645.

In some ways *Tetrachordon* improves on the first divorce pamphlet. Despite the fact that its form is controlled by discussion, in series, of the four chief passages in the Bible that treat of divorce, Milton seems far less tied to the reconciliation and exegesis of texts. It becomes clear that he really opposes obedience to the letter of any law that is a clog or restriction on the human spirit, regardless of the origin of that law. 'The law is to tender the liberty and human dignity of them that live under the law.'

Moreover, the issue of divorce is discussed in more universal and less personal terms. Milton's bitterness has diminished. He shows an even clearer realization of the nature of a true marriage. He develops the idea of a wife as a second self, able to be a perpetual source of delight to her husband. He is still an impassioned apostle of human liberty, but he can no longer be charged with fanaticism.

331

TETRACHORDON:

EXPOSITIONS

UPON THE FOUR CHIEF PLACES IN SCRIPTURE
WHICH TREAT OF MARRIAGE OR NULLITIES IN
MARRIAGE

Genesis i. 27

'So God created man in his own image, in the image of God created
he him; male and female created he them.

28. 'And God blessed them, and God said unto them, Be fruitful,' etc.

Genesis i. 27

'So God created man in his own image.'] To be informed
aright in the whole history of marriage, that we may know for
certain, not by a forced yoke, but by an impartial definition,
what marriage is, and what is not marriage, it will undoubtedly
be safest, fairest, and most with our obedience, to inquire, as
our Saviour's direction is, how it was in the beginning. And
that we begin so high as man created after God's own image,
there want not earnest causes. For nothing nowadays is more
degenerately forgotten, than the true dignity of man, almost in
every respect, but especially in this prime institution of matrimony, wherein his native pre-eminence ought most to shine.
Although if we consider that just and natural privileges men
neither can rightly seek, nor dare fully claim, unless they be
allied to inward goodness and steadfast knowledge, and that the
want of this quells them to a servile sense of their own conscious unworthiness; it may save the wondering why in this age
many are so opposite both to human and Christian liberty,
either while they understand not, or envy others that do; con-
tenting, or rather priding themselves in a specious humility and
strictness, bred out of low ignorance, that never yet conceived the
freedom of the gospel; and is therefore by the apostle to the
Colossians ranked with no better company than 'will-worship
and the mere show of wisdom.' And how injurious herein they
are, if not to themselves, yet to their neighbours, and not to them
only, but to the all-wise and bounteous grace offered us in our
redemption, will orderly appear.

'In the image of God created he him.'] It is enough determined, that this image of God, wherein man was created, is meant wisdom, purity, justice, and rule over all creatures. All which, being lost in Adam, was recovered with gain by the merits of Christ. For albeit our first parent had lordship over sea, and land, and air, yet there was a law without him, as a guard set over him. But Christ having 'cancelled the handwriting of ordinances which was against us,' Col. ii. 14, and interpreted the fulfilling of all through charity, hath in that respect set us over law, in the free custody of his love, and left us victorious under the guidance of his living Spirit, not under the dead letter; to follow that which most edifies, most aids and furthers a religious life, makes us holiest and likest to his immortal image, not that which makes us most conformable and captive to civil and subordinate precepts: whereof the strictest observance may ofttimes prove the destruction not only of many innocent persons and families, but of whole nations: although indeed no ordinance, human or from heaven, can bind against the good of man; so that to keep them strictly against that end, is all one with to break them. Men of most renowned virtue have sometimes by transgressing most truly kept the law; and wisest magistrates have permitted and dispensed it; while they looked not peevishly at the letter, but with a greater spirit at the good of mankind, if always not written in the characters of law, yet engraven in the heart of man by a divine impression. This heathens could see, as the well-read in story can recount of Solon and Epaminondas, whom Cicero, in his first book of 'Invention,' nobly defends. 'All law,' saith he, 'we ought to refer to the common good, and interpret by that, not by the scroll of letters. No man observes law for law's sake, but for the good of them for whom it was made.' The rest might serve well to lecture these times, deluded through belly doctrines into a devout slavery. The scriptures also affords us David in the shewbread, Hezekiah in the passover, sound and safe transgressors of the literal command, which also dispensed not seldom with itself; and taught us on what just occasions to do so: until our Saviour, for whom that great and godlike work was reserved, redeemed us to a state above prescriptions, by dissolving the whole law into charity. And have we not the soul to understand this, and must we against this glory of God's transcendent love towards us be still the servants of a literal indictment?

.   .   .   .   .

Genesis ii. 18

'And the Lord God said, It is not good that man should be alone; I will make him a help meet for him.

23. 'And Adam said, This is now bone of my bone, and flesh of my flesh; she shall be called Woman, because she was taken out of man.

24. 'Therefore shall a man leave his father and his mother, and shall cleave unto his wife, and they shall be one flesh.'

Genesis ii. 18

'For man to be alone.']   Some would have the sense hereof to be in respect of procreation only; and Austin contests that manly friendship in all other regard had been a more becoming solace for Adam, than to spend so many secret years in an empty world with one woman.   But our writers deservedly reject this crabbed opinion; and defend that there is a peculiar comfort in the married state beside the genial bed, which no other society affords.   No mortal nature can endure, either in the action of religion, or study of wisdom, without sometime slackening the cords of intense thought and labour, which, lest we should think faulty, God himself conceals us not his own recreations before the world was built: 'I was,' saith the Eternal Wisdom, 'daily his delight, playing always before him.'   And to him, indeed, wisdom is as a high tower of pleasure, but to us a steep hill, and we toiling ever about the bottom.   He executes with ease the exploits of his omnipotence, as easy as with us it is to will; but no worthy enterprise can be done by us without continual plodding and wearisomeness to our faint and sensitive abilities.   We cannot, therefore, always be contemplative, or pragmatical abroad, but have need of some delightful inter-missions, wherein the enlarged soul may leave off a while her severe schooling, and, like a glad youth in wandering vacancy, may keep her holidays to joy and harmless pastime; which as she cannot well do without company, so in no company so well as where the different sex in most resembling unlikeness, and most unlike resemblance, cannot but please best, and be pleased in the aptitude of that variety.   Whereof lest we should be too timorous, in the awe that our flat sages would form us and dress us, wisest Solomon among his gravest proverbs countenances a kind of ravishment and erring fondness in the entertainment of wedded leisures; and in the Song of Songs, which is generally believed, even in the jolliest expressions, to figure the spousals of the church with Christ, sings of a thousand raptures between these two lovely ones far on the hither side of carnal enjoyment. By these instances, and more which might be brought, we may imagine how indulgently God provided against man's loneliness; that he approved it not, as by himself declared not good; that he approved the remedy thereof, as of his own ordaining, consequently good; and as he ordained it, so doubtless proportionably to our fallen estate he gives it; else were his ordinance at least in vain, and we for all his gifts still empty handed. Nay, such an unbounteous giver we should make him, as in the fables Jupiter was to Ixion, giving him a cloud instead of Juno; giving him a monstrous issue by her, the breed of Centaurs, a neglected and unloved race, the fruits of a delusive marriage; and lastly, giving him her with a damnation to that wheel in hell, from a life thrown into the midst of temptations and disorders. But God is no deceitful giver, to bestow that on us for a remedy of loneliness, which if it bring not a sociable mind as well as a conjunctive body, leaves us no less alone than before; and if it bring a mind perpetually averse and disagreeable, betrays us to a worse condition than the most deserted loneliness. God cannot in justice of his own promise and institution so unexpectedly mock us, by forcing that upon us as the remedy of solitude, which wraps us in a misery worse than any wilderness, as the Spirit of God himself judges, Prov. xix; especially knowing that the best and wisest men amidst the sincere and most cordial designs of their heart, do daily err in choosing. We may conclude, therefore, seeing orthodoxal expositors confess to our hands, that by loneliness is not only meant the want of copulation, and that man is not less alone by turning in a body to him, unless there be in it a mind answerable; that it is a work more worthy the care and consultation of God to provide for the worthiest part of man, which is his mind, and not unnaturally to set it beneath the formalities and respects of the body, to make it a servant of its own vassal: I say, we may conclude that such a marriage, wherein the mind is so disgraced and vilified below the body's interest, and can have no just or tolerable contentment, is not of God's institution, and therefore no marriage. Nay, in concluding this, I say we conclude no more than what the common expositors themselves give us, both in that which I have recited, and much more hereafter. But the truth is, they give us in such a manner, as they who leave their own mature positions like the eggs of an ostrich in the dust; I do but lay them in the sun; their own pregnancies hatch the truth; and I am taxed of novelties and strange producements, while they, like that inconsiderate bird, know not that these are their own natural breed.

'I will make him a help meet for him.'] Here the heavenly institutor, as if he laboured not to be mistaken by the supercilious hypocrisy of those that love to master their brethren, and to make us sure that he gave us not now a servile yoke, but an amiable knot, contents not himself to say, I will make him a wife; but resolving to give us first the meaning before the name of a wife, saith graciously. 'I will make him a help-meet for him.' And here again, as before, I do not require more full and fair deductions than the whole consent of our divines usually raise from this text, that in matrimony there must be first a mutual help to piety; next, to civil fellowship of love and amity; then, to generation; so to household affairs; lastly, the remedy of incontinence. And commonly they reckon them in such order, as leaves generation and incontinence to be last considered. This I amaze me at, that though all the superior and nobler ends both of marriage and of the married persons be absolutely frustrate, the matrimony stirs not, loses no hold, remains as rooted as the centre: but if the body bring but in a complaint of frigidity, by that cold application only this adamantine Alp of wedlock has leave to dissolve; which else all the machinations of religious or civil reason at the suit of a distressed mind, either for divine worship or human conversation violated, cannot unfasten. What courts of concupiscence are these, wherein fleshly appetite is heard before right reason, lust before love or devotion? They may be pious Christians together, they may be loving and friendly, they may be helpful to each other in the family, but they cannot couple; that shall divorce them, though either party would not. They can neither serve God together, nor one be at peace with the other, nor be good in the family one to other; but live as they were dead, or live as they were deadly enemies in a cage together: it is all one, they can couple, they shall not divorce till death, no, though this sentence be their death. What is this besides tyranny, but to turn nature upside down, to make both religion and the mind of man wait upon the slavish errands of the body, and not the body to follow either the sanctity or the sovereignty of the mind, unspeakably wronged, and with all equity complaining? what is this but to abuse the sacred and mysterious bed of marriage to be the compulsive sty of an ingrateful and malignant lust, stirred up only from a carnal acrimony, without either love or peace, or regard to any other thing holy or human?

This I admire, how possibly it should inhabit thus long in the sense of so many disputing theologians, unless it be the lowest lees of a canonical infection liver-grown to their sides, which, perhaps, will never uncling, without the strong abstersive of some heroic magistrate, whose mind, equal to his high office, dares lead him both to know and to do without their frivolous case-putting. For certain he shall have God and this institution plainly on his side. And if it be true both in divinity and law, that consent alone, though copulation never follow, makes a marriage, how can they dissolve it for want of that which made it not, and not dissolve it for that not continuing which made it and should preserve it in love and reason, and difference it from a brute conjugality?

'Meet for him.'] The original here is more expressive than other languages word for word can render it; but all agree effectual conformity of disposition and affection to be hereby signified; which God, as it were, not satisfied with the naming of a help, goes on describing another self, a second self, a very self itself. Yet now there is nothing in the life of man, through our misconstruction, made more uncertain, more hazardous and full of chance, than this divine blessing with such favourable significance here conferred upon us; which if we do but err in our choice, the most unblamable error that can be, err but one minute, one moment after those mighty syllables pronounced, which take upon them to join heaven and hell together unpardonably till death pardon; this divine blessing that looked but now with such a humane smile upon us, and spoke such gentle reason, straight vanishes like a fair sky, and brings on such a scene of cloud and tempest, as turns all to shipwreck without haven or shore, but to a ransomless captivity. And then they tell us it is our sin; but let them be told again, that sin, through the mercy of God, hath not made such waste upon us, as to make utterly void to our use any temporal benefit, much less any so much availing to a peaceful and sanctified life, merely for a most incident error, which no wariness can certainly shun. And wherefore serves our happy redemption, and the liberty we have in Christ, but to deliver us from calamitous yokes, not to be lived under without the endangerment of our souls, and to restore us in some competent measure to a right in every good thing both of this life and the other? Thus we see how treatable and distinctly God hath here taught us what the prime ends of marriage are—mutual solace and help. That we are now, upon the most irreprehensible mistake in choosing, defeated and defrauded of all this original benignity, was begun first through the snare of antichristian canons long since obtruded upon the church of Rome, and not yet scoured off by reformation, out of a lingering vainglory that abides among us to make fair shows in formal ordinances, and to enjoin continence and bearing of crosses in such a garb as no scripture binds us, under the thickest arrows of temptation, where we need not stand.

AUTOBIOGRAPHICAL
EXTRACTS

AUTOBIOGRAPHICAL EXTRACTS

I. FROM THE SECOND DEFENCE OF THE ENGLISH PEOPLE
(1654)

This is a translation, done with great spirit by Robert Fellowes, from the *Defensio Secunda* of Milton. The passage selected gives a general account of Milton's life and of his prose works.

I MUST crave the indulgence of the reader if I have said already, or shall say hereafter, more of myself than I wish to say; that, if I cannot prevent the blindness of my eyes, the oblivion or the defamation of my name, I may at least rescue my life from that species of obscurity, which is the associate of unprincipled depravity. This it will be necessary for me to do on more accounts than one; first, that so many good and learned men among the neighbouring nations, who read my works, may not be induced by this fellow's calumnies to alter the favourable opinion which they have formed of me; but may be persuaded that I am not one who ever disgraced beauty of sentiment by deformity of conduct, or the maxims of a freeman by the actions of a slave; and that the whole tenor of my life has, by the grace of God, hitherto been unsullied by enormity or crime. Next, that those illustrious worthies, who are the objects of my praise, may know that nothing could afflict me with more shame than to have any vices of mine diminish the force or lessen the value of my panegyric upon them; and, lastly, that the people of England, whom fate, or duty, or their own virtues, have incited me to defend, may be convinced from the purity and integrity of my life, that my defence, if it do not redound to their honour, can never be considered as their disgrace.

I will now mention who and whence I am. I was born at London, of an honest family; my father was distinguished by the undeviating integrity of his life; my mother, by the esteem in which she was held, and the alms, which she bestowed. My father destined me from a child to the pursuits of literature; and my appetite for knowledge was so voracious, that, from twelve years of age, I hardly ever left my studies, or went to bed before midnight. This primarily led to my loss of sight.

341

My eyes were naturally weak, and I was subject to frequent head-aches; which, however, could not chill the ardour of my curiosity, or retard the progress of my improvement. My father had me daily instructed in the grammar-school, and by other masters at home. He then, after I had acquired a proficiency in various languages, and had made a considerable progress in philosophy, sent me to the University of Cambridge. Here I passed seven years in the usual course of instruction and study, with the approbation of the good, and without any stain upon my character, till I took the degree of Master of Arts.

After this I did not, as this miscreant feigns, run away into Italy, but of my own accord retired to my father's house, whither I was accompanied by the regrets of most of the fellows of the college, who showed me no common marks of friendship and esteem. On my father's estate, where he had determined to pass the remainder of his days, I enjoyed an interval of uninterrupted leisure, which I entirely devoted to the perusal of the Greek and Latin classics; though I occasionally visited the metropolis, either for the sake of purchasing books, or of learning something new in mathematics or in music, in which I, at that time, found a source of pleasure and amusement.

In this manner I spent five years till my mother's death. I then became anxious to visit foreign parts, and particularly Italy. My father gave me his permission, and I left him with one servant. On my departure, the celebrated Henry Wootton, who had long been King James's ambassador at Venice, gave me a signal proof of his regard, in an elegant letter which he wrote, breathing not only the warmest friendship, but containing some maxims of conduct which I found very useful in my travels. The noble Thomas Scudamore, King Charles's ambassador, to whom I carried letters of recommendation, received me most courteously at Paris. His lordship gave me a card of introduction to the learned Hugo Grotius, at that time ambassador from the Queen of Sweden to the French court; whose acquaintance I anxiously desired, and to whose house I was accompanied by some of his lordship's friends. A few days after, when I set out for Italy, he gave me letters to the English merchants on my route, that they might show me any civilities in their power.

Taking ship at Nice, I arrived at Genoa, and afterwards visited Leghorn, Pisa, and Florence. In the latter city, which I have always more particularly esteemed for the elegance of its dialect, its genius, and its taste, I stopped about two months; when I contracted an intimacy with many persons of rank and learning; and was a constant attendant at their literary parties; a practice which prevails there, and tends so much to the diffusion of knowledge, and the preservation of friendship. No time will ever abolish the agreeable recollections which I cherish of Jacob Gaddi, Carolo Dati, Frescobaldo, Cultellero, Bonomatthai, Clementillo, Francisco, and many others. From Florence I went to Siena, thence to Rome, where, after I had spent about two months in viewing the antiquities of that renowned city, where I experienced the most friendly attentions from Lucas Holstein, and other learned and ingenious men, I continued my route to Naples. There I was introduced by a certain recluse, with whom I had travelled from Rome, to John Baptista Manso, Marquis of Villa, a nobleman of distinguished rank and authority to whom Torquato Tasso, the illustrious poet, inscribed his book on friendship. During my stay, he gave me singular proofs of his regard: he himself conducted me round the city, and to the palace of the viceroy; and more than once paid me a visit at my lodgings. On my departure he gravely apologized for not having shown me more civility, which he said he had been restrained from doing, because I had spoken with so little reserve on matters of religion.

When I was preparing to pass over into Sicily and Greece, the melancholy intelligence which I received of the civil commotions in England made me alter my purpose; for I thought it base to be travelling for amusement abroad, while my fellow-citizens were fighting for liberty at home. While I was on my way back to Rome, some merchants informed me that the English Jesuits had formed a plot against me if I returned to Rome, because I had spoken too freely on religion; for it was a rule which I laid down to myself in those places, never to be the first to begin any conversation on religion; but if any questions were put to me concerning my faith, to declare it without any reserve or fear. I, nevertheless, returned to Rome. I took no steps to conceal either my person or my character; and for about the space of two months I again openly defended, as I had done before, the reformed religion in the very metropolis of popery.

By the favour of God, I got safe back to Florence, where I was received with as much affection as if I had returned to my native country. There I stopped as many months as I had done before, except that I made an excursion for a few days to Lucca; and, crossing the Apennines, passed through Bologna and Ferrara to Venice. After I had spent a month in surveying the curiosities of this city, and had put on board a ship the books which I had collected in Italy, I proceeded through Verona and Milan, and along the Leman lake to Geneva. The mention of this city brings to my recollection the slandering More, and makes me again call the Deity to witness, that in all those places in which vice meets with so little discouragement, and is practised with so little shame, I never once deviated from the paths of integrity and virtue, and perpetually reflected that, though my conduct might escape the notice of men, it could not elude the inspection of God.

At Geneva I held daily conferences with John Deodati, the learned professor of Theology. Then pursuing my former route through France, I returned to my native country, after an absence of one year and about three months; at the time when Charles, having broken the peace, was renewing what is called the episcopal war with the Scots, in which the royalists being routed in the first encounter, and the English being universally and justly disaffected, the necessity of his affairs at last obliged him to convene a parliament.

As soon as I was able, I hired a spacious house in the city for myself and my books; where I again with rapture renewed my literary pursuits, and where I calmly awaited the issue of the contest, which I trusted to the wise conduct of Providence, and to the courage of the people. The vigour of the parliament had begun to humble the pride of the bishops. As soon as the liberty of speech was no longer subject to control, all mouths began to be opened against the bishops; some complained of the vices of the individuals, others of those of the order. They said that it was unjust that they alone should differ from the model of other reformed churches; that the government of the church should be according to the pattern of other churches, and particular the word of God. This awakened all my attention and my zeal. I saw that a way was opening for the establishment of real liberty; that the foundation was laying for the deliverance of man from the yoke of slavery and superstition; that the principles of religion, which were the first objects of our care, would exert a salutary influence on the manners and constitution of the republic; and as I had from my youth studied the distinctions between religious and civil rights, I perceived that if I ever wished to be of use, I ought at least not to be wanting to my country, to the church, and to so many of my fellow-Christians, in a crisis of so much danger. I therefore determined to relinquish the other pursuits in which I was engaged, and to transfer the whole force of my talents and my industry to this one important object.

I accordingly wrote two books to a friend concerning the Reformation of the church of England. Afterwards, when two bishops of superior distinction vindicated their privileges against some principal ministers, I thought that on those topics, to the consideration of which I was led solely by my love of truth and my reverence for Christianity, I should not probably write worse than those who were contending only for their own emoluments and usurpations. I therefore answered the one in two books, of which the first is inscribed, Concerning Prelatical Episcopacy, and the other Concerning the Mode of Ecclesiastical Government; and I replied to the other in some Animadversions, and soon after in an Apology. On this occasion it was supposed that I brought a timely succour to the ministers, who were hardly a match for the eloquence of their opponents; and from that time I was actively employed in refuting any answers that appeared.

When the bishops could not longer resist the multitude of their assailants, I had leisure to turn my thoughts to other subjects; to the promotion of real and substantial liberty; which is rather to be sought from within than from without; and whose existence depends, not so much on the terror of the sword, as on sobriety of conduct and integrity of life. When, therefore, I perceived that there were three species of liberty which are essential to the happiness of social life—religious, domestic, and civil; and as I had already written concerning the first, and the magistrates were strenuously active in obtaining the third, I determined to turn my attention to the second, or the domestic species. As this seemed to involve three material questions, the conditions of the conjugal tie, the education of the children, and the free publication of the thoughts, I made them objects of distinct consideration.

I explained my sentiments, not only concerning the solemnization of the marriage, but the dissolution, if circumstances rendered it necessary; and I drew my arguments from the divine law, which Christ did not abolish, or publish another more grievous than that of Moses. I stated my own opinions, and those of others, concerning the exclusive exception of fornication, which our illustrious Selden has since, in his Hebrew Wife, more copiously discussed; for he in vain makes a vaunt of liberty in the senate or in the forum, who languishes under the vilest servitude to an inferior at home. On this subject, therefore, I published some books which were more particularly necessary at that time, when man and wife were often the most inveterate foes, when the man often staid to take care of his children at home, while the mother of the family was seen in the camp of the enemy, threatening death and destruction to her husband.

I then discussed the principles of education in a summary manner, but sufficiently copious for those who attend seriously to the subject; than which nothing can be more necessary to principle the minds of men in virtue, the only genuine source of political and individual liberty, the only true safeguard of states, the bulwark of their prosperity and renown. Lastly, I wrote my *Areopagitica*, in order to deliver the press from the restraints with which it was encumbered; that the power of determining what was true and what was false, what ought to be published and what to be suppressed, might no longer be entrusted to a few illiterate and illiberal individuals, who refused their sanction to any work which contained views or sentiments at all above the level of the vulgar superstition.

On the last species, of civil liberty, I said nothing, because I saw that sufficient attention was paid to it by the magistrates; nor did I write anything on the prerogative of the crown, till the king, voted an enemy by the parliament, and vanquished in the field, was summoned before the tribunal which condemned him to lose his head. But when, at length, some presbyterian ministers, who had formerly been the most bitter enemies to Charles, became jealous of the growth of the Independents, and of their ascendancy in the parliament, most tumultuously clamoured against the sentence, and did all in their power to prevent the execution, though they were not angry, so much on account of the act itself, as because it was not the act of their party; and when they dared to affirm that the doctrine of the protestants, and of all the reformed churches, was abhorrent to such an atrocious proceeding against kings; I thought that it became me to oppose such a glaring falsehood; and accordingly, without any immediate or personal application to Charles, I showed, in an abstract consideration of the question, what might lawfully be done against tyrants; and in support of what I advanced, produced the opinions of the most celebrated divines; while I vehemently inveighed against the egregious ignorance or effrontery of men who professed better things, and from whom better things might have been expected.

That book did not make its appearance till after the death of Charles; and was written rather to reconcile the minds of the people to the event, than to discuss the legitimacy of that particular sentence, which concerned the magistrates, and which was already executed.

Such were the fruits of my private studies, which I gratuitously presented to the church and to the state; and for which I was recompensed by nothing but impunity; though the actions themselves procured me peace of conscience, and the approbation of the good; while I exercised that freedom of discussion which I loved. Others, without labour or desert, got possession of honours and emoluments; but no one ever knew me either soliciting anything myself or through the medium of my friends, ever beheld me in a supplicating posture at the doors of the senate, or the levees of the great. I usually kept myself secluded at home, where my own property, part of which had been withheld during the civil commotions, and part of which had been absorbed in the oppressive contributions which I had to sustain, afforded me a scanty subsistence. When I was released from these engagements, and thought that I was about to enjoy an interval of uninterrupted ease, I turned my thoughts to a continued history of my country, from the earliest times to the present period.

I had already finished four books, when, after the subversion of the monarchy and the establishment of a republic, I was surprised by an invitation from the council of state, who desired my services in the office for foreign affairs. A book appeared soon after, which was ascribed to the king, and contained the most invidious charges against the parliament. I was ordered to answer it; and opposed the Iconoclast to his Icon. I did not insult over fallen majesty, as is pretended; I only preferred Queen Truth to King Charles. The charge of insult, which I saw that the malevolent would urge, I was at some pains to remove in the beginning of the work; and as often as possible in other places. Salmasius then appeared, to whom they were not, as More says, long in looking about for an opponent, but immediately appointed me, who happened at the time to be present in the council. I have thus, sir, given some account of myself, in order to stop your mouth, and to remove any prejudices which your falsehoods and misrepresentations might cause even good men to entertain against me.

II. FROM THE REASON OF CHURCH GOVERNMENT (1641)

The occasion of this treatise on the theory of Church Government is related in the preceding extract. The present extract forms the preface to the second book of it. It is noticeable that, when he wrote it, Milton was still convinced of the divine right of Presbyterianism. Before he wrote the *Areopagitica* (1644), probably by the time that he wrote the *Doctrine and Discipline of Divorce* (1643), he had come to think otherwise.

How happy were it for this frail, and as it may be called mortal life of man, since all earthly things, which have the name of good and convenient in our daily use, are withal so cumbersome and full of trouble, if knowledge, yet which is the best and lightsomest possession of the mind, were, as the common saying is, no burden; and that what it wanted of being a load to any part of the body, it did not with a heavy advantage over-lay upon the spirit! For not to speak of that knowledge that rests in the contemplation of natural causes and dimensions, which must needs be a lower wisdom, as the object is low, certain it is that he who hath obtained in more than the scantiest measure to know anything distinctly of God, and of his true worship; and what is infallibly good and happy in the state of man's life, what in itself evil and miserable, though vulgarly not so esteemed; he that hath obtained to know this, the only high valuable wisdom indeed, remembering also that God, even to a strictness, requires the improvement of these his entrusted gifts, cannot but sustain a sorer burden of mind, and more pressing, than any supportable toil or weight which the body can labour under, how and in what manner he shall dispose and employ those sums of knowledge and illumination, which God hath sent him into this world to trade with.

And that which aggravates the burden more, is, that, having received amongst his allotted parcels certain precious truths, of such an orient lustre as no diamond can equal, which never-theless he has in charge to put off at any cheap rate, yea, for nothing to them that will; the great merchants of this world, fearing that this course would soon discover and disgrace the false glitter of their deceitful wares, wherewith they abuse the people, like poor Indians with beads and glasses, practise by all means how they may suppress the vending of such rarities, and at such a cheapness as would undo them, and turn their trash upon their hands. Therefore, by gratifying the corrupt desires of men in fleshly doctrines, they stir them up to persecute with hatred and contempt all those that seek to bear themselves uprightly in this their spiritual factory: which they foreseeing, though they cannot but testify of truth, and the excellency of that heavenly traffic which they bring, against what opposition or danger soever, yet needs must it sit heavily upon their spirits, that being, in God's prime intention and their own, selected heralds of peace and dispensers of treasure inestimable, without price, to them that have no peace, they find in the discharge of their commission, that they are made the greatest variance and offence, a very sword and fire both in house and city over the whole earth.

This is that which the sad prophet Jeremiah laments: 'Wo is me, my mother, that thou hast borne me, a man of strife and contention!' And although divine inspiration must certainly have been sweet to those ancient prophets, yet the irksomeness of that truth which they brought was so unpleasant unto them, that everywhere they call it a burden. Yea, that mysterious book of revelation, which the great evangelist was bid to eat, as it had been some eye-brightening electuary of knowledge and foresight, thought it were sweet in his mouth and in the learning, it was bitter in his belly, bitter in the denouncing. Nor was this hid from the wise poet Sophocles, who in that place of his tragedy where Tiresias is called to resolve King Oedipus in a matter which he knew would be grievous, brings him in bemoaning his lot, that he knew more than other men. For surely to every good and peaceable man, it must in nature needs be a hateful thing to be the displeaser and molester of thousands; much better would it like him doubtless to be the messenger of gladness and contentment, which is his chief intended business to all mankind, but that they resist and oppose their own true happiness. But when God commands to take the trumpet, and blow a dolorous or a jarring blast, it lies not in man's will what he shall say, or what he shall conceal. If he shall think to be silent as Jeremiah did, because of the reproach and derision he met with daily, 'And all his familiar friends watched for his halting,' to be revenged on him for speaking the truth, he would be forced to confess as he confessed: 'His word was in my heart as a burning fire shut up in my bones; I was weary with forbearing, and could not stay.' Which might teach these times not suddenly to condemn all things that are sharply spoken or vehemently written as proceeding out of stomach, virulence, and ill-nature; but to consider rather that, if the prelates have leave to say the worst that can be said, or do the worst that can be done, while they strive to keep to themselves, to their great pleasure and commodity, those things which they ought to render up, no man can be justly offended with him that shall endeavour to impart and bestow, without any gain to himself, those sharp but saving words which would be a terror and a torment in him to keep back.

For me, I have determined to lay as the best treasure and solace of a good old age, if God vouchsafe it me, the honest liberty of free speech from my youth, where I shall think it available in so dear a concernment as the church's good. For if I be, either by disposition or what other cause, too inquisitive, or suspicious of myself and mine own doings, who can help it? But this I foresee, that should the church be brought under heavy oppression, and God have given me ability the while to reason against that man that should be the author of so foul a deed; or should she, by blessing from above on the industry and courage of faithful men, change this her distracted estate into better days, without the least furtherance or contribution of those few talents which God at that present had lent me; I foresee what stories I should hear within myself, all my life after, of discourage and reproach.

'Timorous and ungrateful, the church of God is now again at the foot of her insulting enemies, and thou bewailest. What matters it for thee, or thy bewailing? When time was, thou couldst not find a syllable of all that thou hast read, or studied, to utter in her behalf. Yet ease and leisure was given thee for thy retired thoughts, out of the sweat of other men. Thou hast the diligence, the parts, the language of a man, if a vain subject were to be adorned or beautified; but when the cause of God and his church was to be pleaded, for which purpose that tongue was given thee which thou hast, God listened if he could hear thy voice among his zealous servants, but thou wert dumb as a beast; from henceforward be that which thine own brutish silence hath made thee.'

Or else I should have heard on the other ear: 'Slothful, and ever to be set light by, the church hath now overcome her late distresses after the unwearied labours of many her true servants that stood up in her defence; thou also wouldst take upon thee to share amongst them of their joy: but wherefore thou? Where canst thou show any word or deed of thine which might have hastened her peace? Whatever thou dost now talk, or write, or look, is the alms of other men's active prudence and zeal. Dare not now to say or do anything better than thy former sloth and infancy; or if thou darest, thou dost impudently to make a thrifty purchase of boldness to thyself out of the painful merits of other men; what before was thy sin is now thy duty, to be abject and worthless.'

These, and such like lessons as these, I know would have been my matins duly, and my evensong. But now by this little diligence, mark what a privilege, I have gained with good men and saints, to claim my right of lamenting the tribulations of the church, if she should suffer, when others, that have ventured nothing for her sake, have not the honour to be admitted mourners. But if she lift up her drooping head and prosper, among those that have something more than wished her welfare, I have my charter and freehold of rejoicing to me and my heirs. Concerning therefore this wayward subject against prelaty, the touching whereof is so distasteful and disquietous to a number of men, as by what hath been saith I may deserve of charitable readers to be credited, that neither envy nor gall hath entered me upon this controversy, but the enforcement of conscience only, and a preventive fear lest the omitting of this duty should be against me, when I would store up to myself the good provision of peaceful hours: so, lest it be still imputed to me, as I have found it hath been, that some self-pleasing humour of vain-glory hath incited me to contest with men of high estimation, now while green years are upon my head; from this needless surmisal I shall hope to dissuade the intelligent and equal auditor, if I can but say successfully that which in this exigent behoves me; although I would be heard only, if it might be, by the elegant and learned reader, to whom principally for a while I shall beg leave I may address myself.

To him it will be no new thing, though I tell him that if I hunted after praise, by the ostentation of wit and learning, I should not write thus out of mine own season when I have neither yet completed to my mind the full circle of my private studies, although I complain not of any insufficiency to the matter in hand; or were I ready to my wishes, it were a folly to commit anything elaborately composed to the careless and interrupted listening of these tumultuous times. Next, if I were wise only to my own ends, I would certainly take such a subject as of itself might catch applause, whereas this hath all the disadvantages on the contrary; and such a subject as the publishing whereof might be delayed at pleasure, and time enough to pencil it over with all the curious touches of art, even to the perfection of a faultless picture; whenas in this argument the not deferring is of great moment to the good speeding, that, if solidity have leisure to do her office, art cannot have much. Lastly, I should not choose this manner of writing, wherein knowing myself inferior to myself, led by the genial power of nature to another task, I have the use, as I may account, but of my left hand.

And though I shall be foolish in saying more to this purpose, yet, since it will be such a folly wisest men go about to commit, having only confessed and so committed, I may trust with more reason, because with more folly, to have courteous pardon. For although a poet, soaring in the high region of his fancies, with his garland and singing robes about him, might, without apology, speak more of himself than I mean to do; yet for me sitting here below in the cool element of prose, a mortal thing among many readers of no empyreal conceit, to venture and divulge unusual things of myself, I shall petition to the gentler sort, it may not be envy to me.

I must say, therefore, that after I had for my first years, by the ceaseless diligence and care of my father (whom God recompense!), been exercised to the tongues and some sciences, as my age would suffer, by sundry masters and teachers, both at home and at the schools, it was found that whether aught was imposed me by them that had the overlooking, or betaken to of mine own choice in English, or other tongue, prosing or versing, but chiefly by this latter, the style, by certain vital signs it had, was likely to live. But much latelier in the private academies of Italy, whither I was favoured to resort, perceiving that some trifles which I had in memory, composed at under twenty or thereabout (for the manner is, that everyone must give some proof of his wit and reading there), met with acceptance above what was looked for; and other things, which I had shifted in scarcity of books and conveniences to patch up amongst them, were received with written encomiums, which the Italian is not forward to bestow on men of this side the Alps; I began thus far to assent both to them and divers of my friends here at home, and not less to an inward prompting which now grew daily upon me, that by labour and intense study (which I take to be my portion in this life), joined with the strong propensity of nature, I might perhaps leave something so written to aftertimes, as they should not willingly let it die.

These thoughts at once possessed me, and these other; that if I were certain to write as men buy leases, for three lives and downward, there ought no regard be sooner had than to God's glory, by the honour and instruction of my country. For which cause, and not only for that I knew it would be hard to arrive at the second rank among the Latins, I applied myself to that resolution, which Arios to followed against the persuasions of Bembo, to fix all the industry and art I could unite to the adorning of my native tongue; not to make verbal curiosities the end (that were a toilsome vanity), but to be an interpreter and relater of the best and sagest things among mine own citizens throughout this island in the mother dialect. That, what the greatest and choicest wits of Athens, Rome, or modern Italy, and those Hebrews of old did for their country, I, in my proportion, with this over and above, of being a Christian, might do for mine; not caring to be once named abroad, though perhaps I could attain to that, but content with these British islands as my world; whose fortune hath hitherto been that, if the Athenians, as some say, made their small deeds great and renowned by their eloquent writers, England hath had her noble achievements made small by the unskilful handling of monks and mechanics.

Time serves not now, and perhaps I might seem too profuse, to give any certain account of what the mind at home, in the spacious circuits of her musing, hath liberty to propose to herself, though of highest hope and hardest attempting; whether that epic form whereof the two poems of Homer, and those other two of Virgil and Tasso, are a diffuse, and the book of Job a brief model: or whether the rules of Aristotle herein are strictly to be kept, or nature to be followed, which in them that know art, and use judgment, is no transgression, but an enriching of art; and lastly, what king or knight, before the conquest, might be chosen in whom to lay the pattern of a Christian hero. And as Tasso gave to a prince of Italy his choice whether he would command him to write of Godfrey's expedition against the Infidels, or Belisarius against the Goths, or Charlemain against the Lombards; if to the instinct of nature and the emboldening of art aught may be trusted, and that there be nothing adverse in our climate, or the fate of this age, it haply would be no rashness, from an equal diligence and inclination, to present the like offer in our own ancient stories; or whether those dramatic constitutions, wherein Sophocles and Euripides reign, shall be found more doctrinal and exemplary to a nation.

The scripture also affords us a divine pastoral drama in the Song of Solomon, consisting of two persons, and a double chorus, as Origen rightly judges. And the Apocalypse of St John is the majestic image of a high and stately tragedy, shutting up and intermingling her solemn scenes and acts with a sevenfold chorus of hallelujahs and harping symphonies: and this my opinion the grave authority of Paraeus, commenting that book, is sufficient to confirm. Or if occasion shall lead, to imitate those magnific odes and hymns, wherein Pindarus and Callimachus are in most things worthy, some others in their frame judicious, in their matter most and end faulty. But those frequent songs throughout the law and prophets beyond all these, not in their divine argument alone, but in the very critical art of composition, may be easily made appear over all the kinds of lyric poesy to be incomparable.

These abilities, wheresoever they be found, are the inspired gift of God, rarely bestowed, but yet to some (though most abuse) in every nation; and are of power, beside the office of a pulpit, to imbreed and cherish in a great people the seeds of virtue and public civility, to allay the perturbations of the mind, and set the affections in right tune; to celebrate in glorious and lofty hymns the throne and equipage of God's almightiness, and what he works, and what he suffers to be wrought with high providence in his church; to sing victorious agonies of martyrs and saints, the deeds and triumphs of just and pious nations, doing valiantly through faith against the enemies of Christ; to deplore the general relapses of kingdoms and states from justice and God's true worship.

Lastly, whatsoever in religion is holy and sublime, in virtue amiable or grave, whatsoever hath passion or admiration in all the changes of that which is called fortune from without, or the wily subtleties and refluxes of man's thoughts from within; all these things with a solid and treatable smoothness to paint out and describe. Teaching over the whole book of sanctity and virtue, through all the instances of example, with such delight to those especially of soft and delicious temper, who will not so much as look upon truth herself, unless they see her elegantly dressed; that whereas the paths of honesty and good life appear now rugged and difficult, though they be indeed easy and pleasant, they will then appear to all men both easy and pleasant, though they were rugged and difficult indeed. And what a benefit this would be to our youth and gentry, may be soon guessed by what we know of the corruption and bane which they suck in daily from the writings and interludes of libidinous and ignorant poetasters; who, having scarce ever heard of that which is the main consistence of a true poem, the choice of such persons as they ought to introduce, and what is moral and decent to each one, do for the most part lay up vicious principles in sweet pills to be swallowed down, and make the taste of virtuous documents harsh and sour.

But because the spirit of man cannot demean itself lively in this body, without some recreating intermission of labour and serious things, it were happy for the commonwealth, if our magistrates, as in those famous governments of old, would take into their care, not only the deciding of our contentious law-cases and brawls, but the managing of our public sports and festival pastimes; that they might be, not such as were authorized a while since, the provocations of drunkenness and lust, but such as may inure and harden our bodies by martial exercises to all warlike skill and performance; and may civilize, adorn, and make discreet our minds by the learned and affable meeting of frequent academies, and the procurement of wise and artful recitations, sweetened with eloquent and graceful enticements to the love and practice of justice, temperance, and fortitude, instructing and bettering the nation at all opportunities, that the call of wisdom and virtue may be heard everywhere, as Solomon saith: 'She crieth without, she uttereth her voice in the streets, in the top of high places, in the chief concourse, and in the openings of the gates.' Whether this may not be, not only in pulpits, but after another persuasive method, at set and solemn paneguries, in theatres, porches, or what other place or way may win most upon the people to receive at once both recreation and instruction, let them in authority consult.

The thing which I had to say, and those intentions which have lived within me ever since I could conceive myself anything worth to my country, I return to crave excuse that urgent reason hath plucked from me, by an abortive and foredated discovery. And the accomplishment of them lies not but in a power above man's to promise; but that none hath by more studious ways endeavoured, and with more unwearied spirit that none shall, that I dare almost aver of myself, as far as life and free leisure will extend; and that the land had once enfranchised herself from this impertinent yoke of prelaty, under whose inquisitorious and tyrannical duncery no free and splendid wit can flourish.

Neither do I think it shame to covenant with any knowing reader, that for some few years yet I may go on trust with him toward the payment of what I am now indebted, as being a work not to be raised from the heat of youth, or the vapours of wine; like that which flows at waste from the pen of some vulgar amourist, or the trencher fury of a rhyming parasite; nor to be obtained by the invocation of dame memory and her siren daughters; but by devout prayer to that eternal Spirit, who can enrich with all utterance and knowledge, and sends out his seraphim, with the hallowed fire of his altar, to touch and purify the lips of whom he pleases: to this must be added industrious and select reading, steady observation, insight into all seemly and generous arts and affairs; till which in some measure be compassed, at mine own peril and cost, I refuse not to sustain this expectation from as many as are not loth to hazard so much credulity upon the best pledges that I can give them.

Although it nothing content me to have disclosed thus much beforehand, but that I trust hereby to make it manifest with what small willingness I endure to interrupt the pursuit of no less hopes than these, and leave a calm and pleasing solitariness, fed with cheerful and confident thoughts, to embark in a troubled sea of noises and hoarse disputes, put from beholding the bright countenance of truth in the quiet and still air of delightful studies, to come into the dim reflection of hollow antiquities sold by the seeming bulk, and there be fain to club quotations with men whose learning and belief lies in marginal stuffings; who, when they have, like good sumpters, laid ye down their horse-loads of citations and fathers at your door with a rhapsody of who and who were bishops here or there, ye may take off their pack-saddles, their day's work is done, and episcopacy, as they think, stoutly vindicated. Let any gentle apprehension, that can distinguish learned pains from unlearned drudgery, imagine what pleasure or profoundness can be in this, or what honour to deal against such adversaries.

But were it the meanest under-service, if God by his secretary conscience enjoin it, it were sad for me if I should draw back; for me especially, now when all men offer their aid to help, ease, and lighten the difficult labours of the church, to whose service, by the intentions of my parents and friends, I was destined of a child, and in mine own resolutions: till coming to some maturity of years, and perceiving what tyranny had invaded the church, that he who would take orders must subscribe slave, and take an oath withal, which unless he took with a conscience that would retch, he must either straight perjure, or split his faith; I thought it better to prefer a blameless silence before the sacred office of speaking, bought and begun with servitude and forswearing. Howsoever, thus church-outed by the prelates, hence may appear the right I have to meddle in these matters, as before the necessity and constraint appeared.

INDEX